Charles Wesley

A Biography

G. M. Best

 EPWORTH

British Library Cataloguing in Publication data

A catalogue record for this book is available
from the British Library

0 7162 0615 3/978 0 7162 0615 6

First published in 2006
Second impression 2007
by Epworth
4 John Wesley Road
Werrington
Peterborough PE4 6ZP

Typeset by Regent Typesetting, London
Printed and bound in Great Britain by
William Clowes Ltd, Beccles, Suffolk

Charles Wesley

Contents

Introduction

For most people Charles Wesley is only a hymnwriter. They regard his brother John as being the sole founder of Methodism and the most eminent of all eighteenth-century Protestants. John's constant preaching around the country over half a century has become the stuff of legends, especially in the years when he faced tough opposition from mobs. Historians have viewed his perseverance and strength of will, which brooked no opposition, as critically important in providing the religious discipline necessary to shape the turbulence generated by religious fervour. As a consequence there has been a never-ending succession of books about John Wesley and his contribution not only to religion but also to the very nature of British society. Yet increasingly modern research has shown that John was not the single-handed shaper of Methodism that his writings or early historians proclaimed. There were many other people, both clerical and lay, who played a vital role in the creation of Methodism and who have been largely ignored. Among the many other creators of Methodism there were certainly two who played just as important a role as John. They were George Whitefield and Charles Wesley.

Like John, George Whitefield has been the subject of many books and this is understandable. He was the first of the three to experience a conversion sufficiently powerful to make him initiate a religious revival. He was the first to draw immense crowds and decide that open-air preaching was essential. He was the first to create societies which adopted the name 'Methodist' and the first to accept the use of lay preachers. It was in fact Whitefield who for many years was known as the founder of Methodism and who held the first ever 'Methodist Conference'. He was also the first to announce that the world was his parish, seeking to create a religious revival which would extend far beyond the borders of Britain. For that reason it was he who was the first great awakener of Methodism in America. It has to be said that John's much-vaunted itinerancy almost pales into insignificance beside that of this inveterate preacher. However, John Wesley had the advantage of living far longer and so he was able to rewrite the history of Methodism and so diminish Whitefield's role.

In comparison to John Wesley and George Whitefield, Charles has been terribly ignored. Yet it was Charles who founded the Oxford Holy Club, which is so often seen as the precursor to Methodism, and who brought Whitefield under its influence. It was Charles who provided the warmth of character which kept many loyal to his more autocratic and severe brother. It was Charles and not John who was often judged the most effective preacher in Methodism whenever Whitefield was absent in America. Charles became the mentor for the lay preachers and was the mainstay for the development of the Methodist societies in London and what was then Britain's second-largest city, Bristol. Without Charles' many friends – George Whitefield, Benjamin Ingham, Howell Harris, William Grimshaw, John Fletcher, and many more – John would not have been anything like as successful. Indeed, it was Charles who blocked time and again moves to have John's leadership of Methodism removed. He constantly supported his brother, even when they disagreed, and by becoming the hymnwriter of the movement, he embodied its message far more effectively in his verse than John was ever able to achieve through his prose. And it was Charles who long delayed the separation of Methodism from the Anglican Church.

All this makes it quite remarkable that Charles has been so little studied – indeed the last major biography of him was written in the nineteenth century! This book tries to redress the balance. It is therefore a history of all three men and early Methodism but with Charles at the centre, rather than John or George. It shows how the 'man made for friendship' (as Charles was described by one who knew him well) was not just a great hymnwriter but centrally important to the creation of Methodism. Writing the book has been an exciting journey of discovery for me and I am grateful to all those who have helped me in its production, especially my wife, Frances, for all her unfailing support and patience, and Dr Ralph Waller, the Principal of Harris Manchester College, for all his encouragement to turn my studies into a book and the time he gave me to study in Oxford. I would also like to record my gratitude to the governors of Kingswood School for granting me a sabbatical to help me complete some of my research. Finally, my thanks go to my mother who inspired me with a love of history and who sent me as a child to our local Methodist Church, thus introducing me to a movement which has certainly shaped my own life.

Fifty years ago on the 250th anniversary of Charles' birth the *Methodist Recorder* published the following verse about him by Maldwyn Edwards:

Prophet speaking to all time
Ageless accents in your song:
God's word caught within your rhyme,
God's fire lighting on your tongue.

Let that song in thunder come
To the deafened ears of man;
Show once more the soul's true home,
Raise our hearts to God again.[1]

To achieve that on the occasion of the 300th anniversary it is time for a fuller account of his contribution.

G. M. Best

---

1 'Prophet For All Time' in *Methodist Recorder*, December 1957.

A Church Upbringing

Jesus in earth in heaven the same
Accept a parent's vow,
To Thee, baptized into Thy name
I bring my children now:
Thy love permits, invites, commands
My offspring to be bless'd:
Lay on them, Lord, Thy gracious hands,
And hide them in Thy breast.

To each the hallowing spirit give
Even from their infancy,
And pure into Thy church receive
Whom I devote to Thee:
Committed to Thy faithful care,
Protected by Thy blood,
Preserve by Thine unceasing prayer,
And bring them all to God.[1]

Today Charles Wesley is best remembered as the hymnwriter who helped his brother John found Methodism. Such an epitaph would not have pleased him because, like most of the eighteenth-century evangelicals, Charles believed those converted to Christianity were best served by remaining within the Church of England, not by becoming members of a separate dissenting faction. In origin Methodism was about reviving the Church not challenging it, and Charles' hymns were simply his way of communicating God's forgiving love as revealed in the life, death and resurrection of Jesus Christ. To understand Charles' love of the Church one has only to look at his upbringing by his parents, Samuel and Susanna, who had both rejected the religious dissent associated with their respective families in order to become strong advocates for the Church of England when it was reshaped in the 1660s to meet the needs of all Christians.

Charles knew his nonconformist ancestors had attacked the Church of England because initially it had stemmed from little more than the pope's refusal to annul Henry VIII's marriage to Catherine of Aragon. What this new 'Protestant' Church should therefore be like in terms of its theology, its organization and its worship was understandably the matter of intense debate for over a century. The more Catholic-minded sought to retain traditional forms of worship and structure in the hope of one day returning the Church to papal control, while the more radical Protestant groups encouraged people to appreciate salvation depended upon direct personal religious experience and demanded church services should be purified from 'the rags of the Papacy'. Many of the latter became known as 'Puritans' and both of Charles' great-grandfathers were in that category.

Charles' great-grandfather on the paternal side, Bartholomew Westley (the 't' was later dropped), was a Puritan doctor who became Rector of Charmouth in Dorset. John White, his mother's grandfather, was a Puritan lawyer who became a Member of Parliament for Southwark and the author of a parliamentary report on 'the scandalous immoralities of the clergy'. He urged the abolition of bishops and other clerical roles which stemmed from the Church of England's Catholic origins, and was described as a 'burning, shining light' of the Puritan movement.[2] It was the combined religious and political demands of Puritans like Westley and White that eventually plunged the country in 1642 into a destructive civil war. Both Charles' great-grandfathers aligned themselves with the Parliamentarians in this conflict because they felt Charles I was too inclined towards Catholicism. White did not long survive the outbreak of the war, dying in 1644, but Bartholomew Westley went on to become an avid supporter of Oliver Cromwell when he emerged as the main Parliamentarian commander. Legend says that, after the beheading of the king in 1649, Bartholomew was only prevented from arresting the future Charles II because he was too busy saying prayers of thanksgiving to notice the prince's flight through his parish!

Charles grew up among a generation who viewed Puritanism as having achieved nothing but strife and anarchy. Stamped on memories were the worst excesses of extremists: the shocking disruption of any worship which they deemed unacceptable, the wanton destruction within churches of any symbol or statue or stained-glass window deemed Catholic, the banning of traditional pastimes and pleasures, the vicious treatment of those alleged to be guilty of witchcraft or heresy, the denial of any kind of traditional authority, and the endless division into factious sects because of increasingly bitter wrangling over theological issues.

Ferocious religious wars between Catholic and Protestant in Europe provided further evidence, if it were needed, of the intolerance that religious extremism could engender. Eventually the increasingly autocratic government of Cromwell and his strident imposition of a narrow morality on the population generated a backlash in favour of the restoration of the monarchy and the creation of a more traditional and less 'enthusiastic' Church.

Central to the restoration of Charles II was the 1662 Act of Uniformity, which tried to create the ideal of a single, all-inclusive, national Church with its worship controlled by a single prayer book. This Church offered the 'via media' or middle way between the authoritarianism of Catholicism and the excessive individualism of radical Protestantism. Church and State were to be inextricably bound together so that they could work together in harmony. The Church of England thus became one of the key pillars of the nation's unity and, not surprisingly, those who refused to accept this were viewed with distaste and concern as undesirable religious enthusiasts. The importance of replacing passion with reason was encouraged by the many scientific advances of the seventeenth century and by both geographical exploration and early colonization, which made many intelligent people realize the creator of the world was beyond humanity's petty theological divisions. When the first major English dictionary was produced by Dr Samuel Johnson, it defined religious enthusiasm as 'a vain belief of private revelation; a vain confidence of divine favour or communication'.

Charles was therefore brought up by his parents to be a rational enthusiast and avoid the worst excesses of religious intolerance. Samuel Wesley in particular made clear that he expected his children to support the Church of England and decried the way in which his own father, John, and grandfather, Bartholomew, had entered the ranks of the dissenters by refusing to accept the Act of Uniformity. This act of defiance had led to their expulsion from the Church alongside two thousand others. Bartholomew had ceased to be the Rector of Charmouth and John had lost his position as Vicar of Winterborn Whitchurch in Dorset. Samuel knew the painful cost of this to the family. His father had been subsequently imprisoned four times, dying at the relatively young age of 42 in 1670. A heartbroken Bartholomew did not long survive him. This left the fatherless Samuel to be brought up in poverty by his mother. From his perspective his father and grandfather would have achieved far more by remaining within the Church and fighting for what they believed than by stepping outside it. It was a message deeply instilled into Charles.

After his father's death, Samuel was sent to Dorchester Grammar School, which was run by Henry Dolling, a highly respected churchman.

Under his influence it is likely Samuel started challenging the dissenting views of his family because he was soon moved, first to a dissenting academy in Stepney and then to another at Newington Green. Among his later teachers was the well-known republican Charles Morton. Despite this, Samuel made clear at the age of 21 that he wished to become a priest and, in August 1683, went as a 'pauper scholar' or 'servitor' to Exeter College, Oxford. Years later his son John claimed that his father took this decision when he was asked to publicly defend the views of the dissenters. Having studied how he would do this, Samuel concluded it was an impossible task and instead gave his full allegiance to the Church. The change of name from Westley to Wesley may possibly date from this rejection of dissent, though some think the 't' was dropped earlier.

Samuel had to fund the cost of board and lodging at the university by serving richer undergraduates. He found life tough, 'some days getting meat, and others none' but, as a sincere Christian, he still put the needs of others before those of his own. On one occasion he describes giving the only pence he possessed to a starving child. Fortunately others matched Samuel's generosity. His mother sent him food, his tutor paid his college bills, and a relative sent him money. His studies led him to accept the High Anglican views then prevalent within the university. High Anglicans valued the role of the Church in interpreting the truths of scripture through the catechism, the creeds and the prayer book, and believed the role of bishops was essential because they represented the apostolic succession. They thus offered a religion which replaced the Puritan emphasis on individual salvation with one based on self-denial and salvation experienced through the worship of the Church. In particular they thought God's grace was experienced through baptism and taking communion, activities which the Puritans had denigrated. One can see this High Anglican influence in Charles' respect for the role of bishops as true guardians of both religious orthodoxy and the social order, and in the importance he attached to receiving the sacraments as an essential means of receiving God's grace.

Charles was to struggle throughout his life with whether it was acceptable or not to reject aspects of the way in which the Church he loved operated. This was partly because he recognized his ancestors had been men of conscience and he sought to emulate that. Whatever the reservations of his father, he knew Bartholomew and John Westley had only acted as they did because of their fears that the rites and ceremonies incorporated into the new Church of England were steps to returning the country to Catholicism. They had little faith in a king whose court was openly immoral and who was known to be a secret Catholic. As a consequence early Methodist writings were often to be critical of the government's harsh response to such men:

> The true pastors of the flock were expelled from the fold; and hire-lings, who cared more for the fleece and the fat than for the sheep, climbed over the wall, and seized on flocks to which they had no right, either Divine or human.[3]

The reason why Charles was prepared to sometimes place his own conscience before the rules of the Church probably owed much to his mother Susanna's reverence for her father, Dr Samuel Annesley, who had also rejected the Act of Uniformity. This grandfather was held up to Charles as a conscience-driven Christian whose life showed you could be a sincere enthusiast without becoming an intolerant fanatic. Highly religious (he was reading 20 chapters of the Bible every day at the age of five), Annesley had studied at Oxford University and become first a chaplain in the parliamentary navy and then vicar of a church in Kent. His strong principles meant he was not afraid to denounce any-one or anything that he judged wrong. For that reason he had been one of the Puritans deprived of office for refusing to support the execution of Charles I. Restored to favour after Cromwell's death, he had become a popular minister at St Giles' Church, Cripplegate until his expulsion for his refusal to accept the Act of Uniformity.

Even when deprived of office, Annesley had continued to inspire many by his charitable lifestyle and strong Christian witness. One of his pupils was the great writer Daniel Defoe and he later said this inspiring man had 'nothing in him that was little or mean'.[4] Much of Susanna's approach to Charles' education was based on her upbringing by her father. He had not only educated her far beyond what was normal for women at that time, but also constantly encouraged her to think for herself and challenge whatever she was not prepared to accept. In particular he had stressed the importance of judging religion by its outcome in a person's life, proclaiming 'faith without morality ... is but downright hypocrisy'.[5] Even though one of her first acts as a teenager had been to reject dissent, Susanna never expected her children to have unquestioning allegiance to the Church – if it was not doing what it should, then the role of a Christian was to challenge it. This was to be an important factor in why Charles and his brother John were sometimes prepared to act in ways that were 'irregular' to more conventionally minded clergy.

The reason why Susanna abandoned dissent probably owed much to her meeting Samuel Wesley, who had moved to London after completing his degree in 1688. While at university Samuel had supplemented his meagre income by writing humourous poems which attacked contemporary vices under the title 'Maggots: Or Poems on Several Subjects Never Before Handled'. These had been published by an eccentric called John Dunton, who was the son-in-law of Annesley. Through this contact Samuel was introduced to the family as a newly ordained deacon with a promising clerical future ahead of him. He immediately saw Susanna as an ideal prospective wife. She was beautiful, intelligent and well educated, and her family was connected to the lesser aristocracy. Being six or seven years younger than Samuel, Susanna was flattered by his attentions. One of Samuel's associates, Charles Gildon, describes him as being a warm and witty man who combined concern for the welfare of others with zeal for the gospel and a detailed knowledge and understanding of scripture.

The marriage of Samuel and Susanna on 11 November 1688 coincided with the 'Glorious Revolution' of 1688–9 in which the Catholic James II was deposed in favour of his Protestant daughter Mary and her Dutch husband, William of Orange. Having personally witnessed the king's autocratic behaviour during a royal visit to Oxford, Samuel judged James II to be a tyrant not worth saving, but in this he differed from most High Anglicans, who did not approve of the dethronement of a king, even if he was a Catholic. Among the outspoken critics were William Sancroft, Archbishop of Canterbury, and Thomas Ken, Bishop of Bath and Wells, who is now better remembered as the author of the hymn 'Praise God, from whom all blessings flow'. They and many others refused to swear loyalty to the new monarchs and were consequently debarred from holding office in the Church. Unlike Samuel, Susanna was sympathetic to these men of conscience, sharing their view that it was wrong to dethrone a God-anointed king. It was the first indicator that Samuel and Susanna were not perfectly matched in their views.

A number of High Anglicans subsequently became members of the 'Jacobite' party (from the word *Jacobus*, which is Latin for James). This was dedicated to restoring James and, after his death, his descendants. Susanna's sympathies towards Jacobite views were to later cause problems for her and her children, including Charles. In contrast Samuel welcomed the Glorious Revolution because he felt such a clear rejection of Catholicism made dissent unnecessary. This was embodied in the Toleration Act of 1689, which accepted people could worship outside the confines of the Church of England (providing they registered their preachers and their places of worship), while discouraging them from doing so by imposing penalties. Thus Catholics were denied all political and civil rights while Protestant dissenters – Presbyterians, Congregationalists, Baptists, Quakers and others – were denied political office and access to any university education. These penalties were designed to be fierce enough to discourage without being cruel enough to generate martyrs.

Samuel knew it would now be difficult for him to gain promotion in a Church which viewed High Anglicans with suspicion and so he went out of his way to continuously stress his loyalty to the crown. He later tried to inculcate a similar loyalty into all his children. Having sworn his obedience to the new Queen, Samuel was fully ordained on 24 February 1689 by the Bishop of London. His first clerical appointment was as a curate at St Botolph's, Aldersgate, but it soon proved impossible for him and Susanna to live on his small salary of £28 per year. The eighteenth-century Church has often been accused of being corrupt because of the practice of 'pluralism', by which many clergy held more than one post. However, this ignores the fact that many parishes were so poor that clergy could not survive without combining them together. About 10 per cent of the clerical positions in the country were worth under £20 a year and an uneducated labourer might earn around £15. About half the clergy, even if they held more than one position, earned no more than £80 a year.

Samuel was forced to make ends meet by accepting a post as a chaplain aboard a Royal Navy man-of-war in the Irish Sea. This was worth £70 per year but he found the conditions too appalling to stay in the job for long. Moreover, Susanna, who had temporarily returned to live with her father, discovered she was pregnant. She gave birth to a son on 10 February 1690 and named him Samuel after both his father and his grandfather. After only six months on board ship, Samuel returned to take up a post as curate at Newington Butts in Surrey and the young couple with their infant son moved into lodgings in a cheap boarding house. The salary for the new post was only £30 a year but Samuel hoped to be able to supplement his limited income by writing articles on religious topics for *The Athenian Gazette*. Published by his brother-in-law John Dunton, it was designed for literary circles and was very popular in the new coffee clubs which were springing up all over the capital. Some of its other contributors, such as Daniel Defoe and Dean Swift, were later to become quite distinguished authors. Samuel's contributions were less noteworthy.

In October 1691 Samuel became Vicar of South Ormsby, a small village of between two and three hundred people about 25 miles east of the cathedral city of Lincoln. Over half of all appointments to parishes were in lay control and South Ormsby was in the patronage of Lady Massingberd, whose son, the Marquis of Normanby, was connected with the Annesleys. Samuel described his new home as 'a mean cot, composed of reeds and clay',[6] but in fact it was a step up for him and his family and a much needed one because Susanna was pregnant again. Four children followed in rapid succession over the next four years, though only one survived. This child was named Emily and she was baptized in January 1693. The death of their other children was not unusual because the average death rate among infants at this time was around 50 per cent.

Samuel's income from the parish was only £50 a year. To make ends meet he took on additional curacy work in the parish of South Thoresby and continued writing for *The Athenian Gazette*. In 1693 he tried to gain royal patronage by dedicating to the Queen a very ambitious heroic poem in ten books on the life of Christ. It was reasonably well received and the poet laureate Nahum Tate compared it to the epic works of John Milton. In 1694 the Marquis of Normanby nominated him for an Irish bishopric but Samuel's hopes were dashed when he failed to win the appointment. The next year Samuel tried again to win royal favour by publishing his *Elegies on Queen Mary*, but critics claimed the queen liked the binding more than its contents! That same year Samuel was driven out of South Ormsby because he refused to allow his wife to associate with the mistress of a local magnate, John Saunderson, later Earl of Castlebar. Like his forebears, Samuel had put principle before personal considerations and he was reduced to taking up an ill-paid curacy in Swaby.

In 1696 Susanna's father died but their hopes of acquiring some of Annesley's money to offset their mounting debts were dashed because he bequeathed most of his estate to three of his other children. Susanna only received one shilling! The Wesleys were again rescued by the Marquis of Normanby, who had Samuel appointed as Rector of St Andrew's Church in Epworth. This was deemed to be worth potentially £150 to £200 per year but in other respects it was not a good appointment. Epworth was a small farming parish of about 1,100 inhabitants in northwest Lincolnshire. There was not even a road within a 40-mile radius of the village and it was so surrounded by fenland it was often reduced to an island in the winter months. The chances of gaining recognition for one's talents were non-existent because no one of any social worth ever visited Epworth. Moreover, its sizeable estate meant the holder of the living had to become a part-time farmer, and Samuel was far from suited to such a role.

This unprepossessing place was to become Charles' birthplace. It contained an unusually high percentage of dissenters, including about 70 Anabaptists, who were prone to insult any clergyman at every opportunity. When Samuel arrived there in 1697 with his family, he estimated that less than one in 20 of the population could recite the Lord's Prayer and even fewer the Creed. Only about 20 people regularly attended the church services. The only thing in Epworth's favour was that the family's debts now amounted to around £300 and it offered a larger income. Unfortunately, the very process of buying furniture and setting up home incurred more borrowing. Samuel also appears to have had to borrow money to prevent his mother going into prison for debt. By 1700 Samuel was complaining to the Archbishop of York that, although he had been able 'to stop the mouths of my most importunate creditors', he was still spending more than his income warranted and he feared part of the reason was 'not understanding worldly affairs'.[7]

Despite the pressures, Samuel proved a very conscientious minister in Epworth, offering two services every Sunday, mid-week prayers on Wednesdays and Fridays, and monthly communion services (the norm in rural areas was only about three or four times a year). He visited all his parishioners regularly, even allegedly when they did not want to see him! In 1700 he ordered books and tracts from the newly created Society for the Promotion of Christian Knowledge and encouraged eight of the more receptive of his parishioners to form themselves into a London-style religious society to study the Bible and encourage each other to adopt a more Christian lifestyle. He hoped this would lead to further societies being created, each with no more than a dozen members. The Epworth society was undoubtedly an influence on Charles' later creation of a 'Holy Club' in Oxford. Samuel also continued to publish religious tracts on a variety of subjects, including the role of the ideal cleric. Charles thus grew up in an environment where writing and publishing were the norm – this was to encourage him and his brother John to do the same.

Up until their time in Epworth Samuel appears to have felt his wife was a model of modesty and restraint, who 'graced my humble roof, and blest my life'.[8] He liked her passionate love for the Church and appreciated the value of her Puritan upbringing with its emphasis on personal devotion and a strict moral lifestyle. However, there was evident friction between the couple within a short time of their arrival at Epworth. Despite a number of infant deaths, they had six children by 1702. In addition to Samuel and Emily, there was Susannah (born 1695 and nicknamed Sukey), Mary (born 1696 and nicknamed Molly), Mehetebel (born 1697 and nicknamed Hetty), and Ann (born 1702 and nicknamed Nancy). The constant pregnancies not only inevitably affected Susanna's health but also made Samuel increasingly resentful of his ever-increasing family. It kept him tied to a parish which offered little job satisfaction and no hope of advancement. He warned his son to 'burn romances', 'shut his eyes and heart against any sexual urges', and never marry because 'there was never a truly great man who could not bridle his passions'.[9]

Outwardly Susanna continued to show Samuel the respect he expected, including calling him 'Sir' and 'My Master', but privately she resented his domineering and dogmatic approach. Samuel's main weakness was his inability to listen to those who had a different view from his own and Susanna later confessed to her children: 'Tis an unhappiness almost peculiar to our family that your father and I seldom think alike.'[10] He and Susanna had always had different opinions about the validity of the Glorious Revolution of 1688 because she had never accepted the dethronement of a God-anointed king. Now Samuel chose to make her views a reason for ending their marriage. The death of Queen Mary and the decision of the government to accept her husband William as sole king acted as the trigger because Susanna found it impossible to accept that this Dutchman had any proper claim to the throne. She refused to say 'Amen' to her husband's prayers for William. Samuel told her: 'You and I must part; for if we have two Kings, we must have two beds.'

The resulting separation was certainly about more than differing attitudes to William of Orange because the king was killed in a riding accident on 8 March and yet the dispute continued. Samuel wanted an excuse to leave his family. He told Susanna he would accuse her of treason before the Bishop of Lincoln and the Archbishop of York, and then, on 5 April, he left Epworth to spend Easter in London, saying he was looking to return to a naval chaplaincy. The deserted Susanna wrote for advice to Lady Yarborough, a noblewoman who was known to support the restoration of James II. She advised Susanna to seek the advice of Dr George Hickes, the Suffragan Bishop of Thetford, who had lost his post as Dean of Worcester Cathedral for refusing to swear his loyalty. Susanna duly obliged, and Hickes told her to stick to what her conscience told her to do because Samuel could not expect her to perjure herself by making promises that ran contrary to her beliefs. Susanna told Samuel this when he returned from London, and he immediately cursed her and walked out of the house, saying this time he intended to leave her forever. He had been back home for less than two days.

According to Susanna, Samuel did not get very far because 'he met a clergyman to whom he communicated his intentions ... and he prevailed with him to return'.[11] It has been suggested the real reason for his return was that the Epworth Rectory was set ablaze. Susanna later said the fire was the product of a careless accident by a servant, but some historians have surmised it was arson by a disaffected parishioner. Two-thirds of the rectory was destroyed. The fire was so coincidental on Samuel's curse that both he and Susanna thought it was 'the finger of God'[12] in judgement on their quarrel. Talk of him leaving his family was dropped. The immediate fruit of their reunion was the birth of a son nine months later on 17 June 1703. They named him John (after Samuel's father). However, their marriage remained unhappy and Samuel spent as much time as he could away in London. Fear of the consequences of marriage was to be instilled into his second son, John, and with disastrous consequences.

Samuel determined that his elder son should not be doomed like him to live in a backwater. By this time the young Samuel was showing academic promise, largely due to the coaching first of Susanna and then a schoolmaster called John Holland, a teacher who frequently 'showed his kindness on his pupils' knuckles'.[13] Samuel's intelligence had come as a surprise because he had initially been deemed backward as a result of his not speaking till he was five years old. Legend says his first words were 'Here I am, mother', spoken to Susanna when she could not find him because he had hidden under the family table. In 1704 Samuel decided it would be worth sending his son away to study at Westminster School in London, even though the family could ill afford the cost. Alongside Eton and Winchester, Westminster was a main feeder school for Oxford and Cambridge and it was regarded as the training ground for society's future leaders in both Church and State. Samuel hoped his son would mix with the sons of many influential people, thus opening up avenues for a successful career.

Susanna was anxious whether her son would be corrupted by the other boys. She wrote regularly to him, telling him to remain true to his faith:

In all things endeavour to act upon principle, and do not live like the rest of mankind, who pass through the world like straws upon a river, which are carried which way the stream or wind drives them.[14]

Her constant theme was the importance of religion as something which should be expressed in his daily living and in his attitude to others, especially those less fortunate than himself: 'We express our love to God by being friendly and beneficent to all that bear his image.'[15] Within three years Samuel won himself a scholarship and he soon became the protégé of Francis Atterbury, the Dean of Westminster. He was also specially selected to read at night to the elderly Bishop of Rochester, Dr Thomas Sprat, then deemed one of the country's finest scholars. Samuel's success encouraged his father to seek similar opportunities for John and Charles by also sending them to London for their education.

His son's attendance at Westminster gave Samuel greater excuse to go to London, as did his appointment as a member of Convocation. Samuel now made no effort to hide how much he disliked working in a remote

parish. He was too intellectual in his approach for the Epworth parishioners and he disliked being away from where all the latest news was
so avidly discussed and debated. He was painfully aware his charitable
activities had failed to win over his parishioners' affections and they remained hostile to his High Anglican approach to worship and his almost
Puritanical dedication to church discipline. For example, they hated the
way he insisted on any person found guilty of adultery being made to
stand for three successive Sundays 'on the damp mud floor in the centre
of the church, without shoes or stockings; bareheaded; covered with a
white sheet; and shivering with cold ... as a warning to others.'[16] In reply
ill-wishers maimed his cattle and vandals molested his property.

In 1705 Samuel succeeded in offending some key local figures by supporting the wrong candidates in a parliamentary election. As a result
he and his family faced a screaming mob which fired guns at the house.
Susanna had only recently given birth and the family nurse was so frightened she inadvertently smothered the child. This tragedy may have led to
Samuel's enemies deciding to act by more legal methods. They demanded
that Samuel pay money he owed because it was known he lacked the necessary funds to do so. This led to his immediate arrest and imprisonment
for debt. Repairing his house after the fire of 1702 and paying for his
elder son's education were factors in his excessive borrowing, but much
of the problem lay in his bad management and frequent absence, which
meant he often failed to collect tithes from hostile parishioners. One of
his daughters commented, 'My father will never be worth a groat, as the
saying is, and we of the female part of the family consequently left to get
our own bread or starve.'[17]

Samuel tried to bear his imprisonment in Lincoln Castle with Christian
forbearance, asking God to not let him hate those who had put him there
or become 'querulous, or impatient, or envious'.[18] Susanna sent him the
little jewellery she possessed, including her wedding ring, so he could
purchase better treatment from his gaolers, but he refused to accept
her sacrifice. Publicly he tried to make a virtue out of his imprisonment
by offering Christian witness to his fellow prisoners and saying he was
better treated there than in Epworth. Privately he was devastated and he
commenced what eventually proved his best prose work, *Dissertations
on the Book of Job*. It was an apt topic for a man in his position.

Samuel stayed in prison for three months while his friends gradually
raised the funds to pay his debts and secure his release. In a letter to
the Archbishop of York Samuel wrote how in his absence his wife was
facing terrible persecution. This included someone attacking their cows
and their house-dog with a scythe. Such appalling behaviour must have
deeply scarred the family's view of Epworth. There is also evidence that

Susanna made herself ill by not eating properly in order to feed her children. Understandably it was galling to her that her husband's talents were wasted in Epworth:

> I should think it a thousand pities that a man of his brightness, and rare endowments of learning and useful knowledge, in relation to the church of God, should be confined to an obscure corner of the country, where his talents are buried.[19]

While in prison Samuel pinned his hopes on winning promotion by writing patriotic verse. Since 1701 Britain had been at war with France and Spain as part of a long process to weaken the power of the French king Louis XIV. The main commander of the British forces was John Churchill, Earl of Marlborough, and in 1704 he had won the first of a series of very important victories at the Battle of Blenheim. Samuel produced a celebratory poem entitled 'Marlborough or the Fate of Europe'. It cannot have pleased Susanna because she found nothing to celebrate in a war between Christian nations. She prayed to God 'to put a stop to the effusion of Christian blood, and in His own goodtime to restore us the blessing of public peace'.[20] It is interesting that both John and Charles Wesley in later life were to share their mother's views on the undesirability of war.

The poem was well received by Marlborough, who offered Samuel an army chaplaincy, but the pay was less than his income from Epworth. Some of his friends advised him to accept in the hope it would lead to other positions, but Samuel hoped for a better offer and his pride made him reluctant to leave Epworth so shortly after his time in prison lest his enemies see that as a victory. He wrongly hoped that more poetry would bring a better post. In reality his verse was not as good as he thought it was, and even Samuel's publisher thought he wrote too fast to write well. Charles was to far outshine his father's poetic talent. The only hymn Samuel wrote that achieved a degree of success was one on the crucifixion entitled 'Behold the Saviour of Mankind'. Interestingly, the crucifixion was equally to inspire some of Charles' best hymns.

Once released, Samuel still made repeated visits to London, though he could not afford to do so. Many years later one of Susanna's brothers, Samuel Annesley, expressed surprise that his sister had put up with her husband's incompetence as a provider for his family for so long. Susanna replied she was loyal to Samuel whatever his faults, but the tone of her letter has been taken by some to imply she stayed more from Christian duty than from love. As far as Samuel was concerned, spending time with his family was far less exciting than being involved in the debates and discussions taking place in London on issues like the signing of the 1707 Act of Union, which formally united England and Scotland into Great Britain. His main contribution to the family was to continue making Susanna repeatedly pregnant on his infrequent visits home. Susanna suffered further miscarriages and infant deaths, but she successfully added three more children to the family: Martha (born 1707 and nicknamed Patty), Kezziah (born 1710 and nicknamed Kezzy) and Charles, who was born two months prematurely on 18 December 1707. Their third son was possibly named after the martyred monarch of that name. In total it is thought Susanna had 19 children by her husband but only ten of these had survived infancy.

Susanna's entire world became her children and even Samuel had to admit she was 'the best of mothers'.[21] It was only her constant care that ensured the infant Charles did not die. She wrapped him up in soft wool until the time at which he should have been born and for those weeks he neither cried nor opened his eyes. It has been suggested some of Charles' later health problems stem partially from his premature birth. Once his life was not in jeopardy the normal family rules were applied. He was taught to 'cry softly' in order to escape 'abundance of correction' (presumably because Samuel was too much prone to beat any child who disturbed him with 'that most odious noise of crying').[22] As soon as the young Charles could speak, Susanna taught him to say the Lord's Prayer. It is said he inherited his father's short temper and was given to childish tantrums but, if so, he was soon taught greater self-control by being made to 'fear the rod'. Susanna had little time for those parents who ignored wilful behaviour out of 'foolish fondness' and thereby doomed their children to bad habits.

Both Susanna and Samuel believed all their ten children should be made to do exactly what they were told, even in small matters. They had to seek permission before doing anything, even leaving the room. The family sat down together for three set meals a day, so proper table manners were learnt. No one was permitted to shout for what they wanted at table. They had to make whispered requests instead. The children had to eat what they were given and they were not permitted to have any snacks between meals. If sick, they had to take medicine without complaint. When they played they had to do so quietly so as not to disturb others and Susanna monitored with whom her children mixed because she felt 'a clownish accent and many rude ways' were easily transferred between children if left unobserved.[23] Susanna was also particularly concerned to warn them against excessive drinking when they were older.

It was instilled into Charles that self-control alone could conquer and control his innate sinfulness:

Self-will is the root of all sin and misery, so whatever cherishes this in children insures ... [their] wretchedness and irreligion; whatever checks and mortifies it promotes their future happiness and piety ... Religion is nothing else than doing the will of God, and not our own ... The parent, who studies to subdue self-will in his child, works together with God in the renewing and saving a soul. The parent who indulges it does the devil's work; makes religion impracticable [and] salvation unattainable.[24]

Some historians have tended to represent Susanna's disciplinary methods as unduly harsh. A few have implied she wrecked her children's lives by crushing their wills so that even as mature adults they found it difficult to do anything but obey her. However, Susanna did not want to crush their spirit, merely their selfishness, and she actively encouraged independent thinking – hence John and Charles' willingness to challenge the customs of the age. She also saw religion as something joyful rather than life-denying. Charles later reflected her motivation in one of his hymns:

To time our every smile or frown
To mark the bounds of good and ill:
And beat the pride of nature down,
And bend or break his rising will.[25]

And John wrote in a treatise on education that a parent's role was 'to correct with kind severity' rather than see a child become ill-disciplined.[26]

Much of the modern criticism of Susanna reflects the child-rearing philosophies of a later age and distorts her views. It ignores the fact she felt punishment should never take place without due cause or without appropriate restraint. She believed that by physically punishing a child when very small, he or she soon learnt to obey and this made later punishment unnecessary. Just to raise the voice or wag an admonishing finger became sufficient. Once a parent and child had the right kind of relationship Susanna felt 'a great many childish follies and inadvertencies may be passed by'.[27] She constantly stressed the importance of both praise and forgiveness, saying every act of obedience 'should be always commended and frequently rewarded' and that parents should make allowances for their children because of 'the weakness of their reason, and immaturity of their judgements'. If a child did something wrong but the intention was good, that should be taken into account, and there was no need for punishment if a child confessed his or her guilt and promised to amend.

Charles certainly felt his mother's approach was based primarily on love not punishment. He later reflected her views in one of his hymns on bringing up children:

We would persuade their hearts to obey;
With mildest zeal proceed;
And never take the harsher way
When love will do the deed.[28]

Above all, Susanna taught by example, believing parental actions always speak louder than words:

Religion is not to be confined to the church, or closet, nor exercised only in prayer and meditation. Everywhere we are in the presence of God, and every word and action is capable of morality.[29]

Charles was, of course, too young to remember the famous rectory fire, which occurred in 1709 when he was still just 18 months old. The blaze started in the middle of the night and it may have been another arson attack. Susanna, who was almost eight months pregnant at the time, afterwards wrote how the family had no time to don clothes and ran naked out of their burning home. Her legs and face were burnt when three times she ran back into the flames to try and ensure all her children were saved. Charles owed his escape to a maid who carried him out of the burning building. The five-year-old John was trapped upstairs in a bedroom but a resourceful parishioner told another to climb on his shoulders and so reach him. John was snatched to safety literally minutes before the burning thatch roof collapsed into the room and he later referred to himself as 'a brand plucked from the burning'. In reality the whole family felt their escape was miraculous.

The house and all its contents were totally destroyed and rebuilding their home was to lead to real hardship for many years. Though the Ecclesiastical Commissioners paid part of the cost, it is estimated Samuel had to add at least £400 to his existing debts. Initially the children were sent temporarily to live with friends, except for two of the girls, Sukey and Hetty, who went to live with their uncle, Matthew Annesley, who was a prosperous apothecary in London. Sukey never returned home. Instead, she was asked to live with another of her mother's brothers, Samuel Annesley, and eventually married in 1721 a tax officer called Richard Ellison, whom Susanna felt was 'little inferior to the apostate angels in wickedness'.[30] The little information we have indicates he treated Sukey harshly and despotically. Hetty did return once the shell of a new rectory had been erected, but her time in London had made her resentful of its restricted and isolated lifestyle and this was to cause future family problems.

Despite the problems generated by the fire, Samuel continued travelling frequently to London. He wanted to be involved in the debates that were taking place within the Church over its organization and role. Some clergy resented the way in which the bishops had subordinated their religious role to their political one and felt it was time for the Church to assert its independence. Others wanted to end even the limited tolerance being shown to dissenters. Many were increasingly involved in the party politics between Whigs and Tories over what should happen to the monarchy if Queen Anne died childless. The choice lay between the son of the deposed James II and the Elector of Hanover, who had a distant claim to the throne but who had the advantage of being a staunch Protestant.

In 1709 the inherent tensions erupted following a speech by an ambitious and publicity-seeking High Anglican clergyman called Dr Henry Sacheverell, who was a Fellow of Magdalen College, Oxford. He was impeached for his 'furious rant against dissenters, occasional conformists, unlicensed schools, "moderate" bishops ... and all who gainsaid the primitive doctrine of loyalty and obedience'.[31] Dr Sacheverell's trial was held in March 1710 in Westminster Hall before the House of Lords amid scenes of massive public unrest over his alleged persecution. Sacheverell's defence was placed in the hands of Francis Atterbury, the Dean of Westminster. According to John Wesley, his father assisted Atterbury in his preparation for the trial. The Dean proved a brilliant defender, saying Sacheverell was just a loyal priest who had been grievously misrepresented by spiteful opponents. This did not prevent the House of Lords finding Sachaverell guilty, but it was only by a narrow majority of 17 votes, and he was given the minimum possible sentence of three years' suspension from preaching. He left the court a national hero.

Samuel's increasing life in London contributed to the increasing poverty experienced by his family. An absent clergyman simply could not expect to extract his proper revenue from his estates and Susanna recorded her disappointment that, however much she tried to save money by 'care, frugality, and industry', the family always appeared to end up in greater difficulties than her 'boasted prudence' could have foreseen. Nor can it have helped that the family had to find funds not only to rebuild their home, but also to pay for the young Samuel to go from Westminster to Christ Church College, Oxford, in 1711. One of his sisters recorded: 'For seven winters my father was in London, and we at home in intolerable want and affliction ... vast income but no comfort or credit from it.'[32]

Family hardships and frequent illnesses did not prevent Susanna undertaking some of her absent husband's duties. As a former dissenter, she was used to lay people leading sessions of prayer and reading sermons to congregations so she increasingly took on this role. Her personal version of the Apostle's Creed is admired more than any of the writings of Samuel and recent collections of her prayers have shown Susanna had a way of using words to let her faith shine out. Initially she intended her sessions of prayers and readings to be only for her family, but her reputation soon grew and her sessions of worship became far more popular than her husband's services had ever been. It is said up to three hundred people attended them. She had an extraordinary breadth of interest and knowledge of what was happening in religious circles. Among the things she read out to the parishioners of Epworth were accounts of missionary work being undertaken by Germans in India!

In 1712 Samuel challenged what she was doing because he was stung by the harsh comments of his fellow clergy, who were very hostile to anyone, especially a woman, undertaking what they regarded as priestly functions. A righteously indignant Susanna stuck to her guns:

> In your absence I cannot but look upon every soul you leave under my care as a talent committed to me under a trust by the great lord of all the families of heaven and earth ... It came into my mind, though I am not a man nor a minister of the gospel, and so cannot be employed in such a worthy employment ... yet if my heart were sincerely devoted to God, and if I were inspired with a true zeal for his glory and did really desire the salvation of souls, I might do somewhat more than I do.[33]

She told him she would only stop if he took full responsibility for any souls that might be damned as a consequence of her inaction. Their mother's refusal to give up her preaching was to be something that Charles and John Wesley were to remember when they subsequently faced opposition from clergy over their decision to make use of lay preachers. The saving of souls outweighed all else.

Following Charles' fifth birthday in December 1712 Susanna began teaching him his alphabet. She believed it was only from this age that a child was ready for more formal instruction. Studying meant six hours per day of 'vigorous application' in which no excuses were accepted and play was not permitted, but she appears to have been a charismatic teacher. Her children later spoke with affection of their lessons:

> Learning here placed her richer stores in view,
> Or, winged with love, the minutes gaily flew.[34]

It is said within a day Charles was able to read all his letters and to read the first verse of Genesis. At a time when rote learning was the norm, Susanna encouraged true understanding. Hence her son John's later comments that schools should avoid turning children into mind-less parrots.[35] Part of her success lay in her incredible patience. On one occasion Samuel was amazed to hear his wife go over a topic 20 times with one of the children and he told her he could not understand how she could do that. She replied, 'If I had satisfied myself by mentioning it only nineteen times, I should have lost all my labour. It was the twentieth time that crowned it.'[36]

In January 1714 Charles' brother John was sent away on a scholar-ship to Charterhouse, one of two London charity schools associated with almshouses for the poor (the other being Christ's Hospital). The nomination for John's scholarship came from the former Marquis of Normanby, now Duke of Buckinghamshire. The timing appeared per-fect because his elder brother Samuel had become a teacher in West-minster School thanks to the influence of Francis Atterbury, who had been appointed Bishop of Rochester the previous year. Samuel was well placed to keep an eye on John's welfare. This was important because ever since the fire of 1709 Susanna had viewed John as specially chosen by God and had vowed 'to be more particularly careful of the soul of this child'.[37] Charles' subsequent readiness to obey John may well have stemmed from imbibing his mother's belief.

John's departure meant Charles was left in an essentially female household for the next two years. Susanna gave each of her children her undivided attention on a given day and for Charles this was every Satur-day. Susanna taught him the importance of getting into the right habits in order to live a good life. Her advocacy of adopting a methodical pat-tern to their day was to play an important part in the later development of Methodism with its emphasis on religious routines. The strict family guidelines on expected behaviour included that Charles should keep his promises, be honest in all he said, and admit any mistakes. He had to be courteous to others (including the servants) and respect other people's property. This included never invading 'the property of another in the smallest matter, whether it were but the value of a farthing or a pin'.[38] None of the children were permitted to borrow anything without the full consent of its owner.

Charles grew up in a household where singing psalms, saying prayers and reading passages from the Bible were regular daily features and where religion was a way of life and not just a matter of certain outward observances. Susanna told one of her daughters:

'Tis not learning these things by rote, nor the saying a few prayers morning and evening, that will bring you to heaven; you must under-stand what you say, and you must practise what you know.[39]

Her father had taught Susanna to give her studies what he called 'heart-room' and part of this process of meditation involved regular self-examination. She strongly commended this approach to all her own children.

By April 1716 Charles was himself old enough to leave the female-dominated environment of home and go to school in London. He later summed up his gratitude for the education he had received at the hands of both his parents in the following hymn:

> With thanks I rejoice
> In Thy fatherly choice
> Of my state and condition below;
> If of parents I came
> Who honoured Thy name,
> 'Twas Thy wisdom appointed it so.[40]

Charles went to Westminster School because his brother Samuel had agreed to pay his brother's fees there and give him board and lodging. Samuel was 17 years older and by temperament well suited to become a second father to him. Susanna was happy because there was clearly less chance that attending the school might corrupt Charles.

The year of Charles' departure from home saw very strange events take place at Epworth Rectory. On 2 December one of the family's servants, Robert, heard knockings on the door when no one was there and, when he retired to bed, saw a strange object whirling to the accompaniment of sounds which were similar to a gobbling turkey-cock. The next day a maid heard knockings in the dairy and then it was the turn of Charles' sisters, Molly and Sukey, to hear strange sounds. Susanna was initially inclined to disbelieve their accounts, but then she heard the sound of a rocking cradle in a room where there was none. When Susanna told Samuel, he was extremely angry at their credulity. However, that evening Samuel performed family prayers and 'a thundering knock attended the Amen'. The whole family was frequently subjected to the apparently supernatural noises until the end of January 1717.

It is likely Charles was told of these strange events. His brother Samuel tried to persuade the family that there was a rational explanation, such as servants playing tricks or animals in the house. Susanna replied that she had long sought to explain away the noises by arguing it must be 'only rats or weasels that disturbed us', but in the end she had had to admit 'that it was beyond the power of any human creature to make such strange and various noises'.[41] She eventually decided the noises and disturbances might be an indicator that her brother Samuel Annesley, who was serving in the East India Company, was dead, but this was erroneous.[42] Emily Wesley told her brother John she thought it stemmed from witchcraft because they had thrice seen what looked like a headless badger. Historians have tended to see the strange events as a practical joke engineered either by those parishioners who still wanted to get rid of the Wesleys or by one of the family themselves (usually this is identified as the spirited and rebellious Hetty).

For many years afterwards the family still continued to record hearing occasional unusual noises and items moving of their own accord. We do not know why but eventually they attached the name 'Old Jeffery' to their poltergeist. As far as we know Charles never encountered 'Old Jeffery', but it is thought his brother John did. 'Old Jeffery' may well explain why both brothers were at times to show an overreadiness to accept the supernatural in their future dealings with people, despite their normal emphasis on the importance of using reason to determine what one believed.

Charles, of course, was facing other excitements at this time as he embarked more fully on his education in London. Being able to spend time with his two elder brothers must have given him especial pleasure. Less happy was that national events had provided a severe setback to the career hopes of his oldest brother. In 1714 Queen Anne had died and the Whig Party quickly ensured its candidate, George Louis, Elector of Hanover, became King George I before the Tories could effect sufficient support for the son of James II. In 1715 the most committed of the Jacobites had tried in vain to reverse this with an abortive rebellion in Scotland, thereby tainting the names of Tory and High Anglican with the suspicion of treason. This was a serious blow to any chance of the Wesleys gaining clerical promotion. The one consolation for Charles was that this meant his brother Samuel stayed at Westminster. His influence on Charles was to become very considerable over the next ten years.

It is sometimes forgotten that it was Samuel who was viewed as the model son by his parents, rather than John or Charles. Samuel's faith appears to have had none of the doubts that were to assail his younger brothers. By all accounts he was a very committed Christian with a real calling 'to strengthen such as do stand [firm in their faith], to comfort and help the weak hearted, to raise up those that fall, and finally to beat down Satan'.[43] At a time when it was regarded as undesirable to show emotion in one's religion, he wrote hymns that were often unashamedly passionate, especially if they were about Christ's sacrifice on the cross:

My sins give sharpness to the nail,
And pointed every thorn.[44]

As a student at Christ Church College, Oxford, he had 'gained a reputation beyond most of his contemporaries, being thoroughly skilled in the learned languages, and master of Classics to a degree of perfection, perhaps not very common'.[45] His circle of friends included a number of gifted intellectuals, including the future famous poet and satirist Alexander Pope.

This clever, conscientious and charitable man was prepared to spend much of his income on bailing out his parents whenever their debts reached crisis proportions and on contributing very significantly towards the costs of educating both his younger brothers. Not surprisingly they 'always spoke of him with the highest reverence, respect and affection'.[46] He took his responsibility as their guardian very seriously, and Charles was largely brought up by him and his wife. She was the daughter of a cleric called John Berry, who boarded some of Westminster's young pupils and it was because of this Samuel was able to suggest Charles could exchange his family home in Epworth for one in London. The character of Samuel's wife is not easy to depict because we have contradictory accounts. Samuel clearly loved her deeply and thought she combined 'plain sense and humble sweetness'.[47] Charles felt she needed careful handling and her sisters-in-law found her waspish. This may have been because she resented how much Samuel financially gave to his family.

Living with Samuel undoubtedly helped mould Charles' views on the nature of the Church of England, inspiring him with a deep love of its modes of worship. Westminster School functioned literally within the shadow of Westminster Abbey, which served as the school's chapel, and it has been surmised that its worship and other activities must have made an impact on a boy brought up (unlike some of his peers) to be religious, even if he later claimed he was inattentive at public worship. We know, for example, that Charles was expected to write about the sermons he heard preached and sometimes translate them into Latin. At the age of 11 Charles witnessed a particularly memorable religious event: the midnight burial of the poet, politician and essayist Joseph Addison, who was famous for his many articles in the leading periodicals of the day. Samuel had been on very friendly terms with Addison and almost certainly Charles would have been one of the pupils chosen to stand round the open grave with tapers in their hands to light the ceremony. Charles probably took pride not only in attending such a ceremony, but in the fact that his eldest brother moved in such exalted circles and was respected as a poet in his own right.

Charles found conditions at Westminster School to be even more spartan than those back home. The boys had to rise at 5.15 am and, after reciting the morning collect on their knees and washing with cold water, attend Latin prayers at 6.00 am. They then studied Latin grammar and Greek until it was time for their 8 am breakfast. Further study then took place until supper time, interrupted only by dinner at midday. Monitors, who 'kept them strictly to the speaking of Latin', maintained strict discipline. The boys were expected to go to bed at 8.00 pm. Even though the change was eased by initially living with Samuel, it must have come as an enormous cultural shock for Charles to move from isolated, rural and sparsely populated Epworth to the noisy clamour of the crowded streets of London and to exchange his home-schooling within a predominantly female family for the hurly-burly of a school of over four hundred rumbustious boys, most of whom came from far wealthier homes. Poor 'foundationers' were in a tiny minority and most of his classmates had fathers who were leading bishops, generals, admirals, politicians and the like.

Though there was rigid discipline within the classroom, there was often lawlessness outside it, and the richer of the school's pupils had a reputation for immoral and drunken behaviour. One contemporary commented that 'schools offer a system of premature debauchery that only prevents men from being corrupted by the world, by corrupting them before they enter the world'.[48] Not surprisingly, Charles wrote in later life of how he had to resist the temptations from his fellow pupils to be led astray:

What but a miracle of grace
Could keep my soul within
The mouth of hell, the murderer's ways,
The public schools of sin;
Where troops of young corrupters tried
In wickedness to excel,
Lewdness their vile delight, and pride
Their boasted principle?[49]

He also wrote about how boys take a 'wicked delight' in mocking each other, in destroying the innocence of others, and in learning to curse and swear and fight.[50]

The headmaster at the time when Charles was there was Dr Robert Friend, who wanted to produce the finest classical scholars in the country. Schools at this time paid little attention to mathematics and science. They focused their attention on studying ancient Greece and Rome as models of civilization and on developing in their pupils the art of thinking, writing and speaking. It was judged that classical writers were the best teachers of how to use language and the art of rhetoric was regarded as an essential skill to be studied. Among the many famous old boys of Westminster School who had benefited from this approach were George Herbert, Christopher Wren, John Locke and John Dryden. The teaching at Westminster undoubtedly significantly contributed towards Charles' later skills as a preacher and hymnwriter.

Samuel was central to this education and by all accounts a very fine teacher. When he later became a headmaster it was said of him that he was 'nearly idolized' and that 'children were sent from all quarters to be placed under his tuition'.[51] He rapidly communicated his own classical scholarship to Charles and encouraged him to especially love poetry, introducing him to far better examples of that medium than anything their father had produced. Charles soon came to greatly admire many of the classical poets and in particular Virgil. He could quote by heart many sections of the 'Aeneid'. Samuel was a prolific poet in his own right, writing in a variety of metres (something Charles was later to emulate) and producing an endless string of odes and satires, hymns and songs, elegies and epigrams, many of them very witty.

Samuel reinforced their mother's teaching that religion was real only if expressed through daily living. Contemporaries thought his life embodied 'useful charity'.[52] This was highlighted in 1719 when he became a key figure in establishing an infirmary at Westminster for the relief of the sick and needy (this later became St George's Hospital on Hyde Park Corner). Charles admired his brother's generosity and strong social conscience and later made clear in his hymnwriting that to serve the poor was to serve Christ. He became highly critical of clergy who did not undertake charitable work:

> Ambitious, covetous, and vain,
> Priests who in ease and pleasure live,
> They persecute their Lord again,
> His members vex, his Spirit grieve.[53]

We know little more of Charles' time as a schoolboy except that he earned himself a reputation as a courageous and skilful fighter. This was probably necessary in order to survive the school's rather harsh environment. One of the stories told of his time at Westminster concerns his defence of a new boy called James Murray, who was being bullied partly because he had a Scottish accent and partly because his family were viewed as Jacobites. Politics certainly impinged on the lives of the boys because some of them regularly visited the nearby Westminster Hall, which was the stage for some of the great dramas of the day. In the aftermath of the Jacobite Rebellion of 1715 many a treason trial featured there and it is not surprising some boys felt inspired to emulate the proceedings. Charles' defence of James Murray must have been very courageous and may have been inspired by the pro-Jacobite sympathies of his mother and eldest brother. Murray was obviously grateful for Charles' timely support because in later life he became Lord Chief Justice and used his position to help Charles when he came under attack because of his Methodism.

Charles was a lively pupil and it was soon evident he had the makings of an excellent classical scholar (more so than his brother John at Charterhouse). Charles' hard work was encouraged by his awareness that his family were clearly struggling to pay his fees. In 1719 assistance came from the purse of an Irishman from County Meath called Garrett Wesley, who had no children of his own. He hoped to adopt Charles simply because he bore his name, even though was no direct family connection. However, when Charles refused to go to Ireland, Garrett looked elsewhere. He eventually opted to leave his fortune to a relative called Richard Colley on condition he took the name of Wesley or, as it later became, Wellesley. Colley's son was later the father of both the Duke of Wellington, who defeated Napoleon at the Battle of Waterloo, and the Marquis of Wellesley, who was a key figure in the British conquest of India.

In 1720 the 13-year-old Charles strove to win a free education at his school by becoming a King's Scholar (as his brother Samuel had been). This involved him in weeks of extensive extra study, mostly undertaken in the early hours of the morning and with the assistance of an older boy who acted as his tutor (and caned him if he did not perform well!). Once he was ready, Charles faced examination through a series of 'challenges' in which he and the other candidates for scholarship went twice a day before the headmaster and took it in turns to ask each other the most difficult questions they could devise. These challenges took place about three days a week for about eight to ten weeks so it was a demanding process. To his family's delight Charles won one of the nine scholarships on offer and this not only eased the financial problem of keeping him at the school but also meant he could move into the school itself rather than boarding with Samuel.

Because of Samuel's role at Westminster, Charles had less freedom than his brother John at Charterhouse. However, John stayed with Samuel and his wife on many occasions and one has to assume that the remarkably deep friendship which Charles showed throughout his life for 'Jack' (as he affectionately called John) had its origins in the four years when both were at school in London. Unfortunately there is very little evidence about their time together in these years, probably because both men were subsequently rather ashamed they had not fully lived up to the ideal expected of them either by their mother or brother! John later admitted he committed a number of sins while at school. Charles was thought to be 'exceedingly sprightly and active, very apt to learn, but arch and unlucky, though not ill-natured'.[54] That probably means that when he did get up to relatively innocent escapades he usually got caught!

In June 1720 John left London to go as a student to Christ Church College in Oxford. Five years later Charles was to join him there and open a new chapter in the lives of them both.

The Holy Club

Come, thou holy God and true!
Come, and my whole heart renew;
take me now, possess me whole,
form the Saviour in my soul:
    In my heart thy name reveal,
    stamp me with thy Spirit's seal,
    change my nature into thine,
    in me thy whole image shine:
Happy soul, whose active love
emulates the Blessed above,
in thy every action seen,
sparkling from the soul within:
    Thou to every sufferer nigh,
    hearest, not in vain, the cry
    of widow in distress,
    of the poor, the shelterless:
Raiment thou to all that need,
To the hungry dealest bread,
To the sick givest relief,
Soothest hapless prisoner's grief:
    Love, which willest all should live,
    Love, that over all prevails,
    Love, that never, never fails.
    Love immense, and unconfined,
    Love to all of humankind.[1]

Charles' years at Westminster School were very successful ones but his achievements were overshadowed by the clash between his elder brother Samuel and powerful figures in government. Samuel's loyalty to his patron and friend, Francis Atterbury, Bishop of Rochester, was an ever-increasing liability to his career prospects. Unlike his fellow bishops, Atterbury had refused to sign a declaration of loyalty during the abortive Jacobite Rebellion of 1715 and he had subsequently become a major critic of the Whig government led by Sir Robert Walpole. In 1722 this culminated in his arrest for treason. Atterbury was imprisoned in the Tower of London and sentenced to banishment. Had Samuel been less loyal to him it is thought he might have become the headmaster of Westminster, but his denunciation of the government's treatment of Atterbury removed all chances of such promotion.

Another blow to the hopes of the Wesleys occurred in 1724 when Samuel Annesley mysteriously disappeared. As the wealthiest of their connections, they had assumed he might financially help his nephews and nieces on his return from East India. Susanna travelled to London to meet his ship. It was the first time she had been out of Epworth since going there and her arrival must have been a great thrill for Charles who had not seen her since entering his school. However, when the ship docked Samuel Annesley did not disembark to greet his waiting sister. Neither he nor his money was ever heard of again and it is now assumed he may have been murdered. It was a particular blow to Charles' remaining unmarried sisters because all hope of obtaining dowries to attract husbands died with his disappearance.

A particular tragedy then struck Charles' favourite sister, the fun-loving but headstrong Hetty. She was educated to a level unusual in women of the day, being proficient in Latin and Greek by the age of nine. She hated Epworth, describing it in verse as a place 'debarred of wisdom, wit, and grace' and its inhabitants as 'asses dull, on dunghills born ... a sordid race'.[2] She had long feared she might end up as a spinster given her isolated existence and her father's 'sour-faced' attitude towards any potential suitor,[3] but in 1724 she fell in love with a very handsome and intelligent graduate from Oxford called John Romley. He had been appointed as her father's curate when Samuel acquired a second living to add to that of Epworth. This was the parish of Wroote and it added about £50 to the family income, as well as enabling Samuel and Susanna to move into its parsonage so they could rent out the Epworth rectory to their daughter Sukey and her much disliked husband Richard Ellison, to whom Samuel owed money.

Unfortunately for Hetty, her father overheard John Romley singing a song which Samuel deemed vulgar and so he dismissed him and banned him from the house. When Hetty secretly communicated with Romley, Samuel packed her off to serve as a lady companion to a family in the town of Kelstern. She wrote to her brother John in March 1725:

I had far rather have gone to my grave! ... I am in no great measure careless what becomes of me. Home I would not go to, were I reduced to beggary, and here I will never stay ... I intend to try my hand in London ... [Here] I am condemned to constant solitude.[4]

Trying her hand in London was her coded way of saying she had decided to elope with a local lawyer called Will Atkins. In her desperation she had chosen the worst kind of man. She was forced to return home after only one disastrous night in which it became clear that sex rather than marriage was the lawyer's only desire.

Samuel refused to forgive his daughter and, when he discovered she was pregnant, insisted on her immediately marrying another man as soon as he could find anyone prepared to have her. This proved to be a poorly educated glazier and plumber called William Wright from the nearby town of Louth. It is said only one of Hetty's sisters, the crippled Mary, had the courage to try to stop this, telling her father: 'You are seldom kind and rarely just ... You are a tyrant to those you love; and now in your tyranny you are going to do ... a downright wickedness.'[5] Hetty and Wright were married on 13 October 1725. It was a disastrous match made worse by her husband's tendency towards heavy drinking. In the circumstances it is not surprising that Hetty's child proved frail and only survived a couple of months.

This was the situation when the 19-year-old Charles completed his final term at Westminster. By then he had earned himself the honour of being appointed 'Captain of School', which made him the chief liaison person between the masters and the boys, and he had won a king's scholarship to Christ Church College in Oxford by coming top in his final examinations. He had also become a delightful young man as those whom he was to meet at university were shortly to testify:

Charles Wesley was a man made for friendship; who, by his cheerfulness and vivacity, would refresh his friend's heart; with attentive consideration, would enter into and settle all his concerns; so far as he was able, would do anything for him, great or small; and, by a habit of openness and freedom, leave no room for misunderstanding.[6]

Unfortunately, the scholarship, which was worth £100 per year, was insufficient to entirely fund him going to Oxford and for some months in 1726 Charles was unsure of whether his family could afford the remainder, especially as his father suffered a partial stroke, possibly through the strains imposed by Hetty's behaviour.

It was in this state of uncertainty that Charles walked the 170 miles from London to Epworth with his brother John, who was equally unhappy about his future. Having completed his degree and embarked on an MA, John had been ordained as a deacon by John Potter, Bishop of Oxford, the previous September. Through the contacts of his brother Samuel he had also, in March 1726, been elected as a Fellow of Lincoln College. This fellowship gave John an income of £30 per year without any onerous duties being attached. However, his father was demanding he replace the disgraced Romley as his curate and take up residency at Wroote. This had no attractions compared to life in Oxford because, in the words of his brother Samuel, Wroote's thatched parsonage was only made lively by the mingled music of 'kittens and whelps', 'pigs and porkets', 'bellowing kine and bleating lambs, quacking ducks and fluttering hens'.[7]

John and Charles entered into a home still traumatized by what had happened to Hetty. As far as we know it was the first time Charles had been home since he left Epworth at the age of eight. John invited the family to hear him preach at Wroote on 28 August 1726 and wrote a sermon on forgiveness. The motive was not lost on his mother, who told him: 'You wrote this sermon for Hetty.'[8] Susanna decided to visit her erring daughter even though her husband had not appreciated being lectured at in public. Unfortunately, she found Hetty greeted her arrival 'without the least emotion of joy or grief' and listened to her 'with great indifference ... [seeming] not pleased that I supposed she stood in need of my pardon':

> I then proposed a reconciliation between her and Mr Wesley and ... she told me she had no desire to see him, because she knew he would reproach her with what was past, and that she could not bear ... I returned home strangely mortified, neither pleased with her nor myself.[9]

Samuel Wesley hated the fact that John had taken Hetty's part, partially because he feared John's own sexual behaviour was suspect. It was a condition of John's Oxford fellowship that he should not marry and the only serpent in the Epworth Eden[10] was seen to be John's fondness for attaching himself to young ladies in ways his parents thought inappropriate. John's looks and character made him attractive to women and he loved flirting with them. To his parents' way of thinking John's theological discussions about the love of God seemed easily to encourage expressions of human love. Nor was this concern limited to them. Their oldest daughter Emily warned John he must avoid a Hetty-style emotional entanglement: 'Let me have one relation that I can trust.'[11]

Samuel wrote to his oldest son, Samuel, saying John was defending immorality. When Samuel asked his brother for clarification, John explained his actions:

My sister Hetty's behaviour has ... been innocent enough since her marriage ... [but our father is] inconceivably exasperated against her ... and never spoke of her in my hearing but with the utmost detestation ... [My] sermon was to endeavour ... to convince them ... some tenderness was due to her still.[12]

Their father turned to Charles for support. Charles wanted to back John's attempts at a family reconciliation, but he found it impossible to stand up to his father whom he held in great awe. He therefore agreed to remonstrate with John for disrespectfully challenging their father's actions.

Charles told John his sermon amounted to open defiance and it had understandably caused their father considerable grief. Chastened by his brother's words, John agreed that he would only do what his father wanted. Charles thus effected John's reconciliation with his father but at Hetty's expense. Was it just coincidence that shortly afterwards a grateful Samuel informed Charles that he had scraped the money necessary for him to return to London and prepare for his departure to Oxford? It was left to other family members to come to Hetty's rescue. Her brother Samuel offered her what limited financial support he could and, more importantly, her uncle Matthew paid for her to leave Epworth and move with her husband to London, where he set Wright up in business.

Charles was not happy at the outcome of his actions. When he returned to London briefly in January 1727 he visited Hetty 'almost continuously' for a week without telling his father, and then wrote to John:

Poor sister Hetty! ... In a little neat room she had hired did the good-natured, ingenuous, contented creature watch, and I talk, over a few short days which we both wished had been longer. As yet she lives pretty well ... though I fancy there is another [child] coming. Brother Sam and sister are very kind to her, and I hope will continue so ... She begs you write to her.[13]

Hetty tried to make her own reconciliation with her father, but he took further offence when she told him: 'As you planted my matrimonial bliss, so you cannot run away from my prayer when I beseech you to water it with a little kindness.'[14] Samuel had not entirely thrown off his Puritanical background and Christian duty ranked higher in his thinking than Christian forgiveness. A letter dating from 1729 shows she felt he was still forever finding fault with her. Sadly, she was only to find happiness in the final years of her life when she became for a short time a helper in John and Charles' evangelistic work.

In October 1726 Charles was probably very pleased to be out of Epworth and entering Oxford. It was a relatively small place (just one mile in length and less in breadth) but a city of contrasts. The beauty and learning associated with the university was mixed with the squalor and industry of the town, and many of its fellows and students were more renowned for seeking pleasure than seeking wisdom. Nevertheless, the university was the chief centre for training clergy and ensuring their views were free of any subversive Catholic or Protestant thinking, even if its reputation for orthodoxy had been weakened by the support shown by some dons for the Jacobite cause. Studying was based on traditions inherited from the Middle Ages and therefore its academic courses centred on reading classical authors and gaining an understanding of the Aristotelian 'sciences' of logic, rhetoric, morals and politics. Some critics felt this educational focus was far too much linked to passing on received wisdom rather than engaging in debate over the new ideas being promoted by scientists such as Isaac Newton and philosophers like John Locke.

Charles went to the same college as his older brothers and he must have easily uncovered tales of what 'Jack' had got up to while studying for his first degree. We know John had spent considerable time boating and swimming, drinking with friends, flirting with young women, and playing backgammon, chess or billiards, and that he later expressed regret at 'the sensual pleasures, the desire of the sexes, and [the] pernicious friendships' of his youth. Charles felt he was equally entitled to a similar freedom before settling fully to his studies, especially as for the first time in his life he was not under the watchful eye of either his parents or his oldest brother. All that held him back was a dire shortage of cash. Indeed, such was Charles' poverty that one of the college tutors, Henry Sherman, suggested he should share a garret with another student so that he could rent out his own room.

John also returned to Oxford that October, partly to complete his studies for his MA and partly because Lincoln College wanted him to undertake some tutoring. He opposed Sherman's suggestion, possibly because he preferred to keep Charles' actions restricted by inadequate finances. John had become a far more serious person. As his father's curate, he had studied more religious works and reading Jeremy Taylor's *Holy Living and Holy Dying* had made him resolve to dedicate all his life to God.[15] The unfortunate affair of his sister Hetty and his own attachment for a time to a beautiful and vivacious young woman called Sally Kirkham (until her marriage to another man) had also affected his outlook. So too had the witness of a very poor college porter, who was continually giving thanks to God. John is said to have asked him to explain how a man who had 'nothing to wear, nothing to eat and no bed to lie upon' could be grateful to God. The porter replied: 'I thank Him that He has given me life and being; and a heart to love Him and a desire to serve Him.' John felt this was the faith he should seek.[16]

Nevertheless, at this stage John was still willing to continue flirting with the opposite sex, and he introduced Charles to a circle of lady friends who lived in the Cotswold villages of Buckland, Broadway and Stanton, Gloucestershire. These included Nancy Griffiths, Anne Granville, Mary Pendarves, Fanny Tooker, and the three sisters, Sally, Betty and Damaris Kirkham, who were daughters of the Rector of Stanton Harcourt. Nicknaming himself 'Cyrus', John had given each of these women nicknames. Thus, for example, Sally Kirkham was known as 'Varanese', while Mary Pendarves was called 'Aspasia' and Anne Granville 'Selima'. Charles soon acquired his own nickname of 'Araspes' and he entered into regular correspondence with them. Charles later wrote: 'My first year at college I lost in diversions.'[17]

However, John soon took the decision that he and leisure had to part company[18] and he began keeping a diary to monitor his Christian progress (as was then fashionable among evangelical circles). He devised his own secret code so that no unauthorized person could ever read its contents. Forgetting his own early time at university, he began accusing Charles of studying too little and paying only conventional allegiance to Christian beliefs and observances. He found it very annoying that Charles would burst into his rooms in Lincoln College unannounced, reciting scraps of poetry and flicking through whatever papers happened to be on John's desk, often leaving them in great disorder. He equally disliked Charles' habit of asking questions and then not listening to his answers: 'If I spoke to him about religion, he would warmly answer, "What, would you have me a saint all at once?" and would hear no more.'[19] Charles claimed he was 'very desirous of knowledge' but that he was not as academic as his brothers and so found himself 'bewildered' in reading anything difficult: 'My head will by no means keep pace with my heart, and I'm afraid I shan't reconcile it in haste to the extraordinary business of thinking.'[20]

It must have been a relief to Charles when John returned to Wroote and largely stayed away from Oxford in 1727, even if the earliest known verse by Charles is one reassuring John that his influence remained:

Nor yet from my dim eyes THY form retires!
Nor cheering image of thine absent fires.

His freer lifestyle threw him into debt and he was forced to write to John in January 1728 asking for money:

'Twill most certainly have one of two widely different effects upon me: make me a very hard student or none at all: an excellent econo- mist or a poor desperate scoundrel ... 'Tis in the power of a few ... Epworth guineas and clothes to give things the favourable turn, and make a gentleman of me.[21]

However, in the course of 1728 Charles became far more religious and studious. It has been suggested that this arose because of a narrow escape from the clutches of a London actress called Molly Buchanan, who was appearing in *The Virgin Queen* at the Theatre Royal in Lincoln's Inn. Charles had formed an attachment to her on his visits to the capital:

Satan and sloth had smoothed my way,
To pleasure's paradise,
Yet still I paused, afraid, to stray,
Or plunge the gulf of vice.[22]

Molly's mother had endeavoured to ensure that Charles would seduce her daughter in order to force his hand into marriage. Charles later con- fided to John:

To do the Old Lady justice, she did give us opportunities enough could I have had the Grace to have laid hold of them ... Hints were lost upon so dull stupid a Fellow as I was; and as such no doubt I have been since sufficiently laughed at.[23]

As far as we can gather, it was John who helped Charles deal with the emotional aftermath of all this. Charles determined to learn from the incident: 'From henceforth ... I shall be less addicted to gallantry ... and liking woman simply for being woman ... But enough of her – I'll blot my brain and paper no longer with her.'[24] The frivolous manner that had so often annoyed John and his parents became suddenly solemn and prayerful. He promised to abandon all diversions, start reading seri- ously, and follow his brother's example in keeping a daily record of his spiritual progress. He told John:

It is through your means that, I firmly believe, God will establish what He hath begun in me; and there is no one person I would so willingly have to be the instrument of good to me as you.[25]

In verse Charles summed up his youthful errors and thanked God he had been led to a more religious life:

> Bolder I with my fellows grew,
> Nor yet to evil ran,
> But envied those who dared break through,
> And copy lawless man;
> From parents' eye off removed,
> I still was under thine,
> And found, for secret sin reproved,
> The government divine.[26]

Unfortunately Charles did not find Oxford conducive to seriousness. He later described the university as a place 'where learning keeps its loftiest seat, and hell its firmest throne'.[27] His newfound devotion to religion and study simply made him a joke to most other students, and he informed John:

> Christ Church is certainly the worst place in the world to begin a reformation in. A man stands a very fair chance of being laughed out of his religion at his first setting out, in a place where 'tis scandalous to have any at all.[28]

By January 1729 Charles was finding it very difficult to withstand the temptations offered by other students and he felt he could not succeed in becoming a better Christian unaided:

> One who has for almost thirteen years been utterly inattentive at public prayers can't expect to find there that warmth, he has never known, at his first seeking ... [But] I look upon this coldness as a trial ... [and] I won't give myself to leisure to relapse for I'm afraid if I have no business of my own, the Devil will soon find me some.[29]

Charles told John he needed to surround himself with a supportive group of like-minded friends. He persuaded a couple of his fellow students to join him in attending weekly communion. One was Robert Kirkham, who was a student at Merton College and the brother of Sally, whom John Wesley had at one time courted. The other was a fellow student at Christ Church called William Morgan, who was the elder son of a prominent Dublin lawyer. Charles told John that Morgan was 'a modest, humble, well-disposed youth' who, with his encouragement, 'resolved to spare no pains in working out his salvation'.[30] The three young men agreed they would observe the latest statutes of the university, dating from the previous December. In these the authorities had recommended 'the frequent and careful reading [of] the Scriptures and such other books as may serve more effectually to promote Christianity, sound principles, and orthodox faith'.[31]

Charles confessed to John that he found Kirkham's commitment to be lacklustre: 'you can't imagine how wretchedly lazy he is and how small a share of either Piety or Learning will content him'.[32] He was therefore reluctant to continue visiting Kirkham's home at Stanton, especially as he knew the enjoyable company of Robert's sisters 'would be dangerous to one in my unconfirmed condition'.[33] Instead he visited Hetty and some of his old contacts at Westminster in the summer of 1729, walking from Epworth to London to save expense. While there Charles described to John how much people felt he had changed:

> I have lost my stomach ... [and] they wonder here I'm so strangely dull (as indeed mirth and I have shook hands and parted) and ... they pay the compliment of saying I grow extremely like you.[34]

Though Charles undoubtedly looked to John as his role model, his brother was not the paragon Charles thought. That autumn John had to be sent away from Epworth because he had started paying too much attention to a friend of his sisters called Kitty Hargreaves. John wrote in code in his diary that he would 'never touch Kitty's hand again' and resolved 'never to touch any woman's breasts again'.[35] This crisis at home coincided with a demand from Lincoln College for John to earn his salary as a Fellow by doing some tutoring in logic and Greek. Thus, in November 1729, a chastened John returned to Lincoln College with a determination not to be sidetracked from his studies. In January 1730 he began tutoring Charles and his two friends in the classics and encouraging them to read more religious works.

A pattern developed of meeting to study in Charles' room every Tuesday evening, in Robert Kirkham's every Thursday, in John's every Saturday, and in William Morgan's every Sunday. They also normally attended the university sermon together in St Mary's every Sunday unless John had been invited to preach in one of the country parish churches around Oxford. John, Charles and William developed a particular friendship and often went for walks together. They also occasionally rowed on the river or attended some of the university's musical concerts. Towards the end of the month the three men travelled together to London to spend time with Samuel Wesley and, among other things, visit the House of Commons.

By this time Charles had completed his degree and, like John, he had become a college tutor, much to his family's delight. His father told Charles that he ought to give this new role his whole attention:

[Take] the utmost care to form their minds to piety as well as learning ... You are now launched fairly, Charles. Hold up your head and swim like a man ... and so God send you a good voyage through the troublesome sea of life, which is the hearty prayer of your loving father.[36]

In March Charles invited another Christ Church student and a former pupil at Westminster School called Francis Gore to join 'our society'. In June John was assigned 11 students as his tutees and he decided to also invite any of them who showed interest. Thus the circle of friends became a religious society whose members would live 'according to the method laid down in the Bible'.[37]

There was nothing remotely new in this idea. Over half a century earlier two Lutheran ministers, Johann Arndt and Philip Jakob Spener, had become founders of a movement in Germany to encourage Christians to meet together for study, prayer and mutual support. Their followers, who were dubbed 'Pietists', advocated the creation of mutual-support groups as a means of promoting inner godliness and outer good works. Pietist-style religious societies had first appeared in London in the 1670s in reaction to the immorality prevalent in society after the Restoration of Charles II. Their great advocate was a German minister in the Savoy Chapel, Dr Anthony Horneck, and he commended the creation of societies nationwide as 'an effectual means for restoring our decaying Christianity to its primitive life and vigour, and the support of our tottering and sinking Church'.[38] It was a book by Horneck that had led Samuel Wesley to create a religious society in Epworth in 1702.

Charles and John therefore did not have to devise what their society should do because the rules of religious societies to promote 'real holiness of heart and life' were already well established:

To pray many times every day ... to partake of the Lord's Supper at least once a month ... to practise the profoundest meekness and humility ... to accustom themselves to holy thoughts in all places ... to shun all foreseen occasions of evil [and] evil company ... to examine themselves every night, what good they have done in the day past ... to keep a private fast once a month ... to mortify the flesh with its affections and lust ... to shun spiritual pride and the effects of it ... to read pious books ... [and] to walk so circumspectly that none may be offended or discouraged ... by what they see.[39]

The main guide to their thinking became the writing of the Cambridge scholar and ascetic William Law. His two main books, *Christian Perfection* and *A Serious Call to a Devout and Holy Life,* had been published respectively in 1726 and 1729. The latter in particular influenced Charles' thinking and he later referred to him as 'our John the Baptist'[40] because of his role in calling him and his brother to repentance. He said: 'All that I knew of religion I learned from him.'[41] Law laid great emphasis on developing a rational faith: 'If you are afraid of reason hurting your religion, it is a sign that your religion is not as it should be.'[42] He argued that Christianity required a total renunciation of the world. Instead of seeking worldly pleasures, the Christian should seek perfection and model his life on that of Christ. This included devoting less time to studying classical grammar in 'the pagan pits of learning'[43] and spending more time saving souls and helping lives.

In early August the kind-hearted William Morgan took it upon himself to visit a condemned murderer in Oxford Castle, which had been used as a jail since the Middle Ages. It made him realize there was real Christian work to be done in helping prisoners. John was initially cautious, saying dons and students should not be visiting prisons, but Morgan's enthusiasm would not be gainsaid and he acquired an ally in a new recruit to the group called John Boyce, who was the son of a former Mayor of Oxford. On 24 August John and Charles agreed to go to the prison and were shocked by what they saw. Certain moments are life-shaping and this was undoubtedly one of those. Both brothers were converted to the need to help not only its inmates but also those in the Bocardo, a prison for debtors above the north gate of the city.

At this time prisons were subject to no regulations and gaolers were not paid by fixed salaries. They lived upon the fees they extorted from the prisoners and conditions varied according to an inmate's ability to pay. Sometimes needy prisoners died of hunger in their cells before their trial was heard at the local assizes. Overcrowding and unsanitary conditions made the prisons open to all kinds of disease and it was not uncommon for the bodies of the dead to await removal for days so the corpses simply decayed in the same cells as the living. Even if eventually acquitted of the charges brought against them, some prisoners were unable to return to freedom because they had incurred too many debts to their warders to make their release acceptable. Charles and John felt the least they could do was to read the prisoners prayers, teach those who were illiterate to read, and to provide what financial and legal help they were able.

Samuel Wesley was delighted by his sons' new interest because he had suffered so much while in a debtors' prison. For over 50 years Charles and John were to make helping prisoners one of their constant aims. Charles was to write many hymns based on his experiences and the very last publication he produced in 1785 was a collection of hymns for 'Condemned Malefactors'. He saw prisoners as the most obvious symbol of humanity's need for salvation because all people were imprisoned by their innate sinfulness and needed both forgiveness and freedom:

> Faithful and true, Thy word we plead,
> Met in Thy name to intercede
> For these sad sons of woe,
> Cut off by man, to death consign'd
> And, justly swept from earth, to find
> Severer pangs below ...[44]

William Morgan also collected children from some of the villages around Oxford in the hope he could instruct them in religion. He took Charles and John to see an elderly, sick woman and urged they should undertake other charity work. John sought advice on the desirability of widening their activities and encouragement came from his father:

> I have the highest reason to bless God that he has given me two sons together in Oxford to whom he has given grace and courage to turn the war against the world and the devil ... I think I must adopt Mr Morgan to [also] be my son.[45]

John therefore sought the approval of the Bishop of Oxford and, when this was granted, the young men had a new agenda: to imitate Christ by feeding the hungry, clothing the naked, teaching young children, visiting the sick and imprisoned, and 'making all these actions subservient to a higher purpose, even the saving of souls from death'.[46] Charles later embodied his feelings on the subject of helping the poor and others in need in his beautiful *Songs for the Poor*.

The charitable activities attracted more students to join them, including William Golburne, Thomas Horne, Christopher Rhodes and John Spicer from Christ Church College, Robert Bulman from Lincoln College, Morgan Graves from University College, and Richard Watkins from Wadham College. The young men mostly met together within their friendship groups, but the more enthusiastic began to also meet regularly in John Wesley's room in Lincoln College and John assumed leadership over Charles. A later recruit commented that John dominated not only because he had 'more learning and experience than the rest' but also because of his 'singleness of heart' and 'the authority in his countenance'. After prayer John showed 'a serenity of countenance that was next to shining'.[47]

What was happening soon attracted ridicule. To see religion taken to this level of seriousness was simply something more worldly-minded students found ludicrous. In November 1730 some of them began jokingly calling John and Charles' society 'the Holy Club' or 'the Godly Club', though it was not in any sense an organization. There were no rules of membership, no rites of initiation, no fixed times of meeting. All that John was promoting (with Charles' assent) was that the young men in their circle should meet three or four times per week in small groups of three to six in order to pray and meditate, self-examine themselves about what each had done, and study the Bible and other religious works. In addition they attended public worship and regularly took communion. In trying to put their faith into practice, they sought to avoid mixing in bad company, and to serve Christ by helping the less fortunate, denying themselves needless luxuries and eating and drinking in moderation. Charles' father wrote in December, telling his sons not to worry about their critics:

> Preserve an equal temper of mind, under whatever treatment you meet from a not very just or well-natured world ... He by whom all actions and intentions are weighed will both accept, esteem, and reward you. I hear my son, John, has the honour of being styled 'the Father of the Holy Club': if it be so, I must be the grandfather of it.[48]

One of the recruits to the 'Holy Club' was a student at Christ Church called John Gambold, who was the son of a Welsh minister. A rather introspective youth, he had found it difficult to make any friends until befriended by Charles. He soon recognized how much Charles obeyed John:

> I never observed a person have a more real deference for another than he constantly had for his brother. Indeed, he followed his brother entirely. Could I describe one of them I should describe both.[49]

This meant that between 1731 and 1733 it was John who shaped what the group should do. He saw self-examination as vital and so devised a series of 15 or so questions which were designed to encourage everyone to take greater note of what they were thinking, saying and doing. He recommended they engage in this 'general examination' on a daily basis. They had to ask whether they had seized opportunities for good and served their neighbour, and whether they had tackled evil and been evangelical enough in spreading the gospel. They had to show how they were conveying that religion was something positive and not negative, and demonstrate that they had engaged in sufficient private prayer and public worship. They also had to support each other by pointing out each other's weaknesses and faults but only in a kind way and for loving reasons.

In addition, John compiled a list of questions on aspects of the Christian faith and expected these to be asked weekly. The questions focused each individual's attention on the love of God every Sunday, the love of humanity every Monday, the importance of humility every Tuesday, resignation and meekness every Thursday, and thankfulness every Saturday. The questions every Wednesday and Friday related to mortification and self-denial and were linked to fasting. On those days John asked members of the group to forego their breakfast and evening meal and only eat a modest lunch. He was determined to make them 'Bible-Christians'[50] so he also expected them to study the scriptures in English, Greek and Hebrew. This earned the group nicknames like 'the Bible moths' or 'the Bible bigots'. One of the later recruits, Benjamin Ingham, wrote in his diary: 'We ought to try all human writings by the test of Scripture and only approve of them in so far as they agree with Scripture ... The Holy Scripture is our Master.'[51]

John began recommending an increasingly long list of appropriate books for study, ranging from biblical commentaries to studies on the nature of worship, and from advice on Christian living to collections of prayers and sermons. Central to this list were books on meditation and self-examination, such as Francis de Sales' *An Introduction to a Devout Life*, Thomas Ken's *Meditations*, Anthony Horneck's *The Happy Ascetic*, Robert Nelson's *Practice of True Devotion*, and Jeremy Taylor's *Holy Living* and *Holy Dying*. John specially abridged for them Joseph Hall's *Art of Divine Meditation* because he found it particularly useful. Some of John's recommendations show the influence of the Pietists in his thinking, such as Thomas à Kempis' *The Imitation of Christ* and John Goodman's *The Penitent Pardoned*. Others were biographies or autobiographies designed to provide good role models of a Christian life. Among these were Ambrose Bonwicke's *A Pattern for Young Students at University*, William Burkitt's *Young Man's Guide*, and William Hamilton's *The Life and Exemplary Character of James Bonnell*.

Though the young men's reading was mainly religious, it was not entirely so. We know they also read classical works by Homer, Cicero, Virgil, Juvenal, Plutarch and others, and the best modern poetry, including John Milton's *Paradise Lost* and the verse of George Herbert and Alexander Pope. They also read those magazines which reflected on the political and social issues of the day, such as *The Spectator, The*

Guardian and *The Tatler*. Some even read popular works of drama and fiction. There were also books on John's list designed to provide salutary warnings against allowing sin to rule in one's life, such as Richard Sault's *The Second Spiral*, which was subtitled 'a fearful example of an atheist ... who died in despair'.

Gradually John became obsessed with encouraging an ascetic lifestyle. For example, he recommended they all get up by 4.00 am. We have an interesting account in the diary of a later member, Benjamin Ingham, of his failure to succeed in rising early, despite all his best efforts. Among other things, he tried sleeping without a mattress or sheets, asking a friend to sit sentry by his bedside, purchasing a mechanical alarm, and imposing penalties on himself (such as forgoing meals). John's request they all fast on Wednesdays and Fridays was ignored by many, in part because missing meals in college inevitably made them appear very different from other students. However, Charles and William Morgan did obey John. One of Charles' doctors was to attribute the repeated bouts of ill health which Charles faced in later years to excessive fasting while at Oxford, and William Morgan's father was certainly alarmed at the impact on his son's health:

> They imagine they cannot be saved if they do not spend every hour, nay minute, of their lives in the service of God ... They almost starve themselves to be able to relieve the poor and buy books for their conversion. They endeavour to reform notorious whores and allay spirits in haunted houses. They fast two days a week, which has emaciated them to that degree they are a fearful sight.[52]

This was not just the mutterings of an overly anxious parent. In June 1732 William Morgan was taken seriously ill and had to return home to Ireland. Friends began to be concerned at what was happening. The family of Robert Kirkham criticized John and Charles for adopting a lifestyle that was 'righteous over much' and for 'laying burdens on ourselves too heavy to be born, and consequently too heavy to be of any use to us'.[53] Some called them 'Super-Rogation Men' because of their overobservance of ceremonies laid down by the Church, especially in relation to fasting. To any criticism John replied that he felt the contempt of others was 'part of the cross which every man must bear if he follows Christ'.[54] By 1732 their father felt he had to intervene and he told John to stop behaving like 'a wild enthusiast or fanatic'.[55] Their sister Emily was equally dismissive, saying the constant self-questioning by members of the group 'seems to me like Church tyranny, and assuming to yourselves a dominion over your fellow creatures which was never designed you by God'.[56]

In May their brother Samuel came to see at first hand what John and Charles were doing in Oxford and he was not impressed by John's obsessive asceticism. Samuel advised Charles to continue serving others but to avoid anything that would injure his health or even threaten his life. He posed in verse the problem as he saw it:

Safe march they on, 'twixt dangerous extremes
of mad profaneness, and enthusiasts' dreams?[57]

Samuel almost certainly thought it was time John paid more attention to what was happening back in Epworth. We know from Emily Wesley that the family was 'in intolerable want and affliction ... [and] in scandalous want of necessaries'.[58] John's reaction to the family's criticism was to become increasingly uncommunicative. Even Charles complained John's attitude was becoming offensive.

Their 69-year-old father desperately wanted John to take over the running of his parish. In 1731 he had had a serious accident, falling from a wagon onto his head, and it was clear his health was rapidly deteriorating. Moreover a firmer hand than his was required to sort out the family's fortunes. Sukey Wesley had been forced to leave her husband, Richard Ellison, because of his mistreatment of her and their four children. It is surmised that the final straw was his setting fire to their home, presumably while drunk. Financially supporting Sukey and her children was a burden none had envisaged. Nor were matters helped by the fact Samuel was helping fund through university a young man called John Whitelamb, who had been educated in the charity school he had set up in Wroote. He was judged to be 'a valuable person, of uncommon brightness, learning, piety, and industry',[59] and Samuel wanted to reward him for having saved him from drowning when a ferry boat sank. Even with free tutoring provided by John Wesley, this was something the family could ill afford.

The financial pressures on the Wesley family are well illustrated by what happened to Charles' sister Kezzy at this time. She had gained herself a place as a pupil-teacher in Lincoln but her father had insufficient money to help her purchase the clothes required for her role so she was forced to relinquish her post and return home. When Susanna's brother, Matthew Annesley, visited Epworth Rectory, he was horrified at the poverty he saw. In response he chose to help out by providing enough money to enable his oldest niece Emily to set up her own school at Gainsborough. Other help came from her brother Samuel and even from Charles, though he had precious little income himself. Indeed in one of his letters Charles says his brother Samuel could bear witness to his own 'proficiency in begging'.[60]

In the summer of 1732 it looked as if the religious society in Oxford might fade away because three of its original key members, William Morgan, Robert Kirkham and John Boyce, all left the university. No one now talked of the existence of any 'Holy Club' because all that remained were loosely connected student groupings. However, fresh impetus to continue came from a tutor at Brasenose College called John Clayton, who had been running his own religious society. He now took over from Morgan as the chief promoter of charitable activities. He raised money to pay for a teacher to run a school for the children whom William Morgan had been helping and he encouraged visits to one of the local workhouses in the parish of St Thomas. The conditions within it were almost as bad as in the prisons. Most people felt the only good pauper was a dead pauper and the inmates were treated with contempt. The brutal regime within the workhouses was designed to speed them on their way to their grave.

Financial backing for charitable activities came from a number of Clayton's contacts, including his close friend, Sir John Phillips, a blind former MP who was also a benefactor of the Society for Promoting Christian Knowledge. John Wesley joined the organization and a recruit to their circle called Thomas Broughton later became a highly respected leader of the SPCK (from 1743 to 1777). Clayton also encouraged the Wesleys to expect everyone to spend more of their time in private and public worship. John suggested they all say a brief 'ejaculatory' prayer every hour and use special collects four times a day. Throughout 1733 he gradually developed a compilation of useful prayers and these were subsequently edited and published in 1734 as *A Collection of Forms of Prayer for Every Day in the Week*.

Clayton was the well-educated son of a Manchester bookseller and he urged the Wesleys to particularly study the writings of the early Church Fathers. This had a tremendous impact on both John and Charles (hence the allusions to them in so much of Charles' later hymnwriting). They concluded the early Church's success was based on its simplicity of message and the fact it had not permitted theological differences to become a source of deep disunity. The focus of the early Church Fathers was simply to 'have the mind of Christ and walk as he walked'.[61] As Charles later wrote, ultimately religion was something to be lived rather than fought over:

All united in Thy name,
Let us think, and speak the same:
Then the world shall know and own
God Himself hath made us one.[62]

The Wesleys regarded taking communion as even more important once they appreciated the early Christians took the sacraments almost daily as a means of receiving God's grace. Watching the Wesleys and their friends publicly walk through the streets every Sunday to celebrate the Lord's Supper at the university church of St Mary's led to some scoffing students naming them 'the Sacramentarians'. Over a decade later Charles was to publish 166 hymns on the Lord's Supper to show his continued strong feelings on the importance of communion:

We see the blood that seals our peace,
Thy pardoning mercy we receive:
The bread doth visibly express
The strength through which our spirits live.[63]

He talks of the symbolic wine and bread focusing people's attention on the sacrifice of Christ on the cross and becoming 'the channels of grace' to convey God's love to every heart. He describes how communicants receive 'the sense of sins forgiven' and 'a taste of heaven', and how they experience their hearts filled 'with all the life of God' so that it was like 'a pledge of glory in our heart'.[64] Charles believed anyone not engaging in frequent communion was simply ignoring the wishes of Christ.

Most of those students connected to the Wesleys continued to meet largely in friendship groups of two or three, but three key larger groups now emerged – one meeting with John in Lincoln, one meeting with Clayton in Brasenose, and one meeting with Charles in Christ Church. By September 1732 a new word was being applied to them – 'Methodist'. This may have been used because they were seeking to be 'methodical' both in their worship and their lifestyle. A contemporary dictionary, published in 1706, defined a 'Methodist' as 'one that treats of method or affects to be methodical'.[65] However, the word may also have been used because other students sensed that Clayton and the Wesleys were increasingly seeking to earn their salvation by what they were doing. The word 'Methodism' had first been coined about 90 years earlier as a term of abuse for those nonconformists who followed the teaching of Jacobus Arminius. This Dutch theologian had argued that even those Christians who felt assured of their salvation could have their faith undermined or destroyed by ill living and that every Christian had to methodically undertake a holy life.

That autumn Clayton left Oxford to take up a church living in Salford, near Manchester. His departure coincided with the news that William Morgan had died on 26 August at his home in Ireland. Though he suffered from tuberculosis, it was alleged his death was a consequence of excessive fasting and self-mortification and a mind deranged by religious hysteria. An anonymous letter writer sent an account of the undesirable behaviour of 'the Methodists' and their 'enthusiastic madness' to a London newspaper called *Fogg's Weekly Journal*:

> The University at present is not a little pestered with those sons of sorrow … They avoid … any pleasant and grateful sensation. All social entertainments and diversions are disapproved of, and in endeavouring to avoid luxury, they not only exclude what is convenient, but what is absolutely necessary for the support of life.[66]

This public condemnation gave the word 'Methodist' a prominence that earlier nicknames had lacked and so the name stuck, even though neither John nor Charles liked it. Susanna Wesley comforted her sons, saying she supported their charitable work and their stance against a frivolous lifestyle, but even she was cross at how John's excessive asceticism had impacted on Charles, who was unable to 'eat a full meal, but must presently throw up again'.[67] John asked William Morgan's father to entrust his younger son, Richard, to him as a tutee and so end the rumours that he was to blame for William's death. It is not clear why Morgan's father acceded to this but it appears to have been Charles' intervention that was critical.[68] Even so he laid down ground rules that Richard was not to undertake the ascetic lifestyle of his elder brother:

> I would have him lead a sober, virtuous and religious life … but for young people to pretend to be more pure and holy than the rest of mankind is a dangerous experiment.[69]

Richard was very unhappy at his father's decision:

> The whole college makes a jest of me … By becoming his pupil I am stigmatised with the name of a Methodist, the misfortune of which I cannot describe … If I am continued with Mr Wesley I shall be ruined.[70]

John preached a sermon on Christian Perfection in St Mary's Church, Oxford, on 1 January 1733. It was the first of many sermons in which John argued that striving for perfection was a natural human response to the call of Christ to 'be perfect as your Father in Heaven is perfect'. Charles held that John's search for perfection was doomed to fail but he accepted it was the only goal worth seeking:

Whilst we can be better than we are, we are not to think of ourselves as perfect ... When we have done all the good we can, we are still to seek opportunities of doing more ... There is no resting in the mid way between heaven and hell. We must pursue our way to the former, or we shall infallibly make quick advances towards the latter. All virtue consisteth in habit: and habits, we know, are only to be obtained by constant and repeated acts ... [He] that would attain to real Christian charity must never cool in his labour of love.[71]

The next month a small anonymous pamphlet appeared called 'The Oxford Methodists'. It defended the Wesleys and their followers, saying 'their notions and principles were better considered and digested than their ill-willers generally imagine them to be'.[72] Support also came from John and Charles' brother, Samuel, who published a poem to celebrate Morgan's devotion to good works, which 'preached the unhoped for gospel to the poor':

Glad'ning the poor, where'er his steps he turn'd,
Where pine'd the orphan, or the widow mourn'd;
Where prisoners sigh'd beneath guilt's horrid stain,
The worst confinement, and the heaviest chain.[73]

The Oxford Methodists not only survived the crisis over Morgan's death, but increased in number, largely because John Clayton had encouraged them to fall upon their friends, 'by which means I hope in God we shall get at least an advocate for us, if not a brother and fellow labourer, in every College in town'.[74] By 1734 there were tiny Methodist groups in eight of the university's colleges (Christ Church, Lincoln, Exeter, Brasenose, Pembroke, Merton, Queen's and Magdalen) as well as a group run by a 'Mrs Potter'. These groups each developed their own patterns of behaviour and had a fluctuating membership, and some students attended more than one group. John remained a very influential figure but he was not the dominant figure to whom all looked. That Charles was an equally important figure in these years is illustrated by the fact that he was directly responsible for attracting the two students who, more than any others, were to play a key role in the later creation of Methodism. These were Benjamin Ingham and George Whitefield.

Born at Ossett in Yorkshire, Ingham had become an usher at Batley Grammar School before entering Queen's College in October 1730. In 1733 he was befriended by Charles who taught him to emulate John's ascetic lifestyle and to keep a coded diary about his religious development. In the resulting diary there are almost four times as many references to him associating with Charles as there are with John. Ingham proved a very dedicated disciple: 'I trust that by God's mercy and grace I shall be enabled to inure myself to hardship and to fight manfully against the world, the flesh, and the devil.'[75] Charles persuaded him to visit the inmates of the workhouse in the parish of St Thomas in January 1734 and Ingham was so moved he 'promised to continue and go two or three times a week to teach the children to read and [to] read to the old people'.[76] Other students from Queen's College also offered to help.

Ingham renounced all 'the pomps and vanities of the world ... all proud and vain thoughts of my own worth ... [and] all the sinful ways of the flesh'.[77] He and a fellow student called James Hervey began visiting the workhouse at Whitefriars in Gloucester Green and working with the poor at St Batholomew's Hospital and in the slum street in West Oxford known as 'the Hamel'. James Hervey told his sister they were rejecting the normal passions of youth in order 'to walk humbly with God' and become 'angels of light'.[78] Hervey was later to become best known for his religious writing. His most famous book, *Meditations and Contemplations*, was for a time ranked with John Bunyan's *The Pilgrim's Progress* in terms of its popularity and impact. Though both Ingham and Hervey sometimes looked for spiritual advice to John, they had reservations about him. Neither chose to attend meetings in his rooms in Lincoln. Ingham in particular much preferred to go to the group that met with Charles in his rooms in Christ Church. He also set up his own group at Queen's, which developed into one of the largest (with a dozen members). It met on Wednesdays, Saturdays and Sundays. He and his friends developed a set of coded hand signals so that they could secretly warn each other if they felt someone was saying or doing something in public that was contrary to their faith.

In late August or early September 1733 Charles Wesley befriended George Whitefield, who was to become the most important of all the recruits the Oxford Methodists ever gained. This future inspirational evangelist was one of seven children born to a Bristol-born innkeeper who had become the proprietor of 'The Bell Inn', the largest and finest hostelry in Gloucester. His father had died when he was just two years old and so the family business had very much fallen on George's mother until her remarriage. Whitefield later described his childhood in unflattering terms, saying he had been given over to 'lying, filthy talking, and foolish jesting' and that he had frequently stolen money from his mother to engage in undesirable activities, such as gambling:

> Some of the things I did at the grammar school had a natural tendency to debauch the mind, to raise ill passions and to stuff the memory with

48

things as contrary to the Gospel of Jesus Christ as light to darkness, Heaven to Hell.[79]

His stepfather ruined the reputation of the inn and then deserted the family. The resulting financial problems meant George was denied the university education his mother had long planned for him. Instead he had to become just a servant at the inn. He turned to religion for consolation. Accidentally learning he could have his university fees paid if he acted as a servitor to wealthier students, Whitefield persuaded his mother to scrape together enough to send him back to school so he could acquire the knowledge of Latin and Greek which a university education demanded. In November 1732, shortly before his eighteenth birthday, he was judged ready to go to Pembroke College in Oxford. His inferior status as a servitor meant he was not supposed to associate with the other students but that did not stop him watching what they were doing. It was in this way that Whitefield became a secret admirer of the Oxford Methodists:

> For about twelve months my soul longed to be acquainted with some of them, and I was strongly pressed to follow their good example, when I saw them go through a ridiculing crowd to receive the Holy Eucharist at St Mary's.[80]

He finally made personal contact when he sought out Charles to ask him whether he would come to the aid of a poor woman who had attempted suicide in one of the workhouses:

> He sent an invitation to me ... to come to breakfast with him the next morning. I thankfully embraced the opportunity; and blessed be God! it was one of the most profitable visits I ever made in my life. My soul, at that time, was athirst for some spiritual friends to lift up my hands when they hung down, and to strengthen my feeble knees. He soon discovered it, and, like a wise winner of souls, made all his discourses tend that way.[81]

Charles ignored the rules that said he should not be friendly with a servitor and became mentor to the shabbily dressed Whitefield. He lent him books to shape his Christian thinking, and introduced him to his circle of friends. Whitefield later wrote:

> [He] instructed me as I was able to bear it. By degrees he introduced me to the rest of his Christian brethren. They built me up daily in the

knowledge and fear of God, and taught me to endure hardness as a
good soldier of Jesus Christ. I now began, like them, to live by rule ...
Never did persons strive more earnestly to enter in at the strait gate ...
They were dead to the world, and willing to be accounted as the dung
and offscouring of all things, so that they might win Christ. Their
hearts glowed with the love of God.[82]

Whitefield faced immediate hostility from other students for attaching
himself to the Methodists: 'I daily underwent some contempt at college.
Some have thrown dirt at me; others by degree took away their pay
from me; and two friends that were dear to me ... forsook me.'[83] Charles
helped him cope with such persecution and also rescued him from taking self-denial too seriously when Whitefield locked himself in his study
and tortured himself over his inability to avoid temptation:

> My honourable friend, Mr Charles Wesley ... came to my room, soon
> found out my case, apprised me of my danger, if I would not take
> advice; and recommended me to his brother John, as more experi-
> enced in the spiritual life ... John advised me to resume all my external
> [activities] ... and I was delivered from those wiles of Satan.[84]

Whitefield always remembered Charles' early kindness to him, saying he
owed him 'the greatest deference and respect' for changing his life and
setting him out on the path of faith.[85] Charles remembered their first
meeting with equal affection:

> A modest, pensive youth, who mused alone,
> Industrious, the frequented path to shun,
> An Israelite, without disguise or art,
> I saw, I loved, and clasped him to my heart,
> A stranger as my bosom-friend caressed,
> And unawares received an angel-guest.[86]

This is not surprising. Whitefield was to become the great pioneer of
Methodism in both Britain and America and the man responsible for
launching first John Wesley's and then Charles' careers as open-air
evangelists.

The fact Charles was 'a man made for friendship' meant he could play
an increasingly vital role among the Oxford Methodists when John's
behaviour became ever stranger. John adopted an 'almost neurotic
grid-system'[87] on which he listed his daily activities hour by hour and,
after daily self-interrogation rather than meditation, rated his 'temper

of devotion' on a scale of 1 to 9. His obsession with the state of his faith made him resentful of his parents' increasing desire to see him return to Epworth. In 1733 he tried to resolve this by urging his father to appoint John Whitelamb as his curate. The latter strengthened his cause by courting the slightly deformed but very kind Mary Wesley (or 'Molly' as she was known within the family). Charles commented on her that 'she would be glad if she could spend her whole life doing good to fellow creatures'.[88] Samuel agreed to their marriage and handed over the living of Wroote to Whitelamb, though financially he could ill afford to do so. Sadly, Molly died in childbirth in November 1734 and Whitelamb's faith was shattered by the experience.

Even before this tragedy had unfolded, Samuel demanded John's return. A partial stroke and a series of accidents had taken their toll and he knew Susanna would be evicted from the family home when he died unless one of his sons took over first. Charles was not ordained and Samuel had just become headmaster of Blundell's School in Devon, so this only left John. However, John refused in a long and rather selfish letter home, saying his income as a fellow at Lincoln College was more than adequate to meet his needs and that 'a parish would crush my own soul and make me useless to others'.[89] He rather cruelly told his father that he had no wish to repeat his father's failures and no desire to work among 'lukewarm Christians' when his personal salvation demanded he should stay in Oxford. He also largely stopped writing to his mother.

All this incensed his older brother, who told him: 'I see your love to yourself but love to your neighbour I do not see.'[90] There was undoubted truth in this. At the university John could have as much or as little company as he pleased, and he had acquired half-a-dozen close friends who were entirely of his own way of thinking. The money from his fellowship gave him the privilege of being able to attend worship and serve the poor without having to worry about 'worldly cares'. More fundamentally, John's desire for holiness had led him to become entirely inward-looking. In contrast, Charles was still as open and friendly as ever. In the summer of 1734 he invited Benjamin Ingham to meet his family at Epworth. Ingham recorded in his diary having 'religious and useful talk with John, Charles Wesley, their mother, and three sisters (Molly, Kezzy, and Patty)'.[91] Samuel Wesley was ill in bed and Ingham sat with him for a time.

On Christmas Day 1734 Samuel Wesley made a far more impassioned plea for John to take over his work at Epworth. John once again refused, claiming that he could better serve God in Oxford. Charles knew the impact on his parents was immensely distressing, but appears to have been caught between conflicting loyalties. In March 1735 he cancelled a planned visit to his brother Samuel, saying he needed to give time to the family:

> My father declines so fast that before next year he will, in all probability, be at his journey's end; so that I must see him now, or never more with my bodily eyes. My mother seems more cast down at the apprehension of his death than I thought she could have been; and what is worse, he seems so too.[92]

The imminence of their father's death and the impact that would have on their mother finally made John relent. Belatedly he approached one of his friends, James Broughton, who had become a chaplain in the Tower of London, and he asked him to lobby his contacts in government and ensure the parish of Epworth passed to him on his father's death. On 15 April Boughton told John that the Bishop of London, Edmund Gibson, had decided he was not a fit successor because he was a fanatic given over to an unhealthy strictness. Boughton urged John to see if he could persuade the Bishop of Oxford to challenge Gibson over the matter. But it was too late because ten days later the 72-year-old Samuel Wesley died.

Charles was present at his father's death and was overcome with grief. Though their relationship had been in many ways very formal (Charles addressed his father as 'Honoured Sir'), there is no doubting his deep filial affection. He wrote to his brother Samuel, who had not been able to return home in time:

> You have reason to envy us, who could attend him in the last stage of his illness. The few words he could utter I saved, and hope never to forget ... He appeared full of faith and peace ... [and] often laid his hand upon my head, and said, 'Be steady. The Christian faith will surely revive in this Kingdom. You shall see it, though I shall not.'[93]

When the news came that the parish had been given to another clergyman, there was a degree of bitter irony that it fell to John Romley, the man whom Hetty had wished to marry. He was to prove a bitter critic of the Wesleys until his eventual death in 1751. Charles looked to his brother Samuel rather than to John to help him get a job so that 'I may do something in this shipwreck of the family for somebody, though it be no more than furnishing a plank.'[94] He told him of the seriousness of the plight of their mother and unmarried sisters, who were having to sell their few possessions to pay off outstanding debts. Samuel paid some of the debt himself to prevent his mother's arrest and invited Susanna to come and stay with him. He also started to make arrangements as to where his remaining unmarried sisters could live. He wrote their father's epitaph in the form of a poem:

> A Parish Priest, not of the pilgrim kind,
> But fix'd and faithful to the post assign'd,
> Through various scenes with equal virtue trod,
> True to his oath, his order, and his God ...
> In converse free; for ev'ry subject fit;
> The coolest reason join'd to keenest wit ...
> He mourn'd with those who pain or want endure,
> A guardian angel to the sick and poor ...[95]

In these circumstances a remorseful John announced he would leave Oxford and undertake missionary work abroad. He demanded Charles and Benjamin Ingham accompany him and so George Whitefield agreed to take over the leadership of the remaining Oxford Methodists, though most of its members had either left or were about to leave. It had become an increasingly disparate group whose members disagreed on many aspects of religion – indeed a number were to become outspoken critics of the later development of Methodism. Nevertheless, the small mutually supportive student groups had served their purpose of encouraging a greater commitment to Christianity. Most of their members became, in the words of one early historian of Methodism, 'sincere, earnest, laborious, successful ministers of Christ'[96] and many played prominent religious roles, some locally and others nationally. Robert Potter, who was Bishop of Oxford during the early 1730s, later reflected on the Oxford Methodists: 'These gentlemen are irregular; but they have done good; and I pray God to bless them.'[97]

Neither John nor Charles foresaw the future development of a Methodist movement – they simply now looked to open a new chapter and find their salvation in the New World.

3

American Adventure

Long have I seemed to serve thee, Lord
With unavailing pain;
Fasted, and prayed, and read thy Word,
And heard it preached – in vain.

Oft did I with th'assembly join,
And near thy altar drew;
A form of godliness was mine –
The power I never knew.

I rested in the outward law,
Nor knew its deep design.
The length and breadth I never saw
And height of love divine.

To please thee thus, at length I see,
Vainly I hoped and strove:
For what are outward things to thee
Unless they spring from love?[1]

Charles initially became interested in America through his brother
Samuel's links with the MP for Haslemere, James Edward Oglethorpe,
a former Captain-Lieutenant in the Queen's Guards and Aide-de-Camp
to the famous commander Prince Eugene of Savoy. The two men had
become friends when Samuel received both moral and financial support
from Oglethorpe to make more permanent his scheme to operate an
infirmary for the sick poor in Westminster. In 1728 Oglethorpe agreed
to become chairman of a parliamentary committee to investigate conditions in all the country's gaols, following the death of an architect
friend who had been placed in prison simply for debt. This investigation
interested the whole Wesley family because of their father's earlier imprisonment and they welcomed the resulting report which detailed the
appalling overcrowding and the cruelty with which inmates were treated

by many warders. Oglethorpe suggested it would be preferable to send debtors to the colonies as a punishment and proposed the creation of a new colony in North America expressly for this purpose.

Samuel gave his friend's scheme enthusiastic support, describing Oglethorpe as 'a guardian angel' come to the rescue of suffering prisoners:

> Their only bed dank earth, unpaved and bare,
> Their only covering is the chains they wear:
> Debarr'd from cheerful morn, and human sight,
> In lonely, restless, and enduring night;
> The strongest health unsinew'd by disease,
> And Famine wasting life by slow degrees ...[2]

Oglethorpe cleverly proposed to name the new colony 'Georgia' after King George II and said its success would be guaranteed by also encouraging worthy religious refugees from Europe to seek new lives there. Parliament viewed the scheme favourably because it offered a way of promoting further trade while creating a geographical barrier between the Carolinas and the still expanding Spanish empire in Florida. Therefore on 9 June 1732 a special royal charter was obtained and Oglethorpe obtained £10,000 towards the cost of putting his scheme into practice. Trustees managed to raise a further £36,000.

In November 1732 Oglethorpe set sail for America with the first batch of debtors and other men keen to apply their trades in a new colony. They disembarked on the banks of the Savannah River the following February and named the first settlement in Georgia after it. There were only 35 families but the local Indians proved friendly and soon arrangements were in hand to build a second town, Ebenezer, as a haven for German Lutherans seeking their freedom from religious persecution in Salzburg. The Georgia Trustees had little confidence in the ability of debtors to run their own lives and so laid down very strict rules as to how the colony should operate. Thus no elected assemblies were permitted and land was allocated to the settlers on almost feudal principles, with the colonists promising obedience and, if required, military service. The Trustees wanted to maximize the number of farms worked by whites and so took the unusual step of banning slavery and creating small compact farms which were unsuitable for development into plantations. The colonists were expected to cultivate hemp (to make rope), flax (to make linen), grapes (to make wine) and, most importantly, mulberry (to feed silkworms). It was hoped a silk industry would guarantee Georgia's commercial success.

In June 1734 Oglethorpe arrived back in England to raise more funds and to collect a second batch of debtors for the emerging colony. Samuel Wesley senior wrote expressing his warmest approval at Oglethorpe's creation of a colony 'in the midst of wild woods and uncultivated deserts, where men may live free and happy'.[3] He suggested Oglethorpe should consider publishing his commentary on the book of Job because it was based on his bitter personal experience of prison. His son Samuel wrote to John and Charles to ask them to attend a public meeting in Oxford to raise funds for the colony. It is not clear whether Charles went but we know John did because he then expressed a wish not to get particularly involved in the Georgia scheme. It was guilt over his behaviour prior to his father's death which made John rethink the matter. Knowing the colony had been dear to his father's heart, he agreed to accept an invitation from a trustee of the scheme, John Burton, who was a well-known don at Corpus Christi College, to meet Oglethorpe, who had decided to become the colony's governor. Oglethorpe proved highly persuasive in encouraging John to return with him to offer religious support to the colonists and act as a missionary to the native Indians.

John Burton informed the Society for the Propagation of the Gospel that John was a man 'inured to contempt of the ornaments and conveniences of life' and prepared to endure 'bodily austerities'[4] and it agreed to pay him a salary of £50 a year as the new colony's chaplain. Any remaining reservations were removed by John's correspondence with John Clayton and William Law because they both supported him going to Georgia. However, John laid down one condition: Charles and a couple of their friends would have to accompany him. This must have come as a great shock to Charles, who had no desire to leave Oxford and their brother Samuel thought Charles' frail health made John's proposal a nonsense. However, in his determination to do penance for not taking on the rectory at Epworth, John refused to recognize either Charles' reluctance or Samuel's concern: 'My chief motive, to which all the rest are subordinate, is the hope of saving my own soul. I hope to learn the true sense of the Gospel of Christ by preaching it to the heathen.'[5]

John believed the forthcoming hardships would guarantee an ascetic lifestyle and he was extraordinarily naïve about what the Indians would be like, saying they would be 'like little children, humble, willing to learn, and eager to do the will of God'.[6] He also wrongly hoped that living in a place where there would be few women, except for Indians who were 'of a different species from me', would solve the problem of sexual temptation. To Samuel's intense annoyance, Charles felt he could not deny John's request and so agreed to go with him. He later wrote his brother 'always had the ascendant over me'.[7] The only person who might have persuaded

Charles to ignore John was their widowed mother, Susanna. Instead she gave her blessing to their joint departure, saying: 'Had I twenty sons, I should rejoice that they were thus employed.'[8] She told them not to worry about what would happen to her in their absence because she was content to go and live with her eldest daughter Emily at Gainsborough.

Such an option was only possible because John had helped arrange for Emily to marry an apothecary called Robert Harpur. Like her sister Hetty, Emily had not had a happy love life. As a young woman staying with her uncle Matthew in London, she had fallen in love with a man called Leybourne but her family had opposed the match and made the couple part. Emily had bitterly grieved over the separation and for four years had spoken of death as 'a consummation devoutly to be wished'.[9] As a mature woman she had fallen in love with a local doctor. Her family had again disapproved, largely because he was a dissenting Quaker. Emily felt compelled to drop the relationship, though the doctor's possessive nature may also have contributed to their break-up. Now John pushed her into marriage with a man she did not love. It was rapidly to prove a terrible mistake, so much so that Susanna did not stay with the unhappy couple beyond September 1736.

A later regretted marriage also took place for Martha Wesley, the sister so like John in looks that it was said only their attire distinguished them. Susanna had sent Martha to live with her uncle Matthew in London in the hope she would acquire a better husband than was possible within the confines of Epworth. However, she had been very unhappy there and had sought consolation in the friendship of a man called Westley Hall, who was one of John's tutees and a member of the Holy Club. Samuel said Hall was 'too smoothe'[10] for his liking, but John dismissed his brother's concern. Nevertheless, Samuel's judgement was right because Hall secretly betrothed himself to Martha and then, without her knowing, began to court her youngest sister, Kezziah, who equally knew nothing about his relationship with Martha. In 1734 Hall sought and gained the family's approval to marry 'Kezzy'. An outraged Martha then forced him to honour his original commitment to her, but their marriage shocked Charles. He assumed Martha had pinched Kezzy's lover and said her marriage would justify 'the curse of God'. He later viewed Kezzy's subsequent increasing ill health and eventual early death as a direct consequence of Hall's unseemly behaviour.

However, John was more concerned to ensure that Westley Hall should accompany him to America than about which sister he married. Indeed, he encouraged poor Kezzy to live with Martha because she would soon be without her American-bound husband! However, Hall was as indecisive over going to Georgia as he was choosing a bride, and eventually he declined to go. After leaving Emily, Susanna was to stay with Martha and Westley but their unhappiness led to her moving yet again and going to live with Samuel. Hall was to prove not only a poor husband but also a very unreliable minister, inflicting on Martha a series of mistresses and, as an older man, involving himself with increasingly dubious groups within the Church.

Given all these events, one is tempted to think that John was more concerned about going to Georgia than about the best interests of any of his brothers and sisters. He not only remained totally oblivious of Charles' genuine desire not to go but also insisted that Charles should be ordained as a minister before going, even though Charles had no calling to be a minister and said it was something he 'exceedingly dreaded'.[11] At one level the experience of trying to live a holy life among like-minded fellow students had paid Charles a disservice because an emphasis on showing one was saved by performing good works had only succeeded in making him feel his faith was inadequate and his lifestyle unworthy of a true Christian. This was not the context in which he thought it was right to consider becoming a clergyman responsible for the souls of others let alone undertaking missionary work abroad. Nevertheless, despite such grave doubts, Charles surrendered to John's insistence and agreed to accept ordination and become Oglethorpe's personal secretary and the colony's Secretary of Indian Affairs.

Charles was ordained as a deacon by John Potter, Bishop of Oxford, (1715–37) on 21 September and as a minister by Edmund Gibson, Bishop of London, on 29 September. Charles' sad comment on these events was: 'Jack knew his strength and used it ... I freely own 'twas the will of Jack, but am not yet convinced 'twas the will of God.' [12] The same insistence was used to persuade two Oxford Methodists to accompany them. John urged Benjamin Ingham to take Hall's place: 'Fast and pray, fast and pray; and then send me word whether you dare go with me to the Indians.'[13] Initially Ingham was reluctant, saying he felt there were enough heathens in England without seeking them out in America, but his deep friendship for Charles eventually led him to accept. John hoped to also take one of his tutees, a young man called Matthew Salmon. When the youth's parents vetoed this, John persuaded another tutee to take his place. This was the 21-year-old Charles Delamotte, who was the son of a Middlesex sugar merchant and magistrate.

John expressed his delight at the prospect of the ascetic life which lay ahead:

The pomp and show of the world have no place in the wilds of America
... I cannot hope to attain the same degree of holiness here, which I

may there ... [I will be] cut off from all occasions of gratifying those desires which, unless speedily rooted out, will drown ... [the] soul in everlasting perdition.[14]

Samuel grieved that John had 'robbed him' of Charles, but put a brave face on matters and published a celebratory poem called 'Georgia' in honour of their undertaking. On 14 October 1735 the four missionaries set sail from Gravesend in a ship called the *Simmonds* with 257 passengers and crew. Alongside this sailed a second ship called the *London Merchant*. Near the outset of the voyage the two ships stopped at Cowes on the Isle of Wight, where they were joined by a government sloop called *The Hawk*, which was to escort them and then chart the Georgia coastline. Storms delayed their departure till 10 December.

While they were waiting, the four young men went for walks to discuss their forthcoming work. They agreed that they would totally support each other in the challenges that lay ahead because it would be 'impossible to promote the work of God among the heathen without an entire union among ourselves' and they mutually vowed they would fully consult each other about everything they did and accept majority decisions.[15] The newly ordained Charles was selected to preach several times. In one of his sermons he voiced his regret at the human weakness that made people reluctant to give up all for the gospel:

> The world with her pomps and vanities, pleasures and delights, entertainments and diversions, has monopolised a large share of our affections ... We have offered part of our service to other masters ... [yet] the gospel informs us that to be disciples of Christ we must forsake ... [everything] which the world counts dear.[16]

All four hoped they would show that the Anglican Church offered a vibrant version of Christianity and was not just a by-product of the commercial creation of colonies in Virginia, Maryland, the Carolinas, and now Georgia.

Once they were properly at sea, the four young men adopted a regular daily routine throughout the two-month voyage to America. Benjamin Ingham has left us with an account of this. They rose early, prayed for an hour, and studied passages from the Bible and from books on the history of Christianity. They then had breakfast before engaging in public prayers and further study. At midday and mid-afternoon they led public worship and the rest of their time was spent discussing with each other how best to live a Christian life. Thus the former Oxford Methodists transferred their daily routine from university campus to an ocean-going vessel. Not surprisingly, some of the ship's officers poked fun at them for their constant religious activities but Oglethorpe came to their defence: 'Do you take these gentlemen for tithe-pig parsons? They are gentlemen of learning and respectability. They are my friends and whoever offers an affront to them insults me.'[17]

Behind the public façade, Charles agonized over whether he should have embarked with his brother. The seas were very rough and he suffered from appalling sea-sickness and this helped plunge him into an increasingly deep depression: 'I find no words to express myself. There is no writing down my sensations. I feel the weight and misery of my nature, and long to be freed from this body of corruptions.'[18] Charles confided how much he loathed his life in a letter to his friend, Sally Kirkham: 'In vain have I fled from myself to America; I still groan under the intolerable weight of inherent misery! ... Go where I will, I carry my Hell about with me; nor have I the least ease in anything.'[19] He urged Sally to fulfil the Christian life better than he could:

> I cannot follow my own advice, but yet I advise you – Give God your heart: Love Him with all your soul; serve Him with all your strength. Forget ... Riches, Pleasure, Honour – in a word, whatever does not lead to God ... Whatever ye speak, or think, or do, let God be your aim, and God only! ... Have one design, one desire, one hope! ... To love God and be beloved by Him is enough ... He shall fill you with Peace and Joy and Love.[20]

It cannot have helped that John's behaviour was not all it should be on the journey. As far as we can tell both Charles and Benjamin Ingham were concerned that too much of John's time was taken up by Beata Hawkins, the wife of the ship's surgeon, and her pregnant friend, Anne Welch, who was the wife of a carpenter. Some of the other would-be colonists viewed Mrs Welch and Mrs Hawkins as little better than common prostitutes and Charles thought John was blind to the fact their flirtatious attentions probably had less than honourable motives.

When the ship faced tremendous storms, the four young missionaries discovered they were terribly afraid of dying. John in particular could not help contrasting his screams of terror with the calm assurance shown by a small group of 26 German Moravians, who had joined the expedition to escape religious persecution. They sang hymns as the waves struck. John commented to his brother and friends: 'O how pure a heart must he be, who would rejoice to appear before God without a moment's warning!' Their faith perfectly matched the words of a well-known hymn:

Let mountains from their seats be hurled
Down to the deep and buried there,
Convulsions shake the solid world,
Our faith shall never yield to fear.[21]

The Moravians were the spiritual descendants of the fifteenth-century Hussite movement which had broken away from the Roman Catholic Church in Bohemia. In the 1720s a small group had fled from persecution in their homeland and sought refuge in Saxony. There they had been given asylum by a German Count called Nikolaus Ludwig Graf von Zinzendorf. He was a Lutheran minister who had been deeply influenced by the Pietist movement. Zinzendorf created a home for the refugees at Herrnhut on his estate at Berthelsdorf and preached to them about the need for personal faith and spiritual renewal. Their positive response led him to develop an organization called the Unitas Fratrum (Unity of the Brethren). Its members were soon labelled 'the Moravians' because of the geographical area from which they came.

The Moravians laid great emphasis on each person developing his or her personal heartfelt faith through quiet prayer and reflection but they also expressed their individual faith through communal living, liturgical worship and helping others. John and Charles noticed they were prepared to undertake all the lowly tasks which no one else was prepared to do and, if threatened, were prepared to turn the other cheek. Their leader, David Nitschmann, began teaching John German. Benjamin Ingham later wrote of how impressed he and the others were:

> They are more like the primitive Christians than any church now existing … They live together in perfect love and peace, having for the present all things in common. They are more ready to serve their neighbours than themselves. In business they are diligent, in all their dealings strictly just; and in everything they behave themselves with meekness, sweetness and humility.[22]

Unlike John, Charles did not fret that the Moravians appeared more advanced in their Christian witness. Instead he hoped simply to keep his eye fixed on the way marked out for him 'so I may in good time gain the crown which God in Christ Jesus hath proposed to me'. In running the Christian race he was convinced no one could be immune from continued temptation because even Christ had been tempted. What was necessary in the face of failure was 'vigour and industry and perseverance' and recognition that the search for Christian perfection, while unachievable, was 'the goal of our religious race … [because] Heaven is a matter

of such consequence that nothing else is worthy our seeking besides it'.[23]
He therefore described himself as 'a prisoner of hope':

> I am come to a crisis ... I shall either be converted or lost ... Obstinate
> pride, invincible sensuality stand betwixt God and me. The whole
> bent of my soul is to be altered. My office calls for an ardent love of
> souls, a desire to spend and to be spent for them, and earnestness to
> lay down my life for the Brethren.[24]

The would-be colonists arrived in Georgia on 5 February 1736. John
Wesley later recorded his impressions of the country, detailing its
weather patterns, its changing seasonal temperatures, and its differing
and difficult terrain, which ranged from land covered with pine and oak
(which made it very difficult to clear land for farming) to disease-ridden
swamp and marsh. He recounts how they quickly came to appreciate that
much of the land reclaimed from pine forest yielded little return for the
effort put into it, though it was suited to the growing of peaches, grapes,
mulberries, water melons and certain types of bean. Long-term fertil-
ity only existed in the land which was reclaimed from the oak forests
that bordered the swamps. Charles wrote more succinctly of his feelings: 'God has brought an unhappy, unthankful wretch hither, through
a thousand dangers, to renew his complaints, and loathe the life which
has been preserved by a series of miracles.'[25]

For the first five weeks they lived sometimes on board ship and sometimes in an encampment on the shore. Oglethorpe introduced them to
a young Moravian called August Gottlieb Spangenberg, who had come
out to Georgia on an earlier ship, and John struck a friendship with
him. Almost identical in age and both university-educated, the two men
found they had much in common because both favoured erudite conversation or solitude to frivolous company. However, Spangenberg's
Moravian background made him certain of his own salvation in a way
John found disconcerting. He told John it was important to restrict one's
learning only to that which really contributed to the soul's welfare and
to recognize that no one could earn their way into heaven by good works
– assurance of salvation came only from the rebirth offered by the Holy
Spirit. At the time John was not ready to listen, but Spangenberg was
sowing seeds that were to later bear fruit not only in the life of John but
also in Charles.

The Georgia Trustees had underestimated the hardships that they
would face. Savannah proved to be only a small town of about a hundred houses, just beginning to emerge from the wilderness. Its inhabitants were fearful of attack not only from Indians but from the Spanish.

It only had four public buildings: a courthouse, a prison, a storehouse
and a public mill for grinding corn. The courthouse doubled up as the
colony's church. Initially the log-cabin rectory was still occupied by
John's predecessor as chaplain, the Revd Samuel Quincey, so John took
up temporary residence in a communal room with the Moravians, and
so did Charles Delamotte. They began visiting the sick and bereaved
and educating the children. John removed his shoes and taught barefoot
in the newly created log classroom to counteract the contemptuous way
in which the richer children treated any barefooted classmates. Inspired
by Moravian hymn-singing, John also began compiling *A Collection
of Psalms and Hymns* and this was published in 1737 by a publisher in
Charleston.

John was initially impressed by the settlers' willingness to crowd into
church and 'the deep attention with which they received the word'.[26]
Some of the settlers appeared to take him to their heart. They told him
they were thankful to God for 'all the goodness ... [and] great many
benefits'[27] arising from his ministry. However, gradually John became
disillusioned as more and more colonists criticized him. They disliked
the fact he supported the colony's anti-slavery policy because they could
not help comparing their harsh existence with the lifestyle of white plan-
tation owners in the Carolinas. Equally they hated his support for the
colony's strict trading laws and its ban on the drinking of rum. Increasingly they were also offended by his outspoken preaching, which was
very critical of their morality.

The position of Charles and Benjamin Ingham was worse. They accompanied Oglethorpe to set up a new settlement called Fort Frederica on St
Simon's Island, which was 100 miles south of Savannah. The colonists
there only had a few tents and huts. It is not surprising that Charles
found living in a tent surrounded by wilderness a very depressing experience after the joys of Oxford. He wrote home saying he might not
survive for very long:

> I wandered to the north end of the island and stood upon the narrow
> point which ... [projects] into the ocean. The vastness of the watery
> waste, as compared with my standing place, called to mind the brief-
> ness of life and the immensity of its consequences.[28]

Matters were not helped by the fact Charles found he was spending
hours just writing letters and Oglethorpe proved a hard and at times
ungracious and hot-tempered taskmaster.

Nevertheless, Charles determined to make a success of his new life
and he asked if he could take on the role of chaplain to the settlement,

leaving Ingham, who had originally been assigned that task, to do missionary work with the Indians. Oglethorpe agreed and Charles wrote in his diary that his depression lifted because 'God gave me, like Saul, another heart'.[29] In the absence of any church building, Charles led four services a day in the open air, summoning people to these devotions by beating a drum. At least half of the sermons he preached had been written for him by his brother. This was not unusual because using the sermons of someone you admired was standard practice in the eighteenth century. Unfortunately John's sermons contained more about fearing God's vengeance than about responding to God's forgiveness and love. Their style and content did not endear Charles to the colonists. Living in such difficult conditions, the last thing they wanted to hear was that they should deny themselves still further because any worldly pleasure was vain and sinful.

Charles soon ran into problems that were not of his making. Oglethorpe banned any shooting on Sundays and Charles was wrongly blamed as the instigator behind this very unpopular decision. On 18 March he was lucky to escape injury when a gun was fired 'from the other side of the bushes'.[30] Whether this shot was accidental or deliberate is uncertain. Three days later Hawkins, the former ship's surgeon turned colony doctor, publicly challenged the ban by firing his gun while Charles was conducting a service. He was arrested and his wife, Beata, publicly attacked Charles 'with the utmost bitterness and scurrility':

> [She said] she would blow me up, and my brother ... [and that] she would be revenged, and expose my dammed hypocrisy, my prayers four times a day by beat of drum, and abundance more, which I cannot write, and thought no woman ... could have spoken.[31]

Charles wrongly thought he could ignore her but she was supported by her friend, Anne Welch. These were the two ladies who had sought to make themselves attractive to the Wesleys on the voyage across to America. They saw themselves as 'the queen bees of the colony'[32] and Beata Hawkins made it her business to make much of her husband's arrest. She fired a gun herself and then ran around 'like a mad woman' saying she would resist arrest and kill the first man who came near her.[33] With the help of Anne Welch, she began encouraging other women to get their husbands to accuse Charles of being a troublemaker in the colony.

Charles started avoiding meeting people in public, fearful that anything he said or did might be misinterpreted. On 25 March Oglethorpe summoned him and accused him of filling the colonists with dread and confusion:

He charged me with mutiny and sedition; with stirring up the people to desert the colony ... My answer was ... I know nothing of their meetings or designs ... I never incited anyone to leave the colony. I desire to face my accuser face to face.[34]

The next day Charles wrote: 'Innocence is not the least protection; but my sure trust is in God.'[35] Unfortunately his troubles had just begun. While Hawkins was in prison a pregnant woman lost her child and Charles was horrified to discover this was attributed to him for having had the doctor arrested in the first place. Charles was painfully aware that only Oglethorpe could protect him: 'I know my life is in your hands ... My safety depends on your single opinion of me.'[36]

Sadly Charles' naivety made him fall victim to the lies of the very people who were undermining him. Beata Hawkins and Anne Welch pretended they were sorry for their actions and then confided to him that Oglethorpe had seduced them on board the *Simmons*. Despite his earlier misgivings about the two women, Charles very foolishly believed them and distanced himself still further from his employer. The two women then went to see Oglethorpe and warned him that Charles was spreading false tales about him being an adulterer. They also accused Charles of having attempted to rape Mrs Welch. An incandescent Oglethorpe refused to communicate with Charles and instructed everyone to ignore him. The impact was immediate and devastating:

Knowing I was to live with Mr Oglethorpe I had brought nothing with me from England except my clothes and books, but this morning, asking a servant for something I wanted (I think a tea-kettle), I was told Mr Oglethorpe had given orders that no one should use any of his things. I answered that order I supposed did not extend to me. 'Yes, sir', says she, 'you was excepted by name' ...[37]

Charles interpreted his position as God testing him and wrote to his brother Samuel, asking him to pray he might respond by proving a true disciple of Christ. However, the departure for Savannah on 28 March of his one source of comfort, Benjamin Ingham, sunk Charles 'into deeper dejection than I had known before'.[38] Convinced that Oglethorpe was now the chief of his enemies, Charles adopted the stance of a Christian martyr:

I find the Scripture an inexhaustible fund of comfort ... I give my back to the smiters, and my cheeks to them that plucked off the hair. I hid not my face from shame and spitting. For the Lord God will help me, therefore shall I not be confounded. Therefore have I set my face like a flint ... Behold the Lord God will help me: who is he that shall condemn me?[39]

This only encouraged his enemies and the situation deteriorated further:

[I was] abused and slighted ... [and] trampled upon ... The people have found out I am in disgrace ... My few well-wishers are afraid to speak to me. Some have turned out of their way to avoid me ... The servant that used to wash my linen sent it back unwashed.[40]

While expressing his continued faith in the ultimate triumph of good, Charles bemoaned the difficulty of anyone attempting to lead a Christian life:

Experience shows us that even those who are Christians indeed, who serve God with all their strength, may go on their way weeping ... They are followers of him who was a man of sorrows and acquainted with grief. And if any man will come after him, he must deny himself and take up his cross ... [and] be made perfect through sufferings.[41]

Beneath the outward façade Charles was in torment at his failure. In a letter home to his brother Samuel he despairingly questioned whether he should ever have become a minister because of his inadequate faith. Samuel's reply was not to reach him till the autumn. In it Samuel pointed out Charles' decision to go to America had been taken against his advice, but he did not believe that Charles was unworthy. The very fact he had such a high view of what a clergyman should do was testimony that he was fitted to the role. Moreover, all the years he and his wife had spent with Charles made them absolutely sure of his genuine awareness of God:

Your wishing yourself out of the reach of temptation is but wishing yourself in Heaven ... That you [fear] you had lived eighteen years without God I either do not understand, or I absolutely deny ... Never spare unburdening yourself to me ... God grant a happy end and ... [that we meet again].[42]

By 1 April Charles had taken to his bed with a fever and three days later he was also suffering from what he describes as 'the bloody flux', an extreme form of diarrhoea. He escaped death only through the kindness of a colonist called Davison and his wife. Hearing from Benjamin Ingham of his brother's plight, John travelled to Frederica to see if he could sort out the chaos. Arriving on 10 April, he found Charles ill with fever and dysentery on the floor of his tent because Oglethorpe had vindictively confiscated his bed. Even John, who was a great advocate of fasting, was shocked to see that Charles was starving himself in his determination to avoid seeking help from the colonists. John used all his skills and persuaded Oglethorpe to listen fully to Charles' version of affairs. When they met, Charles told Oglethorpe:

> Life is bitterness to me ... You have been deceived as well as I. I protest my innocence of the crimes I am charged with, and take myself now to be at liberty to tell you what I thought never to have uttered.[43]

When he heard how Anne Welch and Beata Hawkins had deceived both of them, Oglethorpe was immediately contrite. He kissed Charles 'with the most cordial affection', condemning himself for not investigating the matter properly.[44] As a gesture of renewed goodwill he promised to build a proper house for Charles and give him whatever he wanted. In return Charles expressed his readiness to forgive his enemies. However, in his journal Charles confesses he was galled by the hypocritical return of his congregation and 'their provoking civilities'.[45]

All these events took place at a time when the colonists lived in daily fear of a possible Spanish attack. There were constant false alarms and panics so that 'every one seemed under a consternation'.[46] The night-time watch was doubled, scout boats were sent out, innocent boats were mistakenly fired on, and Oglethorpe had to patrol the coast in a man-of-war. According to Charles, the general uncovered some Spaniards hiding at Point St George and forced them to flee out to sea. Such rumours and events did not make Charles' recovery any easier because they brought home to him the inherent dangers of remaining at Fort Frederica. Nor did it help him to know that John now hated being in Georgia. Oglethorpe had told them they would find the native Indians were Christian in their behaviour and that all that was required was for John 'to explain to them the system of Religion'.[47] Now John appreciated the Indians had 'no inclination to learn anything; but least of all Christianity' and he viewed them as completely lawless and immoral:

> Everyone doeth what is right in his own eyes; and if it appears wrong to his neighbour, the person aggrieved usually steals on the other un-awares, and shoots him, scalps him, or cuts off his ears ... They are likewise all ... gluttons, drunkards, thieves, dissemblers, liars. They are implacable [and] unmerciful ... Whoredom they account no crime,

and few instances appear of a young Indian woman's refusing any one ... They know not what friendship or gratitude means.[48]

Even John's love for Charles could not keep him long in such a horrible settlement as Fort Frederica and, to Charles' distress, his brother rapidly returned to Savannah. By May his continued ill health forced Charles to request leave to return to England. Whatever Charles' failings, Oglethorpe was clearly concerned that the Trustees might send him a less congenial replacement. He therefore asked Charles to consider resuming his post once he had physically recovered, but he also added it might be prudent for him to marry before he returned. Oglethorpe thought Charles' ministry would have fared better if a wife had been around to protect him from the wiles of other women: 'You are of a social temper, and would find in a married state the difficulties of working out your salvation exceedingly lessened and your helps as much increased.'[49] Charles headed back to Savannah to await a ship home.

John agreed to return to Fort Frederica with Charles Delamotte and become Oglethorpe's secretary, leaving Benjamin Ingham to run the church in Savannah. Ingham had discovered the existence of a religious society led by a colonist called Robert Hows and he hoped it could be developed into an American version of Oxford Methodism. Unfortunately, having got rid of Charles, the settlers were in no mood to have his brother as their minister, especially as he was also a High Churchman and therefore to their eyes a Catholic. John's position soon became untenable. A spokesman for the colonists told him:

I like nothing that you do; all your sermons are satires upon particular persons ... We cannot tell what religion you are of ... We know not what to make of it ... All the quarrels that have been here since your arrival have been because of you; and there is neither man nor woman in the town who minds a word you say.[50]

John and Charles Delamotte were forced to ignominiously return to Savannah.

While waiting in Savannah for news of a ship to take him home, Charles had been trying to assist Ingham. Here, for example, is his account of helping a terminally ill teenager:

I visited a girl of fifteen, who lay a-dying of an incurable illness. She had been in that condition for many months ... I started at the sight of a breathing corpse. Never was real corpse half so ghastly. Her groans and screams alone distinguished her from one. They had no intermission: yet she was perfectly sensible, as appeared by her feebly lifting up her eyes when I bade her trust in God, and read [her] prayers ... We were all in tears. She made signs for me to come again.[51]

But his heart was constantly looking homewards and he confided in his journal: 'I was overjoyed by my deliverance out of this furnace, and not a little ashamed for being so.'[52] He wrote to his brother Samuel of his forthcoming return – and this letter brought great rejoicing when it arrived.

On 7 July Charles was lucky not to be seriously injured or killed. He and Charles Delamotte went swimming in the river and only narrowly escaped the jaws of an alligator. Charles must have breathed a sigh of relief when three weeks later he finally left the colony, setting out with John for Charleston in the neighbouring colony of Carolina to embark on a ship for England. Arriving in Charleston on 31 July, Charles was horrified to witness at first hand the cruelties inflicted on African slaves. He thought the practice of giving young white children slaves of their own only encouraged them to grow up believing it was perfectly acceptable to tyrannize and torment anyone of a black colour. He met one man called Star who delighted in nailing a slave to a wall so he could then be whipped 'in the severest manner' before having scalding water thrown over him. Other men would punish by pulling out a slave's teeth or mutilating them:

> One Colonel Lynch is universally known to have cut off a poor Negro's legs; and to kill several of them a year by his barbarities ... Mr Hill, a dancing-master in Charleston, whipped a she-slave so long that she fell at his feet for dead. When, by the help of a Physician, she was so far recovered as to show signs of life, he repeated the whipping with equal rigour; and concluded with dropping hot sealing-wax upon her flesh. Her crime was over filling a tea-cup.[53]

Charles could not condone such 'horrid cruelties' or the slave laws that effectively condoned what frequently amounted to murder. The penalty for killing a slave (should the matter ever go to court which was itself unlikely) was just seven pounds! Many years later Charles wrote hymns for masters and servants. In them he asked servants to remain quietly submissive if faced with a cruel master:

> Insults and wrongs in silence bear,
> And serve with conscientious care
> [He] whom I can never please ...[54]

But he asked masters to behave in a truly Christian way towards their servants by acting 'with mild paternal sway':

> Brethren in our Creator's eyes,
> I dare not injure, or despise
> The workmanship of God,
> Who me their earthly lord confess,
> Heirs of my Saviour's righteousness,
> And bought with all His blood.[55]

On 11 August Charles said a painful farewell to John and set sail for home. His health was still very poor and he soon suffered from 'flux and fever' again. Matters were not helped by the fact that the ship's captain, a man called Indivine, had let out Charles' cabin to someone else. Charles was reduced to sleeping in a chest rather than a bed. Even worse, he had nowhere to go to escape from Indivine, who was frequently drunk:

> [He was] the most beastly man I ever saw: a lewd, drunken, quarrel-some fool; praying, and yet swearing continually. The first sight I had of him was upon the cabin floor, stark naked and dead drunk.[56]

Charles soon discovered that 'while any of his half-hogshead of rum remains, here will be nothing but … drunkenness without end'[57] and that such drunkenness endangered the lives of everyone on board.

One of Charles' fellow passengers was a young Dutchman called Thomas Apee, who had also been on the same ship as Charles on the outward journey to Georgia. Apee had preyed on Charles' good nature and borrowed money he had no intention of returning. Now he shocked Charles by laying aside his mask of friendship and brutally detailing why he felt the Wesley brothers were failures. He alleged that Oglethorpe thought Charles was a man who only did what he did because of his brother's orders and whose faith therefore lacked sincerity.[58] It was time Charles admitted that Georgia had no attractions for him and abandoned the hypocritical pretence of wanting to please God. If he could abandon the pointless strict lifestyle that his brother encouraged, he would be a far happier man and far better company. Charles' response was to rebuke Apee for using lewd language. In reply Apee 'increased his beastliness' and abused Charles 'plentifully'.[59] Charles' revenge was to speak to him in Latin and Greek, knowing Apee could understand neither.

On 20 September there was a terrible storm and Charles records how this led to a major clash between the drunken captain and his first mate, a man called Graham. Indivine was incapable of recognizing that the winds were driving the ship towards the shore and that there was every likelihood of them striking a shoal of rocks. When Graham persisted in reporting their potential danger, Indivine ordered him to simply ensure they had a good look-out. Graham indicated he felt the captain was failing to give any sensible orders. He accused him of failing in his duty as master of the ship by not being on deck during such a storm. The captain said he did not need to be on deck to know exactly where his ship was. Graham asked how that could be possible when Indivine had not personally taken any observations of the ship's course for a fortnight, nor let his men take any for four days. After an hour of wrangling the mate gave up trying to get Indivine to issue any orders and the captain concluded the meeting by asking for a further dram to drink. It was left to Graham to ensure that the ship reached Boston four days later, while the captain was 'dead drunk on the floor, without sense or motion'.[60]

While the ship was repaired and resupplied, Charles enjoyed a brief respite in a city, which he found far more attractive than Savannah: 'The temperate air, the clear rivulets, and beautiful hills and dales, which we everywhere met with, seemed to present the very reverse of Georgia.'[61] Its citizens were far more civilized and, after visiting the city's governor, Charles undertook some preaching, even though his health was still very poor. By the 6 October he was writing to John in a fit of enthusiasm to tell him that he had decided that he would return if at all possible to Georgia rather than return to living in Oxford or with their brother Samuel in Tiverton: 'Georgia alone can give me the solitude I seek after [even if] I cannot look for a long life there.'[62] Unfortunately, a sudden return of severe dysentery made this change of heart not feasible. He 'vomited, purged, bled, sweated, and took laudanum', but this drained him of the little strength he had left.[63] He became desperate just to recover sufficiently to risk taking the next ship home.

On 25 October friends more or less carried him on board a ship called the *Hannah*, which was under the command of a Captain Corney. Charles agreed to share a smaller cabin rather than face having to share the state-room with Thomas Apee, who was also on board. By now Charles had learnt more of the man's past, including that Apee had had to travel to America not to escape religious persecution (as he and John had thought) but to avoid arrest for robbing his father of 300 guineas. The return journey was not without incident because the ship was so overladen that any bad weather caused a real threat of it sinking. Charles wrote that often 'the sea streamed in at the sides so plentifully, that it was as much as four men could do, by continual pumping, to keep her above water' but his faith grew stronger as fear made him constantly

pray: 'I prayed for power to pray, for faith in Jesus Christ, continually repeating his name, till I felt the virtue of it at last, and knew that I abode
under the shadow of the Almighty.'

The worst time was a ten-day storm shortly after leaving Boston.
When the captain was reduced to cutting down the ship's mizzen mast
to prevent them sinking, the impact on Charles was enormous:

> In this dreadful moment, I bless God, I found the comfort of hope;
> and such joy in finding I could hope, as the world can neither give nor
> take way. I had that conviction of the power of God, present with me,
> overruling my strongest passion, fear, and raising me above what I am
> by nature, as surpassed all rational evidence, and gave me a taste of
> the divine goodness ... Toward morning the sea heard, and obeyed,
> the divine voice, 'Peace, be still'.[64]

He was later to recall this experience in verse:

> Headlong we cleave the yawning deep,
> And back to highest heaven are borne,
> Unmoved, though vapid whirlwinds sweep,
> And all the watery world upturn.
> Roar on, ye waves! Our souls defy
> Your roaring to disturb our rest:
> In vain to impair the calm ye try,
> The calm in a believer's breast.[65]

For much of the remaining journey he continued to suffer from dysentery and he records 'I often threw myself upon the bed, seeking rest, but
finding none'.[66] It was a seriously sick man who gave thanks for his safe
return when, after facing yet more storms, the ship landed at Deal on 3
December 1736: 'I knelt down and blessed the Hand that had conducted
me through such inextricable mazes.'[67] Charles immediately travelled to
London. Given his education at Westminster, it was in many ways his
'home', more than either Epworth or Oxford.

Many sections of London were unpleasant because its rapidly rising
population was generating increasingly squalid gin-ridden slums but,
nevertheless, large sections of the capital were still both countrified and
attractive, filled with the gilded mansions of the rich. London Bridge
was the only highway across the Thames so Bethnal Green, Brixton,
Camberwell, Clapham, Islington, Hackney, Peckham and the like were
essentially country villages while Chelsea, Knightsbridge, Marylebone
and Tottenham Court were all in open country. Belgravia was farmland,

Lambeth a garden area, and Stepney a collection of scattered houses surrounded by fields. Moorfields, which was to become the main area for Charles' subsequent work as an evangelist, was a park intersected with gravel walks where people could seek exercise and relaxation.

Charles went to the home of the publisher Charles Rivington, who was an old family friend, and lodged at his home in St Paul's Yard. Then he went to stay with another friend, James Hutton, who lived in Great College Street, Westminster. Hutton's father was a minister who had taken in boarders from Westminster School and he was a very close friend of Samuel Wesley. Charles was warmly welcomed because the newspapers had erroneously printed a story that his ship had been lost at sea: 'My reception was such as I expected from a family that entirely loved me, but had given me over for dead.'[68]

Charles was pleased to discover that James Hutton had started a religious society for prayer and Bible study in his bookshop 'The Bible and Sun' in Little Wild Street, near Drury Lane. Its members were delighted to have a genuine missionary in their midst and Charles revelled in their adulation. Charles pretended his return was primarily the product of the need to convey information about the colony to the Georgia Trustees. He reported on the colony's affairs not only to them but also to the Bishop of London, though his health was in such a very parlous state that he sometimes could not speak aloud and had to rely on others to read out what he wanted to say. He told his friends that he was determined to return to Georgia as a missionary once he was recovered. George Whitefield wrote from Oxford offering to take his place if his health remained poor because he had received a letter from John asking for his help because 'the harvest is great and the labourers few'.[69] However, not all were so keen on the American enterprise. When Charles visited his uncle just before Christmas, Matthew bestowed 'abundance of wit on my brother, and his apostolical project'.[70]

On 26 December Charles' doctor told him he had to remain in bed or he would kill himself. Despite this, Charles continued to visit those people who might support the colonists in Georgia and he dealt with Captain Corney over the refitting of the ship before its return journey, though this was hindered because it was discovered Apee had misappropriated some of the funds set aside for this purpose. On the 7 January 1737 Oglethorpe arrived back in England to deal with accusations from some of the colony's Trustees that he had abused his authority and was misapplying funds. Charles worked with Oglethorpe to try and silence some of the detractors. He also met up with the Moravian community in London to enlist their support and met their leader, Count Zinzendorf, who had recently arrived in the capital.

Ill health continued to dog him. Charles compared his sufferings to those of Job. When he called on a family friend, Mary Pendarves, he found her reading a letter, which wrongly was reporting his death, and he commented: 'Happy for me had the news been true! What a world of misery would it save me.'[71] His illness was not just physical. He felt he had hid the real nature of his experience in America from his friends, putting on a hateful mask:

A goodly formal saint,
I long appeared in sight;
By self and Satan taught to paint
My tomb, my nature, white.
The Pharisee within
Still undisturbed remained;
The strong man, armed with guilt of sin,
Safe in his palace reigned.[72]

Moreover, he found the religious life of London equally hypocritical. The importance of Christianity was being given physical expression in the city at this time because in 1711 an Act of Parliament had authorized the creation of 50 new churches and by the 1730s not only had the first 15 of these made their appearance but also Westminster Abbey had been enlarged. These projects had involved the most distinguished architects in the city. However, Charles was aware neither the new nor the old were attracting many people. The churches might be outwardly fine but they were inwardly failing. Overall the number of churches offering daily services was falling and less than a dozen were offering weekly communion. Almost half of the churches in the diocese of London were failing to even deliver a morning and evening service every Sunday. It did not help that many of the richer churches engaged in the practice of renting out their pews to the wealthy (as an obvious deterrent to the poor!) and that many of the poorer churches relied on very poorly paid and often inadequate curates.

Charles' spiritual depression found expression in the verses which later were known as the 'Hymn for Midnight':

When midnight shades the earth o'erspread,
And veil the bosom of the deep,
Nature reclines her weary head
And Care respires and Sorrows sleep:
My soul still aims at nobler rest,
Aspiring to the Saviour's breast.

Fain would I leave this earth below,
Of pain and sin the dark abode;
Where shadowy joy or solid woe,
Allures or tears me from my God;
Doubtful and insecure of bliss
Since death alone confirms me His.

Absent from thee, my exiled soul
Deep in a fleshly dungeon groans;
Around me clouds of darkness roll,
And labouring silence speaks my moans;
Come quickly, Lord, thy face display,
And look my midnight into day ...[73]

In February Charles visited friends in the Oxford area. Former members of the Holy Club gave him a warm welcome, especially John Gambold, Robert Kirkham and Charles Kinchin. He urged his friends to continue supporting each other and took time to renew his own contact with some of the inmates of the Oxford prison. He was also careful to inform the authorities at Lincoln College of the activities of his brother and was delighted by the affectionate reception given to him by its rector. After a fortnight he returned to London, having decided he would tell Oglethorpe he would return to Georgia but not as his secretary. He travelled to visit his brother Samuel and his mother in Tiverton so he could inform them of this decision. Aware just how frail her son's health had become, Susanna urged him to reconsider returning to America. Doubtless, Samuel was equally opposed. As a consequence Charles decided he would encourage George Whitefield to accompany him.

By this time George was clearly in a class of his own as a preacher and he had none of the inner turmoil facing Charles. He had come to understand before the Wesleys that salvation cannot be earned and that ultimately a person is saved only through God's grace. Just before Easter 1735 he had felt God had truly transformed his life:

O! with what joy – joy unspeakable ... was my soul filled, when the weight of sin fell off, and an abiding sense of the pardoning love of God, and a full assurance of faith broke in upon my disconsolate soul! ... My joys were like a spring tide, and, as it were, overflowed the banks. Go where I would, I could not avoid singing of psalms almost aloud.[74]

Neither Charles nor John were to experience that kind of freedom from the burden of having to justify their salvation until 1738.

Whitefield had temporarily left Oxford in the spring of 1736 to return to his home town of Gloucester to agonize over whether he should seek ordination. He feared that it might lead to him becoming 'puffed up with pride'.[75] While he deliberated he had formed two religious societies – the first Methodist-style ones to be spawned outside Oxford. On the occasion of his ordination as a deacon by Dr Martin Benson, the Bishop of Gloucester, in June 1736, the 21-year-old Whitefield felt his 'heart melted down' and stunned the majority of the congregation by his eloquence. When a few detractors complained to the bishop that Whitefield's emotional preaching had driven 15 people mad, Benson is said to have replied he hoped in that case the madness would prove permanent! Whitefield's comment on his impact was more prosaic: 'I trust I was able to speak with some degree of Gospel authority.'[76]

In order to take control over the Oxford Methodists, Whitefield had declined the offer of small livings offered by Dr Benson and returned to Oxford, determined to complete his Master's degree so he could become a minister and 'be first a saint and then a scholar'.[77] However, in the spring of 1737 he accepted an invitation from his friend, Thomas Broughton, to preach for two months at the chapel of the Tower of London. 'The boy parson'[78] (as Whitefield was soon nicknamed) was surprised by the response he evoked. A delighted Charles commented, 'his preaching is not in persuasive words of human wisdom but in the manifestation of the spirit and of power'.[79] Charles Kinchin, who had become a fellow at Corpus Christi, asked Whitefield to cover his parish duties as Rector of Dummer in Hampshire. It was while he was there that Charles persuaded George to accompany him to Georgia, saying Kitchin could take over the remaining Oxford Methodists.

Charles' health was still too poor for the two men to even begin to contemplate the journey so Charles spent the next few months visiting friends and lobbying important people to support the Georgia colony. This included talking to the Archbishop of Canterbury and the Bishops of London and Oxford, as well as to various members of the nobility, notably Lady Hastings. He also gave evidence to the Board of Trade on the trading problems facing the colony. His sterling work may well have been the reason why the Trustees were keen in June to endorse his brother's work. It was also why in August the archbishop arranged for Charles to visit Hampton Court and subsequently dine with the royal family at St James' Palace. Charles also visited friends, including John Gambold and, on his return from America, Benjamin Ingham. Charles was a particularly frequent and welcome guest in the houses of the Delamottes of Blendon and the Bensons of Cheshunt because he was a gifted conversationalist and his friends loved hearing his beautiful speaking voice read aloud in the evenings to them and any assembled guests.

Charles made a number of visits to members of his family. This included seeing his uncle, who was ill and who died on 12 August. He entered into more regular communication with his sisters Hetty and Kezzy, warning them of the 'danger of lukewarmness and resting in negative goodness'. He told them resignation, self-renunciation and obedience were the great Christian virtues.[80] In September he was delighted by Kezzy's increasing faith because she was 'full of earnest wishes for divine love' and 'owned there was a depth in religion she had never fathomed'.[81] Hetty showed a similar response and was 'quite melted down'.[82] Charles sought to strengthen his own faith by twice meeting the famous William Law, whose writings he had long admired, but this proved a disappointment. The increasingly irrational Law was depriving himself of adequate sleep, having become obsessed with seeing it as a wasteful sin. He told Charles: 'Nothing I can either speak or write will do you any good.'

All Charles' actions paled into insignificance alongside those of George Whitefield. Wishing to say farewell to friends before accompanying Charles to America, he had gone travelling. In Bristol he began preaching four or five times per week and it was as if denominations did not count. Quakers, Baptists, Presbyterians and other dissenters flocked to hear him as much as did those who belonged to the Church of England. He wrote:

> It was wonderful to see how the people hung upon the rails of the organ loft, climbed upon the leads of the church, and made the church itself so hot with their breath that the steam would fall from the pillars like drops of rain. Sometimes almost as many would go away from lack of room as came in.[83]

He repeated this success in Bath where the fashionable rich began demanding his sermons should go into print. When he joined Charles in London in late August, Whitefield hoped to spend the time before their departure to America reading and praying but he was compelled by popular demand to spend considerable time preaching. That autumn he delivered about a hundred sermons and Charles wrote: 'The churches will not contain the multitudes that throng to hear him.'[84] Even members of the aristocracy came to hear him, among them the Duchess of Marlborough.

It is clear Whitefield's preaching combined evident personal commitment and zeal with a unique delivery:

> Every accent, every emphasis, every modulation of voice, was so perfectly tuned and well placed, that … [it gave the listener] a pleasure

of much the same kind with that received from an excellent piece of music.[85]

He was good at depicting what he called 'the pains of hell' but he was even better at presenting the joys of heaven:

Hark! Methinks I hear them chanting their everlasting hallelujahs and spending an eternal day in echoing triumphant songs of joy. And do you not long, my brethren, to join this heavenly choir? Do not your hearts burn within you? ... Behold then a heavenly ladder reached down to you, by which you may climb to this holy hill ... By this we, even we, may be lifted into the same blissful regions, there to enjoy an eternal rest with the people of God, and join with them in singing ... songs of praise.[86]

Living in a society where virtually everyone believed in God's existence, Whitefield did not see his role as to convert people. Rather he was 'awakening' them to what God could do to change their lives and the lives of others around them. After preaching he never called people to come out to the front of a church and make public profession of their faith. Instead he would seek out those who felt they wanted to know more and offer them his time and advice, even though this was hugely time-consuming and meant his lodgings were often besieged by visitors. He saw religious societies as the best mechanism of offering further encouragement to such people, and inevitably began talking of his experience among the Oxford Methodists. Because his preaching led to a significant increase in the number of religious societies in London, the name of 'Methodism' became well known in a way it had not before.

Jealousy soon evoked clerical opposition. Some described Whitefield as 'a spiritual pickpocket' because of his willingness to preach in any parish, and others criticized his willingness to speak to dissenters. Whitefield hoped the best way to bring them round 'was not by bigotry and railing, but by moderation and love, and by undissembled holiness of life'.[87] Interestingly, the jealousy extended even to Benjamin Ingham who felt that Whitefield was monopolizing Charles. He wrote to John Wesley complaining Charles 'neither writes to me, nor comes to see me'.[88] Charles may have been ignoring Ingham because he had been critical of what Charles and John had achieved in Georgia. Ingham wrote to Charles that autumn:

Dear Brother ... Am I your enemy because I tell you the truth? ... Perhaps I was too severe. Forgive me then. However, I am sure that, by soaring too high in your own imaginations, you have had a great downfall in your spiritual progress. Be lowly, therefore, in your own eyes. Humble yourself before the Lord and He will lift you up. I do assure you it is out of pure love, and with concern, that I write.[89]

In October Charles informed Ingham he was confident God intended him to return to America as a missionary. A factor in this was that Charles had survived an attack from a highwayman while travelling to Westminster and he took this as a sign of God's favour. That same month religious circles in London were taken by storm by the evangelical Jonathan Edwards' account of the religious revival taking place in America. Charles told Count Zinzendorf: 'I would once more play the warrior and force my way into freedom … It seems that the Spirit of God is moving here over the face of the waters. Would that it might reach me, even me!'[90]

Part of Charles' reason for wanting to return was that his ability as a preacher was beginning to receive recognition:

Last Sunday I preached such a sermon at Wakefield church as has set all about us in an uproar. Some say the devil is in me; others that I am mad … Others again extol me to the sky. They say it is the best sermon they ever heard in all their life; and that I ought to be a Bishop. I believe indeed it went to the hearts of several persons; for I was enabled to speak with great authority and power; and I preached almost the whole sermon without book. There was a vast large congregation, and tears fell from many eyes.[91]

In November he revisited his brother Samuel and his mother Susanna in Tiverton but they made him face up to the reality that he was simply not fit enough to return to Georgia.

It was finally agreed Whitefield would go out alone. George embarked for America on 30 December, despite entreaties from many sides that he should not abandon the religious revival he had so strongly initiated. To those who depicted that he was going to a wilderness inhabited by savages, he commented: 'God give me a deep humility, a well-guided zeal, a burning love, and a single eye, and then let men or devils do their worst!'[92] While he was waiting to sail out of the port of Deal, a ship called the *Samuel* arrived from America. It contained John Wesley who, unknown to anyone, had decided to return, having judged his time in America a total failure. A thoroughly depressed John made no attempt to see George but simply sent him a note telling him to return to London. George tried to meet him but found John had already left for the capital.

Unsure of what had happened, Whitefield felt obliged to ignore the note, partly because he felt to return to London would be judged an act of cowardice by his enemies, and partly because he felt it was not right for the colonists, even if they were 'a stiff-necked and rebellious people', to be 'left without a shepherd'.[93]

It is said that during the subsequent voyage Georgia Whitefield 'succeeded in turning a rowdy troop ship into a floating beehive of piety'[94] and his courage in the face of storms and other perils earned him the nickname 'the Rock'. However, his departure radically impaired the progress of the religious revival he had initiated in London. He had put his friendship for Charles before what others saw as more important, but his departure left a vulnerable Charles alone to face the full impact of his brother's unexpected return. John's depressed state was to herald a new phase in both their lives.

4

A Moravian Conversion

And can it be that I should gain
an interest in the Saviour's blood?
Died he for me, who caused his pain;
for me, whom him to death pursues.
Amazing love! How can it be
that thou, my God, shouldst die for me!
'Tis mystery all: the Immortal dies!
Who can explore his strange design?
In vain the first-born seraph tries
to sound the depths of love divine.
'Tis mercy all! Let earth adore
let angel-minds enquire no more.
He left his Father's throne above –
so free, so infinite his grace –
emptied himself of all but love,
and bled for Adam's helpless race.
'Tis mercy all, immense and free;
for, O my God, it found out me!
Long my imprisoned spirit lay
fast bound in sin and nature's night;
thine eye diffused a quickening ray –
I woke, the dungeon flamed with light,
My chains fell off, my heart was free,
I rose, went forth, and followed thee.
No condemnation now I dread;
Jesus, and all in him, is mine!
Alive in him, my living Head,
and clothed in righteousness divine,
bold I approach the eternal throne,
and claim the crown, through Christ, my own.[1]

'Our body, soul, and spirit, are infected, overspread, consumed with the most fatal moral leprosy.'[2] These words come from one of John

Wesley's sermons which was preached by Charles on at least ten occasions in both America and England. Its theme was how sin had 'effaced the image of God' and how 'the one thing needful' was to wholeheartedly hand oneself over to God, relying on Christ's 'miracles of love':

> To re-exchange the image of Satan for the image of God, bondage for freedom, sickness for health! ... to be born again, to be formed anew after the likeness of our Creator.[3]

When saying these words Charles was preaching as much to himself as to his congregation because he yearned for God to grant him a true rebirth:

> All his providences, be they mild or severe ... are all designed ... to unite us to what is worthy of our affection ... Every pain cries aloud, 'Love not the world, neither the things of the world.'[4]

When John unexpectedly returned to London Charles was surprised to discover his brother was equally if not more convinced of his own insufficient faith. Events in Georgia after Charles' departure had led the colonists to reject John's ministry and this had plunged him into a spiritual depression. Some historians have attributed John's failure to his overemphasis on ascetic living and the unrealistic demands he placed on himself and the colonists. However, this is overly simplistic because, for example, it ignores his belief in 'the winning easiness of love'[5] and oft-stated view that true religion had 'nothing sour, austere, unsociable, [and] unfriendly in it'.[6] John's real Achilles heel had proved to be that he liked the company of women yet believed any sexual feelings were a sign of an inadequate Christian commitment. This meant he appeared to women to court their attention only to then reject them. Such behaviour explains why, for example, Anne Welch was so angry at John she attacked him with a pair of scissors so that his partly shorn head would make him a laughing stock.

John's flight from America arose largely from his inept handling of his love for Sophy Hopkey, the 18-year-old niece of Thomas Causton, Savannah's chief magistrate. There is no doubt that Sophy wanted to marry John and set out to catch him. She constantly made excuses as to why she should visit him in his lodgings. She deliberately wore white dresses because she knew he liked them. She ousted Charles Delamotte and personally nursed John through a bout of sickness. Ostensibly John became her tutor but, as he admitted:

> Unless I prayed without ceasing ... [I] could not avoid some familiarity or other which was not needful. Sometimes I put my arm round her waist, sometimes took her by the hand, and sometimes kissed her.[7]

Although she was neither as beautiful nor educated as some of the other women he had known, he began hinting at marriage because 'her words, her eyes, her air, her every motion and gesture, were full of such softness and sweetness'.[8] But always he held back. John could hardly imagine his family liking the relatively uneducated Sophy or her deceitful uncle, who was in Georgia because of his fraudulent activities. More importantly, John believed his search for personal perfection required celibacy: 'I cannot take fire into my bosom and not be burnt.' Groaning under 'the weight of unholy desires',[9] John was reduced to drawing lots with friends, marked 'Marry', 'Think not of it this year' and 'Think not of it at all'![10]

As time passed Causton decided John was just playing with Sophy's affections and, in March 1737, he announced his niece would marry a colonist called William Williamson. John was so distraught he could not even pray. He said the thought of losing her 'was as the piercing of a sword'.[11] Yet he neither offered to marry her nor stopped her marriage to Williamson. Subsequent rumours that she had been seeing Williamson while still going out with him drove John to fury. He refused to offer her communion because of her 'deliberate dissimulation' and his accusations against her good conduct were blamed for the miscarriage of her first child. In August the infatuated and frustrated Wesley found himself summoned before the Savannah court for 'meddling into the affairs of private families' and for his uncharitable and unreasonable abuse of his role as a minister. This was not surprising. Causton tolerated no opposition from any source, let alone from a minister, and he totally controlled the colony's judicial system, having made sure all his cronies occupied the key positions in the colony's primitive administrative and judicial systems.

Causton literally threw every charge against John he could conceivably find. Among the accusations brought against him were alterations to the liturgy, his use of unauthorized hymns, and his refusal to baptize children unless they submitted to full immersion. In November John was found guilty by a jury which had been selected largely from those who most disliked him. John's position became untenable. Every day there were fresh accusations of 'words I never said and actions I never did' and he concluded, 'the hour was come for leaving this place'.[12] He jumped bail and took ship from Charleston for England on Christmas Eve, saying his relationship with Sophy had proven that his faith was just 'a summer religion' unable to weather the realities of life.[13] Charles Delamotte assisted his escape, even though to do so meant he had to stay behind.

John's unexpected return angered Oglethorpe and amazed Charles, especially when his brother's loss of confidence in his faith became apparent. John wrote in his journal: 'I, who went to America to convert others, was never myself converted to God.'[14] It probably did not help matters that London was still bubbling from the impact of Whitefield's successful preaching. Many religious societies, though founded independently, were seeking to forge links because of Whitefield's influence, and some were observing days of special prayer and fasting together. Printers were competing to produce editions of his sermons and many clergy were being compared to Whitefield and found wanting. John's depression rekindled Charles' doubts about his own faith:

> [When people first become Christian] they will often have peace with God ... [But then temptation reappears and the Christian] treads the same dreadful round of sin ... His comfort is withdrawn, his peace is lost: he prays, resolves and strives, but all in vain; the more he labours, the less he prevails; the more he struggles, the faster is he bound: so that after a thousand thousand repeated defeats he finds at last that sin is irresistible.[15]

John joined Charles in staying at the home of the parents of James Hutton. Aware of how much the Wesley brothers admired the Moravians, Hutton took them to the house of a Dutch merchant called Weinantz on 7 February and there they were introduced to a group who had just arrived that day in London en route to America. Among these Moravians was a gifted and highly intelligent man called Peter Böhler, a 26-year-old who had studied theology at Jena and been converted by Count Zinzendorf, the founder of the movement. Böhler was only in London briefly while he waited to embark as a missionary to the Negro slaves in South Carolina. The Wesleys immediately liked him because he was very much a man after their own heart. They agreed to assist the Moravians in finding accommodation and Charles said he would help improve Böhler's command of English.

Over the next few days Charles and John could not help but compare their unhappiness with Böhler's deep sense of Christian peace. The Moravian recognized they were both in a spiritual mess and talked to them about 'the necessity of prayer and faith'.[16] He urged them to focus less on what they wanted to achieve for God and more on what God could do for them, trying to make them see that if they relied on God for forgiveness they would lose their constant sense of guilt and serve humanity better. He thus reinforced the earlier messages of August Spangenberg in Georgia. As he got to know them better, Böhler felt John needed to give more of his heart and less of his head to Christ, while Charles needed to stop viewing himself as being so worthless as to be beyond God's grace. He wrote: '[Charles] is very much distressed in mind and does not know how he shall begin to be acquainted with the Saviour.'[17]

On 17 February Charles and John took Böhler to meet some of their friends in Oxford. John rapidly returned to London, leaving Charles to show Böhler around the University. The two men spent considerable time together debating the nature of faith and Böhler was invited to preach at a number of the college chapels. However, they had only been in Oxford a week when Charles fell seriously ill. Initially he complained of toothache and was given some medicine mixed with honey. When this failed to provide any relief, he was encouraged to smoke tobacco to dull the pain but this made him vomit. Charles' fear of dying provided Böhler with the opportunity to demonstrate the stronger nature of his faith:

> At eleven I waked in extreme pain, which I thought would quickly separate soul and body. Soon after Peter Böhler came to my bedside ... and prayed for my recovery ... He took me by the hand, and calmly said, 'You will not die now.'[18]

Böhler asked Charles whether he hoped to be one of the saved. Charles replied that he did because he had used his best endeavours to serve God. Böhler indicated that this was not grounds for guaranteeing salvation and Charles weakly reflected: 'What, are not my endeavours a sufficient ground of hope? Would he rob me of my endeavours? I have nothing else to trust to.'[19] There is no clearer statement of how much Charles had come to accept John's views on the need to earn salvation. Böhler commented it was no wonder he and John plagued and tormented themselves until at heart they were very miserable.[20]

The illness proved to be more serious than anyone had first envisaged. Charles developed pleurisy (an inflammation of the membranes that surround the lungs and line the chest cavity). His sister, Kezzia, acted as his chief nurse and two doctors called Manaton and Fruin did all they could to ensure his recovery with the limited medicines at their disposal. They bled him on three occasions, although this did little to help. Charles attributed his eventual recovery to divine rather than human action:

> Jesus to my deliv'rance flew,
> Where sunk in mortal pangs I lay:

Pale Death his ancient conqueror knew,
And trembled, and ungrasp'd his prey!
The fever turn'd its backward course,
Arrested by almighty Power;
Sudden expired its fiery force,
And Anguish gnaw'd my side no more.[21]

The illness had two important consequences. First, it put out of question once and for all Charles ever returning to Georgia because, as he told his brother, 'the Doctor tells me to undertake a voyage now would be certain death'.[22] This meant Charles had to start giving more serious thought to what he would do with the rest of his life. He officially handed in his notice on 3 April at about the same time as his brother John also formally resigned his post as minister of Savannah. Second, and even more importantly, Charles' close encounter with near death confirmed in his mind just how weak his faith was because he had feared dying and entering the presence of Christ:

'Twas not the searching pain within
that fill'd my coward flesh with fear;
nor conscience of uncancell'd sin;
nor sense of dissolution near.
Of hope I felt no joyful ground,
The fruit of righteousness alone;
Naked of Christ my soul I found,
And started from a God unknown.[23]

It confirmed for him that he was not a reborn Christian but 'unchanged, unhallow'd, unrenew'd'.[24] He desperately wanted to feel transformed by God:

My nature re-exchange for Thine;
Be Thou my life, my hope, my gain;
Arm me in panoply divine,
And death shalt shake his dart in vain.[25]

And he said he would never rest till this happened because, without such assurance, his ministry was doomed:

How shall I teach the world to love,
Unchanged myself, unloosed my tongue?

Give me the power of faith to prove,
And mercy shall be all my song ...[26]

There was also a third outcome of Charles' illness. His brother took over as Böhler's chief companion and thus John received the brunt of the Moravian's probing questions about the nature of faith and how one acquired a place in heaven. The Moravians believed people were truly saved only if they passed six tests. A true Christian was one who experienced the three gifts of joy and peace and love in his life and who felt no fear, experienced no doubt, and was guilty of no sin. Chastened by his experience in America, John was prepared to admit he failed all six of these tests. He therefore began questioning whether he was fit to be a preacher, but Böhler told him: 'Preach faith till you have it and then, because you have it, you will preach faith.'[27]

John agreed to put Böhler's words to the test. He visited Oxford prison and consoled a man called William Clifford, who was about to be hanged for assault, burglary and desertion from the army. Whereas before John would have assumed the condemned man was destined for hell, he knelt with him and prayed extempore that he should be saved by God's grace. The prisoner responded positively, saying: 'I am now ready to die. I know Christ has taken away my sins; and there is no more condemnation for me.' When Clifford was hung, Wesley noted 'in his last moments he was ... . enjoying a perfect peace'.[28] From Oxford John travelled with his friend Charles Kinchin to the latter's home in Manchester, stopping at several places en route. He again tested out preaching Böhler's message to a range of people from different backgrounds and was surprised how in almost every case it led to a deep-seated emotional response. Once he was in Manchester, he preached at St Anne's Church on the text: 'If any man be in Christ, he is a new creature.'

Towards the end of March John returned to Oxford and he and Böhler began further debating the nature of faith with a partially recovered Charles. The truths Böhler tried to convey were simple ones. No one can earn their salvation because it is a gift of God's grace. All God seeks is an open heart. Constantly seeking to prove that you are perfect is an indication that you have not fully entrusted your life to God's transforming power. People who are saved are no longer anxious and afraid because they know God has forgiven their sins and pardoned them. For that reason peace is also a gift of God's grace. So too is love because God instantly transforms people's lives if they will let him, removing the mastery of sin. Living a truly Christian life becomes thus also a gift of God's grace. Böhler promised to introduce the Wesleys to a number of Christians in London who would vouchsafe the truth of what he was saying. He fulfilled his promise and the impact on John was immediately apparent because he began using extempore prayer:

> My heart was so full that I could not confine myself to the forms of prayer which we are accustomed to use ... Neither do I purpose to be confined to them anymore, but to pray ... as I may find suitable to particular occasions.[29]

Not all were impressed by the change. A number of churches closed their doors to him because of his association with the Moravians. One of his former Oxford friends, John Clayton, told him to avoid 'vehement emphasis' and to abandon extempore preaching in which 'few or none were edified'.[30] The parents of both James Hutton and Charles Delamotte expressed concern that John was becoming a religious extremist. John's family also voiced their concern. Samuel's strong opposition may well explain why Charles temporarily turned against Böhler's ideas and began taking issue with John. The scale of the family tensions is hinted at in Charles' journal when he records a rare example of a major row between him and John over whether faith could arise gradually rather than having to be the product of one instantaneous moment of revelation. Charles found John's advocacy for instantaneous conversion deeply worrying, not least because that was not his experience of faith:

> I was much offended at his worse than unedifying discourse ... I stayed and insisted a man need not know when first he had faith. His obstinacy in favouring the contrary opinion drove me at last out of the room.[31]

The squabbles with family and friends reduced John to 'constant sorrow and heaviness'. What made matters worse was that John knew he lacked the kind of instantaneous conversion experience deemed so vital by the Moravians:

> I could not understand how this faith should be given in a moment: how a man could at once be turned from darkness to light, from sin and misery to righteousness and joy in the Holy Ghost.[32]

He wrote in his journal: 'I could now only cry out, "Lord, help Thou my unbelief!"'[33] Remarkably the answer to this prayer came five days later on 28 April when Charles was struck down again by pleurisy. Both brothers took this as a sign from God that he was displeased with Charles for challenging John and not listening properly to Böhler.

The Moravian visited the suffering bedridden Charles in the house of James Hutton:

> He stood by my bedside and prayed over me, that now at least I might see the divine intention, in this and my late illness. I immediately thought it might be that I should again consider Böhler's doctrine of faith.[34]

Charles was flung into a spiritual crisis. He was filled with 'sighs and groans unutterable' and 'tears that flowed freely' until he finally accepted that salvation did come entirely through God's grace.[35] Weary of struggling with pain, worn down by his failure to live up to his ideals, he did as Böhler asked and turned to God:

> Speak, gracious Lord, my sickness cure,
> Make my infected nature pure;
> Peace, righteousness, and joy impart,
> And pour Thyself into my heart.[36]

While Charles lay suffering, John worked with Böhler and James Hutton to draw up the statutes for a new religious society which was to meet in a room in Fetter Lane, off Fleet Street. Böhler clearly intended that this should become the first truly Moravian society in Britain. In addition to themselves, they identified eight potential members and six of these were former Oxford Methodists: Charles Wesley, George Whitefield, Benjamin Ingham, Charles Kinchin, John Hutchings and Westley Hall. It was agreed the Fetter Lane Society would ask its members to meet in small bands for mutual confession and prayer every week. They would also join together occasionally for both fasts and love-feasts. On 4 May Böhler had to leave to commence his voyage to America. He urged both John and Charles to make sure they continued to avoid 'the sin of unbelief'. They agreed to act as pastors of the Fetter Lane Society, though Charles' frail health left John to become its real leader.

The Fetter Lane Society initially had more honorary members than real ones – and those few it did have were not from the educated classes, with the exception of James Hutton and a lawyer called John Shaw. As far as we know, the other early members were a poulterer, a clogmaker, a wine cooper, a brazier and two barbers. James Hutton later wrote about the great debt everyone felt they owed to Böhler. Their attempts to earn salvation had led only to 'a dry morality', whereas salvation by faith had opened up a new and exiting world:

> It was with indescribable astonishment and joy, that we embraced the doctrine of our Saviour, of His merits and sufferings, of justification

through faith in Him, and of freedom, by it, from the dominion and guilt of sin. This was something so very new to us, so universal, so penetrating.[37]

John wrote to his former mentor William Law and told him to stop misleading people into thinking they had to work so hard at earning salvation. Law replied he had never set himself up as John's teacher, and he would not now be criticized for John's inadequacies. As far as he was concerned, Christ expected his followers to take up their cross and there was no easy-fix salvation.

Charles found Böhler's departure difficult because he had not yet resolved all his spiritual uncertainties:

For some days following I felt a faint longing for faith, and could pray for nothing else ... God still kept up the little spark of desire, which he had enkindled in me; and I seemed determined to speak of, and wish for, nothing but faith in Christ.[38]

Moreover, his increasing frailty was leading to a situation where he required more physical care. James Hutton's parents expressed their readiness to look after him but Charles knew they were very hostile to the Moravians. If he remained permanently under their roof, he knew they would do all in their power to undo Böhler's influence. Having known him and John since they were boys, the Huttons would not tolerate any talk of them not being proper Christians. The growing tension surfaced when John wrote an account of the instantaneous conversion of a Scottish Presbyterian called Haliburton, and asked James Hutton to publish it. Hutton's father intervened and banned this happening. In retaliation Charles insisted on reading out aloud sections of his brother's work, even though this clearly upset the entire household.

It may have been this incident that led to Charles deciding to move to alternative accommodation offered by a member of the Fetter Lane Society called John Bray, a brazier whose home was above a shop in Little Britain, near Smithfield. Charles was too ill to walk there so he had to be carried by sedan chair. James Hutton's parents were understandably hurt and shocked that Charles should decline their hospitality to go to the home of 'a poor ignorant mechanic'.[39] They took it as another sign of the Moravian madness affecting the Wesleys and their own son James. But Charles wrote later that Bray's simple faith was exactly what he needed 'to supply Böhler's place':

Mr. Bray ... knows nothing but Christ ... We prayed together for faith. I was quite overpowered, and melted into tears ... I was persuaded I should not leave his house before I believed with my heart unto righteousness ... I longed to find Christ, that I might show him to all mankind.[40]

A succession of friends visited Charles, anxious over his prolonged sickness and concerned lest he was falling into the trap of believing that a Christian lifestyle no longer mattered. He assured them that he still regarded as useless any faith which did not lead to a loving life. All he wanted was to acquire the ability to rely on God for forgiveness rather than on his own merits and, in the process, acquire a faith 'productive of all good works and all holiness'.[41] Charles confessed his problem was that he still felt far too unworthy to receive God's forgiveness:

At last I own it cannot be
That I should fit myself for Thee:
Here then to Thee I all resign;
Thine is the work, and only Thine.[42]

On 17 May a commercial painter called William Holland brought Charles a copy of Martin Luther's *Commentary on the Galatians*. Reading this showed that Protestantism had been founded on the concept of salvation by faith and so Böhler's ideas did not deserve the derogatory treatment they had received from the hierarchy of the Church. Charles said he was 'astonished' that he had ever viewed Böhler's ideas as 'new'[43] and he read out key passages to the people gathered round him. William Holland later recorded the amazing impact this had on him:

There came such a power over me as I cannot well describe; my great burden fell off in an instant; my heart was so filled with peace and love that I burst into tears. I almost thought I saw our Saviour! My companions, perceiving me so affected, fell on their knees and prayed. When I afterwards went into the street, I could scarcely feel the ground I trod on.[44]

The rest of that evening Charles spent 'in private with Martin Luther'[45] but the excitement caused a physical relapse. His pleurisy returned with a vengeance, making it difficult for him to breathe and giving him a terrible pain in his heart.

For the next two day Charles again received medical treatment, including being bled. Seeing his weakened state, some feared he might die, but this only made Bray and his associates more determined to help Charles spiritually. In his journal Charles records a particularly helpful

conversation with a woman called Mrs Turner, who was one of those
who came to visit him. She told him that God would only let him rise
from his bed when he truly believed that he was saved. She claimed that
she herself had 'perfect peace':

> I would be glad to die at this moment; for I know all my sins are blot-
> ted out ... He has saved me with his death; he has washed me with his
> blood ... I have peace in him, and rejoice with joy unspeakable.[46]

In response Charles spent the night 'with prayers, and sighs, and unceasing desires', bemoaning the fact that while his brain told him to believe
God was ready to offer him full forgiveness of his sins, his heart refused
to accept this was really possible, given his many failings.

On 20 May John Bray entered Charles' room, opened his Bible and
turned to a page at random, and read out the text. It was the story of
the paralysed man brought before Jesus on a bed in chapter 9 of Math-
ew's Gospel. Fighting back tears at its aptness, Bray read out the key
words: 'Son, be of good cheer, thy sins be forgiven thee.' Charles was
overwhelmed: 'I saw herein, and firmly believed, that his faith would
be available for the healing of me.'[47] The next day was Whit Sunday
and Charles later wrote he awoke 'in hope and expectation of His coming'. His optimism was strengthened by an early morning visit from
his brother John and some of his friends. After they had gone Charles
prayed a simple prayer: 'Thou art God, who canst not lie. I wholly rely
upon thy most true promise. Accomplish it in thy time and manner.' He
then decided to have a sleep 'in quietness and peace'.

Charles' rest was disturbed by William Bray's sister, Mrs Musgrave.
When she told him: 'In the name of Jesus of Nazareth arise and believe,
and thou shalt be healed of all thy infirmities!' Charles felt as if the
words were striking his heart: 'I sighed, and said within myself, "O that
Christ would but speak thus to me!"' After musing on this he called
John Bray and asked him to pray with him. Bray told Charles he had
no doubt that Charles was a true believer and suddenly the certainty of
salvation that Charles had so long lacked flowed over him:

> The Spirit of God strove with my own, and the evil spirit, till by
> degrees he chased away the darkness of my unbelief. I found myself
> convinced, I know not how nor when; and immediately fell to inter-
> cession ... I now found myself at peace with God, and rejoiced in hope
> of loving Christ.[48]

His newfound reliance on God's saving grace produced 'a strange palpi-
tation of the heart'.[49] It was as if he suddenly was 'in a new heaven and

a new earth'. He told his friends he now felt 'under the protection of Christ' because he had given himself 'soul and body to Him'.[50]

According to John Wesley, the experience of knowing he was saved cured Charles' physical sickness because 'his bodily strength returned also from that hour'.[51] However, Charles' journal tells a different story. It reveals that Charles continued to suffer and that he believed the devil was inflicting pain on him in the hope this would make him lose patience with God. Charles expressed his gratitude that his newfound faith enabled him instead to turn his illness into 'an occasion of resignation'.[52] He was grateful to God for keeping him 'in a constant sense of my own weakness'.[53] Nevertheless, Charles feared a return to his former uncertainty and he asked not only for continued assurance for himself but also that his brother John might share what he had experienced. On 24 May Charles took communion with some of his friends and was horrified at the extent to which his old 'accustomed deadness' of heart had returned. He says he received the bread and wine 'without any sensible devotion, much as I used to be'.[54] However, he tried to remain calm and to focus on participating in singing, praying and talking with his friends.

That same day John had reluctantly agreed to accompany James Hutton to a meeting of a religious society at Nettleton Court, off Aldersgate Street in London. There he listened to a reading of Luther's version of justification by faith and John's own spiritual breakthrough happened:

> About a quarter before nine, while he was describing the change which God works in the heart through faith in Christ, I felt my heart strangely warmed. I felt I did trust in Christ, Christ alone for salvation; and an assurance was given me that He took away my sins, even mine, and saved me from the law of sin and death.[55]

Towards ten that evening John went to share with his brother the exciting news that he now also felt assured of salvation. Charles was delighted and the news made his own fears fly away:

> At midnight I gave myself up to Christ; assured I was safe, sleeping or waking ... [I] had continual experience of his power to overrule temptation; and confessed with joy and surprise, that he was able to do exceedingly abundantly for me, above what I can ask or think.[56]

Historians have sometimes described these events as John crossing 'his religious Rubicon',[57] but this is just as true for Charles:

> Is this the soul so late weigh'd down
> By cares and sins, by griefs and pains?

Whither are all thy terrors gone?
Jesus for thee the victory gains;
And death, and sin, and Satan yield
To faith's unconquerable shield ...[58]

However, the 'strangely warmed' hearts of the brothers did not make either of them unquestioning in their faith. Like all Christians, they had spiritual ups and downs throughout their lives. Once his initial elation had worn off, Charles' life became a rollercoaster of emotions. For example, he refers in his journal on three successive days in June to being 'utterly dead' spiritually and 'exceedingly heavy and adverse to prayer'. He says 'I could not help asking myself: "Where is the difference between what I am now, and what I was before believing".' For that reason Susanna Wesley sensibly made clear to Charles that he would have to stop thinking that true faith had to be the product of an instantaneous moment:

> I do not judge it necessary for us to know the precise time of our conversion ... nor is the work of regeneration begun and perfected at once. Some (though rarely) are converted by irresistible grace ... Christians go through many degrees of grace, be first infants, or babes in Christ, as St Paul calls them, before they become strong Christians. For spiritual strength is the work of time as well as of God's Holy Spirit.[59]

Charles said he felt more at peace with God but confessed to his mother his new birth was not bringing him the joy he had expected. Susanna told him to be patient because the joy would follow if he but patiently tried to do what God wanted. Charles heeded her advice and he began referring to the 21 May 1738 as the time when he only received 'the first grain of faith'.[60] Because of this experience, he developed a tremendous empathy with those who felt God was sometimes very distant:

> Surrounded, sunk in deepest night,
> To God how can I speak aright,
> In order all my wants declare,
> Or offer an accepted prayer?
> Alas, I know not what to say,
> I know not how to plead or pray.[61]

John Wesley also returned to his more normal emotional level but this made him feel his faith was still too 'rational': 'I go in an even line, being very little raised at one time or depressed at another.' He felt he had achieved a greater trust in God, but he was disappointed how little this seemed to be changing his life. He still experienced doubt and fear, he still sometimes found his mind wandering during worship, he still experienced sexual feelings towards women and, like Charles, he still had 'no settled, lasting joy'.[62] In January 1739 he wrote to his brother Samuel:

My friends affirm that I am mad because I said I was not a Christian a year ago. I affirm I am not a Christian now ... for a Christian is one who has the fruits of the Spirit of Christ ... I have ... [not got] a peace which passeth understanding ... I have not the fruits of the Spirit of Christ.[63]

The problem for both Charles and John was that they tended to believe other people when they said their lives were totally transformed and so they assumed their own continued weaknesses were indicators of a lack of faith. Nevertheless, both men knew their faith had undergone a substantial change in May 1738. Both now fully accepted they could not earn their salvation and were released from the fear of condemnation and damnation that had paralysed so much of their previous Christian witness. Knowing they did not have to achieve perfection to achieve salvation, they were happier to strive towards the perfection that human frailty made unattainable. This was embodied in one of Charles' greatest hymns, 'And can it be that I should gain', which was written to mark the momentous change that had taken place in his thinking. The impact was to release a dynamic energy which made both men far more effective in their daily Christian living and at times made them truly inspirational preachers.

The Wesley brothers' response to God's overwhelming grace is best embodied in the prayer contained in the Covenant service John later produced for all Methodists:

I am no longer my own, but Thine. Put me to what Thou wilt, rank me with whom Thou wilt; put me to doing, put me to suffering; let me be employed for Thee or laid aside for Thee, exalted for Thee or brought low for Thee; let me be full, let me be empty; let me have all things, let me have nothing; I freely and heartily yield all things to Thy pleasure and disposal. And now, O glorious and blessed God, Father, Son, and Holy Spirit, Thou art mine, and I am Thine. So be it. And the covenant which I have made on earth, let it be ratified in Heaven.[64]

In May 1738 none of their friends foresaw what lay ahead for Charles and John and a number questioned whether the events of Whit Sunday had been desirable. On 6 June the mother of James Hutton wrote to Samuel Wesley:

> Your brother John seems to have turned a wild enthusiast, or fanatic, and, to our very great affliction, is drawing our two children into these wild notions, by their great opinion of Mr John's sanctity and judgment.[65]

She informed him he would not think John 'a quite right man' when he heard how his brother was going round saying that 'he was not a Christian ... and the way for them all to be Christians was to believe and own that they were not now Christians'. She claimed that if John was not stopped, he would cause great mischief among the ignorant but well-meaning Christians with whom he was associating. She felt her own son was at risk of being infected because he was already ignoring his parents' commands, saying he wished to focus on God's glory. She concluded her letter to Samuel: 'You will see what I never expected, my son promoting rank fanaticism. If you can, dear Sir, put a stop to such madness.'

Mrs Hutton most feared that John was going to lead his brother and others into becoming Moravians. This fear was not unfounded. The new Fetter Lane Society was clearly dominated by Moravian thinking and both John and Charles were talking of going over to Germany to see the original Moravian communities at first hand so they could better understand the movement's worship and organization. Because Charles' health was not good enough to risk the travelling, John decided to set out for Germany with Benjamin Ingham instead. Before they left, John visited the two people he most wanted to understand what was happening. He went to Salisbury to talk to his mother and to Oxford to talk to John Gambold. Neither was very happy at his actions. Undeterred, John preached his newfound vision in the Church of St Mary the Virgin in Oxford on Sunday 11 June:

> The Christian faith is ... not only an assent to the whole gospel of Christ, but also a full reliance on the blood of Christ; a trust in the merits of His life, death, and resurrection ... [through which] his sins are forgiven, and he reconciled to the favour of God.[66]

John might feel his faith was of a different order but the selfish streak that sometimes made him put his own purposes before the needs of anyone else was still evident. He left the country with Benjamin Ingham without even telling Charles. His rapid departure devastated their sister Emily, who had been expecting John to visit her, given he knew her circumstances had changed dramatically for the worse. Deserted by the useless husband John had more or less forced on her before he had left for America, she was desperately in debt and reduced to selling her clothes for bread. Only some money from Samuel Wesley had enabled her to survive the previous summer. When John subsequently contacted her by letter to talk about the wonderful time he was having in Germany, she was understandably bitter at his selfishness:

> For God's sake, tell me how a distressed woman, who expects daily to have the very bed taken from under her rent, can consider the state of the churches in Germany … I loved you tenderly. You married me to a man, and as soon as sorrow took hold of me you left me to it … You, who could go to Germany, could you not reach Gainsborough?[67]

Over the next three months John and Ingham visited Jena University, consulted with the Moravian leader, Count Zinzendorf, and stayed at the Moravian settlements in Herrnhut and Marienborn. They were both very impressed. John wrote home saying that he was 'with a Church whose conversation is in Heaven':

> Young and old they breathe nothing but faith and love, at all times and in all places … [I have] seen with my own eyes more than one hundred witnesses of that everlasting truth, 'Every one that believeth hath peace with God; and is freed from sin; and is in Christ a new creature'.[68]

Whereas the three months' experience turned Ingham into a committed Moravian, it did not have that effect on John. He thought the communities paid too much homage to Zinzendorf and, more importantly, that they were at times 'unscriptural'. Instead of seeing all scripture as being divinely inspired, they viewed the Bible as simply a collection of ancient texts of variable worth because they felt God was continuing to reveal deeper insights to successive generations. Consequently their main focus was an almost obsessive focus on the sufferings of Christ, which they referred to as 'blood and wounds teaching'.

Some Moravians thought John's refusal to abandon his Church of England roots revealed he was still far from truly reborn. They preferred Ingham and described John as a troubled person who allowed his head to rule his heart.[69] What John's travels did confirm was that Christians required a strong organization to bring out the best in each other. Three features of Moravian life were to stay with him and become a feature of future Methodism. These were their focus on the importance of education, their love-feasts which were informal religious conversations with bread and water (or wine), and their holding of occasional services modelled on the all-night vigils of the early Church.

Charles spent the rest of May and most of June physically recovering from his illness. He initially commented on the 'continual experience' of God's power 'to overrule all temptation'[70] and, in particular, how he was less hot-tempered and no longer given to drink alcohol: '[I was] amazed to find my old enemy, intemperance, so suddenly subdued, that I almost forgot I was ever in bondage to him.'[71] Charles may well be overstating this but, if not, it may indicate that his unhappiness in America had led to him turning overmuch to alcohol for comfort. Encouraged by what had happened, he began attending church and started visiting his friends. Only his poor health prevented him taking to the pulpit. However, it was not long before Charles realized that resisting bad inclinations was still a problem even for the reborn Christian: 'I never knew the energy of sin till now that I experience the superior strength of Christ.'[72]

Charles' newfound enthusiasm had a touch of naivety about it. For example, he began taking decisions as to what God wanted him to do by opening the Bible at random and looking at the first verse that caught his eye or by writing options on different pieces of paper and then picking up one once they were face down. He even took natural phenomena as indicating God's intended action so that, for example, the heavy rain that followed thunder and lightning was 'a sign that the skies would soon pour down righteousness'.[73] However, his naivety was accompanied by what has been described as 'a tidal wave of spiritual energy and action'.[74] He read the Bible constantly and spoke to everyone he met of the importance of God's saving grace.

Among the first to feel the impact was a minister with whom he had become particularly friendly. This was Henry Piers, Vicar of Bexley. Not only were Piers and his wife won over to Charles' views on salvation by faith but so too was Mary their maid, who had overheard his conversations with the family. Charles next turned his attention onto the family of Charles Delamotte. His sisters soon fell under his influence and so too did his brother Jack, who confided to Charles how his message had sunk into his soul, filling him with delight and joy. At first William Delamotte was less receptive, saying it was unjust of God 'to make sinners equal with us, who had laboured perhaps many years'.[75] His dislike of 'instantaneous faith' was shared by Mrs Delamotte, but both eventually surrendered to Charles' impassioned preaching. William wrote of his mother's conversion:

Christ hath spoken peace to her soul ... [Seeing Christ] she loved, believed, adored. Her prayers drew him still nearer ... [until] she received the kiss of reconciliation. Her own soul could not contain the joys attending it.[76]

Even the Delamotte's gardener told Charles: 'Was I to die just now, I know I should be accepted through Jesus Christ'[77] when he overheard Charles reading aloud one of his brother's sermons on faith.

Charles was particularly keen to share his newfound faith with his sisters. He visited the guilt-ridden Hetty and was delighted that, after a few meetings, she 'declared that she could not but believe Christ died for her'.[78] When he was more recovered, he travelled to Oxford to see Kezzy, who was living with John Gambold and his wife. She was quick to respond positively to her brother's views. It must have come as something of a shock to Gambold and another of Charles' friends, Charles Kinchin, when Charles accused them of not yet being true re-born Christians. However, they proved not unreceptive and for a time Kitchin became Charles' 'inseparable companion'.[79] The only person Charles avoided was his brother Samuel. He knew from his brother's correspondence that Samuel was too hostile to listen.

By July Charles felt fit enough to try public preaching. His first service was at Basingshaw and he described it as 'wonderfully animating' to preach salvation by faith to such 'a deeply attentive audience'.[80] Charles tried to encourage passing strangers to also benefit from his evangelical fervour – as is illustrated by his account of travelling in a coach:

> I preached faith to Christ. A lady [in the coach] was deeply offended; avowed her own merits in plain terms; asked if I was not a Method-ist; threatened to beat me. I declared I deserved nothing but hell; so did she; and must confess it, before she could have a title to heaven. This was most intolerable to her. The others [in the coach] were less offended; began to listen; asked where I preached; a maid servant devoured every word.[81]

He became convinced that people were open to instantaneous conver-sion. He recounts, for example, in his journal a conversation with a poor man called Heather, who had heard him preach. Charles asked him whether he felt his sins were forgiven. The man replied he did not but, having heard Charles, he was sure Christ could forgive him. Charles asked him whether he believed God would respond to the prayers of the faithful. When Heather assented, Charles replied he would pray for faith for him. Hearing this, the man responded by saying, 'Then I believe I shall receive it before I go out of the room.'[82]

Charles initially preached as he had before – by using one of John's sermons or by producing a sermon which was largely based on the writings of John and others. However, in August he began carefully putting together a far more personal sermon of his own based on Galatians 3:22 and for the first time wrote entirely without any input from his brother. The few remaining written sermons from this time may not be entirely representative of his preaching, but they reflect something of his new evangelical style:

> Whether your lives are stained with outward visible enormities, or less observable abominations, it makes no great difference ... The careless and the debauched, the scandalous and the reputable sinner, the filthy and the ignorant thoughtless one, are held in equal abomination with God. Nay, he seems to loathe the lukewarm person even worse than him who is cold ... Turn unto the Lord your God, for he is gracious and merciful, slow to anger and of great kindness ... God is not far from every one of you. For you there is about to be joy in heaven, and the angels are tuning their harps ... if ye hearken unto God more than unto man ... He can translate thee this moment out of darkness into his marvelous light, out of bondage into the glorious liberty of the sons of God ... Pray without ceasing, till he is formed in your hearts by faith.[83]

That summer Charles increasingly developed a friendship with George Stonehouse, Vicar of Islington. Initially he did not accept Charles' views on salvation by faith but he recognized Charles was a powerful communicator and so asked him to act as his unofficial curate. Charles saw in Stonehouse someone wracked by his inability to lead a perfect life. The poor man was even declining to marry the woman he loved lest God disapprove of such an action. In August Charles succeeded in winning an ally by converting Stonehouse's maid, Thomasin. He recorded she told him she had found such great peace, comfort, and joy that 'her very inside ... was changed'.[84] By December Charles had also won over Stonehouse to the fact salvation came from God's grace and could not be earned and that his marriage was therefore perfectly permissible.

Throughout the summer months Charles flung himself into as much charitable work as his health permitted. He understood you have to practise what you preach. The test of true faith was still a godly life:

> Therefore let us do good works ... adding to our faith virtue, and to virtue knowledge, and to knowledge temperance, and to temperance patience, and to patience godliness, and to godliness brotherly kindliness, and to brotherly kindliness charity ... If these fruits do not fol-

low, we do but mock God, and deceive ourselves and others ... Let it be your constant employment to serve and relieve ... [the] poor.[85]

Charles found his greatest satisfaction in visiting prisons. For example, in July 1738 he records in his diary visiting ten men who were imprisoned in Newgate under sentence of death. This was one of the worst prisons in the country: 'a place of calamity ... a habitation of misery, a confused chaos ... a bottomless pit of violence, a Tower of Babel where all are speakers and no hearers'.[86] One of the prisoners he saw was a Negro found guilty of murdering his master. Day after day Charles offered him comfort in his loathsome cell by telling him how God sent his son to save the world and by describing the crucifixion and resurrection of Christ:

> He listened with all the signs of eager astonishment. The tears trickled down his cheeks while he cried, 'What, was it for me? Did God suffer all this for so poor a creature as me?' I left him waiting for the salvation of God.[87]

Other prisoners were also 'amazingly comforted' by the knowledge Christ had died for them.

Charles and John Bray agreed to be locked in the cells overnight with the condemned – a remarkable testimony to their faith:

> We wrestled in mighty prayer. All the criminals were present; and all delightfully cheerful ... Joy was visible in all their faces. We sang:
> Behold the Saviour of mankind,
> Nail'd to the shameful tree!
> How vast the love that him inclined
> To bleed and die for thee ...
> It was one of the most triumphant hours I have ever known.[88]

Charles also agreed to accompany all his converts to their execution at Tyburn. He prayed and sang hymns with them, offered them communion, accompanied them to the place of execution, and comforted them as they were one by one hung before the assembled crowds:

> They were all cheerful; full of comfort, peace and triumph; assuredly persuaded Christ had died for them, and wanted to receive them in paradise. None showed any natural terror of death, no fear or crying or tears ... I never saw such calm triumph, such incredible indifference to dying. We sang several hymns ... [and] when the cart drew

off, not one stirred, or struggled for life, but meekly gave up their spirits ... That hour, under the gallows, was the most blessed hour of my life.[89]

Such experiences fed into his hymnwriting, which became far more prolific. One of the hymns which dates from this time in his life reflects how much he felt imprisoned sinful humanity could rejoice at the fact death had lost its victory in the face of Christ's passion and resurrection:

> Christ the Lord is risen today:
> > Alleluia!
> Sons of men and angels say:
> Raise your joys and triumphs high;
> Sing, ye heavens; thou earth reply:
> Love's redeeming work is done,
> Fought the fight, the battle won;
> Vain the stone, the watch, the seal;
> Christ hath burst the gates of hell.[90]

Initially clergy were willing to let Charles preach. He was even permitted to speak about salvation by faith in Westminster Abbey. What he said on that occasion is not recorded but it was probably similar to what we know he was preaching on that topic the following spring: that no one could earn their salvation, that Christ's death alone paid the ransom for humanity's sin, and that once assured of salvation a person was moved to constantly praise God and to live a very different life, in which the aim became 'to do good to every man'. The message was not well received by most of his fellow clergy. The church authorities preferred to see salvation as something which people had to try throughout their life to earn. Some critics soon unfairly began calling both Charles and John 'antinomians'. This was originally a name applied to some of the early followers of Luther who had declared those assured of salvation need not worry about their lifestyle. Antinomians were associated with anarchy, promiscuity and communism.

It was not long before the invitations for Charles to preach began to fall away. His reputation suffered in part because of his known links with Whitefield, whose reputation had suffered as a result of the publication of an unauthorized *Journal* by an enterprising publisher called Cooper. This contained edited copies of some of Whitefield's letters from Georgia and there were many passages which George would never have wanted printed. Indeed Charles had tried in vain to stop Cooper's publication. However, it was Charles' allegiance to the Fetter Lane Society that really damaged his reputation. It had become what has been described as 'a religious pollen factory',[91] attracting a cross-section of the various religious groups functioning in the capital, including not only German Moravians and English Calvinists but French Huguenots. Not surprisingly orthodox clergy judged it politically suspect and condemned its strange mixture of religious ecumenism and social egalitarianism.

In the face of mounting criticism, Charles was delighted when John returned to London on 17 September and he took 'sweet counsel'[92] with him. He listened with interest to John's Moravian experiences and John was surprised at the change in Charles' confidence. The two brothers readily agreed to work together and, while remaining loyal to the Church, continue modelling some of their activities on the Moravians. Encouraged by Charles, John visited Newgate prison and met with a very positive response. He said the whole prison 'sang with the cries of those whom the word of God cut to the heart'. As a result, he agreed with Charles that prison-visiting should become a central feature of their work. The appalling conditions in which the poor lived promoted crime and prostitution and an endemic violence that made Christian pity almost an unknown virtue. The Wesleys felt that if they could evoke religious fervour among the criminal classes, then they could make a serious inroad into converting the poor who both feared and admired them, knowing they were often as sinned against as sinners. Indeed, some criminals, such as highwaymen like Edward Bonner and Dick Turpin, were hailed as heroes for their attacks on the rich.

As Charles came into more contact with the lower strata of society, his style of preaching began to radically change. On 15 October he partially abandoned his preaching notes and preached extempore at Stonehouse's church in Islington. On 20 October he delivered a sermon at St Anthony's Church without any pre-written notes and was surprised at how more effective this made his preaching. From then on the words 'and added much extempore' appear in his journal and he talks of 'expounding' rather than 'preaching' because he was no longer tying himself to formal written notes. Instead of preparing sermons, he opened the Bible and took his theme from whatever text first presented itself to him.[93] This not only led to more inspirational preaching but also gave him more time to do his hymnwriting. Within two years he was to criticize those preachers who unnecessarily preplanned what they were going to say.

John's lecture-like preaching was not as effective as that of Charles, especially as John focused sometimes too much on theological issues and tended to think he had to offend his hearers in order to capture their attention. Charles felt the theology could come later and simply sought to engage the hearts of his audience. Their former companion in Georgia, Charles Delamotte, told John:

> You are better than you was in Savannah. You know that you was then quite wrong; but you are not right yet. You know that you was then blind; but you do not see now. I doubt not that God will bring you to the right foundation ... [but currently] you have a peace, but it is not a true peace: if death were to approach, you would find all your fears return.[94]

Though they regularly worshipped in churches, the Moravian-style Fetter Lane Society was the real focus for the spiritual lives of both Charles and John throughout the autumn of 1738. Its members had agreed they would focus on 'holiness and the things that make for peace'[95] and not squabble over any theological differences, so the society had grown significantly. It now contained just over 60 members. These were divided into groups of between five and ten people, each holding weekly meetings for prayer, singing and mutual confession of faults. Each member was expected to speak freely about the real state of his heart and attend a monthly three-hour love-feast, in which religious conversation was combined with the celebration of communion. New members were admitted under two months' probation and anyone breaking the society's rules was expelled if they failed to respond to three warnings.

Susanna Wesley was sufficiently happy about her sons' attendance at the Fetter Lane Society to sometimes join them. She confessed to Charles she did not understand what all the fuss in May had been about because he had never been devoid of faith, but she praised God for setting his faith afire through those events:

> Blessed be God! that showed you the necessity you were in of a Saviour to deliver you from the power of sin and Satan ... and directed you by faith to lay hold on that stupendous mercy offered us by redeeming love! Jesus is the only physician of souls, his blood the only salve which can heal a wounded conscience. 'Tis not in wealth or honour or sensual pleasure to relieve a spirit heavy laden and weary of the burden of sin ... None but Christ is sufficient for these things.[96]

Her moderate response infuriated Samuel Wesley, who felt he could not condone his brothers' mixing with Moravians or their extempore preaching and prayers to societies in unconsecrated buildings.

On 21 October both John and Charles had to appear before the Bishop of London, Edmund Gibson, to defend themselves against charges that their preaching was heretical and their societies a cover for secret plotting against the government. Gibson had ordained Charles and proved sympathetic because he appreciated the brothers' obvious sincerity and Christian commitment. He accepted that there was nothing wrong in preaching salvation by faith providing that it was also combined with a strong message on the essential importance of living a good life. He also said he did not know enough about the religious societies to judge whether they were seditious gatherings, but he thought it unlikely. However, Gibson made clear he still felt their methods were too irregular to fully sanction. He told them they should only preach in a parish if they first had the permission of its minister and that they must make sure their actions did not bring the Church into disrepute. He also said they could have free access to him if they needed further advice.

Despite this warning, Charles shocked the London clergy by preaching in the open air. On 7 November he and John went to sing hymns with the condemned in Newgate as they were prepared for public hanging. John later wrote: 'It was the most glorious instance I ever saw of faith triumphing over sin and death.' Tears ran down the cheeks of one of the men as the rope was placed round his neck, and he told Charles and John: 'I feel at peace which I could not have believed to be possible. And I know it is the peace of God, which passeth understanding.'[97] In response Charles felt compelled to immediately preach before the assembled onlookers at Tyburn. He later recorded: 'I was melted down under the word I spake.'[98] It was a spur of the moment action and the fact he had preached by necessity in the open air in America made the step less of a jump, but it was outrageous behaviour in the eyes of his fellow clergy, who thought only dissenters and radicals preached in the open.

The impact of Charles' action was evident the very next evening when Henry Piers, Vicar of Bexley, refused to continue attending the Fetter Lane Society 'through fear of the world's threatenings'[99] and said he was no longer prepared to let Charles use his pulpit. Charles was indignant:

> Mr Piers refused me his pulpit, through fear of man; pretending tenderness to his flock. I plainly told him, if he rejected my testimony, I would come to see him no more. I walked back to town in the strength of the Lord.[100]

Charles then made matters worse. He had got into the practice at the religious societies of baptizing any adult who requested him to do so, but he had never sought official approval for this. Now he decided he ought to inform Gibson. The bishop was furious with him because he viewed baptism as entirely the responsibility of the appropriate parish minister.

Charles said that he only baptized people if he had the consent of the proper minister but Gibson told Charles he was not a licensed curate and 'no man can exercise parochial duty in London without my leave'.[101] The bishop refused to give Charles official approval for what he was doing and demanded he stop his activities altogether.

Charles took on the role of belligerent martyr while making clear he had committed no crime. The bishop did not take any disciplinary action but he decided the brothers were probably falling into the trap of becoming antinomians and left Charles in no doubt that he had incurred his displeasure. Once this became public, time and again John and Charles had to mark against churches the words 'Forbidden to preach'. Suddenly the Wesleys realized how vulnerable they were because they had no home of their own and were essentially dependent on the goodwill and financial support of others, such as Henry Stonehouse. A fortnight after his meeting with the bishop, a depressed Charles headed for Oxford to consult his old friends, John Gambold and Charles Kinchin. By then it is estimated that only four pulpits were still open to the brothers: St Giles', St Katharine's, Bexley and Basingshaw. His friends did all they could to cheer Charles up and it was suggested that he should consider taking up a post as a college tutor.

At this critical juncture an exhilarated George Whitefield returned to London from America. He had initially won over the colonists by distributing clothing, food, medicines and various other goods, and by showing he was not concerned to abide by the unpopular rules of the Trustees. He had then captivated them by his powerful preaching and charismatic personality. Now he was back in order to be fully ordained as a minister and to raise the funds to create an orphanage in Georgia. This was a project originally proposed by Charles, who had hated seeing so many children left destitute by the early death of their parents in the harsh conditions of the colony. Four former Oxford Methodists, Benjamin Ingham, Westley Hall, Charles Kinchin and John Hutchings, came to London in December to join with John and Charles in welcoming him. The one thing Whitefield feared was that his friends might seek to persuade him not to return but he hoped God would preserve him from 'the fiery trial of popularity'.[102]

The seven men met for a week of prayer and deliberation about their future evangelical work and were so overwhelmed with the divine presence that they felt as if they had been filled with new wine. Whitefield was delighted that both Charles and John had continued working with the religious societies: 'I perceived God had greatly watered the seed sown by my ministry when last in London.'[103] Charles said the experience made Christmas 'a festival indeed; a joyful season, holy unto the

Lord'.[104] On New Years' Eve John recorded how they met with about 60 Moravians and celebrated a love-feast:

> About three in the morning, as we were continuing instant in prayer, the power of God came mightily upon us, insomuch that many cried out for exceeding joy, and many fell to the ground. As soon as we had recovered a little from that awe and amazement at the presence of his majesty, we broke out with one voice, 'We praise thee, O God; we acknowledge thee to be the Lord!'[105]

Samuel Wesley was almost incandescent that his brothers were refusing to cease their irregular activities. He wrote telling them he disliked 'canting fellows ... who talk of indwellings, experiences, getting into Christ, etc, etc.' and that he was even more appalled by anyone preaching extempore because it was 'a natural inlet to all false doctrine, heresy, and schism'.[106] He said Charles was being misled by John and he could only put down John's behaviour to 'perpetual intenseness of thought [and] lack of sleep'. He concluded: 'I heartily pray God to stop this lunacy.'[107] It says much for what Charles had experienced on 21 May that he was prepared to so offend the brother who had brought him up and whom he deeply loved. He wrote his most famous personal hymn on why the assurance of salvation by faith was so vital to him. In its original form it had 18 verses but the first seven were so personal that they were subsequently edited out of hymnbooks. They included the lines:

> Sudden expired the legal strife;
> 'Twas then I ceased to grieve;
> My second, real, living life
> I then began to live ...
> I felt my Lord's atoning blood
> Close to my soul applied;
> Me, me He loved – the Son of God
> For me, for me, He died! ...[108]

Eight of the remaining ten verses were to become 'Hymn No 1' in the *Methodist Hymn Book* because of their popularity. They were verses inspired by a comment by Peter Böhler: 'If I had a thousand tongues, I'd praise Christ with all of them':[109]

> O for a thousand tongues to sing
> My great Redeemer's praise,
> The glories of my God and King,

The triumphs of His grace! ...
Jesus – the name that charms our fears,
That bids our sorrows cease;
'Tis music in the sinner's ears,
'Tis life, and health, and peace ...[110]

In January 1739 George Whitefield and various others tried to persuade Charles to settle into a vacant parish at Cowley so that his skills could be used to best effect in Oxford, a place he knew and loved. None of his friends felt he had the physical stamina to play a more major role. Charles records in his journal that he found himself 'strongly inclined to go' but felt he could not agree 'without further direction from God'.[111] He was still enjoying his role as unofficial curate to the church in Islington and he was loathe to leave London at the very time Whitefield had returned and would resume his preaching. His journal records him engaged that month in a happy round of preaching, praying, helping others, and accompanying friends 'with the voice of joy and thanksgiving'.[112]

That same month Whitefield travelled to Oxford and was ordained as a minister by Martin Benson, Bishop of Gloucester, who admired the power of his preaching. Benson tried to reassure those clergy who thought his action was inappropriate:

Though mistaken on some points I think him a very pious, well-meaning young man, with good abilities and great zeal ... I pray God grant him great success in all his undertakings for the good of mankind and a revival of true religion and holiness amongst us in these degenerate days.[113]

He did not foresee that Whitefield would soon lead himself and the Wesleys into undertaking action that would stamp their evangelical efforts once and for all with the stigma of fanatical extremism and dissent.

5

A New Faith in Action

I want an even, strong desire,
I want a calmly present zeal,
To save poor souls out of the fire,
To snatch them from the verge of hell ...
My every sacred moment spend
In publishing the Sinner's friend ...
And lead them to thy open side,
The sheep for whom the Shepherd died.[1]

Charles assumed the churches of London would all clamour to hear George Whitefield again, especially as he could talk about his success in America. However, the church authorities were hostile and few invitations arrived. In February 1739 the editor of *The Weekly Miscellany* seized on Whitefield's frequent references to the Oxford Methodists and sought to portray 'Methodism' as a new brand of Puritan dissent:

At first we only looked upon the Methodists as well-meaning, zealous people ... [who] would be righteous overmuch; and there were hopes that, when this devotional effervescence had boiled over, they would return to that proper medium where true piety and Christian prudence fix the centre. But instead ... [they encourage] extempore effusions both in their prayers and expoundings ... [and] pretend to a sort of sinless perfection, and boast of inward joys above other Christians.[2]

Whitefield found it intensely frustrating to be denied access to so many pulpits when the response to his preaching was so positive. He therefore entered into a whirlwind of activity with the small but growing number of religious societies in London. Like the Wesleys, he asked society band members to adopt a daily spiritual routine and to question each other more about their faith. The resulting increased effectiveness of the bands is attested to in many contemporary letters. One admirer of Whitefield later recalled:

> The love I had for Mr Whitefield was inexpressible. I used to follow him as he walked the streets, and could scarce refrain from kissing the very prints of his feet.[3]

However, opponents of the societies began satirizing all of them for their alleged Methodism, saying they were 'void of sense':

> By rule they eat, by rule they drink,
> Do all things else by rule, but think –
> Accuse their priests of loose behaviour,
> To get more in the laymen's favour;
> Method alone must guide 'em all,
> Whence Methodists themselves they call ...
> All men of thought with laughter view,
> Of pity, the mistaken crew.[4]

Gradually Whitefield lost patience and began publicly saying there were too many clergy who 'believe only an outward Christ ... [whereas we] believe that He must be inwardly formed in our hearts also'.[5] He even began to speculate about preaching in the open air as an alternative means of reaching the people, but his friends thought this 'a mad notion'.[6] Given what had happened after his earlier spontaneous preaching to the crowd at Tyburn, Charles strongly opposed open-air preaching. He felt it would only lead to further conflict, especially as it still involved preaching within someone else's parish. He persuaded Whitefield it was preferable to put up with the persecution in the hope attitudes would change:

> Let wicked priests, if God permit,
> Out of the pale with fury cast,
> The servants as the Master treat,
> And nail us to his cross at last.[7]

Whitefield reluctantly said he would leave London and try preaching in other cities because his fund-raising for his orphanage in Georgia was being hopelessly compromised. He left for Bristol, taking with him as a companion William Seward, a stockbroker who had become a regular attendant at the Fetter Lane Society through the work of Charles. En route to Bristol Whitefield preached in various places and made a special detour to Salisbury so he could talk with Susanna Wesley, who at this time was staying with her daughter Martha. Almost certainly he did this because Charles was upset that she was hearing such bad reports of him and John. Susanna was impressed by Whitefield and he gave her a different perspective on what was happening. He pointed out the deficiencies of many clergy and the need for others to compensate for that by travelling the country and speaking to those who would otherwise hear nothing of God. He assured her that her sons were not encouraging dissent but promoting a more vibrant Church, and he praised their remarkable achievements. It was music to her ears.[8]

With Whitefield gone, Charles was again asked to take up the post at Cowley, near Oxford. His response was to randomly open his Bible and read a text. He found the words 'with stammering lips and with another tongue will I speak to this people'[9] and happily interpreted this to mean God wanted him to continue working in London. The church authorities took a different view of his refusal. He and John were summoned before John Potter, the Archbishop of Canterbury, (1737–47) to again explain their actions and defend themselves against the charge of being antinomians. Fortunately Potter was well disposed towards them because of his earlier contact with them in Oxford and he reassured them he would not accept any criticisms at face value:

> He showed us great affection; spoke mildly of Mr Whitefield; cautioned us to give no more umbrage than was necessary for our defence; to forbear exceptional phrases; to keep the doctrines of the Church ... He dismissed us kindly ... [and] assured us ... [of] his joy to see us as often as we pleased.[10]

Edmund Gibson, the Bishop of London, was not as friendly. He acknowledged that Whitefield was 'a pious, well-meaning youth' but warned them he was 'tainted with enthusiasm'.[11] He urged them to moderate their actions and undertake more traditional ministerial roles.

Meanwhile in Bristol Whitefield was dismayed to find he was denied access to pulpits because of his reputation for 'enthusiasm'. Inevitably his mind turned again to the possibility of preaching in the open air, especially as he had heard accounts of a schoolmaster called Howell Harris who was successfully doing exactly that in nearby Wales. Born into a working-class family in Trevecca, Harris had led a pretty loose life until his conversion by the Revd Griffith Jones, Rector of Llandowror, in the spring of 1735. Harris said his heart was melted 'like wax before the fire'[12] and he could not help but exhorting others to experience the same: 'A fire was kindled in my soul and I was clothed with power ... I lifted up my voice with authority ... [and] I thundered greatly.'[13] Harris was an especially controversial figure because he was not ordained. An attempt to train for this in Oxford had floundered when he could not cope with its immoral atmosphere.

Openly contemptuous of any church regulations that prevented people hearing about Christ, Harris wrote to Whitefield, urging him not to let men silence his duty to God. Harris knew he was regarded by some as 'a laughing stock, and a subject of lampoons to all',[14] but he begged Whitefield to do as he did and preach in the fields. Charles Wesley and other friends were not around to put counter-arguments. On 17 February Whitefield chose to preach in the open air on frost-bound Hanham Mount to coal miners as they left the hundreds of forest pits that existed in the Kingswood area. Technically he felt he was not breaking any rule because there was no local church but Whitefield knew most clergy would condemn his actions.

Faced with the power of his preaching, the miners, till then regarded as mere savages beyond redemption, were so moved Whitefield could see 'the white gutters made by their tears, which fell plentifully down their black cheeks' and 'hundreds and hundreds of them were soon brought into deep convictions, which ... happily ended in a sound and thorough conversion'.[15] Energized by his success, Whitefield refused to stop when the religious authorities protested:

> I believe I was never more acceptable to my Master than when I stood to teach those hearers in the open fields. Some may censure me, but if I pleased men I should not be the servant of Christ.[16]

He began preaching regularly in the open in Bristol and the surrounding area, gathering crowds of up to 20,000. He told the Bishop of Bristol: 'God knows my heart. I desire only to promote His glory.'[17]

Though clerics accused him of being 'stark mad', people travelled up to 20 miles to hear him.[18] All the reports on his preaching indicate he had the capacity to move people from any strata of society:

> His deep-toned yet clear and melodious voice ... is perfect music. It is wonderful to see what a spell he casts over an audience by proclaiming the simplest truths of the Bible. I have seen upwards of a thousand people hang on his words with breathless silence, broken only by an occasional half-suppressed sob. He impresses the ignorant, and, not less, the educated and refined ... and few return [from hearing him] unaffected ... He speaks from a heart all aglow with love, and pours out a torrent of eloquence which is almost irresistible.[19]

Whitefield met up with Howell Harris and found him to be an emotional but kind-hearted young man of his own age. He described him as 'a burning and shining light'.[20] Ignoring the fact Harris was not ordained, Whitefield agreed to undertake an evangelical tour with him in Wales, with George preaching in English and Howell in Welsh. Thus was laid the foundation for what was later to become the Welsh Calvinistic Methodist Church. However, Whitefield's main base remained Bristol. By March 1739 there were over 40,000 people coming to hear him at one of the 30 or so meetings he was holding every week. As a result the number of religious societies within the city grew. Knowing he had promised to return to Georgia, Whitefield wrote to ask John Wesley to continue what he had started: 'There is a glorious door opened among the colliers. You must come and water what God has enabled me to plant.'[21]

It was a wonderful opportunity because Bristol was the second largest city in the country with something like 40,000 inhabitants. It was not only a busy and thriving port, trading with Africa and America, but also a developing industrial and manufacturing centre, famed particularly for its porcelain and for chocolate production. The request was more naturally directed to John than to Charles because of Charles' frail health and his declared opposition to open-air preaching. Charles urged John to decline and initially John did, but Whitefield's insistence led him to put the matter into God's hands by casting lots. The result was in favour of him going. He therefore arrived in Bristol on 31 March. He was immediately taken to hear Whitefield preach at 'the Bowling Green', an open space in the centre of the city. It seemed to John to be against all he had been taught about 'decency and order' because 'the savings of souls [was] almost a sin, if it had not been done in a church'.[22] But he was deeply impressed by what he saw.

On 2 April John reluctantly decided he should submit to being 'more vile'[23] and do as Whitefield asked. George gave him money he had raised towards creating a school to educate the miners and their children at Kingswood and then left Bristol to return to London to make the arrangements for his return to Georgia. John did nothing by halves. He delivered 500 sermons between April and December 1739 and only eight were in churches. By his reckoning almost 50,000 people heard his preaching within the first month alone – though he conceded the numbers prepared to listen to him were many thousands less than had been drawn by Whitefield's more powerful style. He told his critics Christ's Sermon on the Mount was 'one pretty remarkable precedent of field-preaching'[24] and, when an ex-member of the Holy Club, James Hervey, voiced his concerns, John replied:

I have now no parish of my own, nor probably ever shall ... [so] I look upon all the world as my parish ... This is the work I know God has called me to, and I am sure that His blessing attends it.[25]

However, he tried to reject the label 'Methodist', because he had no desire to be seen as a leader of a religious sect. Once he realized he was stuck with the word, he turned to emphasizing Methodism required the acceptance of no dissenting creed but only a desire to totally love God.[26]

Charles faced a surge of hostility as reports of George and John's actions filtered through to London. Even in George Stonehouse's church at Islington the congregation now wanted rid of Charles. The church-wardens knew he was acting as their curate only by the request of their vicar and not officially by the appointment of the Church, so they began challenging Charles in the vestry before he took services and demanding he show them his bishop's licence to preach. When this failed to faze him, they hired men to prevent him entering the pulpit. When Whitefield returned to London on 25 April, the churchwardens made clear he also was not welcome, even if Stonehouse gave permission for him to preach. Whitefield's response was to commence preaching in the open air, choosing Moorfields and Kennington Common as his main sites.

Moorfields was an 18-acre parkland not far from Fetter Lane and it was used extensively by people as a place of recreation, especially at weekends, while Kennington Common was a 20-acre site south of the Thames renowned for attracting prostitutes and thieves and all the roughest and lowest elements of London. The first day Whitefield preached at both sites saw thousands turn up to hear him. Some expected him to be injured or killed but he preached without hurt and with immense success. A minister called Joseph Trapp, a former chaplain to the Lord Chancellor of Ireland, denounced what was happening from the pulpit of St Martin-in-the-Fields and had his attack published:

> What is this but an outrage upon common decency and common sense? The height of presumption, confidence and self-sufficiency ... [This] outward show of piety ... is one undoubted sign of ... spiritual pride ... It is folly that approaches very near to madness ... They are schismatical, in their tendency at least, though not so designed ... To pray, preach, and sing psalms in the streets and fields is worse, if possible, than intruding into pulpits by downright violence and breach of the peace ... [Religion is made] ridiculous and contemptible ... Go not after these imposters and seducers; but shun them as you would the plague.[27]

Whitefield encouraged Charles to judge what was happening by standing at his side while he preached in the open. Charles was astounded by the experience of seeing 20,000 people listening to his young 24-year-old friend: 'The cries of the wounded were heard on every side. What has Satan gained by turning him out of the churches?'[28] Impressed though he was, Charles still refused to offend the church authorities by engaging in open-air preaching himself. He also opposed John Bray and others in the Fetter Lane Society when they began talking about undertaking open-air preaching. From his perspective it was wrong to accede to any layman preaching. His brother Samuel felt this response was inadequate and looked to his mother to denounce what George Whitefield and John were doing so that Charles did not fall into the same trap.

The scale of anti-Methodist feeling is exemplified by what happened to a young convert called Joseph Periam, who lived in Bethnal Green. His family was so horrified by his constant praying and fasting and by his decision to give all his possessions to the poor that they had him locked away in a damp and windowless cell within a lunatic asylum. There he was force-fed and for long periods denied the use of any light. Whitefield and William Seward lobbied the committee in charge of the asylum, but its members told him they regarded him and his friends 'as much mad as the young man'.[29] It took all Whitefield's power of persuasion to eventually persuade Periam's father to relent and have his son released.

With his departure to America nearing, Whitefield saw the recruitment of Charles as crucial because there was no way John could single-handedly undertake work in London and Bristol. When Howell Harris visited London, Whitefield asked him to add his weight to the arguments. Charles liked Harris, describing him as 'a man after my own heart',[30] but he still said 'no'. However, towards the end of May Charles accepted an invitation to preach at a church in Broadoaks, an Essex village about 40 miles outside London and, while he was there, he accepted the invitation of a farmer to preach in a nearby field. About 500 gathered to hear him. Shortly afterwards he was denied access to a church at Thaxted and so he again preached in the open air, this time on the invitation of a Quaker. Seven hundred came to hear him and, when he repeated the event the following day, over a thousand. These occasions made him feel maybe his brother and Whitefield were right, even while he continued resisting preaching in the centre of London.

At this critical juncture, Charles was summoned before the Archbishop of Canterbury on a charge of unauthorized preaching in other ministers' pulpits. Potter threatened to excommunicate him and dismissed him 'with all the marks of his displeasure' so that Charles was weighed down 'in great heaviness and discouragement'.[31] Understandably, he felt the Church was pushing him into doing the very thing he wanted to avoid – preaching in the open air. His dilemma about what to do was probably not helped by the fact that he was finding his membership of the

Fetter Lane Society less congenial. Some members, notably John Shaw and William Fish, were pushing towards a break with the Church and therefore were living proof that the church authorities were right to be concerned about how religious societies could generate dissent. Other members, including John Bray, were falling under the influence of a group called the 'Camisards' or French Prophets, a Huguenot sect whose members spoke in tongues, claimed spiritual perfection, and prophesied the imminent return of Christ. Charles judged them to be mere 'pretenders to inspiration'[32] and entered into dispute with one of their prophetesses, a woman with a 'horrible hellish laugh' called Mary Lavington.

When Charles made clear he felt there was no way reborn Christians automatically became perfect, Lavington tried to shout him down: 'She lifted up her voice ... and cried out vehemently, "Look for perfection! I say absolute perfection!"'[33] Matters got far worse when Charles discovered John Bray was sleeping with the prophetess and that she was saying she could 'command Christ to come to her in whatever shape she pleases; as a dove, an eagle, etc.'.[34] George Whitefield wrote that he felt 'the devil is beginning to mimic God's work'.[35] A major confrontation resulted in which the prophetess accused Charles of being a fool who was possessed by the devil. He demanded that the society members should hear his denunciation of her and he won the day only by preaching 'with extraordinary power'.[36]

Charles was delighted when John made a brief return visit to London in mid-June and he went to hear him preach in the open at Blackheath, Moorfields and Kennington Common. Unfortunately he did not find this as reassuring as he had hoped because John's style of preaching evoked an intense and almost hysterical emotional reaction among some of the audience. Whitefield's preaching had moved hearts and aroused tears but not reduced anyone to this kind of behaviour. John later commented:

> Some ... were torn with a kind of convulsive motion in every part of their bodies; and that so violently that often four or five persons could not hold one of them. I have seen many hysterical and many epileptic fits, but none were like these.[37]

This response to John's preaching possibly arose from his vivid portrayal of the hellfire that awaited the damned. One later convert commented: 'I felt so vile that I thought hell was ready to swallow me up.'[38]

John tried to persuade Charles his reservations were more about what other clergy might say than about what he and George were doing. Charles wrote in his journal:

My inward conflict continued. I perceived it was the fear of man ... [and] prayed for particular direction; offering up my friends, my liberty, my life, for Christ's sake, and the Gospel's.[39]

On 24 June Whitefield told Charles he had no option but to preach in the open air because he had announced he would do so. Charles probably acceded to this final pressure because he knew it was what his brother John wanted. He found the resulting experience overwhelming:

I found near ten thousand helpless sinners waiting for the word at Moorfields. I invited them in my Master's words, as well as name, 'Come unto me, all ye that travail, and are heavy laden, and I will give you rest'. The Lord was with me, even me, his meanest messenger, according to his promise ... My load was gone, and all my doubts and scruples. God shone upon my path, and I knew THIS was his will concerning me.[40]

Afterwards he attended a service and took communion in St Paul's Cathedral. Then he again preached in the open air, this time on Kennington Common. The following Sunday Charles spoke to a very different audience. He travelled to Oxford and preached 'with great boldness' on the theme of justification by faith at St Mary's before members of the university. Like Martin Luther before him, Charles said he could do no other than take his stand on what was ultimately true: 'I have declared the truth, I have borne my testimony, I have delivered my soul!'[41] Charles recorded that 'all were very attentive' and 'one could not help weeping', but his words ultimately fell on stony ground. He therefore subsequently put the case for what he and his brother were doing to the vice-chancellor. He found he was not unreceptive to their aims but 'objected to the irregularity of our doing good in other men's parishes'.[42]

Behind a brave public façade, Charles continued to agonize privately over whether the principle of field-preaching was right, especially as he knew his eldest brother hated his and John's growing notoriety.[43] Simultaneously Charles questioned whether he was virtuous enough to preach to others. However, a number of letters from converts indicate Charles' reservations did not prevent him becoming a charismatic preacher, especially with young women. A good example is the case of Margaret Austin, a young woman whose husband had abused her and then deserted her, leaving her with two small children. She went to hear Whitefield but felt unworthy of God's love. John Wesley's preaching made her feel only more a sinner. It was not until she heard Charles that she experienced God's forgiving love and such joy that she 'felt old things passing away and all things becoming new'.[44] She said of what happened to her:

[I was] Awakened by the Reverend Mr Whitefield: Convicted by the Reverend Mr John Wesley: Converted by the Reverend Mr Charles: for the truth of whose Doctrine in the Strength of the Lord I am ready to lay down my Life.[45]

James Hutton has left us a vivid description of the congregations who flocked to hear the open-air preaching:

They were composed of every description of persons, who, without the slightest attempt at order, assembles, crying 'Hurrah!' with one breath, and with the next bellowing and bursting into tears on account of their sins; some poking each other's ribs, and others shouting 'Hallelujah!'. It was a jumble of extremes of good and evil ... Here thieves, prostitutes, fools, people of every class, several men of distinction, a few of the learned, merchants, and numbers of poor people who never had entered a place of worship, assembled in crowds and became godly.[46]

Charles proved a more effective preacher than his brother. John Wesley's first official biographer, who heard both preach, regarded Charles' sermons as more 'awakening and useful' and less 'dry and systematic':

He had a remarkable talent of expressing the most important truths with simplicity and energy; and his discourses were sometimes truly apostolic, forcing conviction on his hearers in spite of the most determined opposition.[47]

Unlike John, Charles did not seek to evoke intense physical reactions because, as his journal reveals, he was sceptical about their sincerity and sometimes for good reason:

I talked sharply to Jenny Dechamps, a girl of twelve years old; who now confessed that her fits and cryings out (about thirty of them) were all feigned, that Mr Wesley might take notice of her.[48]

Charles and George thought John's style of preaching was likely to bring Methodism into disrepute. This is not surprising because the following example is not untypical of John's disconcerting impact:

She lay on the ground gnashing her teeth and after a while roared aloud. It was not easy for three or four persons to hold her, especially when the name of Jesus was named. We prayed the violence of her symptoms ceased ... [but] in the evening I was sent for again. She began screaming before I came into the room; then broke out into a horrid laughter, mixed with blasphemy ... My brother coming in, she cried out, 'Preacher! Field preacher! I don't love field preaching!' This was repeated two hours together, with spitting, and all the expressions of strong aversion.[49]

Whitefield told John:

I cannot think it right in you to give so much encouragement to these convulsions ... Was I to do so, how many would cry out every night? I think it is tempting God to require such signs. That there is something of God in it, I doubt not. But the devil, I believe, interposes. I think it will encourage ... people ... [to] depend on visions, convulsions, etc more than on the promises and precepts of the gospel.[50]

It was inevitable most clergymen opposed what was happening. A minister called Henry Stebbing wrote a book called *A Caution Against Religious Delusion*, which accused the Methodists of overturning respect for authority and creating 'tumultuous assemblies' which disturbed the public peace by promoting 'wild fancies'. Another writer called Tristram Land described the Methodists as:

Young quacks in divinity, running about the city, and taking great pains to distract the common people, and to break the peace and unity of the Church. They ... [look] upon themselves as exquisite pictures of holiness and as patterns of piety, they represent us (the clergy) as dumb dogs, profane, and carnally minded. They talk much of the pangs of the new birth, their inward feelings, experiences, and spiritual miracles; but their faith is an ill grounded assurance [and] their hope an unwarrantable presumption.[51]

Whitefield encouraged Charles and others to regard such attacks as 'the buffetings of a ridiculing world'.[52] He said it was time their opponents put their own house in order:

Let them examine their own lives before they condemn others for enthusiasts. It is manifest that ... [some ministers] make no scruple of frequenting taverns and public houses. They make no conscience of playing several hours at billiards, bowls, and other ... games, which they esteem as innocent diversions ... They don't catechise. They don't visit from house to house. They don't watch over their flocks by examining their lives. They keep up no constant religious conversation in families under their care.[53]

Initially Charles' other close friend, Benjamin Ingham, faced less clerical opposition in his evangelical work in his home county of Yorkshire. He had experienced his own call to be an evangelist while sitting on Woolley Moor, a hill overlooking his native town of Ossett and, when Whitefield met him, he was surprised how much Ingham had 'remarkably grown in grace' since their Oxford days together. George said he hoped he could 'catch some of the holy fire with which his soul was fired'.[54] Ingham was creating many societies of an overtly Moravian nature and his work soon extended into the cities of Leeds and Halifax. Such was his fame that one of the aristocracy, Lady Betty Hastings, invited him to preach in her private chapel at Ledston Hall. Three of her half-sisters, Lady Margaret, Lady Anne and Lady Frances, became strong advocates for Ingham's work. The Hastings family were very well connected because Betty's half-brother, Theophilus, was the ninth Earl of Huntingdon and he was married to Selina Shirley, the daughter of the Earl of Ferrars, who owned extensive properties in the Midlands and Ireland.

This was the situation when, on 6 July, Ingham was officially prohibited from preaching in any of the churches within the Archdiocese of York by a congress held in Wakefield. It had taken longer but the clergy had placed Ingham in the same position as Whitefield and the Wesleys. Needless to say, his response was the same as theirs. He began field-preaching and reached even more people. That same month the Countess of Huntingdon announced her support of his message. She had always struggled with her inability to live as good a life as she desired and so the concept of salvation by faith easily won her heart. The news that a prominent aristocrat had joined the despised Methodists soon dominated the social gossip of London.

In the Bristol area John was not as successful as Ingham but he was very happy. His focus was developing two preaching-houses for those who had been awakened. These would offer safety away from the mobs which sometimes tried to break up meetings. It was agreed one meeting house would be built on the site of the proposed miners' school at Kingswood and the other on land purchased in the Horsefair in Bristol's city centre. The latter, which became known as the 'New Room', was funded by contributions from the 90 members who belonged to the two societies meeting in Nicholas Street and Baldwin Street. They did this because Whitefield backed John in promoting the benefits of having one 'United Society'. In July the Bishop of Bristol, Joseph Butler, summoned John to explain what he was doing:

I once thought Mr Whitefield and you well-meaning men. But I can't think so now ... The pretending to extraordinary revelations and gifts of the Holy Ghost is a horrid thing, a very horrid thing! ... You have no business here. You are not commissioned to preach in this diocese. Therefore I advise you to go hence.[55]

Meanwhile, Whitefield was in a buoyant mood. In just eight months his preaching had been heard by about a million people and he felt he had stopped religion from being something that was only 'skulking in corners'.[56] He was confident that just as John had built on his success in Bristol, so Charles would carry on his work in London and, if anything, with even greater success because he thought Charles had the potential to become England's greatest preacher. Charles demurred, saying yet again he did not feel he was a good enough Christian to tell others how they should live their lives:

I am continually tempted to leave off preaching and hide myself ... [to] have leisure to attend to my own improvement. God continues to work by me, but not in me, that I can perceive. Do not reckon on me, my brother, in the work God is doing; for I cannot expect He should long employ one who is ever longing and murmuring to be discharged.[57]

Charles feared constant preaching might not only further damage his already frail health but also encourage him to pretend to a greater faith than was true:

Yesterday I preached to more than ten thousand hearers; and was so buffeted, both before and after, that were I not forcibly detained, I should fly from every human face. If God does make a way for me to escape, I shall not easily be brought back again. I cannot like advertising. It looks like sounding a trumpet.[58]

John decided to return to London and take command of the revival there once Whitefield left for America. He found it an easy task to persuade Charles to take over the less vital work in Bristol. Charles left London on 16 August and spent almost a fortnight preaching in a large number of places, including Oxford, Evesham, Gloucester and Painswick. The man who feared he was not good enough could not help but be moved by the response of some of the crowds who came to hear him:

Thousands stood in the churchyard. It was the most beautiful sight I ever beheld. The people filled the gradually rising area, which was shut up on three sides by a vast perpendicular hill. On the top and bottom of this hill was a circular row of trees. In this amphitheatre they stood, deeply attentive, while I called upon them in Christ's words, 'Come unto me, all that are weary'. The tears of many testified that they were ready to enter into that rest. God enabled me to lift up my voice like a trumpet; so that all distinctly heard me. I concluded with singing an invitation to sinners. It was with difficulty we made our way through this most loving people.[59]

By the time he arrived in Bristol, he had almost lost his voice because of the sheer number of times he had preached, combined with the strain of making himself heard. However, he soon delighted in his new role: 'I fell all at once into the strictest intimacy with these delightful souls, and could not forbear saying, "It is good for me to be here".'[60] He preached to thousands at various places in the city. He also travelled further afield to places like Bradford-on-Avon and Freshford. In his journal Charles records how he spoke 'with great freedom and power'. We have a first-hand report of his preaching written by a Calvinist dissenter called Joseph Williams:

I found him standing on a table, in an erect posture, with his hands and eyes lifted up to heaven in prayer, surrounded with, I guess, more than a thousand people; some few of them persons of fashion, both men and women, but most of them of the lower rank of mankind ... He prayed with uncommon fervency, fluency, and variety of proper expression. He then preached about an hour ... in such a manner as I have seldom, if ever, heard any Minister preach ... to convince his hearers that ... God is willing to be reconciled to all, even the worst of sinners.[61]

Williams was amazed at how well Charles preached extempore:

Although he used no notes, nor had anything in his hand but a Bible, yet he delivered his thoughts in a rich, copious variety of expressions, and with so much propriety that I could not observe anything incoherent, or inaccurate thro' the whole performance.[62]

He accompanied Charles to a religious society and found the place 'thronged' with people. Charles again prayed and preached and expounded on the hymns they sang:

Never did I hear such praying or such singing – never did I see and hear such evident marks of fervency of spirit in the service of God – as in that society. At the close of every petition, a serious Amen like a rushing sound of waters, ran through the whole society; and their singing was ... the most harmonious and delightful I ever heard ... Indeed they seemed to sing with melody in their hearts ... If there be such a thing as heavenly music upon earth, I heard it there ... I do not remember my heart to have been so elevated, either in collegiate, parochial, or private worship, as it was there and then ... If, therefore, any inquire ... 'Can any good come out of Methodism?' I can only answer ... 'Come and see'.[63]

The Bristol clergy did not share Williams' opinion and soon opposed Charles as much as they had George and John. One even had the audacity to complain at the way his church was being filled with strangers wanting to take communion! In reply Charles offered to assist him cope with the extra numbers at his services. The suggestion met with a frosty response. Others were quick to point out that many of those who responded to Charles' preaching failed to amend their lifestyle. Charles did not refute this because the change in some people was short-lived. He reproved the women 'in love and simplicity for their lightness, dress, and self-indulgence' and 'exhorted the men to self-denial'.[64] He admitted their failings sometimes discouraged him: '[I am] a poor creature on such occasions, being soon cast down.'

However, the long-term impact on some individuals is well reflected in a letter written to Charles by a semi-educated woman called Elizabeth Hinsom:

I was a Pharisee ... [and] a damd sinner ... the lord work mytelly in me and I felt a strong conviction ... And then I trembeld an should have fell done but the people heald me up and I was out of my senses but the lord wakened me with peace be unto you your sins are for giving you. I went home full of ioye ... I have now peace with god and I know that my redemer liveeth to make intersestion for me. I can now look up and say Christ is ful of grace for me.[65]

Charles was often deeply moved by such simple but 'irresistible' faith. He wrote in September: 'We daily discover more and more who are begotten again by the word of God's power, or awakened to a sense off sin, or edified in the faith.'[66]

Charles used his natural wit to win attention and hecklers only seemed to inspire him to greater oratory. Unfortunately the written sermons which have survived lack the spirit and style of his deliberately simpler extempore preaching. He agreed with the philosophy of his brother:

I design plain truth for plain people. Therefore ... I abstain from all nice and philosophical speculations, from all perplexed and intricate reasonings, and, as far as possible, from even the show of learning, unless in sometimes citing the original Scriptures. I labour to avoid all words which are not easily understood ... and in particular those kinds of technical terms that so frequently occur in bodies of divinity ... but which to common people are an unknown tongue.[67]

Sometimes he achieved an impact simply by reading aloud his own religious experience from his journal. One listener commented: 'I saw my Saviour bleeding on the Cross and ... I was astonished and stood amazed to think it was for me.'[68]

But the preaching affected Charles' health. He was often physically exhausted and mentally drained:

When my work is over, my strength, both bodily and spiritual, leaves me ... God by me strengthens the weak hands, and confirms the feeble knees; yet am I myself as a man in whom is no strength. I am weary and faint in mind, longing continually to be discharged.[69]

He frequently complained of headaches and on one occasion he even recorded he got so worked up preaching he bled from the nose for some time afterwards.[70] However, he kept his problems in perspective because the suffering endured by those who responded to his preaching was often greater:

Christianity flourishes under the cross. None who follow after Christ want that badge of discipleship. Wives and children are beaten ... Today Mary Hannay was with me. While she continued a drunkard, a swearer, and company-keeper, it was very well; she and her father agreed entirely. But from the time of her turning to God, he has used her most inhumanely. Yesterday he beat her, and drove her out of doors, following her with imprecations and threatenings to murder her, if ever she returned.[71]

Charles discovered that the time demanded from individuals in belonging to a society was simply not possible for most of the working classes, because they had to work all the hours God gave in order simply to survive and feed their family. As a consequence the society in Kingswood drew its members more from those miners who were sufficiently skilled to engage in individual contracts with the owners of the pits than from the ordinary miners, while the society in the centre of Bristol was made up of skilled workers or middle-class citizens. It included one city merchant, three master mariners, two hoopers, two weavers, two braziers, a house carpenter, a serge-maker, a cork cutter, an upholsterer, a baker, a tailor, a tobacconist, a bell founder, a plasterer, a linen-draper, a haberdasher, a clerk, a writing master, a stuff-maker, a glassmaker, a gunsmith, a broker, and a tea-man.

Charles was therefore keen for society members, who were better-off, to be at the forefront of helping the poor and the sick and the imprisoned in order to show non-society members what a difference Christianity could make to everyone's life. Seeing his pastoral care in action, Joseph Williams urged Charles to make the southwest region a more permanent base for his activities:

> I dearly love your religious society. My heart is knit to them: and my prayers are daily for you and them, that they may abound more and more in grace, in every good word and work.[72]

In October 1739 John returned to Bristol from London and for a time the two brothers worked together. John also visited the tiny remnant left of the Oxford Methodists and undertook a five-day preaching tour in Wales. Samuel Wesley was still incensed at what his brothers were doing and begged their mother Susanna to intervene:

> They design separation [from the Church] ... They are already forbid all the pulpits in London, and to preach in that diocese is actual schism ... As I told Jack, I am not afraid the church should excommunicate him – discipline is at too low an ebb – but that he should excommunicate the church. It is pretty near it ... Love-feasts are introduced and extemporary prayers and expositions of Scripture, which last are enough to bring all into confusion.[73]

On 31 October John headed back to London, where two businessmen called Watkins and Ball approached him to create a preaching house similar but larger to what was happening in Bristol. They suggested he hire and convert a large and derelict brick building in Windmill Street near the northwest corner of Finsbury Square. It was called the Foundery because it had originally been used for the casting of cannon until a major explosion in 1716 had reduced it to a 'vast, uncouth heap of ruins'.[74] Purchasing it would be cheap yet its location was perfect. It was on the edge of the city and a favourite spot for city apprentices to entertain their girlfriends on holiday afternoons because 'the ground situated southward from the Foundery ... was (partly) laid out as pleasure grounds, with walks and promenades, shaded by trees, and in the summertime decorated with flowers and shrubs'.[75] When John pointed out his lack of funds, Watkins and Ball offered to advance him the necessary money on the understanding that this would be repaid by the society bands which used it.

John preached for the first time amid the Foundery ruins on 11 November. The following day he met up with two former members of the Oxford Methodists, John Gambold and John Robson. They agreed that the scale of church opposition required all the evangelicals to co-ordinate their work so they could not be picked off one by one. They drew up a list of Oxford Methodists and others who might help the revival. In addition to Charles and Benjamin Ingham, it included John Hutchings, Westley Hall, George Stonehouse and Charles Kinchin. Always something of a control freak, John was already seeing he could use Whitefield's absence to shape the revival to his own way of thinking. As far as he was concerned, the proof of the value of what he and Charles were doing was embodied in the change that had been wrought in Bristol:

> Kingswood does not now, as a year ago resound with cursing and blasphemy. It is no more filled with drunkenness and uncleanness … It is no longer full of wars and fighting, of clamour and bitterness, of wrath and envyings. Peace and love are there.[76]

Methodism had one opponent less when Samuel Wesley unexpectedly died at the age of 49 after a brief illness. Charles and John left their respective work to travel to Tiverton and comfort their mother. They were told Samuel had died with 'a calm and full assurance of his interest in Christ'[77] and they chose to interpret this as meaning he had belatedly decided what they were doing was God's work. The family inscribed his tombstone with the words:

> A man [known] for his uncommon wit and learning, for the benevolence of his temper, and simplicity of manners. Deservedly beloved and esteemed by all; an excellent Preacher; but whose best sermon was the constant example of an edifying life, so continually and zealously employed in acts of beneficence and charity, that he truly followed his blessed Master's example in going about doing good. Of such unscrupulous integrity that he declined occasions of advancement in the world … and avoided the usual ways to preferment as studiously as many others seek them.[78]

Charles and John told Susanna she could have a new home at the Foundery and she said it was her prayer that God would prosper their work. However, on their return to London a shock awaited them. Control of the Fetter Lane Society had been taken away from them by a Moravian called Philip Henry Molther. He had arrived in London in mid-October, fresh from his theological studies at the University of Jena and en route to Pennsylvania. Born in Alsace, he had grown up hugely influenced by the Quietist movement with its emphasis on personal devotion and so he was shocked at the emotional nature of the society's worship. He had decided it was his duty to urge the members to abandon their sighing and shouting in favour of a quieter approach to worship. To Molther being 'still' was more important than anything else, even charitable work. Initially he had been restricted by his poor command of English but, as this improved, so did his following because he was a powerful preacher. With both the Wesley brothers away, the society had naturally turned to his leadership.

Charles and John discovered some of their closest associates, such as John Gambold, Charles Delamotte and Westley Hall, were now abandoning any expression of their faith in favour of 'being still'. Charles was not averse to contemplation as the following example from his verse indicates:

Open, Lord, my inward ear
And bid my heart rejoice;
Bid my quiet spirit hear
Thy comfortable voice
From the world of sin and noise
And hurry I withdraw;
For the small and inward voice
I wait with humble awe.[79]

But Molther was saying attending communion or engaging in social outreach was unnecessary for those who knew they were saved and Charles called this a 'diabolical stillness'.[80] Both the Wesleys still viewed communion as one of the most important means by which God's grace was experienced and they believed it was essential Christians should express their faith by avidly obeying the commands of Christ.

Molther claimed Charles and John must lack proper faith if they did not understand that, once assured of salvation, any activity became pointless. They disagreed and said Molther should recognize his opinions were not infallible and their impact was destructive because society members were either ceasing to live truly Christian lives or were being plunged into deep self-doubt that their faith was inadequate. Describing Molther's ideas to a friend, Charles wrote:

Many here insist that a part of their Christian calling is liberty from obeying, not liberty to obey ... Lazy and proud themselves, bitter and censorious to others, they ... despise the commands of Christ.[81]

And years later he wrote an epistle on Molther, comparing him to a wolf placed among sheep:

> Ye caught th' Occasion, and with deepest Art
> Labour'd to alienate our Children's Heart,
> Wean of their Fondness for their Absent Guide,
> And turn the lame unsettled Souls aside ...
> How did ye make their helpless Souls a Prey,
> Wide-scattering in the dark and cloudy Day![82]

Charles was particularly upset when John Shaw, who was one of Molther's strongest supporters, backed the claims of a barber called Wolfe in claiming there was no such thing as a call to Christian priesthood and that communion services could be conducted by laymen. Opponents of Methodism tried to persuade the heavily pregnant Selina, Countess of Huntingdon, to abandon her connections with what was happening:

> [They are] mad enthusiasts, who teach ... seditions, heresies and contempt of the ordinances of God and man. They are buffoons in religion and mountebanks in theology; creatures who disclaim sense and are below argument; visionary antics in gowns and cassocks ... composing sermons as fast as they can write and speaking faster than they can think.[83]

However, when Martin Benson, the Bishop of Gloucester, tackled her on the matter in December, she told him it was time he took his role as a bishop more seriously and stopped fussing about whether someone had the legal right to be preaching in somebody else's parish. When Benson told her he regretted ever having ordained Whitefield, seeing how he had led the Wesleys and others astray, she replied: 'My Lord, mark my words, when you come upon your dying bed that will be one of the few ordinations you will reflect upon with complacence.'[84]

Charles urged Whitefield to write from America and back him in securing the eviction of some of the society members, but John's predisposition towards the Moravians made him initially desire a compromise. He even went to the trouble of translating one of Molther's favourite German hymns, 'Now I have found the ground wherein'. In a sermon on New Year's Day John urged everyone 'no longer to subvert one another's souls by idle controversies and strife of words'.[85] But Molther was not a man for compromise and soon John agreed with Charles it was time to start regarding the Foundery as their spiritual home rather than the Fetter

Lane Society. The first main phase of work on the redundant building was completed in February 1740 so they had a large preaching place able to accommodate 1,500 people, mainly on benches. Its front gallery was designated for women and the side galleries for men because the Wesleys believed the early Church had separated male and female worshippers. The Foundery eventually also provided a large room for band meeting, a schoolroom, accommodation for the Wesleys and others, and a coach-house and stables.

Given what was happening at Fetter Lane, John and Charles deliberately refused to name the Foundery a Methodist preaching-house (lest that smack of religious dissent). They described it as the base for 'a United Society' like the one in Bristol (i.e. one that would draw members from existing societies who lacked appropriate facilities). They announced it would hold daily services at around six in the morning and six at night. These would consist of an opening prayer and hymn followed by a half-hour address and a concluding hymn and prayers. It is thought Charles preached there for the first time on 3 April to its first 12 members. Within a fortnight the Foundery Society had its own set of rules and these were deliberately different from those of the Fetter Lane Society in two important respects. First, no decision could be taken without the approval of an ordained clergyman. Second, all members had to agree to fully follow the requirements of the Church, including taking regular communion.

The Foundery provided the Wesleys with a means of surviving the growing rejection of their views among the evangelicals. Most Moravians saw no need to belong to the Church of England and even close associates and friends like John Gambold, Charles Delamotte, George Stonehouse and John Bray were becoming vocal in their opposition to John and Charles. John bemoaned that the meetings at the Fetter Lane Society had become 'cold, weary, heartless, dead': 'I found nothing of brotherly love among them now; but a harsh, dry, heavy, stupid spirit.'[86] Neither he nor Charles could understand how people could believe that because they were fully saved they had no need to undertake any Christian activities. Charles felt Molther was appealing to mankind's 'lazy, corrupt nature'[87] and told John that compromise was no longer possible:

> A separation I foresee unavoidable. All means have been taken to wean our friends of their esteem for us. They say God never used us as instruments to convert one soul ... and George Whitefield ... [is condemned as] an unbeliever ... I think it safest not to converse with such of our misled, misleading brethren.[88]

Not for the first time John decided to let Charles deal with an increasingly difficult situation. He left for Bristol and told Charles to achieve a reconciliation among the evangelicals in London. Charles tried but his journal records his frustration:

> Lazy and proud themselves, bitter and censorious towards others, they trample upon the [Church] ordinances, and despise the commands of Christ. I see no middle point wherein we can meet.[89]

He was upset by the way Molther saw it as 'a sign of my carnal state that I complained of our brethren for withdrawing the people's love from me and my brother'.[90] Increasingly he found it impossible to deal with the increasingly aggressive behaviour of those whom Charles termed 'the strong ones' among Molther's disciples:

> I was in a mild, open, loving frame ... [but they were] brimful of dispute. I was to declare my success at Bristol but they would not permit me. After much thwarting, I told them they did not deserve a true Minister of Christ ... I got home weary, wounded, bruised, and faint, through the contradiction of ... these heady, violent, fierce contenders for stillness. I could not bear the thought of meeting them again.[91]

By this time Benjamin Ingham was viewed as the most successful Moravian preacher in the country, having established 50 societies in Yorkshire, and he came to London to support Charles and try and resolve the matter. Howell Harris also arrived to urge unity among the evangelicals. Neither of them could make headway against Molther and his closest associates. Matters came to a head when James Hutton acquired a chapel for use by members of the Fetter Lane Society. Molther succeeded in having a vote taken to ban Charles from preaching in it. Charles later wrote of his immense pain that Hutton voted against him:

> A Faithless Friend, a weak misguided Youth
> A shortliv'd Boaster of his constant Truth,
> Dearest of all that fell by German Art,
> And still the Burthen of my aching Heart.[92]

Charles turned increasingly for friendship to Howell Harris. The two men admired each other hugely. Howell said whenever he heard Charles preach: 'I thought my soul was almost drawn out of my body to Christ.'[93] Charles waxed equally eloquent about the impact of Harris' preaching at the Foundery:

O what a flame was kindled! Never man spake in my hearing as this man spake. What a nursing-father God has sent us! ... Such love, such power, such simplicity was irresistible. The lambs dropping down on all sides into their shepherd's arms.[94]

On 5 June John returned from Bristol and the next day he went with Charles and Howell Harris to see Molther. John argued it might be better to avoid squabbling by dividing the Fetter Lane Society into separate Moravian and Wesleyan groups but Molther opposed this and John found himself described as 'a child of the devil [and] a servant of corruption'.[95] A proposed meeting to co-ordinate the activity of the evangelical preachers was cancelled. John and Charles agreed there was no alternative but to abandon the Fetter Lane Society altogether and take with them who they could. Such a radical step was possible because the Foundery had become a vibrant society in its own right with some 300 members. Charles subsequently wrote:

The noisy 'still-ones' well knew that they had carried their point by wearying out the sincere ones scattered among them ... [but] Benjamin Ingham seconded us ... We gathered up our wreck ... for nine out of ten are swallowed up in the dead sea of stillness. O why was this not done six months ago! How fatal was our delay and false moderation![96]

Almost all the women members of the Fetter Lane Society transferred their allegiance to the Foundery but only about a third of the men. This is perhaps an interesting comment on the particular appeal of both John and Charles to women. It may explain the rather snide comment of their former friend James Hutton:

Both John and Charles Wesley are dangerous snares to many young women. Several are in love with them. I wish they were married to some good sisters, though I would not give them one of mine, even if I had many.[97]

To Charles' distress among those who did not transfer were Martha Claggett and her daughters, who had been among the first of his converts in June 1738. Martha had found Charles' preaching inspirational:

[I was] in such joy as I never felt before, my Heart overflowed with the love of God, and I could not keep from joining the immortal choir in their hallelujahs.[98]

So too had her teenage daughters Susannah and Elizabeth. However, now they were fully in the Molther camp because he guaranteed them a permanently assigned place in heaven compared to Charles' demand for the reborn to prove their worth. Susannah wrote that in her case she had 'a new awakening of an evangelical kind' in which she no longer had to be filled 'with fright and terror' about her depravity.[99]

Charles returned to Bristol so that he could remodel the societies there on similar lines to the Foundery. Arriving there on 21 June, he could not but contrast what was happening in Bristol with the disharmony in London:

> O that our London brethren would come to school in Kingswood! These are what they pretend to be. God knows their poverty; but they are rich ... without confusion ... Peace, unity, and love are here ... My soul is escaped as a bird out of the snare of the fowler.[100]

As previously, he preached not only in Bristol, where he proved increasingly popular, but also further afield in such places as Malmesbury, Stanton Harcourt and Oxford.

The split with the Fetter Lane Society caused great concern among the wider Moravian community, most of whom did not share Molther's dislike of the Wesleys. Count Zinzendorf sent August Spangenberg to heal the breach. It was known John had a high regard for him ever since their first meeting in Georgia. Spangenberg reported the fault for the division lay largely with Molther and Count Zinzendorf urged him in vain to apologize. In September 1741 the count visited London but this did not help, partly because he was critical of the Wesleys' emphasis on good works, and partly because John had reassessed his attitude towards the Moravians. He said they were placing too much reliance on Luther's muddy and confused thinking and were dangerously wrong in undervaluing the importance of a person's lifestyle.[101] Zinzendorf urged all the religious societies to remain within the Church of England, but Molther ignored this and led the Fetter Lane Society towards total dissent. This was an anathema to the loyal Charles:

> Shall I, too, the sinking Church forsake?
> Forbid it, Heaven, or take my spirit back ...
> While but a fragment of our ship remain,
> That single fragment shall my soul sustain.
> Bound to that sacred plank, my soul defies
> The great abyss, and dares all hell to rise,
> Assured that Christ, on that, shall bear me to the skies.[102]

Charles wrote to George Whitefield, outlining how 'the roaring lion is turned a still lion, and makes havoc of the church'.[103] Whitefield was understandably deeply concerned:

> God grant we may keep up a cordial, undissembled love towards each other, notwithstanding our different opinions. O I long for heaven! Surely there will be no divisions, no strife there.[104]

Charles said the success of the revival now solely rested with the Foundery but in reality the Moravians continued to contribute significantly to the religious revival. If anything, their influence increased rather than decreased. For the next 15 years they were to be engaged extensively in both charitable work and evangelism with Benjamin Ingham as their chief apostle in the north. His close friendship with the Wesleys inevitably faded. It was Ingham's very success that was eventually to prove his undoing. Single-handed he could not sustain the control over the societies he was creating in the way the Wesleys were able to achieve by their slower creation of a more complex system.

The division of interest between Ingham and the Wesleys benefited the latter because Selina, Countess of Huntingdon, turned to the Wesleys when she fell out with Ingham over his wish to marry her sister-in-law, Lady Margaret Hastings. The gossiping tongues at court were scathing about how anyone of any social standing could contemplate marriage to 'a poor wandering Methodist'[105] and she was angry that Ingham had abused his situation to win Lady Margaret's heart. When, in the autumn of 1740, she travelled to London, she decided to avoid the Moravian Fetter Lane Society in favour of attending the Wesleyan Foundery. She thus made her first personal link with the Wesleys. John made at least six visits to further cultivate her interest in his work between April and August 1741. She undoubtedly offered him financial support and this was a factor in why he and Charles could eventually afford to rebuild the New Room in Bristol on a grander scale, so it contained not only meeting rooms and a 'preaching-house' (or 'chapel') but also some small bedrooms for use by John, Charles and any other travelling preachers.

The United Societies in Bristol and London are sometimes described as the first ones to be truly distinctively 'Methodist' even if John avoided calling them that. It is true they made higher demands on their members, expecting them to constantly examine each other's faith:

To keep your armour bright
Attend with constant care,
Still walking in your Captain's sight
And watching unto prayer.[106]

In part this was because of John and Charles' determination to prevent happening to them what had happened to the Fetter Lane Society:

> But worse than all my foes I find
> The enemy within,
> The evil heart, the carnal mind,
> My own insidious sin.[107]

However, what really made the United Societies different was their 'class system' and this did not happen until February 1742. By then the costs incurred in building the Foundery and the New Room had generated such debt that John was forced to ask for financial help. A sea captain named Foy suggested the solution lay in asking every society member to pay a penny a week. The Wesleys pointed out that not all members could afford this so it was agreed it would be better to divide the society up into classes, each of about a dozen people and to make each class responsible for collecting 12 pence per week (i.e. within the class some could give more than others). Each society had to appoint a steward to handle the money thus raised (thereby avoiding any danger of the Wesleys being accused of personally benefiting from it).

The classes, unlike the bands, were not divided by age, sex or marital status and both John and Charles were quick to see that each class leader could play a wider role than just collecting money to pay off debt. He could monitor that members fully contributed to helping the poor and others in need. He could check they attended communion regularly in their parish church. Above all, he could ensure that members were staying theologically sound (which meant they accepted the views of the Wesleys). In effect people were only issued with a quarterly ticket of membership if they conformed. It was left to Charles to put an attractive gloss on this system of control and he did so brilliantly:

> Help us to help each other, Lord
> Each other's cross to bear,
> Let each his friendly aid afford
> And feel his brother's care.[108]

Many of the societies which had nothing to do with the Wesleys soon began copying the class system.

John was later to make out that the two United Societies owed everything to him. In reality they owed as much to Charles, who undertook extensive engagements. For example, he was largely based in Bristol throughout September and October 1739, from June to December 1740, and from April to at least October 1741. In that time he constantly declared 'the two great truths of the everlasting gospel' to be 'universal redemption' and 'Christian perfection',[109] presenting God as a loving father out to forgive every repentant sinner:

> He owns me for His child,
> I can no longer fear;
> With confidence, I now draw nigh,
> And 'Father, Abba, Father' cry.[110]

In this process Charles showed he fully understood why most people felt God could not care for them:

> We are a race of fallen spirits. We are all by nature children of wrath, ignorant of good, and haters of God ... All the powers of men are totally depraved. The whole head is sick and the whole heart feint. From the sole of the foot to the crown of the head there is no soundness in him, but wounds and bruises and putrefying sores: his understanding is darkened, his will perverse, his affections set on earthly things.[111]

And then he waxed lyrical on God's forgiveness and love:

> It is the blood of Christ that cleanses from all sins ... In the moment when a self-despairing sinner looks up with faith to Christ Jesus, in that selfsame moment the power of the Lord is present to heal him; his sins are forgiven ... The faith which justifies ... is not a lifeless, cold, historical faith ... but a divine energy ... Faith does not stand in the wisdom of men but in the power of God.[112]

One of the scriptural passages he most frequently quoted was the call of Christ: 'Come unto me all ye that travail and are heavy laden, and I will give you rest.'

His journal recounts with obvious pleasure the names of people whose lives were transformed, such as Elizabeth Field 'immediately lightened', Mary Branker 'filled with unknown power and comfort', Abigail Savage saved after being 'long in darkness', Joanna Nichols 'justified ... on hearing the word', Margaret Thomas receiving 'the faith which works by love', and Jane Connor 'finding the power of the Lord to heal her'. It was women who particularly responded to him. We have a few surviving letters which record the personal thanks of individuals and the following example (from a woman called Maria Price) gives a flavour of the sense of freedom and release generated by Charles' ministry:

> Dear Sir I came to you as a blind man from his birth that never had no thought of sight … i was like a person that was born blind and that moment received light … i received such light as i never had before i as plainly felt a burden taken of my heart as i could feel one took of my back it was done in a moment it was such a work so plainly felt and so wonderfully wrought that I almost lose my senses to explane it and can not do it.[113]

Reading the letters it is not difficult to see why Charles thought he had no option but to defy the Church he loved and continue his irregular ministry. How could he turn his back on such people? John felt the same. Whenever their travels took them away, their converts pleaded for their return as is illustrated by this letter to Charles from a woman called Martha Sones:

> You and your brother gone we were left as sheep without a shepherd … I was brought into great confusion … I continued in great perplexities and had almost given up my hope when God sent you to us again and on Easter Sunday I heard you preach and the Lord strengthened and confirmed my faith [and] my doubts and fears vanished and the Lord made his way plain before my face.[114]

Charles' pastoral work in Bristol brought him into direct conflict with the Calvinist views then prevalent among many people, especially those awakened by Whitefield. The resulting conflict was to lead him and John into a bitter break with their friend. No one could have foreseen such a major division taking place, nor guessed at the long-term animosity it was to generate. John was later to write accounts of the origins of Methodism in which Whitefield's role as the founder of Methodism was essentially ignored (as was also that of Ingham).

6

The Calvinist Controversy

Will they not? Alas for them,
Dead in sin who Christ refuse!
He did all the world redeem,
All unto salvation choose;
Sinners come, with me receive,
All the grace He waits to give.

In ourselves the hindrance lies,
Stopp'd by our own stubborn will;
He His love to none denies,
He with love pursues us still;
Sinners come, and find with me
Only heaven in His decree.[1]

The clash with the Moravians forced John and Charles to consider how best they could control the theological thinking within the revival. This inevitably brought out the latent tensions between their views and those of Whitefield. He had long had strong leanings towards Calvinism, which held that anyone capable of rejecting the gospel was preordained to be damned and that a preacher could only successfully preach to men and women whom God had chosen to be saved (the so-called 'elect'). In contrast, the Wesleys had been brought up by Susannah to see predestination as 'inconsistent with the justice and goodness of God'.[2] Instead, they accepted the theological views of the anti-Calvinist Dutch writer, Jakob Arminius, who believed salvation was open to everybody but not accepted by all because God had provided people with free will to make their own choice. Charles described the belief in a predetermined eternity as 'the injustice of reprobation'. He felt Calvinism encouraged hypocrisy and arrogance. Those who saw themselves as 'the elect' too often felt free to do as they liked while condemning others as 'the damned'.[3]

The Calvinists thought a person preordained to be saved could never fall from grace, but Arminians believed conversion brought no guarantee of eternal salvation because the faith of the reborn Christian was either confirmed by Christian living or undermined (and even lost) by ill living. Charles' hymns are permeated with the view that a person remains saved only by allowing God's grace to continue functioning in his or her life:

> Thou dost not say, the seed springs up
> Into an instantaneous crop;
> But waiting long for its return,
> We see the blade, the ear, the corn;
> The weak; and then the stronger grace,
> And after that full holiness.[4]

The deep friendship between Charles and George Whitefield undoubtedly restrained both men from letting such profound theological differences jeopardize their working together. John was not so tied and on more than one occasion told Whitefield that Calvinism was an inappropriate belief for a minister of the Church of England. After one heated exchange, Whitefield told John:

> For once hearken to a child, who is willing to wash your feet. I beseech you ... write no more to me about misrepresentations wherein we differ ... I am ten thousand times more convinced of the doctrine of election ... than when I saw you last. You think otherwise. Why, then, should we dispute, when there is no probability of convincing? Will it not, in the end, destroy brotherly love, and insensibly take from us that cordial union and sweetness of soul, which I pray God may always subsist between us?[5]

When Whitefield handed over control of the revival in London and Bristol to the Wesleys, he hoped they would continue to put aside their theological differences in order to focus on the salvation of souls. He specifically asked John not to make the issue of predestination a cause for disunity and, once in America, he was understandably disappointed to hear reports of John's increasing attacks on Calvinist thinking in the first half of 1740. In June he wrote: 'For Christ's sake, let us not be divided amongst ourselves. Nothing will so much prevent a division as your being silent on this head.'[6]

There were many Calvinists among the members of the Foundery and one of them, John Acourt, began showing all the signs of being just as disruptive to the harmony of its membership as Molther had been to the society in Fetter Lane. In June 1740 an exasperated Charles ordered Acourt's exclusion. The Calvinist members appealed to John to reinstate him and Howell Harris backed their case:

If you exclude him from the society and from the fraternity of Methodists for such cause, you must exclude brother Whitefield, brother
Seward, and myself.[7]

John replied there were bigots 'both for predestination and against it'[8]
who needed to be sent a clear message. He and Charles told Acourt they
did not mind him believing in predestination providing he did not constantly trouble others with his views. Acourt refused this compromise,
saying he would not be silenced: 'You are all wrong and I am resolved
to set you right.'[9]

John felt he had no option but 'to strike at the root of the grand delusion' that was Calvinism[10] and Charles agreed to assist him to denounce
'the hellish, blasphemous, explosive lie … the foulest tale … that was
ever hatched in Hell'.[11] John preached a sermon on 'Free Grace' to show
the Calvinist view 'in all its naked, hideous deformity'.[12] The sermon
said Calvinism rendered preaching vain, destroyed any motivation to try
to lead a holy life, and encouraged contempt and coldness towards those
who were allegedly damned. It turned Christ into 'a hypocrite and dis-
sembler … pretending a love which He had not' and made God 'worse
than the Devil', a most cruel tyrant prepared to condemn millions of
souls to everlasting fire for committing sins they were unable to avoid.
This sermon was published, accompanied by one of Charles' hymns
called 'Universal Redemption', which praised God's 'boundless grace':

Mercy for all thy Hands have made
Immense and Unconfin'd,
Throughout thy every Work display'd,
Embracing all Mankind.[13]

It was tantamount to a declaration of war and the publication caused
bitter wrangling, especially in Bristol where Whitefield's sister refused
ever again to offer accommodation to the Wesleys. The leading lay work-
er, John Cennick, said John was acting as if he was a pope who could
stamp his views on everyone, while Charles was behaving like Satan in
'making war with all the saints'. Charles later wrote to Whitefield that
he felt part of the Calvinist response was to destroy his and John's reputation by gross lies:

My brother has been most grossly abused; his behaviour (if I may be
a witness) has been truly Christian. All the bitterness his opposers
have shown, and the woes and curses they have denounced against
him, have never provoked him to a like return, or stirred his temper,
or impaired his charity.[14]

But Whitefield was devastated by the action of the Wesleys: 'How can you say you will not dispute with me ... and yet print such ... O my dear brethren, my heart almost bleeds within me!'[15]

Nevertheless, Whitefield wrote letters urging his fellow Calvinists to show tolerance:

> I hear there are divisions among you. Avoid them, if possible. The doctrines of election ... I hold as well as you. But they are not to be contended for with heat and passion. Such a proceeding will only prejudice the cause you would defend ... Avoid all clamour and evil speaking.[16]

This tolerance is not surprising given his increasing ecumenical approach in America. After creating his orphanage (which he named 'Bethesda'), Whitefield had agreed to undertake three preaching tours organized by Presbyterians, Congregationalists and Dutch Calvinists. In April 1740 he had gone to Philadelphia, which was America's largest city, and there he had worked closely with Peter Böhler and other Moravians. By June he was in New York, proclaiming all Methodists should avoid bigotry and sectarian zeal because 'some of Christ's flock are to be found in every denomination'.[17] At the time of writing his letter in August, he had already visited Charleston and commenced a huge tour of New England, which was to last until December 1740.

This tour was the start of a series of ecumenical evangelical campaigns which were later to be dubbed 'the Grand Awakening'. They were supported by the most powerful preachers in America, including Gilbert Tennant (Presbyterian), Henry Muhlenberg (Lutheran), Theodore Frelinghuysen (Dutch Reformed) and Jonathan Edwards (Congregationalist). By exploiting the proliferation of newspapers and publishing massive numbers of non-denominational tracts, Whitefield was able to preach to crowds of up to 8,000 nearly every day and the audience response was always hugely positive. One man wrote:

> He lookt almost angelical; a young, slim, slender, youth before some thousands of people with a bold undaunted countenance ... clothed with authority from the Great God; and a sweet sollome solemnity sat upon his brow.[18]

By 1745 there were 80,000 copies of his tracts in print (about one for every eleven colonists!) and Whitefield was the most widely known 'American' before George Washington. Unfortunately news of his successes only strengthened rather than reduced Calvinist opposition to the Wesleys.

The divisions may have significantly contributed to Charles becoming seriously ill again in August 1740:

> I was taken with a shivering and then the fever came. The next morning I was bled ... My pain and disease increased for ten days; so that there was no hope for my life ... It was reported I was dead, and published in the papers.[19]

Fortunately a doctor called John Middleton tended him carefully, though Charles attributed his survival to God who 'made all things work for my recovery'.[20] In his 'Physician's Hymn', which he dedicated to Middleton, Charles portrayed Christ as the healer of the sin-sick soul:

> Myself, alas! I cannot heal,
> But thou shalt every seed expel
> Of sin out of my heart;
> Thine utmost saving health display,
> And purge my inbred sin away,
> And make me as thou art.[21]

The illness had important consequences. It made Charles even more enthusiastic about ensuring a religious revival: 'I found myself ... more desirous and able to pray, more afraid of sin, more earnestly longing for deliverance and the fullness of Christian salvation.'[22] And it led him to urge an end to the theological conflict because he saw his illness as a punishment by God for what he and John had done in attacking the Calvinists. He wrote to Whitefield:

> Nothing upon earth, or under the earth, shall part us ... I had rather you saw me dead at your feet, than openly opposing you ... All the lovers of discord, I trust, shall be confounded ... Many, I know, desire nothing so much as to see George Whitefield and John Wesley at the head of different parties, as is plain from their truly developed pains to effect it; but be assured, my dearest brother, our heart is as your heart ... May you, my brother, and I, especially, be all one ... My soul is set upon peace, and drawn out after you, by love stronger than death ... You know not how dear you are to me.[23]

Charles' illness may well have also played a significant part in pushing both him and John to accept the use of lay preachers to support their work. Their main lay helper at the Foundery was a young convert called Thomas Maxfield.[24] It is clear from Charles' journal that he thought

Maxfield was a man 'in the full triumph of faith'[25] and he had increasingly welcomed his support in the struggle against Molther. He often asked Maxfield to accompany him while he was travelling and there is no doubt watching Charles preach in London, Oxford, Bristol and elsewhere must have profoundly influenced this young man. It seemed to him a natural step to offer his assistance in leading worship whenever John and Charles were unavailable. They were unsure about the wisdom of this, but with Charles unwell, there seemed little alternative but to make Maxfield their representative at the Foundery. Knowing his mother had heard Maxfield preach, John sought her advice. Susannah told him that he was 'as truly called of God to preach as you are'.[26] The brothers took the momentous decision that, until more clergy rallied to the evangelical cause, it would be necessary to employ some specially chosen lay preachers.

It says much for the attempt to end the conflict with the Calvinists that the main man chosen to be Maxfield's equivalent in Bristol was John Cennick, a young Calvinist land surveyor from Reading. Like the Wesleys, Cennick came from a staunch Church of England family which had once been prominent in dissent (in his case among the Quakers). By all accounts he was a very strict young man, opposed to frivolity of any kind and very austere in his lifestyle, praying nine times a day and frequently fasting to an unhealthy extent. His parents had planned for him to become a carpenter like Jesus, but their attempts to obtain an apprenticeship for him had failed and, while still a teenager, he had started writing hymns and contemplated a monastic life until he fell under Whitefield's spell. He had joined the Fetter Lane Society and, at Whitefield's request, become a teacher at the school being created at Kingswood. He had preached to a gathering of miners as early as June 1739, but Charles at that time had urged John to stop him because no layman had authority to preach.

Now Charles accepted Cennick should be given the authority to preach along with one of Charles' converts, the 20-year-old Joseph Humphreys. Educated as a dissenter, Humphreys had, as an adolescent, become so conscious of his failings that he had begun 'to query whether religion was not all a cheat'.[27] Like Cennick, he had contemplated retreating into a monastery in the hope of gaining absolution for his sins, but, in May 1739, he had been drawn instead to Methodism by the preaching of first Whitefield and then Charles. His personal assurance of salvation had occurred when listening to Charles preach in April 1740: 'I was brought as it were into a new world ... I found myself born again ... swimming in an ocean of love.'[28]

John called Maxfield, Cennick and Humphreys his 'sons of the

Gospel' and soon added to their number a young Cambridge graduate called Thomas Richards and a very pious Bristol carpenter called
Thomas Westell. All the sons of the gospel appear to have been sensitive
to the unusual role they were being given. John Cennick, for example,
went out of his way to dress in such a way that he could not possibly be
mistaken for an ordained person when he preached. While still having
his reservations, Charles publicly backed the use of these men because
he felt the failure of the Church to support their endeavours gave them
no choice. There is a story that the Bishop of Armagh met the recuperating Charles at the Hotwells in Bristol and challenged him about the use
of lay preachers. Charles replied that the fault lay among the clergy for
their refusal to evangelize among the poor. When the bishop showed his
disgust at the use of 'unlearned men', Charles commented that sometimes God had to use a dumb ass to rebuke the prophet.[29]

Recent research has tended to show that Charles may well have acted
as mentor to the sons of the gospel. Certainly they often accompanied
him and he corresponded with them. He soon felt they showed far more
evidence of Christianity in their lives than those ministers who held
office only 'for filthy lucre's state'. He subsequently embodied his views
in a poem which portrayed the failure of ministers to undertake the
saving of souls and therefore God's rejection of them in favour of using
Spirit-led lay preachers:

> The word, the care, the labouring zeal,
> He doth to others give,
> And laymen now of Jesus tell,
> And urge us to believe:
> Unlearn'd they rise, and scale the sky,
> While Scribes, who all things know,
> Live ignorant of Christ, and die,
> And find their place below.[30]

For most of September 1740 Charles was still frail, but it says much for
his strength of character that he risked his life to deal with a serious riot
among the miners at Kingswood over the rising cost of corn. He persuaded some of them to stop rioting and then supported these when they
were attacked by the remaining rioters:

> I rode up to a ruffian who was striking one of our colliers [who had
> agreed to stop rioting] and prayed him rather to strike me. He would
> not, he said, for all the world, and was quite overcome. I turned upon
> one who struck my horse, and he also sunk like a lamb. Wherever I
> turned, Satan lost ground.[31]

He marched those he could persuade away into a prayer meeting. The rioting ceased and was replaced by negotiations between the miners and the authorities. Charles commented: 'Nothing could have more shown the change in them than this rising.'[32]

Methodism clearly was proving itself a force for change but not all could handle the mobs as well as Charles. That same month William Seward, one of Charles' early converts and a great supporter of George Whitefield, was struck in the eye by a stone and killed while trying to preach in South Wales. In 1741 Howell Harris was to be fortunate to escape with his life when visiting Bala:

> The women ... besmeared him with mire, while ... [the men] be-laboured him with their fists and clubs, inflicting such wounds that his path could be marked in the street by the crimson stains of his blood. The enemy continued to persecute him ... striking him with sticks and with staves, until overcome with exhaustion he fell to the ground ... [and they] abused him, though prostrate.[33]

Howell Harris was not sure how to restore good relations with the Wesleys after their earlier actions against the Calvinists. In October he decided to write a letter to John and Charles, reminding them of what they had in common with him and George Whitefield and urging a full reconciliation:

> I hope we have in some measure drank of the same Spirit, that we fight the same enemies, and are under the same crown and kingdom. We travel the same narrow road, and love the same Jesus ... Let us love one another. And if we really carry on the same cause, let us not weaken each other's hands.[34]

With that in mind he invited Charles to preach in the Calvinist societies in Wales, providing he did not preach against predestination. Charles accepted the invitation and travelled to join Harris in November 1740. He said he thought the Welsh people should recognize they had in Harris 'the greatest benefactor their country ever had'.[35]

Inevitably some Calvinists were not prepared to forget and forgive and Charles found himself at the receiving end of considerable criticism. He could not refrain from promoting that those who were saved still had to seek a life of Christian perfection. Harris begged the Welsh Methodists to be tolerant towards Charles who had 'not yet been delivered from a spirit of Railing',[36] but they thought friendship was colouring Harris' judgement.[37] In Cardiff an irate doctor struck Charles with his cane and would have inflicted severe harm had not others come to the rescue. In the resulting melée some women were injured and the doctor demanded the local magistrate arrest Charles for creating a disturbance. When the magistrate refused, the doctor spread tales that Charles was seeking to prevent people attending theatres. This led to the preaching house being surrounded by a company of irate actors, who threatened to burn the place down. Charles wrote that in response he and others 'prayed and sang with great tranquillity till one in the morning'.[38] One actor, armed with a sword, broke into the house but Charles later wrote the sight of the weapon just further kindled his faith!

Whitefield continued to write from America saying he did not want there to be any disputes: 'I dare not speak of the deep things of God in the spirit of a prize fighter or stage player.'[39] Charles agreed and defended allowing believers in predestination to play their role in the revival. He told Harris: 'I trust we shall never be two in time or eternity'[40] and invited him to speak to the Wesley-run societies in both Bristol and London. When some tried to make him condemn Harris' views on pre-destination, Charles refused, saying their 'hearts were knit together':

> I smiled at Satan's impudence ... [and refused] to enter the lists with my friend. I quashed all further importunity by declaring, 'I am un-willing to speak of my brother Howell Harris, because, when I begin, I know not how to lay off; and should say so much good of him, as some of you would not hear'.[41]

Unfortunately the young John Cennick was to shatter the reforged but still frail return to unity. The societies based in the New Room and at Kingswood owed much to Whitefield for their creation and the major-ity of their members were Calvinists. These were being encouraged by Whitefield's sister to refuse to attend society meetings if either Wesley was preaching. Cennick had no desire to be so confrontational, but he saw no reason why he should hide his dislike of the Wesleys' theological views. He personally believed it was impossible for the justified to fall from grace and, while he was an advocate for living according to the demands of Christ, he refused to accept the Wesleyan view that the saved had still to seek holiness or risk losing their salvation.

When Charles returned to Bristol from London at the end of Novem-ber, he was appalled by what Cennick was preaching:

> The poison of Calvin has drunk up their spirit of love ... Alas! We have set the wolf to keep the sheep! God give me great moderation to-ward him, who, for many months, has been undermining our doctrine and authority.[42]

He countered this by preaching that Christ died for all, but this led Cennick to publicly challenge him. It is easy to see why Charles now saw Cennick as another Molther who would eventually snatch control of the Bristol societies from them and drag them into dissent from the Church. According to Cennick, this led Charles to attack him when they dined together:

> [Charles] began to dispute about election. He fell into a violent passion and affrighted all at the table, and rising from the table, he said he would go directly and preach against me, and accordingly did. He called Calvin the first-born son of the devil and set all the people against me.[43]

Once he had calmed down, Charles tried a conciliatory gesture. He held a meeting with Cennick and 'offered to drop the controversy if he would'.[44] However, Cennick would not budge from his open defiance of Charles' views on universal redemption. On 6 December Charles wrote to his brother 'a full account' of his fears that the Calvinists were setting up a separate church.[45] He also wrote to Cennick to say how much he had abused his role as a son of the gospel:

> My dearest brother, John Cennick, – In much love and tenderness I speak. You came to Kingswood upon my brother sending for you. You served under him in the Gospel as a son. I need not say how well he loved you. You used the authority he gave you to overthrow his doctrine. You everywhere contradicted it ... [and] you have stolen the people's hearts from him ... We deserved [more] at your hands. I say 'we' for God is my witness how condescendingly loving I have been toward you ... I can only commit you to Him who hath commanded us to forgive one another, even as God, for Christ's sake, hath forgiven us.[46]

John hoped he could reconcile Charles and Cennick. He liked Cennick and recognized his popularity made challenging him dangerous. He travelled to Kingswood to repair 'the breaches which had been made ... [and] heal the jealousies and misunderstandings which had arisen'.[47] To his dismay he was treated very coldly by Cennick who had already written to Whitefield to beg him to return and take back command of the revival from the Wesleys. The letter, dated 17 January 1741, showed just how unhappy Cennick had become:

> How glorious did the gospel seem once to flourish in Kingswood! ... Now brother Charles is suffered to open his mouth against the truth,

while the frightened sheep gaze and fly, as if no shepherd was among
them ... Brother Charles pleases the world with universal redemption
and brother John follows him in everything. No atheists can preach
more against predestination than they; and all who believe election
are counted enemies of God, and called so ... If God give thee leave,
make haste.[48]

Whitefield wrote a letter to the Wesleys in which he defended Calvinism,
saying Christ's sacrifice was devalued if it was made effective only by
humanity's free will and that 'dooming millions to everlasting burnings
is not an act of injustice, because God, for the sin of Adam, might justly
have thus doomed all'.[49] He argued that anyone truly saved would live
a holy life so their fears about Calvinists living unholy lives were mis-
placed. This private letter mysteriously found its way into publication,
possibly via a copy sent to Cennick. The printed version was distributed
to members of the society at the Foundery on 1 February 1741. John
symbolically tore up a copy and leapt into print to refute it, describing its
contents as 'one of the greatest absurdities and impositions that folly or
impudence could invent ... a correspondence with evil'.[50] In reply John
Cennick, Howell Harris and Joseph Humphreys wrote in its defence. It
was no accident that it was at this time that John introduced the idea of
issuing tickets of membership to those in his societies and making the
tickets dependent on acceptance of his views.

On 22 February Cennick brought 20 like-minded society members
to petition John to change his attitude. John rebuked him for deceit-
fully generating division behind his back. That evening John used the
occasion of a love-feast at Kingswood to publicly denounce Cennick as
a troublemaker and, a few days later, he announced he was expelling
him from the society along with several of his closest associates. John
made clear the expulsion was not because of his Calvinism. It was a
punishment 'for talebearing, backbiting, and evil speaking' and 'for
dissembling, lying, and slandering'.[51] Joseph Humphreys was asked to
take Cennick's place as the Wesley's chief lay assistant and preacher,
but he refused and publicly burnt a copy of one of John's tracts against
predestination. Howell Harris begged everyone adopt a friendlier
stance:

I trust our Dear Lord will help us ... behave to each other in love ...
Let us then not quarrel ... I feel there remains, I hope, a spark of solid
love ... [When we] meet in love with simple minds, open to the truth,
weighing fully what is said on both sides, and praying much, we shall
be brought to see we aim at the same things.[52]

It was at this critical time that George Whitefield arrived back in England. His experiences in America had undoubtedly made him a stronger and more independent figure, so Howell Harris naturally looked to him to resolve the conflict:

> I think I love you more than any[one] ... as I see more of ... [Christ's] likeness in you, more of his love and meekness, humility and tenderness, and a greater deadness to all parties ... You must imagine these divisions must grieve God's Spirit.[53]

As far as Harris was concerned friendship could still end the dispute:

> Yesterday I breakfasted with ... [John and Charles] and we had a sweet fellowship together ... and parted in great love, being not so far distant in their doctrines as many expressions they drop [publicly] sometimes may seem we are. We must bear till the Light of the Gospel shines more clearly in their souls ... They spend and are spent for the Lord, and are faithful I believe according to their present Light.[54]

John initially refused to see Whitefield so Charles went instead. While their friendship was as strong as ever, both men soon recognized each was not prepared to surrender their theological views. Whitefield himself wrote: 'It would have melted any heart to have heard Mr Charles Wesley and me weeping after prayer that, if possible, the breach might be prevented.'[55] Whitefield was in a quandary. He genuinely felt the Wesleys had portrayed a warped picture of Calvinism and were jeopardizing the revival, yet he had no desire to publicly quarrel with the two men who had been most instrumental in his own conversion. It did not help him that he faced severe financial pressures to resolve the crisis as quickly as possible. He was deeply in debt for the work he had undertaken on his orphanage and his income from his writings had dried up because James Hutton, who had been the main publisher of his work, was refusing to have anything more to do with him as long as he remained friends with the anti-Moravian Wesleys.

It took Charles 11 days to persuade John to meet Whitefield in the hope they could resolve their differences. By then the Calvinists had told Whitefield he 'must not stand neuter any longer' and so he gave what appeared to John a frosty reception, refusing to shake hands and threatening to openly speak against what he and Charles were preaching. John responded by saying he would not permit Whitefield to preach at the Foundery or in the New Room. According to Harris, this devastated George: '[I found him] sick and vomiting, he wept with strong cryings and weeping.'[56] Whitefield told Charles that his heart bled within him over such a rejection. Years later Charles wrote of his regret over what had happened:

> What dire device did the old serpent find,
> To put asunder those whom God had joined?
> From folly and self-opinion rose,
> To sever friends who never yet were foes;
> To baffle and divert our noblest aim,
> Confound our pride, and cover us with shame.[57]

Three days later matters were made worse by the marriage of Elizabeth Delamotte, whom Whitefield loved, to the Moravian William Holland as a direct consequence of her parents' desire to disassociate themselves from the Wesleys and Methodism. For a long time Whitefield had admired Elizabeth, while avoiding 'the passionate expressions which carnal courtiers use',[58] and he had offered her marriage in a letter sent from America to her parents. They now deliberately married her off to Holland, who was still a member of the Fetter Lane Society. Here was painful proof of just how much the Wesleys' actions had divided those involved in the religious revival. Whitefield later commented of this time in his life: 'Busybodies on both sides blew up the coals. We harkened too much to tale bearers.'[59]

Whitefield turned for advice to John Cennick, Joseph Humphreys and another lay preacher called Robert Seagrave. They recommended the building of a wooden meeting house where Whitefield's followers could meet instead of attending the Foundery. Whitefield initially opposed this idea as 'erecting altar against altar'[60] but he was persuaded it was essential. The new 'Spa Fields Tabernacle' opened sometime in April 1741 with Whitefield still making it clear he had no desire to destroy the societies led by the Wesleys:

> My heart does not reproach me for my kindness and friendship to those who differ from me ... I would love all that love the Lord Jesus ... I have not given way to the Moravian brethren or to Mr Wesley ... but I think it best not to dispute when there is no probability of convincing.[61]

That same month saw Charles in full evangelical battle-mode in Bristol:

> The Spirit of power came down, the fountain was set open, my mouth and heart enlarged, and I spoke such words as I cannot repeat. Many

sank under the love of Christ crucified, and were constrained to break out, Christ died for us all.[62]

Sometimes he felt elated by his success. For example, he tells how on one occasion the converted wife of one collier at Kingswood with four of her children burst into a room where he was preaching and said, 'You have got the mother, take the bairns too!'[63] And it must have been encouraging to know that he and John had the increasing support of Selina, Countess of Huntingdon:

> Think what you are set for – the defence of the gospel. Trample on men and devils. The hour is hastening when it will be seen how faithful a Master we serve. Your arm shall be a bow of steel. Believe, believe, all is possible to him that believeth.[64]

However, Charles found predestination was like 'a millstone round the neck'[65] to many hearers of the gospel. He wrote of one extreme case in which a man who 'came home elect' felt so free of any moral constraints that he beat his wife, telling her 'if he killed her he could not be damned'.[66] In other cases, people struggled to believe in a God of love who damned many in advance to hell. Charles spent considerable time dealing with those who were sick. He hated to see how so many of the dying dreaded the prospect of meeting their maker because they were scared witless lest they were among those chosen to be damned. Without Calvinism to colour their judgement, the moment of death more often brought evidence of a Christian's 'holiness or absolute resignation or Christian perfection'.[67]

Despite this, neither he nor John ruled out continued co-operation between the two branches of Methodism. There is even some evidence to suggest Charles was prepared to also reopen contact with the Moravians because Molther had left England and Peter Böhler had returned. John met Böhler on 6 April and commented:

> I marvel how I refrain from rejoining these men. I scarce ever see any of them but my heart burns within me. I long to be with them; and yet I am kept from them.[68]

Charles was even more smitten because he looked to Böhler as the architect of his faith. Whitefield was also open to a general reconciliation. There is a story that a Calvinist asked him whether they would see John Wesley in heaven and Whitefield replied: 'I fear not because he will be so near the throne, and we shall we at such a distance, that we shall hardly get sight of him.'[69]

Samuel Wesley. Nineteenth-century engraving taken after frontispiece of one of his books. (New Room, Bristol)

Susanna Wesley. Engraving from an unknown portrait. (New Room, Bristol)

Samuel Wesley, Charles' brother. (Kingswood School Library).

John Wesley from painting in
Kingswood School Dining Hall

Charles as a student in Oxford.
Section of engraving from Marshall
Claxton's painting 'The Holy Club
in Session'. (New Room, Bristol)

George Whitefield as a young man
(Kingswood School Library)

Benjamin Ingham. Nineteenth-century print (Kingswood School Library)

Charles Wesley preaching to the Indians. Nineteenth-century print (New Room, Bristol)

Peter Boehler. Engraving from a drawing by Krugenstein (New Room, Bristol)

Selina, Countess of Huntingdon
Nineteenth-century print
(Kingswood School Library)

Howell Harris Undated print
(Kingswood School Library)

John Cennick. Undated print
(Kingswood School Library)

Interior of New Room, Bristol (Photograph: G. M. Best)

William Grimshaw from engraving
by J. Thomson in Methodist
Magazine 1821

The Foundery. An old print (New Room, Bristol)

Charles Wesley. Engraving by Jonathan Spilsbury, 1786

Sarah Gwynne Oil painting by John Russell c1749 (New Room, Bristol)

Charles in middle age. Nineteenth-century engraving (Kingswood School Library)

Charles Wesley's House, Bristol. (Photograph: G. M. Best)

John Fletcher Nineteenth-century engraving (Kingswood School Library)

The first Methodist Conference to be held in London 1779. It shows John and Charles and 446 preachers. Old print (Kingswood School Library)

Charles Wesley's son, Charles Portrait in No 4 Charles Street, Bristol (New Room, Bristol)

Charles Wesley's son Samuel Portrait in No 4 Charles Street, Bristol (New Room, Bristol)

Charles Wesley's daughter Sally

Charles in old age (New Room, Bristol)

**Medallion of John and Charles Wesley
in Westminster Abbey.** Executed in
marble by James Adams-Acton 1875
(Photo: G. M. Best)

Statue of Charles Wesley outside New Room, Bristol (Photo: G. M. Best)

Unfortunately for the cause of unity John Gambold and Westley Hall tried to encourage Charles to become a Moravian. A very agitated John Wesley wrote to Charles: 'O my brother, my soul is grieved for you; the poison is in you.'[70] When Charles drew back a little, some of the Moravians prevented him seeing the dying William Delamotte, whom he regarded almost like a son. Their cruel action rekindled all Charles' concerns about co-operating with theologically unsound allies. He published an account of the life and death of one of his converts, a woman called Hannah Richardson, in order to show what a true Christian believed and how this led to a life of service and commitment. A few years later he mourned how the Moravian movement had forced many of his friends to cut their ties with him and leave evangelical work in order to undertake lesser tasks:

I see their cruel Waste with streaming eyes,
And still my Soul in strong abhorrence cries. [71]

Charles and John turned from seeking unity to enhancing the spirituality of their followers. In May 1741 they decided to revive one of the traditions of the Holy Club and engage in a night of prayer prior to attending a Sunday service. They felt such 'watch-night services', lasting up to four hours, would prevent some of their members from spending their evening in less appropriate activities, such as drinking in the local pubs. John argued such services were part of the tradition of the Church, because the early Christians had held vigils and, when facing persecution, midnight assemblies. Being practically minded in an age when street lights were virtually non-existent, it was agreed watch-night services should occur when the moon was near its fullest to provide light for those attending them. Watch-night services were also introduced to the Foundery a year later.

Whitefield focused his efforts on the open-air preaching that was his forte. After five weeks London was sufficiently ringing with his name that he could afford to go to preach in Bristol and the surrounding area. When he arrived there he found he was very uncomfortable with what the Wesleys had been preaching, in particular John's encouragement of society members to seek perfection. Whitefield could not fathom how anyone could consider themselves perfect and bemoaned the pride of those that thought they were:

Today I talked with Brother N[owers]. He tells me that, for three months past, he has not sinned in thought, word, or deed. He says he is not only free from the power but from the very in-being of sin. He now asserts it is impossible for him to sin.[72]

In consequence Whitefield felt he had to pluck up what he called 'the sad tares' sown by John Wesley, even if this caused offence to Charles.

Charles makes only one reference to Whitefield's appearance in Bristol. He describes how one of the loyal society members at Kingswood informed him that Whitefield was preaching 'barefaced reprobation'. Charles said he thought it hugely hypocritical to frighten people with the thought of eternal damnation and then offer the hope of salvation to all while believing only a select few could be saved:

> Vain and empty offers indeed! ... He did not believe them all elect; he could not; therefore he only mocked them with an empty word of invitation ... God, according to his scheme, sent him to deceive the greatest part of mankind.[73]

Despite Charles' opinion, George's preaching proved irresistible and soon Bristol was more firmly pro-Whitefield than pro-Wesley. Only the New Room members remained largely loyal to the Wesleys. Whitefield reported 'at Bristol error is in a great measure put a stop to'.[74] Unable to match his preaching, John began producing an endless succession of publications to present his and Charles' arguments.

Even now reconciliation might have been possible, had not Whitefield been threatened with imprisonment for his debts. He felt compelled to question whether the societies in Bristol did not owe him some money because he had helped purchase the site for the preaching house in Kingswood. John Wesley was furious. He felt that the Bristol societies were entirely a product of his and Charles' personal endeavours. The money originally contributed by Whitefield to the start of the work in Kingswood had only amounted to less than a quarter of the cost. Nevertheless, two-thirds of the membership in Kingswood sided with Whitefield and only John's technical ownership of the building stopped them taking control of it. Cennick began building a rival preaching house and school which, like that in London, became known as 'Whitefield's Tabernacle'.

Whitefield returned to London where he found the press was making much of the disputes within Methodism. The *Gentleman's Magazine*, for example, commented:

> Mr Whitefield tells his auditors that, if they follow Mr Wesley's doctrines, they will be damned, eternally damned ... [while] Mr Wesley tells his congregations that, if they follow Mr Whitefield, it will bring all to distraction and confusion ... Now here is oracle against oracle.[75]

He reluctantly began looking for a new man as his deputy to replace John and Charles. He selected Howell Harris. Together they planned how a nationwide preaching tour by Whitefield might lead to a major religious revival. To coincide with this they planned creating a weekly paper to promote Whitefield's views because publicity had been a major factor in the success of Whitefield in America.

The resulting *Weekly History* not only publicized the work of Whitefield and other leading evangelicals but also encouraged the converted to communicate news of what was happening across the country. Up to 80 per cent of its content became letters and reading these out became a feature of many societies. In this way Methodism rapidly gained more awareness of itself as a national and international movement. The fact that the postal system was gradually becoming more effective encouraged this trend still further. By 1743 Joseph Humphreys was able to write a hymn in which he gave thanks to God for what was happening region by region in England, Wales and Scotland, and for successes in America and the Moravian missions in Africa and Greenland. This hymn praised the work of all three types of evangelical 'Methodist': the Calvinists led by Whitefield and Harris, the Arminians led by John and Charles Wesley, and the Moravians led by Count Zinzendorf and Benjamin Ingham. This is not surprising because Humphreys, like Whitefield, was keen to restore unity to the religious revival.

While planning his evangelical campaign, Whitefield made conciliatory gestures towards the Wesleys. He publicly agreed that both the New Room and Kingswood belonged to the Wesleys; he stopped publishing his journal and any other printed matter that might generate theological conflict; he ceased to preach against John Wesley's views on Christian perfection; and he told his supporters to make no attempt to argue with either the Wesleyans or Moravians. It has been suggested that Whitefield's decision to travel widely rather than focusing his efforts in London and the other traditional centres of his work was a product in part of his wish not to be associated with causing dissension among existing societies:

> It is best for the gospel minister, simply and powerfully to preach those truths he has been taught of God, and to meddle as little as possible with those who are children of God, though they should differ in many things. This would keep the heart sweet, and at the same time not betray the truths of Jesus.[76]

In June 1741 Charles engaged in his own gesture of reconciliation and invited Howell Harris to preach to the Wesleyan society members at

Kingswood. This proved a mistake. Harris could not prevent displaying his Calvinist views in his preaching and he refused to stop when Charles tried to interrupt him. Charles appealed to the congregation who began singing 'as the voice of so many waters, or mighty thunderings' to drown Harris' voice. Harris understandably felt he was being driven out. Charles denied this, saying he had to cease preaching but he could stay as 'a child of God'. When Howell still tried to defend his Calvinist thinking, Charles had the congregation sing:

Praise God, from whom pure blessings flow,
Whose bowels yearn on all below;
Who would not have one sinner lost;
Praise Father, Son, and Holy Ghost.

He then took over the preaching from Harris.[77]

Charles' journal at this time implies he had to battle with the issue of predestination on a regular basis among the dying. For example, in July he visited a dying woman to give her comfort and was reviled for his pains because she said she knew she was destined for hell. In this case he prayed with her and changed her view of the matter before she died: 'God gave us a faint spark of hope.'[78] In the same month he met another woman who believed herself destined to be one of the saved and he commented that never before had he met anyone so 'full of pride, and self, and the devil'.[79] As a result Charles reluctantly concluded: 'I cannot allow them Christ's righteousness for a cloak to their sins',[80] and put his faith before his friendship with Whitefield. He published a book of hymns called *Hymns of God's Everlasting Love* which were specifically designed to counter Calvinist thinking:

Father of mankind, whose love
In Christ for all is free
Thou hast sent Him from above
To bring us all to Thee;
Thou hast every heart inclined
Christ the Saviour to embrace.[81]

Charles also wrote to John in September 1741, urging him to be wary of succumbing to the influence of Whitefield's powerful preaching:

[He] wraps up ... [his Calvinist views] in smoother language than before, in order to convey the poison more successfully. Our Society, on this account, go to hear him, without any scruple or dread. We have sufficiently seen the fatal effects of this devilish doctrine already, so that we cannot keep at too great a distance from it ... Do you know the value of souls! Precious, immortal souls! Yet trust them within the sound of predestination? ... I shall on the first preaching night renounce George Whitefield on the house-top.[82]

Nevertheless, Charles could not entirely forget past friendship. In that same September he defended John Cennick against a local magistrate who was encouraging attacks upon the Calvinist meeting-house. He said he could not believe that a magistrate might turn a blind eye to such violence when it was known that Cennick was encouraging the miners to become more law-abiding citizens:

> We work the works of God ... [Those] who spent all their wages at the alehouse, now never go there at all, but keep their money to maintain their families; and have to give to those in want. Notorious swearers have now only the praises of God in their mouths. The good done among them is indisputable: our worst enemies cannot deny it. None who hears us continues either to swear or drink.[83]

Trying to build on this gesture, Howell Harris wrote letters to Charles and John, as well as George, asking them to rekindle their friendship and regain the revival's lost unity of purpose. John showed some signs of softening his stance, but Charles now proved the sticking block. His experience of caring for the dying had entirely convinced him there could be no compromise over the issue of predestination. Moreover, Charles felt it was time he and John publicly reaffirmed their loyalty to the Church of England. That same month of October he persuaded Selina, Countess of Huntingdon, who had become a strong personal friend, to publicly renounce any connection with Ingham and the Moravians. Selina told John:

> I comfort myself very much that you will approve ... declaring open war with them ... Your brother is to give his reasons for quite separating ... [and] I have great faith God will not let him fall ... His natural parts, his judgment, and the improvement he has made, are so far above the highest of them.[84]

While all this was happening Whitefield's main focus was a preaching tour of Scotland from July through to the end of October 1741. Scotland offered a Calvinist an easy time for the country was deeply rooted in its Presbyterian background. Moreover, for years the more evangelically minded had been running 'societies for prayer' to meet for Bible study and to organize Christian assistance to the poor and sick. Whitefield's extensive tour gave him contact with the bulk of the population. Among those who came to hear him were many nobles of high rank, such as the Earl of Leven, who was His Majesty's Commissioner to the General Assembly of the Church of Scotland. Towards the end of the highly successful tour Whitefield received the good news that John Wesley had been persuaded by Howell Harris to meet him in London. He was also told that Charles was still speaking fondly of him. A delighted Whitefield wrote to John:

> Reverend and Dear brother ... I humbly ask pardon. I love you as much as ever ... May God remove all obstacles that now prevent our union! ... May all disputings cease, and each of us talk nothing but Jesus, and Him crucified! This is my resolution.[85]

In November Whitefield headed for Bristol for talks with the Wesleys. Unfortunately John was not well and so their discussions were more curtailed than might otherwise have been the case. Whitefield decided he had time to attend to other important business – his marriage to a widow called Elizabeth James. She was almost ten years older than him and not particularly attractive, but she was honest and kind and deeply religious. For a long time she had been viewed as a potential wife for Howell Harris, who loved her deeply, but Harris had eventually concluded his Christian commitment made marriage undesirable. She seems to have been willing to transfer her affections to Whitefield, who thought her sufficiently 'a true child of God' to pose no threat to his constant travelling.[86] They were married on 14 November at St Martin's Chapel, near Caerphilly, in the presence of Harris, who afterwards wrote:

> The Lord knows ... with what a heart-breaking I gave her up, though with a resigned will ... God had intended her for another to make her more happy than she would likely be with me.[87]

That same month Benjamin Ingham secretly married Lady Margaret Hastings. When news of this eventually leaked out it scandalized high society. They thought it was monstrous that lowly born Methodists should be telling the aristocracy that they had 'a heart as sinful as the common wretches that crawl upon the earth'[88] and then marry one of their number. Such was the reaction that it forced Selina, Countess of Huntingdon, to come to her sister-in-law's defence. This was gradually to lead to a reconciliation between her and Ingham, much to the concern of the Wesleys, who did not wish to see her move away from them. She had become an important if occasional visitor to the Foundery.

It was in January 1742 that the Countess of Huntingdon first heard Thomas Maxfield preach. Expecting to be bored, she was stunned by his impact on her:

> He is one of the greatest instances of God's peculiar favour that I know ... You can have no idea what an attachment I have to him. He is highly favoured of the Lord ... His power in prayer is very extraordinary.[89]

She began personally endorsing the use of gifted laymen, even subsequently encouraging her coach driver, a man named David Taylor, to participate in the village services around her home at Donington. He was to have a widespread preaching career in Derbyshire, Yorkshire and Cheshire, working initially with Benjamin Ingham and later with John Wesley. It was inevitable that the clergy would object strongly to the increased use of 'unlettered mechanics' by the Methodists. Dr Joseph Trapp, a former Chaplain to the Lord Chancellor of Ireland, said the use of lay people to even read prayers was 'neither laudable nor justifiable', and allowing them to preach promoted 'absurd doctrines'.[90]

It was in such a hostile atmosphere that Whitefield launched a new open-air campaign in London in the spring of 1742. One of his first acts was to hear Charles preach but he afterwards confessed that their subsequent meeting was not as good as either of them had hoped: 'I would meet more than half-way; but we are all too shy.'[91] Unfortunately there were many among the associates of the Wesleys who were prepared to question whether Whitefield was genuine in his approaches to them. In February Whitefield visited Selina, Countess of Huntingdon, to enlist her backing for a move towards unity. Her loyalty to the Wesleys made her cautious. She subsequently told John that Whitefield had talked very sensibly but had wrongly tried to charm her by saying she was one of the elect. Nevertheless, the Countess did question whether it was necessary for Charles to call the Calvinists 'Priests of Moloch', a phrase which had 'much provoked' and upset Whitefield.[92]

It was not until March that John Wesley finally deigned to properly reply to the letters Whitefield had been regularly sending since their split. The letter is lost but Whitefield's reply indicates that he felt Charles' attitude was still the stumbling block to the two branches of Methodism working together. He told John that the only group to benefit from this would be the Moravians and urged John to use his influence with his brother because he would accept no contact with George: 'He is too shy of me.'[93] John met up with Whitefield in April and spent 'an agreeable hour' but was adamant that he was not prepared to disguise his obvious theological differences with the Calvinists. He subsequently concluded: 'I am just as I was. I go on my way, whether he goes with me or stays behind.'[94]

The tragedy was that both Whitefield and the Wesleys shared the same passion to overcome the evils of a country in turmoil. Britain was still essentially a rural society but already industrialization was beginning to move many into the towns, where they had no roots and where no one took responsibility for their needs, both physical and spiritual. Whitefield reached new heights of power with the downtrodden masses in London, despite an assassination attempt on him while he was preaching at Moorfields on 20 April. That same month Charles angrily attacked the failure of the established Church in a sermon delivered before the University of Oxford. By its failure to proclaim the gospel it was dooming many a sinner 'to live and die without the image of God ... [not knowing he is] on the brink of the pit, in the jaws of everlasting destruction', and it was allowing the country as a whole to be dominated by evil speaking, drunkenness, sexual licence, oppression and injustice:

> How much anger and pride, how much sloth and idleness, how much softness and effeminacy, how much luxury and self-indulgence, how much covetousness and ambition, how much thirst of praise, how much love of the world ... is to be found![95]

The Wesleys decided it was time to preach their own views nationwide. The man who triggered this was a Yorkshire stonemason in his 30s called John Nelson, who had travelled to London for work. He heard John preach his first sermon at Moorfields and it had hit immediately home: 'I thought his whole discourse was aimed at me.'[96] Sacked by his employer for becoming a Methodist and refusing to work on Sundays, Nelson had returned home, only to find that his own family saw his newfound faith as an embarrassment:

> They begged I would not tell any one that my sins were forgiven; for no one would believe me; and they should be ashamed to show their faces in the street.[97]

Despite this, Nelson began working with Benjamin Ingham, helping initiate Methodist societies in Leeds, Manchester, Sheffield and York. Now he wanted John Wesley to visit him and assist his work in his hometown of Birstall.

John travelled northwards in May 1742, thus committing him and his brother to a wider role than London and Bristol. John said he was impressed by what 'the artless testimony of one plain man' (i.e. Nelson) had achieved and he preached to several hundreds from the top of Birstall Hill and on Dewsbury Moor. The Countess of Huntingdon urged John to journey further and take the gospel message to the most important English city in the north: Newcastle-upon-Tyne. She even sent one of her protégés called John Taylor, the brother of her evangelical coach driver, to accompany him.

The two men arrived in Newcastle on 28 May and were shocked by the depravity and deprivation they saw everywhere. At 7.00 am on a Sunday morning they took themselves to Sandgate, 'the poorest and most contemptible part of the town', and began singing a psalm. A crowd began to gather and, as Wesley started preaching, this grew until an estimated 1,500 were listening. When he finished, he told them his name and announced he would preach again at 5.00 in the afternoon. Twenty thousand people gathered to hear him. It was by far the largest crowd he had ever addressed and it convinced him that Newcastle should become the third centre of his and Charles' work. John purchased land to build a preaching-house on similar lines to the New Room and Foundery. He called it 'the Orphan House', a name possibly chosen to rival Whitefield's 'Orphan House' in Georgia. Charles declared that he foresaw 'the rude populous north' yielding a greater harvest than either London or Bristol.

While John was in Newcastle, Whitefield was undertaking another preaching tour in Scotland. This included visiting a place called Cambuslang near Glasgow in July. The parish had been experiencing a religious revival following Whitefield's earlier Scottish tour thanks to the efforts of a minister called William McCulloch. On this occasion Whitefield agreed not only to preach but also to hold a communion service in two specially erected tents. By his reckoning over 20,000 turned up for this open-air event. A second communion service was planned for August. People walked many miles to attend and this time there were over 30,000 present. Although there were three tents, it took from 8.30 in the morning to sunset to serve communion to everyone. One witness records that Whitefield was 'so filled with the love of God as to be in a kind of ecstasy ... but the thing most remarkable was the ... gracious and sensible presence of God'.[98] For once the Wesleys would have been delighted because of the importance they attached to the communion service as a way of receiving God's grace.

It did not take long for tracts to appear attacking what had happened at Cambuslang as the product of mass hysteria. Whitefield was described

as a 'mountebank' and 'damned rascal' who was driving people insane.
In reply William McCulloch interviewed many of those who had been
present and recorded their responses. These indicate that many of those
who attended were Christians with a long-standing knowledge of the
Bible. What Whitefield had conveyed to them was that they could know
whether they were saved and by all accounts this had a long-lasting
impact on those who attended at Cambuslang. Nine years later its
minister wrote:

> This work ... embraced all classes, all ages, and all moral conditions.
> Cursing, swearing and drunkenness were given up by those who came
> under its power. It kindled remorse for acts of injustice. It won for-
> giveness from the vengeful ... It bound pastors and people together
> with a stronger bond of sympathy. It raised an altar in the household
> ... It made men students of the Word of God and brought them in
> thought and purpose and effort into communion with their Father in
> heaven.[99]

This was exactly what Methodism was meant to achieve.

Both George Whitefield and John Wesley publicized their activities but
Charles was much less of a self-propagandist. Understandably therefore
historians have tended to underrate his contribution. This is particularly
true in 1742 because he provides no information in his journal at all. Yet
from other sources we can infer that, in addition to producing a fifth
volume of hymns, Charles was very busy travelling in his brother's wake,
preaching throughout the Midlands and the North, including preaching
in Oxford, Leeds and Newcastle. It was probably around this time that
his friendship with John Nelson took shape and, as far as we can tell, the
two men corresponded regularly with each other over the next 30 years.
Charles travelled by horse and he used the time to compose the heartfelt
hymns for which he is now best known:

> My heart is full of Christ, and longs
> Its glorious matter to declare.
> My ready tongue makes haste to sing
> The glories of my heavenly King.[100]

One historian has written of Charles' hymnwriting that 'the hoof-beats
hammered out the rhythm of the song as it shaped itself in his brain'.[101]

Singing hymns had not yet become a feature of most church worship and some people were ashamed to admit they liked the practice.
For example, the Moravian Martha Claggett confessed she sang them

only when no one else was around! However, Charles was convinced of the benefits of hymn-singing. He was told by one convert, Elizabeth Downs, that when she sang hymns she felt her heart was being torn out of her body so strong was their impact.[102] Like John, Charles thought the words of hymns mattered more than the tunes. For that reason John complained whenever he found societies using tunes he deemed too complex or too repetitively banal. He told Methodists to 'attend strictly to the sense of what you sing'.[103] Consequently the Methodist hymnbooks were to become increasingly filled with what Charles produced, especially as he could convey the brothers' theological thinking more effectively by his hymns than John could by his prose.

Amid all the excitement of the summer of 1742, three events cast their shadow over the Wesleys. The first was the departure from the mission field of two of their former companions, Benjamin Ingham and John Gambold. In July 1742 Ingham decided to abandon his evangelical work in favour of becoming a teacher in a Moravian school. Not all his 50 or so societies survived his departure and those that did remained Moravian even if the outside world called them Methodist. John Gambold was also encouraged to cease his evangelical ministry and take up running a Moravian school in Essex. Charles felt this was ridiculous, given Gambold's many talents:

> He sinks with such a weight of blessings crown'd,
> And buries his ten talents in the ground,
> Bids country, friends, and Church, and state, farewell,
> Skulks in a widow's house, – and teaches girls to spell![104]

However, even more distressing at a personal level was the death of Robert Jones, who had been a particularly close friend of Charles since they were both students at Christ Church, Oxford. Jones had transformed the dining room in his family home at Fonmon Castle (in Glamorganshire) into a Methodist chapel for use by the Wesleys. Charles wrote a lengthy poem to commemorate him:

> Constrain'd by ecstasies too strong to bear,
> His soul was all pour'd out in praise and prayer ...[105]

In July 1742 a greater blow struck. Susanna Wesley became terminally ill. Living at the Foundery had proved a mixed blessing in that it had brought her closer to her daughters' problems. She had been deeply distressed by the untimely death of Kezzy in March 1741 and she had been increasingly worn down by having to witness at first hand the misery of four of her other daughters because only Ann was happily married (to a highly successful land surveyor in Hatfield). Sukey was hiding in London from her ex-husband, Richard Ellison; Emily was separated from Robert Harpur and dependent on her brothers' charity; Martha was seeing the first signs that Westley Hall was both a bigot and a philanderer; and Hetty was enduring the torture of her marriage to William Wright, who was shunning her in favour of drinking and worse among 'the scum and refuse of the earth'.[106]

The many years of childbearing and hardship at Epworth finally caught up with Susanna and she collapsed. John and most of her daughters were with her when she died. John wrote to Charles, who had been unable to get back in time:

> I found her pulse almost gone, and her fingers dead, so that it was easy to see her spirit was on the wing for eternity ... I sat down on her bedside, and with three or four of our sisters, sang a requiem to her parting soul. She continued in just the same way as my father was, struggling and gasping for life ... till near four o'clock ... When she called me again to her bedside ... the soul was set at liberty, without one struggle, or groan, or sigh ... She had the faith of God's elect.[107]

The Countess of Huntingdon, who had grown to know and admire Susanna, sent the brothers her deepest condolences.

Her funeral at Bunhill Fields, City Road was attended by masses of people and, after Susanna's body had been committed to the ground near the grave of John Bunyan, John spoke from the text in the book of Revelation on how 'the books were opened and the dead were judged ... according to their works'. Her gravestone was inscribed with words written by Charles, though his grief made him incapable of producing his best verse:

> True daughter of affliction, she
> Inured to pain and misery,
> Mourned a long night of grief and tears,
> A legal night of seventy years ...
> In sure and certain hope to rise
> And claim her mansion in the skies,
> A Christian here her flesh laid down,
> The cross exchanging for a crown.[108]

Charles and John knew their mother had been pleased by the expansion of their influence beyond Bristol and London to many societies in Somerset, Wiltshire, Gloucestershire, Leicestershire, Warwickshire, Nottinghamshire and Yorkshire. But they were acutely aware that their achievement did not match that of Whitefield. He was running over 30 Methodist Societies and over 20 preaching places, scattered not just across the Midlands (Buckinghamshire, Oxfordshire, Warwickshire, Staffordshire and Shropshire), but also the South-East (Essex and Kent) and the South-West (Gloucestershire, Wiltshire, Somerset, Devon, Cornwall). More significantly, he had a wider circle of ministers prepared to support him than the Wesleys and his team of lay preachers or 'exhorters' was stronger, including exceptionally able men of the calibre of Howell Harris, John Cennick and Joseph Humphreys. It numbered 50 by 1748.

For that reason John made tentative approaches to both Cennick and Harris, saying he judged the theological differences between Calvinist and Arminian thinking no longer reason for disharmony:

> Let us rise up together against the evil-doers; let us not weaken but strengthen one another's hands in God. My brother, my soul is gone forth to meet thee; let us fall upon one another's neck. The good Lord blot out all that is past, and let there henceforward be peace between me and thee![109]

He said he could never accept that anyone was preordained to be damned, but he did not entirely disagree with the Calvinist concept that some were specially chosen to be saved because God had given preordained roles to certain individuals such as the apostle Paul.

Cennick was receptive. He told Whitefeld's wife that he had had a vision 'that it would be right in the sight of God that all our preachers, all Mr Wesley's, and all the Moravian brethren should meet together ... as the apostles did'.[110] Howell Harris agreed:

> [I am] dead to all parties, and only a member of Christ['s body], and would wish we had no names among us but that of a Christian ... When prejudice falls away and in love we weigh and ask each other's meaning ... [our differences are] not as great as by some expressions it may seem.[111]

However, a proposed reconciliation meeting never happened, almost certainly because John had second thoughts. It was left to Whitefield to be the one who most consistently tried over the coming years to heal the breach with the Wesleys.

Typical of his approach was a special service in the London Spa Fields Tabernacle on 8 November to celebrate what all the evangelicals were achieving in both Britain and America. It is easy to see why Charles recognized his friend's pre-eminent role in the revival:

> He lets his Light on all impartial shine,
> And strenuously asserts the Birth divine,
> While Thousands listen to th'alarming Song,
> And catch conviction darted from his Tongue.
> Parties and Sects their ancient Feuds forget,
> And fall and tremble at the Preacher's feet ...
> Meek, patient, humble, wise above years
> Unbrib'd by Pleasures, and unmov' by Fears,
> From strength to strength the young Apostle goes,
> Pours like a Torrent, and the Land o'erflows ...[112]

The strength of Whitefield's societies has been often underplayed because of the later success of the Wesleys, yet contemporaries saw him as a great organizer. In January 1743 he was invited to become the moderator of the Welsh Calvinists and three months later he united the English and Welsh strands of the religious revival into 'the Calvinistic Methodist Association' and became its moderator with Howell Harris as his deputy. Whitefield divided his movement into four associations, each headed by a superintendent, and these met four times a year to report and plan. He adopted the Wesleyan policy of having classes as well as bands and he stressed the importance of charitable activities. Thus the Tabernacle in London ran both a school for boys and one for girls and operated schemes to offer help to the poor. There was even a scheme to help find work for the unemployed. The Tabernacle also insisted on its members having membership tickets which were renewed every three months only if the member had lived what was judged a Christian life.

It was to be another 18 months before the Wesleys were able to achieve anything remotely comparable to what Whitefield had achieved in terms of their societies. One recent historian has commented that John's 'much vaunted genius for organization turns out upon closer inspection to have been a ragbag of pragmatic innovations' borrowed from others.[113] Nor did he or Charles have the respect Whitefield was slowly gaining within the ranks of the aristocracy. Two of the most celebrated social figures of the day, Sarah, Duchess of Marlborough, and Catherine, Duchess of Buckingham, were prepared to hear Whitefield preach, and so too was even royalty itself in the form of Frederick, Prince of Wales, and his brother, William Augustus, Duke of Cumberland.

None of this stopped Charles agreeing with John that they had to avoid the 'plague' of Calvinism:

No: while the Breath of GOD these limbs sustains,
Or flows one Drop of Blood within these Veins,
War, endless War, with Satan's Scheme I make,
Full vengeance on the hellish Doctrine take,
Its sworn, eternal Foe, for my own Whitefield's sake![114]

What neither they nor Whitefield could foresee was that Methodism in all its forms was about to face persecution on a massive scale because all their activities were shortly to be judged a cover to raise support for a Jacobite rebellion.

7

Jacobite Allegations

Thanks be to God, the God of power,
Who shelter'd us in danger's hour;
The God of truth, who heard the prayer,
Let all his faithfulness declare ...

His eye observed the dark design,
To blast our rightful monarch's line,
The scheme in Satan's conclave laid,
Improv'd by Rome's unerring head,
To gall us with their yoke abhorr'd,
And plant their faith with fire and sword.

He saw the serpent's egg break forth,
The cloud arising in the north,
He let the slighted mischief spread,
And hang in thunder o'er our head;
And while we scorn'd our abject foes,
The drop into a torrent rose ...

Drunk with the bold aspiring hope,
Behold them march triumphant up;
Of conquest fatally secure,
They vow to make our ruin sure ...

Who was it then dispersed the snare,
And choked those ravening dogs of war?
Jehovah curb'd their furious speed,
Jehovah sent the panic dread,
And damp'd and fill'd them with dismay,
And scared the vultures from their prey ...[1]

By 1743 Charles was part of the inner circle attached to Selina, Countess
of Huntingdon, although this group contained some well-known dis-

senters, including Isaac Watts, then the leading hymnwriter of his day. The countess preferred to invite Charles rather than John because she found him a more empathetic listener when she shared any of her family troubles. John was brusquer in manner and tended to ignore the social niceties – hence his dislike of Charles' insistence that the countess should have her own special seat at the Foundery whenever she attended. Selina urged far more extensive nationwide preaching. The laying of the foundation stone for the Orphan House in Newcastle in January 1743 was in a sense a symbol of the Wesley brothers' readiness to undertake this – and in that month John preached in a huge number of places, including Doncaster and Sheffield, Evesham and Stratford, and Reading and Windsor.

Realizing the task of evangelism required more helpers, John began increasing the number of 'sons of the Gospel'. He appointed at least 40 in the early 1740s and they were drawn from all walks of life and all parts of the country. Each was given a probationary period of one year to prove his worth. Their role was succinctly defined as being: '1. To invite. 2. To convince. 3. To offer Christ; and, lastly, 4. To build up – and to do this in some measure in every sermon.'[2] John said they should study the scriptures, have a clear understanding of salvation by faith, and serve God before all else by setting an example of Christian witness in both word and deed. He also advised them on how to stay healthy while constantly travelling. He recommended cleanliness and not using tobacco ('an uncleanly and unwholesome self-indulgence'), snuff ('a silly, nasty, dirty custom') or spirits ('a sure though slow poison').[3] The preachers were all told to be 'serious, weighty and solemn' in their preaching and to keep to simple texts suited to their audience, avoiding affected gestures and pointless digressions. Above all, they had to speak from the heart.[4] John wrote: 'My test of a preacher is when his congregation go away saying, not, "What a beautiful sermon", but, "I will do something".'[5]

Charles was gravely concerned at this radical increase in lay preachers because he rightly recognized it would decrease the likelihood of other clergy joining them. John tried to appease him by continuously laying down ever-stricter guidelines on their behaviour:

Be diligent. Never be unemployed a moment, never be triflingly employed, never while away time ... Be serious ... [and] avoid all lightness as you would avoid hell-fire ... Touch no woman [but] be as loving as you can ... Believe evil of no one ... Put the best construction on everything ... Speak evil of no one ... [but] tell everyone what you think wrong in him and that plainly ... Do not affect the gentleman

... [because] you are the servant of all ... Be ashamed of nothing but sin ... Take no money of anyone ... Act in all things not according to your own will but as a son in the gospel.[6]

Whatever Charles' misgivings, the role of the lay preachers in spreading Methodism cannot be underestimated. A pattern was established by which John and Charles acted as both the promoter of societies founded by these preachers and the means of checking they stayed theologically sound. In this process three kinds of lay preacher emerged. First, there were the full-time itinerants who travelled around the country. Second, there were those preachers who lived and worked primarily in one area but who occasionally undertook to travel further afield. Third, there were those 'local preachers' who worked in their spare time in their home area only. Men often moved from one category of preacher to another according to their personal or family circumstances, although John often assigned preachers to particular places. Each full-time preacher was expected to undertake at least five hours per day of study, alongside his evangelical endeavours. Some had independent means but most relied on voluntary giving or working part-time. From 1752 there was a yearly clothing allowance and other allowances followed with a Preachers' Fund being eventually created.

In 1743 John's itinerary included 14 weeks in London, 10 weeks in Bristol, 13 weeks in Newcastle, and 15 weeks elsewhere (ranging from Cornwall to the far north). Virtually all his travelling was done on horseback and he filled his saddlebags with books to read as he rode, allowing his horse a slack rein so it could judge the best route across the terrain he was crossing. He slept and ate wherever he could and remained very philosophical about the hardships he endured, saying it was wrong to be rendered unhappy by 'a dinner ill dressed, or hard bed, a poor room, a shower of rain, or a dusty road'. It did not matter to him whether he stayed in a stately home or slept for a fortnight on the floor of a fisherman's cottage. Sometimes friends accompanied him, but they often found his pace too demanding.

When Charles chooses to write about what he was doing, it reveals a man just as active and important – indeed he was more prone than John to go into new areas. Like his brother, he preached indoors in any home, meeting house or church prepared to have him, but was frequently forced to speak in the open, often choosing hills and hollows so that his voice would carry further. In towns he preached in the streets and in yards attached to houses, shops, inns and churches. In villages he often chose the village green or square, but he also spoke in fields, meadows, orchards and gardens. In coastal regions, he spoke on the beaches and

on the cliffs. Often Charles was overjoyed by the positive response he
received but occasionally he was angered by the wealthy who refused to
listen:

> Hear ye this and tremble, you who have turned your back upon a
> Saviour! For to you am I sent to cry aloud and spare not, to lift up
> my voice like a trumpet, and show you your transgressions and your
> sins. How shall you escape who have neglected so great salvation! ...
> Repent therefore of your wickedness.[7]

The difficulty inherent in itinerant preaching should not be underestimated. There were no canals or railways and even the roads were few
and badly created. Some were no more than shifting sand or mud. Even
the main highways were full of deep ruts and, in wet weather, it was easy
for vehicles either to get stuck or be unable to pass each other because
the road surface had become a quagmire. Often roads were made totally
impassable for days or even weeks by flooding or by snow and ice. There
were no lights at night and so it was easy to go astray because there was
little to distinguish the road from the common land. Highwaymen and
thieves made some journeys particularly dangerous and these men were
often far more violent and cruel than they appear in romantic legend.
Most people tried to avoid travelling whenever they could so for the
Wesleys and their preachers to embrace it was testimony to both their
commitment and their courage.

Charles was surprised by the extent of the hostility shown to Methodists but this arose from the movement having all the appearance of a
separatist dissenting church. Most clergy depicted John and Charles as
self-righteous hypocrites who were encouraging people to spend their
time in religious activities that were really the domain of the clergy. They
falsely accused them of encouraging a disrespect for authority, alleging,
for example, they persuaded workmen not to work for their masters.
The less well educated among the clergy were often in the poorest parishes, and these were the areas most targeted by Methodist preachers.
Living as they did often on the verge of poverty, such clergy were swift to
denounce anything that was seen to challenge their livelihood and prone
to believe any misguided rumour.

Clergy who resented Methodist incursions into their parishes could
quickly rouse a volatile populace who were uneducated and unused to
strangers by alleging they were agents of the devil. Rioting was a pretty
regular occurrence at the best of times, although mobs had a tendency
to back down in the face of anyone who exuded authority and bravely
stood up to them. How violent the mob became often relied on how

much the local magistrate was or was not prepared to turn a blind eye to what was happening. Unfortunately for the Methodist preachers, magistrates were not likely to support them in the event of a riot because arguably they were breaking the law by encouraging meetings. The gathering together of working people was specifically banned by Parliament at this time and the Toleration Act only covered premises that were officially licensed as being places of worship for dissenters.

Magistrates viewed Methodist gatherings as particularly suspicious at this time because there was a serious concern that any unauthorized meetings might be a cover for rekindling support for the Jacobite cause. Following the failed attempt of James II's son to regain the British throne in 1715, 'the Old Pretender' (as the Whig party contemptuously called James III) had become just 'the king over the water'. However, his son, Bonnie Prince Charlie, was a far more charismatic figure and the international situation in the early 1740s created the potential for a second Jacobite attempt to replace the Hanoverian dynasty. A new generation of warmongering political leaders had been encouraged by George II in his capacity as Elector of Hanover to engage in a European war over the succession of a woman, Maria Theresa, to the Austrian throne. The war had been initiated in 1740 by the Protestant Frederick II of Prussia, who challenged Maria's right to also become the Holy Roman Emperor, a role associated with Catholicism's political control of central Europe. The initial success of his armies had encouraged France to back the Catholic Elector of Bavaria in putting himself forward as an alternative emperor in 1741. George II had then brought Britain into the war on Austria's side.

The German origins of George II and his use of British forces to defend Hanoverian interests inevitably led some to question whether Bonnie Prince Charlie would not make a better king. In the heightened state of concern among government circles, it was soon rumoured that Methodist activities might be a cover for treason. This is not surprising. All three of the Wesley brothers had attended Oxford University and become High Churchmen, a combination known to generate Jacobitism. Samuel's support for the traitorous Bishop of Rochester had not been forgotten, nor young Charles' defence of a Jacobite boy at school. John had links with Jonathan Colley, the Precentor of Christ Church College, a diehard Tory of strong Jacobite sympathies. As early as 1739 the famed gambler, Beau Nash, had tried to block John entering Bath on the grounds his activities were a cover for promoting political unrest. Charles and John were also known to be in friendly contact with Dr Byrom, the inventor of a secret system of shorthand and author of a famous epigram:

God bless our Lord and King, the Faith's defender;
God bless (no harm in blessing) the Pretender,
But who Pretender is, and who the King –
God bless us all – that's quite another thing.

Yet linking Methodism with Jacobitism was an error. As early as 1733 John had said he was convinced of the lawfulness of swearing loyalty to the Hanoverian monarchy and this was strongly echoed by Charles and by George Whitefield. Unfortunately, encouraging lay preachers to travel around made these words sound hollow. The main unit of local government was the parish so anyone ignoring its jurisdiction by preaching uninvited was automatically committing a political as well as a religious offence. Local justices of the peace had enough to do without having their lives complicated by wandering uninvited suspect strangers. Consequently, the more anti-Jacobite they were, the more willing they were either to turn a blind eye to mob violence against Methodists or actively encourage it.

John's experiences of violent opposition to his presence have been much publicized and written about, but Charles' travels were just as broad, just as challenging, and just as dramatic. In February he travelled from London to the west of England, preaching in various places, including Bath, which he viewed as a modern-day Sodom. In May he went to the Midlands to preach in Staffordshire and then Yorkshire. Charles' extensive knowledge of the Bible is constantly in evidence in his hymns but it is worth quoting the following extract from his journal at this time because it shows just how much his prose writing was also influenced:

By four we came to a land of rest; for the brethren of Birstal have stopped the mouths of gainsayers and fairly overcome evil with good. At present peace is in all her borders. The little foxes that spoil the vineyard, or rather, the wild boars out of the wood that root it up, have no more place among them.

Forty out of these 60 words are quoted from the Bible.[8]

Charles was particularly pleased at the progress made among the miners of Wednesbury: 'Here the seed is taken root, and many are added to the church.'[9] However, at Walsall he faced his first really tough mob and the fact he was attempting to preach in the open made him an easy target:

[They] roared, and shouted, and threw stones incessantly. Many struck, without hurting me. I besought them in calm love to be reconciled to God in Christ. While I was departing, a stream of ruffians was suffered to bear me from the steps. I rose and, having given the blessing, was beat down again. So the third time, when we had returned thanks to God for our salvation. I then, from the steps, bade them depart in peace, and walked quietly through the thickest rioters.[10]

Birmingham and Nottingham proved easier venues, but in Sheffield he found the Methodists 'as sheep in the midst of wolves'.[11] The local clergy roused a mob to pull down a recently built Methodist meeting house. The house where he was staying also came under attack and 'the stones flew thick' so Charles decided to leave it and face the mob. A stone struck him in the face and an army captain accused him of treason:

> The Captain ran at me with great fury ... [and] drew his sword, and presented it to my breast. My breast was immediately steeled. I threw it open, and, fixing mine eye on his, smiled in his face, and calmly said, 'I fear God and honour the King'.[12]

Charles' courage and expression of loyalty made the soldier withdraw but the mob continued to wreck the house where he had been preaching. A further day of rioting followed and the house was entirely demolished. Charles entered another house belonging to a Methodist but that too was attacked. Fortunately he managed to find and read a copy of the Riot Act which forced the constable, who had been encouraging the mob, to arrest one of the main ringleaders so that peace was re-established.

At Thorpe Charles faced more violence in the form of 'stones, eggs and dirt'[13] and he was lucky to escape injury when his horse bolted in fear. His companion David Taylor was less fortunate, being injured in the head. Birstal and then Leeds proved a happier experience with Charles delighting in the staunch witness of society members. On 30 May at Ripley his horse threw him and his companion feared he had broken his neck but Charles recorded that 'my leg only was bruised, my hand sprained, and my head stunned, which spoiled my making hymns'.[14] He moved on with varying degrees of both welcome and opposition. Unlike John, Charles disliked any extreme emotional responses to his preaching, and he had his own way of dealing with this:

> Many counterfeits I have already detected. Today one who came from the ale-house drunk was pleased to fall into a fit for my entertainment, and beat himself heartily. I thought it a pity to hinder him; so ... we left him to recover at his leisure. Another girl, as she began to cry, I ordered to be carried out. Her convulsion was so violent as to take

away the use of her limbs, till they laid and left her without the door. Then immediately she found her legs and walked off.[15]

In Newcastle Charles followed up on his brother's witness because John had been there in March and was disappointed at the number of converts who had fallen away. The reasons varied. Some had left because of the opposition of a partner or parent, others because of the advice coming from other clergy. Some had been prevented from attending by their employers or had been persuaded by the arguments of friends, and others had left because they disliked being laughed at or because they had heard bad things being said about Methodism. Many had been unprepared or unable to devote the necessary time. Others had been expelled for a variety of reasons, ranging from swearing and drunkenness to quarrelling and brawling, from excessive frivolity and laziness to wilful lying and evil-speaking, and from habitual Sabbath-breaking to wife-beating. Charles concluded: 'We have certainly been too rash and easy in allowing for believers on their own testimony.'[16] The importance of Charles' work in the North has often been neglected yet there is no doubt he was an important figure in establishing a strong Methodist presence there. One historian has even gone so far as to describe him as 'the Apostle of the North'.[17]

With Charles' backing, John produced his 'Rules for the United Societies' as a means of trying to ensure that the new societies would develop a better track record. The word 'Methodist' was still being avoided as much as possible by Charles and John lest it imply they were seeking to create a sect. The focus of the Rules was more ethical than doctrinal. Members were expected to not only help each other but to 'do good of every possible sort, and as far as possible to all men'.[18] They were expected to serve the needs of the local community, feeding and clothing the poor, visiting the sick and imprisoned, and comforting the dying. They were told to refrain from drunkenness and contentious arguments and fighting and there was great stress laid on the need for self-improvement. The latter was frequently expressed in Charles' hymnwriting:

Toiling henceforth both day and night
To make our heavenly treasure sure,
O might we every means improve,
And Jesus every moment love![19]

After a gruelling fortnight of preaching in Newcastle, Charles began a preaching tour around the surrounding towns, including Sunderland, South Shields and North Shields, at all of which he faced a hostile audience. He next began his return journey to London, preaching en route, including at Birmingham, where he preached to 'several thousand ... many of whom I observed by their tears were pricked at the heart'.[20] On 28 June he arrived back at the Foundery and undertook to strengthen the witness and worship of the societies' work there and at Seven Dials. He then returned to Bristol in mid-July. Two days later he set out to visit Exeter and the South-West at the request of a ship's captain called Joseph Turner. Methodism had spread into that region even though neither John nor Charles had visited it. It was an area ideally suited to Methodism because the growth of mining communities there had made a nonsense of the county's traditional parochial boundaries. Charles journeyed to Bodmin, Redruth, Carnegie Downs, and many other places. At St Ives he faced yet again considerable problems because local gentry had roused the mob to attack him, but Charles showed his courage:

> I began the hundredth Psalm, and they beating their drum, and shouting ... My soul was calm and fearless. I shook off the dust of my feet, and walked leisurely through the thickest of them, who followed like ramping and roaring lions.[21]

On 22 July Charles was preaching at a house in Morvah to a group of tin-miners when he faced a major assault as bad as anything he had experienced in the Midlands. Led by the town clerk, the mob virtually demolished the entire inside of the building in which he was staying and threatened to murder anyone who supported him:

> Several times they lifted up their hands and clubs to strike me; but a stronger arm restrained them. They beat and dragged the women about, particularly one of great age, and trampled on them without mercy ... I bade the people stand still and see the salvation of God.[22]

Eventually only quarrelling among the rioters brought a temporary end to the disturbance. When Charles resumed his preaching the next day, another riot ensued, this time led by the son of the mayor. Charles managed to persuade him to desist when the mob began beating up women:

> I laid my hand upon him, and said, 'Sir, you appear like a gentleman: I desire you would show it by restraining those of the baser sort. Let them strike the men, or me, if they please, but not poor helpless women and children'. He was turned into a friend immediately and laboured the whole time to quieten his associates ... Some of our bitterest enemies were brought over by the meekness of the sufferers.[23]

Successes made up for the dangers. An open-air meeting at Gwennap Pit drew around 2,000 tin-miners, mostly from Redruth. At Pool the tin-miners were so incensed at a drunkard who tried to stop them listening to Charles, they attacked the heckler and Charles had to intervene to protect him from harm. Nevertheless, the fear of Jacobitism became an ever-increasing factor. This was brought home to Charles in rioting at Wednock on 24 July when local ministers urged a crowd to attack him and his followers because they were 'Popish emissaries'. He could not prevent one of his men being brutally clubbed by ten men.[24] In response Charles began revisiting places to encourage the besieged societies. At St Ives he three times faced mob violence and, on the third occasion, the mayor was so tired of the rioting, he brought in 20 constables to keep the peace.

Charles also continued visiting new places, such as St Just and Zennor. From the latter he walked to Land's End and sang a celebratory hymn:

> Come, Divine Immanuel, come,
> Take possession of thy home ...
> Carry on thy victory,
> Spread thy rule from sea to sea;
> Re-convert the ransom'd race;
> Save us, save us, Lord, by grace.[25]

On 7 August he held a final and very successful rally at Gwennap Pit to his largest-ever Cornish audience and then headed back to London, visiting Okehampton, Exeter, Blandford and Salisbury (where he visited his sister) en route.

Meanwhile enemies of Methodism poured out propaganda that he and John and George Whitefield were all secret Jacobites out to create seditious assemblies. The Moravians were similarly accused. George Whitefield resorted to the courts to defend Methodists after a particularly brutal assault on a lay preacher called Thomas Adams at a small town in the Cotswolds called Hampton. Adams was thrown not only into the local pond but twice into a lime pit, causing considerable injuries. Whitefield lodged charges of assault and the case was heard in Gloucester. The defence argued the Methodists were fanatics who were instigating riots and that the locals were merely defending themselves. Whitefield brought non-Methodist witnesses to prove this was false and made clear his own loyalty to the Crown. The jury found against the rioters and ordered them to pay damages. George then generously declined the money saying his only object was to deter people from believing they could mistreat Methodists without fear of retribution.

John published a defence of Methodism called *An Earnest Appeal to Men of Reason and Religion*. He argued no man of reason could oppose those who proclaimed love to be 'the never-failing remedy for all the evils in a disordered world, for all the miseries and vices of men'.[26] Howell Harris congratulated John on its contents, but it made no difference to the level of persecution because of the growing impact of patriotic fervour. In June George II had personally led British and Hanoverian forces into a battle against French and Bavarian forces at Dettingen. News of his courageous victory – the last time a British monarch undertook such a frontline military task – was a source of pride to most Englishmen, but there were soon rumours that Louis XV of France would seek revenge by offering support to Bonnie Prince Charlie.

On 12 August Charles met up with his brother John and the lay preacher John Nelson, who had ridden south from Newcastle and Yorkshire respectively. In the face of the persecution they hoped to also meet with James Hutton and George Whitefield 'to cultivate a better understanding with each other so that the parties might avoid all unnecessary collision and unite, as far as was practicable, in advancing what they all believed to be the work of God'.[27] However, George did not turn up and James Hutton said the Moravians would not meet with the Methodists without the approval of the Archbishop of Canterbury lest they be classed still further with dissent.

John decided to follow up Charles' work in Cornwall, leaving him to strengthen the societies in London. There is no doubt Charles was a greater sustainer of the work there and in Bristol than John. His charitable witness was also often more direct. For example, John wanted to help the sick so, lacking time to do this himself, he divided London into 23 districts and appointed visitors to the sick in each. In contrast Charles personally spearheaded helping those in prison and then urged others to follow his example:

Now into his dungeon shine,
And sweeten his distress;
Fill his heart with love divine,
And keep in perfect peace.[28]

It was probably Charles who was crucial to the establishment of Methodism's first two chapels. In May 1743 John had purchased a former Huguenot chapel known as 'Seven Dials' in West Street so he and Charles could hold liturgical services and administer communion to the members of societies in an episcopally consecrated building. It was opened on Trinity Sunday and its situation in the heart of the theatre district of the West End made it appear a direct challenge to the frivolous activities of the fashionable rich. Three months later a second chapel was created from a former Unitarian chapel called 'Snowfields' in Bermondsey, Southwark. The services within these chapels strictly observed the rubric of the Book of Common Prayer, but Charles wrote hymns which could be sung during them, including at the point where people were moving to take the bread and wine. These hymns were collected into book-form as *Hymns on the Lord's Supper* in 1745. They were Charles' unique way of showing that communion was a vital source of God's grace:

> Come Holy Ghost, Thine influence shed,
> And realize the sign;
> Thy life infuse into the bread,
> Thy power into the wine.
> Effectual let the tokens prove,
> And made, by heavenly art,
> Fit channels to convey Thy love,
> To every faithful heart.[29]

On 17 October Charles left London to join John, who was back in the Midlands. He reached Nottingham on 20 October and John arrived there the next day. Charles was taken aback by John's ragged appearance.[30] John told Charles of his recent experiences in Staffordshire. The Vicar of Wednesbury had spread rumours that Methodists were seeking to ban all popular amusements and so the houses, shops and workshops of local Methodists had been looted. The house in which John was staying had been twice surrounded by a fierce mob, demanding he should be handed over. After an abortive attempt to see a local magistrate, John had been attacked by another mob from Walsall. They had pulled him through the steep and wet cobbled streets and, had he fallen, he would probably have been killed. As it was, several blows with bludgeons had been deflected only by the fact his small size made him a difficult target. With nose and mouth streaming blood from a blow he had received, John had been dragged before the newly appointed mayor, but this had not stopped him preaching to a crowd baying for his crucifixion. Such had been his courage that the leader of the mob had eventually rescued him, saying: 'Sir, I will spend my life for you. Follow me, and not one soul here shall touch a hair of your head.'

John's ability to turn around the attitude of a mob was to become almost legendary, but Charles' similar bravery has not been as well recognized. On this occasion it was Charles who agreed to return to Wednesbury and preach to the very men who had so threatened his brother. Charles then went on to preach at Birmingham, Evesham, Cirencester, and various other places before reaching Bristol. After preaching at Kingswood and in the Horsefair, he set out for a brief visit to Cardiff and Wenvo and then headed for London, preaching en route in Bath, Cirencester, Evesham and Oxford. On reaching the Foundery on 24 November, Charles devoted himself to producing *Hymns for Times of Trouble*. He found it ironic that those who were seeking to improve lives faced persecution, while those who lived in sin were accepted by society:

> Smitten, we turn the other cheek,
> Our ease, and name, and goods forego,
> Help, or redress, no longer seek
> In any child of man below ...[31]

Hymns for Times of Trouble embodied in verse what his brother John was saying in prose: that loyalty was 'an essential branch of religion' and civil war an anathema. The hymns clearly depicted Charles' view that the Hanoverian king was God's anointed vice-regent, responsible for upholding religious freedom and serving the needs of the British people. Charles repeatedly invoked God's protection for George II against the Jacobites:

> Guard him from all who dare oppose
> Thy delegate and Thee,
> From open and from secret foes,
> From force and perfidy ...[32]

And he offered the early Methodists hope for the future because, like Christ, they were suffering for their faith:

> Be faithful unto death, He cries,
> And I the crown will give:
> Amen, the glorious Spirit replies,
> We die with Thee to live.[33]

Charles' hymns made no difference. In 1744 the attitude of the authorities hardened still further against Methodism in the face of mounting political tensions. By December 1743 Louis XV had agreed to launch a French invasion of Britain and was assembling a force of 10,000 men under the Marshal de Saxe at Gravelines near Dunkirk. The charismatic Bonnie Prince Charlie arrived in Paris on 29 January 1744 to finalize details for a direct drive on London. In February a French fleet headed for the English Channel and British troops were urgently re-called from the continent to face the invasion, which all now expected to take place. Howell Harris reflected on the political situation in a letter to a friend:

> The French fleet now lay at anchor in one of the ports, being come over with a firm resolution to dethrone His Majesty & to see the Pre-tender's son on the throne of England & consequently not only to take away all toleration & liberty of Protestantism but re-establish Popery again ... Next Monday we have settled for fasting & praying for the King and the Nation, we all hold it our duty to preach loyalty to the King & to stand by him with our lives, fortunes & prayers, as he is the King set over us by the Lord & as he is a Protestant & tolerates the true Religion & as he is laid so deeply on our hearts too.[34]

At this critical time personal circumstances had affected George White-field's ability to provide leadership. The previous September his pregnant wife Elizabeth had narrowly escaped injury while touring with him and so he had decided to curtail his travelling and stay in rented accommo-dation in London. It must have been a hostile environment because it is said their landlord hung an iron mechanism on the walls so he could chain up his own wife and prevent her hearing any preaching! White-field's son had been born in November but in February 1744 the child died, having caught a cold on a journey in an unheated coach. In their desire to get away from the scene of the tragedy, George announced he and his wife would return to America, leaving John Cennick in charge of the Calvinist branch of Methodism.

Charles left London on 30 January to journey to Newcastle, preach-ing en route at many places, including Birmingham, Dudley, Wednes-bury, Nottingham, Sheffield and Epworth. We know from an account by Howell Harris that Wednesbury in particular was again the scene of very violent excesses against Methodists, including the looting of homes, public humiliation by stripping society members naked, and dragging men through the streets on ropes. Charles felt the magistrates were en-couraging such hostility:

> The Magistrates ... only stand by ... No wonder that the mob, so en-couraged, should say and believe that there is no law for Methodists. Accordingly, like outlaws they treat them, breaking their houses, and taking away their goods at pleasure; extorting money from those that have it, and cruelly beating those that have not ... What justice can be expected from the chief men of this place ...?[35]

John decided it was necessary to send a personal statement of loyalty to the king on behalf of all 'the Societies in England and Wales in derision called Methodists'. Charles expressed his concern that such a letter would reinforce the opinion that the societies were a sect rather than part of the Anglican Church. John ignored him, but altered his draft to clarify that not only was Methodism not inclined to Catholicism but it was not 'a peculiar sect of men, separating ourselves from the Established Church'.[36]

In late February storms severely damaged the French invasion fleet, but the subsequent public rejoicing caused problems for the Methodists. Charles faced rioting at the hands of drunken revellers in Newcastle and others experienced similar events elsewhere. For example, the Mayor of Nottingham summoned the preacher Thomas Westall and threatened him with prison for his disloyalty, even though he swore 'that King George was our rightful King and no other, and he would take this oath with all his heart'.[37] Charles headed southwards, determined to 'vindicate the loyalty of God's people'.[38] At Leeds he narrowly escaped serious injury when the floor of an upper room in which he was speaking collapsed under the weight of the crowd. He and a hundred others fell through 'heaps upon heaps' to the floor below. Charles, who sustained only a bruised hand and a scraped head, commented: 'Never did I more clearly see that not a hair of our head can fall to the ground without our heavenly Father.'[39]

Shortly afterwards Charles was accused of treason by a cleric called Coleby and a warrant was issued for his arrest. When Charles faced the magistrate at Wakefield, it soon became clear there was no evidence to support the charges. The magistrate announced he was free to depart, but this did not amount to a declaration of innocence so Charles protested that he wanted his name and that of all Methodists cleared from accusations of treason. The magistrate said it was reported Methodist societies constantly prayed for Bonnie Prince Charlie. Charles assured him the reverse was true and their hymns and prayers were all for King George: 'I am as true a Church-of-England man, and as loyal a subject, as any man in the kingdom.'[40] This was contested by his enemies but it soon became clear they again had no evidence. The magistrate moved to release Charles, who again asked first for his innocence to be declared. Reluctantly the court proclaimed his loyalty.

Charles preached in Derby, Sheffield, Nottingham and elsewhere before returning to London. He faced particular problems in Nottingham because its mayor blamed the Methodists for any disturbance, even when it was obvious they were the victims of it. According to Charles, he even ordered the arrest of one prominent Methodist, Daniel Sant, for simply letting people pray in his house. On 22 March Charles returned to the Foundery, where he was given a hero's welcome. His nationwide experiences found expression in more hymns, many of which were designed to appeal specifically to the different sectors of society he had encountered. For example, the ironworkers of Newcastle could sing as they tended their furnaces:

> See how great a flame aspires
> Kindled by a spark of grace.
> Jesu's love the nation fires,
> Sets the kingdoms on ablaze ...

And Welsh quarrymen:

> Strike with the hammer of Thy word,
> And break these hearts of stone!

While Cornish fishermen could sing:

> Teach me to cast my net aright,
> The Gospel net of general grace,
> So shall I all to Thee invite,
> And draw them to their Lord's embrace.[41]

Four days after Charles' return to London John set out to go to Cornwall, where he also witnessed many examples of persecution. In May Charles undertook a brief visit to Bristol and the surrounding area and then returned to London. That same month the talented Methodist preacher, John Nelson, was arrested in Birstal and press-ganged into the army. He was marched through Bradford, Leeds and York to Newcastle. Crowds gathered to see him along the way, some to shout their support, but many to jeer and mock. Charles led public prayers for Nelson's rescue and, when petitions failed to evoke a response, raised money to hire a substitute soldier to take his place. Nelson later wrote:

> Several would have given bail for me, but I was told one hundred pound was refused. I am too notorious a criminal to be allowed such favours. Christianity is a crime which the world can never forgive.[42]

Nelson proved a troublesome soldier and was eventually court-martialled for adopting a pacifist stance and preaching to his fellow soldiers. Interestingly John Wesley did nothing to try and help Nelson. It was Charles who encouraged the Countess of Huntingdon to use her influence to secure his release.

Other Methodist preachers faced the same press-gang method. One of them, Thomas Beard, was so badly treated he had to have an arm amputated. He was then discharged, dying shortly afterwards. There was also a second assassination attempt on Whitefield in Plymouth not long before he and his wife set sail again for America. Charles was so upset by all that was happening he extended his *Hymns for Times of Trouble* and reprinted them as *Hymns for Times of Trouble and Persecution*:

Shepherd of souls, Thy sheep behold
In the dark cloudy day,
The wolf is come into Thy fold,
To scatter, tear, and slay ...[43]

Adopting almost a fortress mentality, John and Charles organized the first Methodist Conference in June 1744, copying the idea from George Whitefield's earlier conference for the 'Calvinistic Methodist Association'. In addition to John and Charles Wesley, it contained four other clergy and four laymen. The ministers were Henry Piers, Vicar of Bexley, John Hodges, Rector of Wenvo in South Wales, Samuel Taylor, Vicar of Quinton near Evesham, and John Meriton, a cleric from the Isle of Man. Charles opened the Conference with 'solemn prayer and the divine blessing'. All the Conference sessions were held in the Foundery but the Countess of Huntingdon entertained its members in her home, probably at 11 Downing Street. They discussed various theological issues and matters of organization, including whether they ought to work again with the societies led by Whitefield and by the Moravians.

However, the main concern of the delegates was to express their loyalty to the Church while stating their reasons for continuing evangelical work. One of the hymns from Charles' 1744 collection totally embodies their determination to fight on:

Ye servants of God, your Master proclaim,
And publish abroad his wonderful name;
The name all-victorious of Jesus extol;
His kingdom is glorious, and rules over all ...[44]

In July Charles travelled again to Bristol and then down to Cornwall, accompanied by John Meriton. Instances of persecution were everywhere. For example, at Middlesey Charles witnessed a baker's boy called John Slocombe 'by his own uncle dragged away to prison'[45] and at St Ives he recorded how the mob 'broke the windows of all who were only suspected of Christianity'[46] and 'one of our sisters complained to the Mayor of some who had thrown into her house stones of many pounds' weight, which fell on the pillow within a few inches of her sucking child'.[47] Despite such experiences, Charles was upbeat about the progress of the societies and he records standing on the Cornish hills to sing, pray and rejoice. When he preached at Gwennap Pit in July he declared:

> Here a little one has become a thousand. What an amazing work hath God done in one year! The whole country is alarmed, and gone forth after the sound of the Gospel. In vain do the pulpits ring of Popery, madness, enthusiasm. Our Preachers are daily pressed to new places, and enabled to preach five or six times a day ... Societies are springing up everywhere.[48]

In mid-August Charles ventured into Wales again, still accompanied by John Meriton. He then visited Kingswood before journeying via Cirencester to Oxford to briefly meet up with his brother and Henry Piers. They went to prayers in Christ Church Cathedral and were publicly mocked during the service. Charles preached in the open to the crowds and John preached in St Mary's but for the last time because he was then banned from its pulpit. The charge of holding illegal assemblies was still much in evidence. Charles persistently denied that he was breaking any law in preaching to assembled crowds. He then travelled back to Bristol but not for a rest. For example, he notes in his journal for the 23 September preaching at 5.00 am in the Horsefair, journeying to Kingswood to take a baptism and communion service, returning to preach in the city centre, travelling back to Kingswood for a love-feast, and finally returning home at midnight prior to an early start for London.

Both brothers found their reputation came under attack from a former convert called Thomas Williams, who had been expelled from the Foundery for his poor behaviour. In retaliation he was spreading as many scandalous rumours about them as possible, including that Charles was guilty of sexual misconduct. He appears to have persuaded a woman to sign an affidavit to that effect and placed it in the hands of Thomas Broughton, a former member of the Holy Club. Broughton took the woman's affidavit to the Bishop of London. Charles swore that he was innocent but to his horror many were prepared to believe the story. This deeply upset Charles who envisaged no end to the rumours till God vindicated him on Judgement Day:

> Lord, my times are in Thy hand,
> Judged in man's unrighteous day,

Let us in Thy judgement stand,
When the wicked melt away
Vindicate Thy servant there,
Clear me at the last great bar.[49]

It is at such time that you know your true friends. George Whitefield, hearing the news, wrote from America: 'Some have wrote me things of your disadvantage. I do not believe them. Love thinks no evil of a friend. Such are you to me. I love you dearly.' [50]

In October Charles headed north again for Newcastle. Once again he visited Nottingham, Epworth, Sheffield, Birstal, Leeds, Bradford and other places on the way. He spent most of November and early December in Newcastle. The strength of continued persecution was matched by the severity of the weather that winter, but it did not prevent him travelling further afield to places like Sunderland. After one horrendous itinerary he only gave himself one day back in Newcastle to rest before embarking again:

Being so feeble that I could not walk; yet I was forced to it the last mile, being almost starved to death in the next to impassable ways. I was led, I know not how, by the brethren, up to my knees in snow, the horses ofttimes sinking up to their shoulders.[51]

The strain on his health was so obvious that a doctor urged him to rest before he killed himself. As the year ended Charles handed over the situation in Newcastle to John Nelson and returned to London, again preaching en route in various places

After the rigours of the previous two years, Charles spent the spring and summer of 1745 working in London except for short almost monthly visits to Bristol. One of his converts at this time was the actress wife of John Rich, the owner of the Covent Garden Opera House and now best remembered as the producer of John Gay's *The Beggar's Opera*. She became a regular attendee at the Seven Dials chapel. Her husband was furious at her becoming a Methodist, not least because she refused to perform on stage again. In retaliation he produced a stage character called 'the Harlequin Preacher' to mock the Methodists. However, Rich eventually was won over – according to the satirist Smollett because of the combined impact of the tyranny of his wife and the terrors of hell-fire! It was through Mrs Rich that Charles met a number of the leading musicians of the day, including the German composer John Frederick Lampe, who was a bassoon player in the Covent Garden orchestra. He agreed to set many of Charles' hymns to music.

Meanwhile international events continued to affect public attitudes. On 30 April the French army under Marshal de Saxe won a decisive victory at Fontenoy in the Austrian Netherlands over a combined army of British, Hanoverian, Dutch and Austrian troops led by George II's son, William Augustus, Duke of Cumberland. This disaster was followed by Bonnie Prince Charlie landing in Scotland and, on 19 August, raising the Jacobite standard of rebellion at Glenfinnan. English Jacobites expressed a readiness to raise a similar standard in England if the French would send them 10,000 men. Preparations began for the French fleet to carry invading forces to Britain and once again this led to strong anti-Methodist riots.

In August 1745 Charles attended the second Methodist Conference, which was held in Bristol. It was attended by three clergy and six of the movement's lay preachers. Its main focus was on ensuring that what was being preached was theologically sound and on taking measures to guarantee the societies were being properly run. John asked whether he could travel less in order to devote more time to writing and publishing, but the others felt they could not afford his loss. The shortage of helpers meant John suggested they should not yet form societies in certain areas. The Conference again pledged loyalty to King George and its members left with a rallying call: 'You have nothing to do but to save souls. Therefore spend and be spent in this work.'

Shortly afterwards Charles was injured in Shepton Mallett. In crossing a field to speak to a crowd, he tripped and 'violently sprained' his leg, so he was reduced to preaching on his knees. His injury, though extremely painful, did not prevent him travelling to Bristol and Cardiff, though he could only hobble on crutches or be carried. When his foot became obviously very inflamed and swollen, his friends insisted he spend three weeks convalescing. On 9 September he resumed his itinerant preaching, though still not fully recovered. He could only sit on a horse if another person sat behind him. It was on his return to Bristol at the end of September that he heard there was a significant chance of a Jacobite invasion of England because Bonnie Prince Charlie had taken control of Edinburgh on 17 September. Charles warned the society members of the dangers this posed and was heartened that they 'seemed to have a strong faith that the Romish Anti-Christ shall never finally prevail in these kingdoms'.[52] They all prayed for the king to be safely delivered from all his enemies.

John Wesley was nearer to what was happening. On 18 September he had entered Newcastle and found the city in an uproar. His Orphan House was just outside the Pilgrim Street Gate and this was walled up as the city prepared its defences against a possible attack. On 21 September news arrived that the Jacobite forces had defeated the British army at Prestonpans. The brutality of the Jacobite forces was much publicized and John's journal vividly records the panic response as many fled the city. The authorities began preparing Newcastle's fortifications. John offered the mayor his support in preaching the need for loyalty and he noted with relief that the cannon on the city's walls were not aimed in the direction of where he was staying! But when the Jacobites failed to immediately press on to Newcastle, John left to go on a preaching tour which extended as far south as Sheffield and Leeds. He returned in late October and was shocked by the lawlessness and wanton blasphemy of the 15,000 troops that had gathered in Newcastle. He offered to preach to them in the hope of improving their morals, but was careful to assure the authorities he was no secret Jacobite agent out to weaken their desire to fight.

All over England suspected Jacobites faced arbitrary arrest and the scale of persecution facing the local preachers was far worse than anything either of the brothers had experienced. In Exeter, for example, Methodists were treated 'with such abuse and indignity as not to be expressed'.[53] This included the women being publicly humiliated. They were semi-stripped, dragged through the streets, and then exposed by having their petticoats pulled over their heads. John left Newcastle on 3 November to rejoin Charles in London for a debate on what they should do. On his arrival, John found Charles was preaching successfully to some of the soldiers gathering to face the Jacobite enemy. Selina, Countess of Huntingdon, wrote to the Secretary of State, Lord Carteret, and declared the loyalty of all Methodists.

By this time the pressure of events had made John Cennick realize he was not cut out to replace Whitefield as leader of the Calvinist Methodists. He was a highly successful preacher and had an excellent record for creating new societies in Wiltshire, but he was not a gifted diplomat when it came to handling internal conflict among the Methodists. Recognizing the greater organizational power of the Moravians, he joined their ranks in December, taking about 400 Methodists from Whitefield's London Tabernacle with him. Whitefield wrote from America in sorrow rather than anger and wished his former ally success with the Moravians. Howell Harris took over control of the Calvinistic Association but his work in Wales prevented him really spending enough time in London to hold the organization properly together. It appeared the Calvinist branch of Methodism might self-destruct.

By 4 December the forces of Bonnie Prince Charlie had reached Derby and there was panic across the country. However, the English Jacobites failed to join the prince. One of the exceptions was the former Oxford

Methodist, John Clayton, who greeted the prince at Manchester. For this treasonable activity Clayton was suspended from his ministerial office. The lack of English support eventually made the Scottish commanders demand the prince begin an ignominious retreat. Almost simultaneously the danger of a French invasion receded because the British fleet severely damaged the French fleet. Amid the resulting national joy the evangelicals renewed their efforts to reunite. For that reason John Wesley met up with Howell Harris in Bristol. They agreed both Calvinists and Wesleyans would achieve more if they avoided slandering each other. The Countess of Huntingdon was delighted and from America Whitefield equally welcomed the fresh accord, but with a note of caution:

> My heart is ready for an outward, as well as an inward union. Nothing shall be wanting on my part to bring it about; but I cannot see how it can possibly be effected till we all speak and think the same things.[54]

This was sensible. James Hutton soon made clear that on no account would the Moravians work with the Calvinists whom they regarded as 'vainly puffed up bitter enemies of Christ'.[55]

Charles remained very active in London, but his health was again troubling him so he had to rely on 'supernatural strength' rather than his own.[56] He saw the Jacobite rebellion as a product of God's displeasure over the immorality prevalent in the country so he was not surprised when Bonnie Prince Charlie's forces defeated the English forces at Falkirk on 16 January. Charles confided to a friend:

> I cannot help expecting the sorest judgements to be poured out upon this land, and that suddenly ... Now is the axe laid to the root of the tree; now is the decree gone forth; now is the day of visitation. It comes so strangely and continually upon me, that I almost think there is God in my prospect of war, famine, pestilence, and all the vials of wrath bursting on our heads.[57]

However, the Jacobites failed to follow up their victory at Falkirk and their morale began to crumble as the prince's commanders forced him to retreat further into the Highlands. On 16 April 1746 the exhausted remnants of the Jacobite forces were cut to pieces by the English artillery at the Battle of Culloden. The English forces suffered only 100 dead while the Jacobites lost over half their remaining army. John Wesley declared: 'The day of public thanksgiving for the victory of Culloden was to us a day of solemn joy' and Charles wrote seven celebratory hymns. Even their most bitter enemies had to begin accepting the Wesleys were not traitors.

Nevertheless, with the country still technically at war, both John and Charles continued to travel less in 1746. This did not stop Charles undertaking a tour of Cornwall in the summer. He was encouraged by what he saw:

> The whole country finds the benefit of the Gospel. Hundreds who follow not with us, have broke off their sins, and are outwardly reformed ... For one Preacher they cut off, twenty spring up. Neither persuasions nor threatening, flattery nor violence, dungeons, or sufferings of various kinds, can conquer them. Many waters cannot quench this little spark which the Lord hath kindled, neither shall the floods of persecution drown it.[58]

At Helston he experienced problems when one of his companions was taken to be Bonnie Prince Charlie in disguise, but generally the worst excesses of mob persecution were ceasing and Charles discovered 'some of those who fell off in the late persecution desired to be present ... [again]'.[59] At a particularly memorable day at Gwennap Pit Charles addressed an estimated 10,000 people. He later commented: 'Seventy years' sufferings were overpaid by one such opportunity.'[60]

In the face of the remaining hostility, the Wesleys grouped Methodist societies into seven regional 'circuits'. Four were named after cities and towns – London, Bristol, Newcastle and Evesham – and three after regions – Cornwall, Wales, and six counties labelled together as 'Yorkshire'. Two years later a lay preacher called John Bennet recommended these circuits begin holding Quarterly Meetings to ensure societies were conforming to the expectations of the Wesleys. The annual Methodist Conference also became a means 'to regulate our doctrine, discipline and practice'. They were held in a variety of places, including London, Bristol, Manchester, Leeds and Newcastle, and at a variety of times, although late July or early August became the norm. John maintained his control by only issuing invitations to preachers who supported him, and from 1765 proper minutes were published to leave no room for questioning Conference decisions. In effect all these moves began the process of creating a national movement out of what had been a mass of local revival groups. For that reason John has been described as 'a great cannibalizer'.[61]

Once the fear of Jacobitism was gone, the main reason behind continued opposition to Methodist preachers was the simple fact they were strangers. In an era when travel was difficult and many did not go much beyond their village, it was easy to be suspicious of visitors, especially as they spoke with a different accent and challenged the existing order of things. In some cases the mobs clearly thought they were supporting their local church and rang the church bells to signal they were repelling an 'invasion'. The emotional response of some of the crowds to Methodist preaching did little to appease those critics who thought Methodism was dangerously fanatical. Equally unhelpful were the comments of some of the preachers, who compared the clergy to the Pharisees of Jesus' day.

In September 1746 Charles visited the home of Vincent Perronet, the Vicar of Shoreham in Kent. This minister, who was of Swiss descent, had become friendly with his brother John two years earlier through the medium of Henry Piers. He was an advocate of what the Wesleys were seeking to achieve in terms of a religious revival within the Anglican Church. Charles became almost instantly the friend of his two sons, Edward and Charles, both of whom were to become lay preachers. Edward was also to become a hymnwriter and among his output was the famous 'All hail the power of Jesu's name'. Vincent permitted Charles to preach at Shoreham but rioters invaded the church and he was stoned. Had not Charles Perronet screened him with his own body, he might have been seriously injured. The incident did not stop Charles in October heading northwards with Edward Perronet to Newcastle. In a number of towns they found placards had been posted inviting people to attack and destroy Methodism. Charles wrote how he had to rely on his preaching to make 'our leopards all become lambs'.[62]

That same month the husband of the Countess of Huntingdon died of a stroke. The devastated Selina contemplated retiring from public life. This was a great blow to the Methodists because they looked to her as their best-placed defender and only hope of obtaining social acceptance. Only a handful of clerics were as yet sympathetic to them. The most important of these was the Revd William Grimshaw, Vicar of Haworth, a tiny village in the midst of the desolate moors of northern Yorkshire. As a young minister he had been rather ungodly and prone to swearing and drinking, but the death of his young wife had transformed him into a genuine Christian. He had had a remarkable vision of the crucified hands of Jesus reaching out to him, 'the nail-holes ... ragged and bluish, and fresh blood streaming from each of them'. Linking himself with the Methodist revival offered Grimshaw a means of showing his repentance. His direct and powerful manner made him a very effective preacher and the rather rough and ready people among whom he worked were more prepared to listen to him than to any travelling stranger. One of his early converts was the future lay preacher Richard Burdsall, who wrote of Grimshaw's impact:

> His voice in prayer seemed to me as it had been the voice of an angel. After prayer he took a little Bible out of his pocket, and read ... [the words of his chosen text]. The Holy Ghost now shone upon my heart ... [and] I wept.[63]

Initially Grimshaw had worked with Benjamin Ingham and John Nelson but this did not mean he saw himself as either a Moravian or a Methodist. He was simply sharing their evangelical fervour. What mattered to him was not a person's theology but his or her lifestyle: "Tis not what we hold, but what we are, that makes us Christians.'[64] His first personal contact with the Wesleys came when John Nelson persuaded Charles to visit Haworth in October 1746. Grimshaw was charmed by Charles and the two men became great friends. He therefore agreed to meet John and, in January 1747, persuaded the religious societies created by a preacher called William Darney to place themselves under the Wesleyan rather than Moravian banner. More importantly, Grimshaw undertook to extend his evangelical preaching to a wider area and to help monitor local societies. He also agreed to train lay preachers and to allow his home to become a base for them as they travelled the region.

Charles was thus very instrumental in helping to recruit a freelance evangelical minister who was to prove the most significant promoter of Wesleyan Methodism in the North Midlands. Many contemporary accounts bear witness to Grimshaw's unique approach. For example, he would often leave the service while psalms were being sung to see if he could round up any parishioners who had failed to turn up. One visitor thought the local pub was on fire because he saw several people jumping out of its windows, but he was subsequently informed it was just men fleeing from the parson!

Inevitably Grimshaw's open support for the Wesleys brought him into disrepute with many of his fellow clergy, but the Archbishop of York found it hard to criticize a minister who was so effective in making parishioners attend church and take communion. There is a story that the archbishop went to personally hear him preach and was so moved he told Grimshaw's detractors: 'I would to God that all the clergy in my diocese were like this good man.' John and Charles were delighted by Grimshaw's increasing willingness to preach outside his own parish to Methodist societies in other parts of Yorkshire and in North Derbyshire, Cheshire and Lancashire. 'Mr Grimshaw's circuit' eventually covered an area of about 8,000 square miles and, though he traversed most of it by horse, he sometimes travelled large areas by foot – 'a robust, stocky, windswept figure familiar all over the moorlands'.[65]

After his first meeting with Grimshaw, Charles spent the whole winter of 1746 in the far north. At Hexham he records that the only place he could gain permission to preach in was the local cockpit. When his enemies then brought their cocks and set them fighting, Charles commented wryly: 'I expected Satan would come and fight me on his own ground.'[66] However, the good experiences outweighed the bad. In Newcastle he found 'they had no feeling of the sharp frost while the love of Christ warmed their hearts'[67] and he wrote in joy at their faith the hymn:

> See how great a flame aspires
> Kindled by a spark of grace!
> Jesu's love the nation fires,
> Sets the kingdoms on a blaze.
> To bring fire on earth he came;
> Kindled in some hearts it is:
> O that all might catch the flame,
> All partake the glorious bliss![68]

In January 1747 Charles returned south via Grimsby, where he faced another violent onslaught when 'several poor wild creatures, almost naked, ran about the room, striking down all they met' until Charles won over their leader and the rest of the mob began fighting among themselves.[69] His preaching took him through many places, including Epworth, Leeds, Birstal, Manchester, Sheffield, Rotherham and Penkridge. At Haworth William Grimshaw was happy to have him in his house but was afraid to let him preach in his church for fear of what might happen. This is not surprising because even Selina, Countess of Huntingdon, was facing angry scenes:

> Our affronts and persecutions here for the Word's sake are scarcely to be described ... They call out in the open streets for me, saying if they had me they would tear me to pieces etc.[70]

At Darlaston Charles saw some of the fiercest persecutors he had ever seen and commented you could always tell the house of a Methodist because its windows were always boarded up.

Charles reached London on 10 February. Shortly afterwards, he travelled with John Meriton to Bristol. He preached widely in the surrounding area, including visiting Devizes on 25 February. As he was preaching to society members in a house, boys began ringing bells outside and then men arrived with a water pump and sprayed water at them. When the local constable intervened and confiscated the pump's nozzle, the men hurried off to fetch the town's fire-engine. The force of the water from this broke the windows and flooded the rooms. Charles and his followers moved upstairs, but not before the growing mob had seized the most prominent of the local Methodists and dragged him off to be thrown into a nearby horse-pond. The number in the mob grew as news of the trouble spread. For three hours some of the rioters continued to regularly pump water into the house, encouraged by some of the richer inhabitants who brought them pitchers of ale to drink. One of the few who opposed what was happening was the wife of the mayor. Charles had converted her son and stopped him running away to sea. She sent her maid to encourage Charles to disguise himself as a woman and so escape. The maid managed to get through the mob but Charles declined to run away.

At this critical juncture the mob looked as if they would forcibly break into the house but the constable, at great risk to himself, declared he would treat any who did so as breaking the peace. This caused the mob to retreat but from his window Charles could see the ringleaders consulting a lawyer. Some of the mob returned and tried to break in at the back door of the house, but were stopped by its owner, who made absolutely clear he would not have his guest turned out. Rumours that Charles had escaped in disguise led some of the rioters to take the water engine to the nearby inn and hose it with water in order to force its landlord to release Charles' horse. Others tried to break into the house of another Methodist but he held them at bay by threatening them with a gun. When it became clear Charles was still in the original house, the mob reformed and some clambered on the roof and began removing its tiles. Charles commented in his journal:

> Upon their revisiting us ... we stood in jeopardy every moment. Such threatenings, curses, and blasphemies I had never heard. They seemed kept out by a constant miracle ... We continued in mutual exhortation and prayer, looking for deliverance. If ever we felt faith, it was now.[71]

The scale of the violence now began to worry the leading citizens who had encouraged it. One of them promised Charles a safe exit if he promised never to preach in Devizes again. Despite Charles' refusal, the masters called off their men and told Charles he could leave. In front of the hostile chanting mob Charles and Meriton were allowed to mount their horses:

We rode a slow pace up the street, the whole multitude pouring along on both sides, and attending us with loud acclamations. Such fierceness and diabolical malice I have not seen in human faces.[72]

The danger was not yet over because one of the crowd released his two bull-dogs and they attacked Meriton's horse, one biting its muzzle and the other its chest. Meriton was thrown off and surrounded by the mob. Fortunately some men pulled off the dogs and permitted Charles to help Meriton remount and both men then rode out without further harm.

From the beginning of March to the latter end of August 1747 Charles was employed alternately in Bristol and London. In the latter he preached frequently to large crowds in the Moorfields. He had the satisfaction of knowing that, despite all the persecution, the religious revival had grown and not diminished. According to estimates based on Moravian sources, their societies contained approaching 6,000 members, the societies run by the Wesleys contained around 12,000 members, and Whitefield's societies had approaching 20,000 members. Little did Charles realize that his brother was about to send him on a journey that was to lead to his marriage and that his relationship with John was about to face its severest test.

8

Marriages Made in Heaven and Hell

Sing to the Lord earth and sky,
Who first ordain'd the nuptial tie,
In Eden yoked the new-made pair,
And bless'd them to each other there ...

God of the patriarchal race,
He still directs us by His grace,
Who Isaaac and Rebecca join'd
He gives us each our mate to find.

He magnified the social state,
And stamp'd our joy divinely great,
When God appear'd His creature's Guest,
And Jesus graced a wedding feast.

That everlasting joy of His
Is shadow'd by the nuptial bliss:
Heaven is the marriage of the Lamb,
And God assumes a bridegroom's name ...

Thanks to our heavenly Adam give,
Who form'd His church the second Eve,
Produc'd her from His wounded side,
And still rejoices o'er His bride:

Praise to the blessed Spirit above
Who fills our hearts with sacred love,
Our faithful hearts to Jesus plights,
And each to each in God unites.[1]

By 1745 the Wesleys had developed a small school catering to the needs of 40 children of the miners at Kingswood. John decided to create alongside this a fee-paying boarding school for the sons of their principal friends. This would be freed from the 'palpable blemishes'[2] of other schools and have teachers 'truly devoted to God'.[3] Charles was very supportive because he felt a truly Christian school would remedy each child's 'sin-sick mind' and inspire not just academic learning but 'a spark of heavenly fire, a taste of God, a seed of grace'.[4] This would stand in sharp contrast to other schools, which only encouraged children to want to be 'caressed, admired, and pampered with applause', thus 'heightening their disease', and which provided only an outward knowledge that was 'learning's shell'.[5] Both the Wesleys accepted the view of the eighteenth-century philosopher John Locke that human perfection was attainable if a child was immersed while young and impressionable in the right environment. Charles wrote:

> Happy the well-instructed youth
> Who in his earliest infancy
> Loves from his heart to speak the truth,
> And, like his God, abhors a lie.[6]

In his *Lessons for Children* John said it was essential to avoid 'making children parrots'. Instead they should be made to question everything they read so as to better understand 'the true meaning of Christianity'.[7] Such an approach would 'turn the bias from self-will, pride, anger, revenge and the love of the world, to resignation, lowliness, meekness, and the love of God'.[8] Charles said the same but in verse:

> Ah, give me other eyes
> Than flesh and blood supplies,
> Spiritual discernment give;
> Then command the light to shine,
> Then I shall the truth receive,
> Know by faith the things divine.[9]

The proposed school was, in the words of Charles, for 'a little flock, a chosen seed', who would 'shun the paths of men' and 'listen for the voice of truth'.[10] Such a school would produce the next generation of religious leaders and 'ambassadors for the King of Kings'.[11]

A foundation stone was laid on 7 April 1746. Financial restrictions meant the school was a very simple building with a schoolroom and dining room on its ground floor and a large dormitory and rooms for staff and visitors on the floor above. The Kingswood meeting place acted as its chapel and pastures and gardens were created on adjacent land.

'Kingswood School' officially opened on Midsummer Day 1748. John preached a sermon based on the text 'Train up a child in the way he should go and when he is old he will not depart from it' and Charles composed a special hymn:

> Error and ignorance remove,
> Their blindness both of heart and mind;
> Give them the wisdom from above,
> Spotless, and peaceable, and kind;
> In knowledge pure their minds renew,
> And store with thoughts divinely true ...
> Unite the pair so oft disjoined,
> Knowledge and vital piety;
> Learning and holiness combined,
> And truth and love, let all men see
> In those, whom up to Thee we give,
> Thine, wholly Thine, to die and live.[12]

In this context 'knowledge' meant acquiring the self-understanding crucial to salvation and not just learning information, while 'vital piety' referred not only to the worship of God but also the social outreach which that should encourage. John said the hallmark of a good student was not just how clever he became but how moral he was because 'without love, all learning is but splendid ignorance, pompous folly, vexation of spirit'.

The school was designed to cater for up to 50 children aged between 6 and 14 (anyone older John deemed already corrupted by the world). Its teachers came from the ranks of the lay preachers and they were told to constantly monitor the welfare of the pupils day and night because they were apt 'to hinder and corrupt one another' if left unobserved.[13] The children were expected to rise at 4.00 am for private devotions, attend a public act of worship at 5.00 am (the time when most workers had to be on their way to work), and then, after a breakfast of porridge or gruel, commence their lessons, which occupied most of the day, except for a brief pause for some bread and butter. The day ended with private devotions at 5.00 pm, a frugal supper at 6.00 pm. public worship at 7.00 pm and early retirement to bed at 8.00 pm Sunday had its own routine, which included private devotions, Bible reading, hymn-learning sessions, and worship in the local parish church. This strictly controlled timetable was accompanied by a very simple lifestyle designed to prevent contact with any luxury that might encourage indulgence, greed, softness or effeminacy.

John produced a four-year course designed to encourage 'useful learn-ing' and wrote all the school's initial textbooks. However, amid the aca-demic rigour, John reminded its masters: 'Beware you be not swallowed up in books. An ounce of love is worth a pound of knowledge'.[14] The Wesleys believed it was not the IQ but the 'I will' that mattered in educa-tion so Charles encouraged its pupils to sing:

> Give us an humble, active mind,
> From sloth and folly free;
> Give us a cheerful heart, inclined
> To truth and piety.[15]

There was to be no play because 'a mixed herd of unruly boys' encour-aged the wrong values. One has to remember that virtually all the sports we associate with schools today had not yet been invented and that the Wesleys had seen enough brutal and debasing forms of fun among adults, such as cockfighting and bull-baiting, to see no long-term bene-fits from encouraging 'sport'. They preferred the pupils' relaxation to take the form of useful tasks, such as gardening or learning music. John made the oft-quoted remark: 'he that plays as a child will play when he is a man'[16] and Charles thought sloth was 'the accursed root whence ten thousand evils shoot; every vice and every sin, doth with idleness begin'.[17] He wrote a hymn to endorse his dislike of unsupervised child-ish behaviour:

> Let heathenish boys
> In their pastimes rejoice,
> And be foolishly happy at play:
> Overstocked if they are,
> We have nothing to spare,
> Not a moment to trifle away.[18]

There were no school holidays because 'children may unlearn as much in one week as they have learned in several'.[19]

Within months of the school opening Charles felt the school was 'lay-ing the foundations of many generations'.[20] Two of the first pupils were Jane and John Grimshaw, the children of the Rector of Haworth. With their mother dead and their father undertaking increasingly extensive itinerant work, this seemed a sensible move. Jane was 10 years old and John was 12. Sadly Jane never reached her thirteenth birthday as she was taken ill and died at Kingswood on 14 January 1750. Charles took re-sponsibility for informing her father, seeing to the funeral arrangements, and comforting her brother. John Grimshaw wrote to his father that his sister had coped with her suffering 'wonderfully' and been 'perfectly resigned' to her death because of her faith. She had even sung to herself one of Charles' hymns:

> He hath loved me I cried,
> He hath suffered and died
> To redeem such a rebel as me.[21]

Grimshaw arrived from the North on 4 February to visit her grave and Charles comforted him as best he could.

Jane's death may have led to the decision to restrict the school to boys. Charles' contribution to their education was at times probably significant. For example, the three school letters that have survived from this time show Charles sorting out disciplinary issues. When one mother was very upset that her son had been sent home for bad behaviour, Charles consoled her about her 'poor wild boy' and said that he would personally look after the boy on his return 'and he shall not be corrected at all if you can have confidence in him that he shall not be mischievous anymore'. He also added that her son would probably recognize it was better to amend his ways at Kingswood than be 'whipped through Westminster or some other great school'.[22]

Charles explained to the pupils that their failings were a natural product of human sin – and he taught them to see that only by the grace of God could they hope to improve. In one of the hymns he wrote for them, he summarized his own personal experience in just eight lines:

> I cannot obey Thy commands
> Unassisted by grace from above;
> No grace I deserve at Thy hands,
> Yet I hope to recover Thy love:
> Thy mercy is promised to all,
> The giver of Jesus Thou art,
> And therefore attend to my call,
> And discover His love to my heart.[23]

John was keen to frighten the boys into good behaviour by depicting the hell that awaited the unrepentant sinner. It is said on one occasion he plunged a naughty child's finger into a candle flame so the boy could experience a taste of the hellfire that awaited him. He was delighted when one of the teachers at Kingswood took the boys to see corpses in the local morgue and reduced them to almost hysterical fear. In his hymns for the boys Charles was equally prepared to depict the 'dark and bottomless' pit of hell where the damned 'die an everlasting death' with 'their tortured bodies ... scorched by the consuming fire'.[24] He urged the boys to avoid dooming themselves to such an appalling fate:

> Shall I, – amidst a ghastly band, –
> Dragg'd to the judgement-seat,
> Far on the left with horror stand,
> My fearful doom to meet?
> Abandon'd to extreme despair,
> Eternally undone ...
> While they enjoy His heavenly love,
> Must I in torments dwell?[25]

Charles visited the school regularly over many years. As far as we know, he taught the boys his hymns by making them learn them two lines at a time. Many of the hymns he wrote for them were eventually collected in his *Hymns for Children*, which was published in 1763. One became particularly well known:

> Gentle Jesus, meek and mild,
> Look upon a little child;
> Pity my simplicity,
> Suffer me to come to Thee.[26]

Looking after other people's children must have brought home to the brothers their own lack of a family. John made a virtue out of this, even though he was no advocate for the imposed celibacy of Catholicism. He claimed the advantage of having no wife or children was having more time to serve God:

> I have no babes to hold me here ...
> I have no sharer of my heart,
> To rob my Saviour of a part,
> And desecrate the whole;
> Only betrothed to Christ am I,
> And wait his coming from the sky,
> To wed my happy soul.[27]

Charles appeared to concur until he fell hopelessly in love en route to visiting Ireland for the first time. The more religiously minded among the troops garrisoned in Dublin had initially been led by a Baptist called

Benjamin La Trobe, whose son was later to emigrate to America and find fame as the architect for the House of Representatives and the Senate in Washington. In 1746 John Cennick had transformed the religious society there into a Moravian organization, though its members were better known as 'Swaddlers' (allegedly because of Cennick's frequent references to the baby Jesus wrapped in swaddling clothes). A rival Methodist society had then been founded by a Wesleyan lay preacher called Thomas Williams, and John Wesley had briefly visited its 200 members in August 1747. Not long after his departure, rioting between rival apprentice gangs had led to the chapel in which the Methodists were meeting being set on fire, and, in response, John decided to send out Charles.

On his journey Charles stopped for a time at Garth, a small village near Builth Wells in South Wales. There he stayed at a large country mansion owned by Marmaduke Gwynne, a local magistrate who had been educated at Jesus College, Oxford, and at Lincoln's Inn. His wife Sarah was a rich heiress and the Gwynnes loved entertaining. They rarely had less than a dozen or so guests staying at their house. Marmaduke had been won over to Methodism by hearing Howell Harris preach and his wife Sarah by reading John Wesley's *An Appeal to Men of Reason and Religion*. Charles was captivated by their pretty, shy 21-year-old daughter, Sally. He later told her 'at first sight my soul seemed pleased to take acquaintance with thee. And never have I found such a nearness to any creature as to you.'[28] She found Charles' personality equally magnetic but neither of them said anything to Marmaduke. Charles was almost twice Sally's age and he lacked the social standing expected in any potential suitor.

Marmaduke Gwynne and Edward Philips, vicar of the nearby church at Maesmynis, accompanied Charles to Dolgelly. The next day Charles got as far as the Bar-Myni Ferry by five in the afternoon but then had to wait two hours because of the stormy weather. To make up lost time he rode almost 25 hours in the saddle with just one brief stop before reaching Holyhead, where he embarked for Ireland. He arrived in Dublin on 9 September and found the Methodists had leased a base for themselves in a weaver's shed in Cork Street. Charles' lodgings proved squalid:

A family of squalling children, a landlady just ready to lie in, a maid who has no time to do the least thing for us, are some of our inconveniences. Our two rooms for four persons ... and I groan for elbow room; our diet answerable to our lodgings; no one to mend our clothes; no money to buy more.[29]

Understandably Sally was very much in his thoughts and so he confided by letter to John that he was considering whether he ought to marry (but without naming her). John 'neither opposed nor much encouraged'.[30]

Charles faced a far more daunting task than his brother had because the city was experiencing one of its not infrequent periods of gang warfare. He saw a woman beaten to death and competing mobs fight each other till the ground ran red with blood. It horrified him when the courts acquitted a man who had killed another by jumping on his stomach. Violence against the Methodists was just a part of this wider lawlessness, but no less frightening for that:

> A mixed rabble of Papists and Protestants broke open our room ... and a warehouse, stealing or destroying the goods to a considerable value; beat and wounded several with clubs, etc; tore away the pulpit, benches, window-cases, etc and burnt them openly ... swearing they would murder us all.[31]

Undeterred, Charles rallied the burgeoning society. He even preached under the very wall of the army barracks so that ordinary soldiers could hear him despite the opposition of their officers. On 7 October he was amused to see how several soldiers, who had subsequently defied orders to attend one of his addresses, 'skulked down, kneeling or sitting on the ground, behind the women' to avoid being seen. [32]

Charles set up two meeting places. One was in the former Moravian meeting-house in Skinner's Alley (because they had moved elsewhere) and the other was a warehouse in Dolphin's Barn Lane where he and his fellow preachers could also stay. He also preached regularly in Dublin gaol. As the crowds listening to him became larger, Methodists became less of a target for those who enjoyed causing problems. Nevertheless, there were still some incidents. For example, Charles was hit by a stone on 30 October but fortunately not seriously hurt, and mob violence again surfaced in the city in November. Nevertheless, Charles decided to risk even greater danger by visiting huge sections of the country in order to spread the revival further afield. Near Athlone stones were hurled at him and his associates and one of them narrowly escaped death when a servant of the local Catholic priest clubbed him in the face.

There was little success in converting Catholics to Methodism (especially as the Methodist preachers spoke in English and not Irish), but there was a very positive response from the Protestant community, especially among craftsmen and shopkeepers who had recently arrived with their families from England, Wales and Scotland. Some of the success was reminiscent of the early work at Kingswood. For example, Charles wrote of a place called Tyril's Pass:

> [Never had I spoken] to more hungry souls. They devoured every word [and] some expressed their satisfaction in a way peculiar to them and whistled for joy ... The people of Tyril's Pass were wicked to a proverb; swearers, drunkards, Sabbath-breakers, thieves, etc, from time immemorial. But now the scene is entirely changed. Not an oath is heard, or a drunkard seen among them. They are turned from darkness to light.[33]

Howell Harris expressed his admiration at what Charles was achieving and encouraged him: 'Go on my dear honoured brother – and blaze abroad the flame of Jesus our God.'[34] From America George Whitefield also rejoiced and urged Charles to 'turn thousands and tens of thousands more into righteousness, and shine as stars for ever and ever'.[35] However, the strain on Charles' health was becoming evident and so it was agreed in March 1748 he would return home. Before he left he wrote a hymn of thanksgiving for the success of his mission:

> I the wandering sheep have found,
> Earth and heaven with praise resound![36]

He headed straight for Garth and another chance to see Sally Gwynne. Landing at Holyhead he crossed the sea between the Isle of Anglesey and the mainland in an overcrowded boat and in the teeth of a gale. After a brief rest overnight, he rode all day through driving wind and rain to Tan-y-bwlch. The next day he was up at five in the morning to once again ride all day through pouring rain. Another overnight stop and another early dawn start saw him press on through appalling weather 'till I could ride no more; walked the last hour; and by five dropped into Garth ... [where] they quickly put me to bed'.[37] He stayed a fortnight in order to recover from the hardships he had faced. By the end of that time he had no doubts that he had fallen in love with Sally.

Back in London, Charles confided his secret to Charles Perronet, who told him it seemed an ideal match because her family was highly respectable and well connected. Charles wrote 17 hymns on the subject of marriage as a means of saying Sally could enhance his ministry rather than diminish it:

> Two are better far than one
> For counsel or for fight.

How can one be warm alone
Or serve his God aright?[38]

In June and July Sally and her father spent time first in Bristol and then in London so they could see Charles' work at first hand. His friends thought she was very agreeable and recognized in her positive response to what she saw that she was a sufficiently committed Christian to accept hardships for the good of the gospel. This may help explain why the Methodist Conference that summer decreed that 'a believer might marry without suffering loss in his soul'.[39] The society at the Foundery had particular occasion to look favourably on her because on 19 July Sally saved the building from a serious fire. Having forgotten something from her room there, she returned only to find the door locked. Fortunately she insisted on the lock being broken so she could enter. It was then discovered the bed sheets were on fire because the servant responsible for the room had accidentally knocked over a lit candle before departing.

By then Charles' private life had been overshadowed by the return of George Whitefield to London on 10 July. Whitefield was surprised by how much the Calvinist branch of Methodism had lost its direction during his absence. Charles promised that, if unity could be restored, George would be 'an equal with his brother'.[40] However, Whitefield appreciated that their doctrinal differences might make a reunion impossible and he confided to Howell Harris that he thought John was far too autocratic to agree to any dual leadership.

Charles agreed to escort the Gwynnes back to their home. On the way he let Sally visit Windsor Castle, undertook some preaching in Reading, and spent three days showing Sally the colleges of Oxford. Once in Bristol, Sally was exposed more deeply to the nature of his preaching work at Kingswood and in the Hotwells and the Horsefair. For someone of her relatively sheltered background, it must have been a real eye-opener to see the wide range of people with whom Charles was dealing. After a brief but very happy interlude at Garth for a week, Charles tearfully parted from Sally on 8 August, but said nothing about marriage because he still feared John's reaction.

Though the hoped-for unity between the Wesleyans and the Calvinists did not materialize that summer, progress was made towards greater cooperation. Both sides agreed not to speak ill of the other and there was a mutual understanding that preachers should endeavour to avoid 'preaching controversially' on themes that would upset the other branch. John thought these agreements were too little to be of any real worth and Charles felt the opportunity for unity had essentially 'come to nought'.

However, Charles welcomed the fact he could now invite Whitefield to again preach in the Wesleyan societies.

Whitefield began carving a new niche for himself with the help of the Countess of Huntingdon. She had become a more frequent attendee at the Moorfields Tabernacle than at the Foundery because of her liking for Howell Harris, who had been a great comfort to her on the death of her husband in the autumn of 1746. The two evangelists used all their influence to persuade her to fulfil a larger role in the revival. Whitefield told her:

> When, like Noah's dove, we have been wandering about in a fruitless search for happiness, and have found no rest for the sole of our feet, the glorious Redeemer is ready to reach out His hand and receive us into His ark. This hand, honoured madam, He is reaching out to you.[41]

The countess decided her role might be to win over the aristocracy and she made Whitefield her chaplain and then invited all her contacts to hear him. On 20 August Whitefield faced his first test, preaching to a congregation that included the Earl of Chesterfield and Lord Bolingbroke. He passed with flying colours. Bolingbroke described him as 'the most extraordinary man of our times'[42] and Chesterfield wrote that Whitefied's 'eloquence is unrivalled – his zeal inexhaustible; and not to admire both would argue a total absence of taste'.[43] Whitefield was pleased but said his new role should not stop him undertaking his wider ministry to the poor. The countess, who was 'all in a flame for Jesus',[44] promised to fund new societies and chapels all around the country, but Whitefield felt America was calling him back. He wrote to John in September 1748 that he would therefore leave him to settle societies everywhere.

Prior to his departure, Whitefield set off for a third tour of Scotland. It was marred by ill health. He described his symptoms as 'pain in my breath' but he was also vomiting and losing 'a great quantity of blood'.[45] Some historians believe he may have burst a blood vessel in his throat by straining his voice too much. Whatever the cause, Whitefield's health was never the same again. In contrast, Charles was taking more care of his physical well-being than ever before. This was undoubtedly the influence of Sally, who urged him to try and sleep in a proper bed each night and for a reasonable amount of time. She therefore encouraged him to abandon John's unreasonable demand that he should always rise at four o'clock in the morning. Charles said he slept better knowing he had 'a friend who constantly attends my slumbers and hovers over me like a guardian angel'.[46]

That autumn Charles undertook a second and more challenging visit to Ireland. At Kinsale, for example, he received a severe blow to the side of his head from one opponent. However, he was delighted by his success, especially in Cork:

> Outward wickedness has disappeared, outward religion succeeded ... At five I took the field again: but such a sight I have rarely seen! Thousands and thousands had been waiting some hours, Protestants and Papists, high and low ... I cried after them for an hour, to the utmost extent of my voice, yet without hoarseness or weariness.[47]

The next day he wrote: 'Wherever we go, we are received as angels of God'[48] and he rejoiced in the effect on ordinary lives:

> One poor wretch told me, before his wife, that he had lived in drunkenness, adultery, and all the works of the devil, for twenty-one years; had beaten her every day of that time; and never had any remorse till he heard us: but now he goes constantly to church, behaves lovingly towards his wife, abhors the thing that is evil, especially his old sins. This is one instance out of many.[49]

The clergy were Charles' main opponents, disliking the arrival in their churches of so many 'strangers' seeking to take communion. At Bandon Charles voiced the pain this caused him: 'We send them to church to hear ourselves railed at.'[50] But in an interesting comment in his journal he confessed he often found it easier to face such clerical opposition than reject the appeals of those members of the church hierarchy who liked him yet wanted him to cease his preaching:

> I do not find it good for me to be countenanced by my superiors. It is a snare and burden to my soul ... Sometimes our waiting on great men ... [is] apt to weaken our hands, and betray us into an undue deference and respect of persons![51]

In September he wrote a special hymn for the Roman Catholics whom he described as 'bound in ignorance and sin' by a clergy whom he felt were prepared to 'sell poor souls for gain':

> Those blinded leaders of the blind,
> Who frighten them from thee,
> And still bewitch the people's mind
> With hellish sorcery:
> Pierced with thy Spirit's two-edged sword,
> They shall no more deceive.[52]

On 8 October Charles embarked for England but with a presentiment of danger. A huge storm developed, wrecked the ship's mainsail, and washed the ship's captain overboard. One of the passengers took over command and ensured the ship was not sunk, but Charles ascribed his survival to God, 'our invisible pilot'.[53] The following day he left Holyhead and travelled across the Welsh mountains in appalling conditions till he reached the Baladan ferry. The crossing proved so rough that it was feared the ferry would sink and Charles said he and the other passengers were 'half-drowned'. One of the women clung to him with such terror that he was aware she would prevent him swimming if the boat did go under, but he told her and the others: 'Fear not ... the hairs of our head are still numbered. Our Father sits at the helm!'[54]

On 13 October Charles finally reached the home of the Gwynnes and remained at Garth for a week. At some stage he proposed to Sally and was accepted, but he put off seeking the formal approval of her parents and his brother. Instead he spent three weeks working in Bristol and the surrounding area, pushing his health to its limits. On 25 October he was quite seriously injured in a fall from his horse. He refers not only to damage to his hand and a crushed foot but also to severe pains in his chest. However, the next month he travelled to London to finally tell his brother about Sally. To his surprise John said he was delighted and that Sally was an ideal choice. Charles then headed for Garth to ask Sally's family for their approval, arriving on 21 December.

Sally's father was supportive of the proposed marriage but feared his wife's reaction. Charles therefore used one of Sally's sisters as an intermediary. She reported back that their mother liked Charles but he would have to be earning at least £100 a year to be regarded as a suitable husband. Charles had virtually no income of his own other than a small legacy. Like the lay preachers, he tended to rely on money from the societies to fund his expenses. His only hope of attaining a regular financial income was by gaining money from the sale of his hymnbooks. Charles told a distressed Sally to place her trust in God:

> The hinge on which it all turns is not Fortune, not even the consent of friends, but the Glory of God and the good of souls (yours especially). If our meeting would really answer these ends, I defy all Earth and Hell to hinder it.[55]

As a lucky omen, Sally purchased the first subscription to Charles' latest two-volume edition of his hymns.

Friends in London welcomed the news of Charles' engagement, except for those ladies who had hoped to persuade him to marry them.

Charles told Sally that in the case of a young lady called Elizabeth Cart: 'My cheerfulness has murdered hers.'[56] Similar opposition came from Edward Philips, the Vicar of Maesmynis, who had hoped to marry Sally. Charles began investigating exactly what revenue he might derive from his share of the royalties from the various publications he and John had produced. He wrote to Mrs Gwynne to explain what he thought he was worth and how she could be reassured he was not after any of her family's fortune. He offered to prove this by committing himself legally to never becoming a beneficiary to any Gwynne money.

Mrs Gwynne refused to accept Charles' word about his potential income so he travelled to see Ebenezer Blackwell, a banking friend in London. He recommended Charles persuade a dozen or so of his wealthier contacts to raise the income he required by annual subscription. However, John would not hear of such a plan, fearing the subscribers would feel they had the right to dictate what Charles should do. Instead, he offered to provide £100 a year himself by paying the money out of his income from his publications. Mrs Gwynne refused to accept this solution because she thought income from writing was too unsure a source. Charles confided his distress to Vincent Perronet, who immediately wrote to her, telling her to be less mercenary and to listen to the voice of God. Lest such an argument fail, he also made clear he felt Mrs Gywnne was misjudging the value of what the Wesleys were publishing: 'They are works which will last and sell while any sense of true religion and learning still remain among us.' [57]

Mrs Gwynne finally gave her approval but, when an overjoyed Charles journeyed to Garth, he found a fresh obstacle. Sally's eldest brother, Howell, now opposed the family becoming linked to a Methodist. Fortunately the rest of the family persuaded him to change his mind. It was agreed that Charles and Sally should marry in April 1749. John Wesley made it a condition that Sally should promise never to persuade Charles to abandon his itinerant ministry (or the vegetable diet John deemed good for his brother's health!). While waiting for the marriage day, Charles returned to his missionary work and corresponded with Sally by post, often writing in verse. To their surprise John suddenly appeared to have second thoughts about their marriage and talked of withdrawing his offer of financial support. This may have arisen because he feared Mrs Gwynne would oppose Charles continuing with his itinerant ministry, but the more likely reason is that John's thoughts were also turning to marriage and so he felt he might not be able to afford to be so generous.

Unknown to anyone, the previous autumn John had fallen in love with Grace Murray, the sweet-natured 32-year-old housekeeper at the

Orphan House in Newcastle. As a teenager Grace had rejected her religious upbringing and run away to London to join her elder sister, becoming a servant in the house of an East India merchant. At the age of 20 she had married a sea captain called Alexander Murray and it was the death of their first child which had acted as the catalyst for Grace joining the Methodists in 1739. Her husband had bitterly opposed this and threatened to place her in a lunatic asylum. His death at sea in 1742 had therefore come as a welcome release. Returning to her hometown of Newcastle, she had become not only the housekeeper of the Orphan House but also a class leader. Her ability to lead devotions and her charitable work with the sick made her a popular figure, and she acted as a loving nurse to any of the travelling preachers who were taken ill. It was when Grace nursed John for a time that he decided she was his potential partner.

Grace was unsure how to respond. She was conscious that her attractive appearance could be a snare to men. A previous suitor called John Brydon had abandoned his faith when she had refused to marry him. However, she was flattered by John Wesley's attentions. Unfortunately, John found it difficult to take the step of formally proposing. The nearest he got to it was saying: 'If I ever marry I think you will be the person.' Grace's situation was complicated by the fact she had previously been courted by a prominent Methodist preacher called John Bennet, whom she had nursed through a six-month illness in 1746. Born in Derbyshire, Bennet was a well-educated man, who had been a magistrate's clerk and a carrier arranging for the transport of goods between Sheffield and Manchester. His faith had been kindled while attending Sheffield races, and in 1743 he had become one of John Wesley's preachers, introducing Methodism into Chester, Rochdale and Stockport. His effectiveness can be judged from the fact that he was invited to the first Methodist Conference in 1744. Grace had told Bennet she did not want a second husband, but they were still in correspondence with each other.

Bennet viewed John's courtship of Grace as an abuse of his position as leader of Methodism to ride roughshod over the love of a preacher. He therefore renewed his suit, telling Grace that God wanted her to marry him and not Wesley. Some historians have accused Grace of being unacceptably flirtatious with the feelings of both her suitors, but this ignores her inherent desire not to upset either of them, and the problem she found in handling two eloquent men who were both above her in terms of their social status and background.

Charles, unaware of all these circumstances, found John's change of heart over his own proposed marriage hurtful, but placed the matter in the hands of God. This did not prevent him becoming 'weary, faint, oppressed' in spirit.[58] Fortunately John eventually relented and again assented to Charles' marriage. A factor may have been Mrs Gwynne's assurance that she would not use her position as mother-in-law to oppose Charles' itinerant work. On 8 April 1749 John married Charles and Sally at Llanlleonfel Church, which was the Gwynne's small family chapel. In the words of an ecstatic Charles, 'not a cloud was seen from morning till night':

> At eight I led my Sally to church ... Mr Gwynne gave her to me, under God. My brother joined our hands. It was a most solemn season of love! I never had more of the divine presence at the sacrament. My brother ... prayed over us in strong faith. We walked back to the house, and joined again in prayer. Prayer and thanksgiving was our whole employment. We were cheerful without mirth, serious without sadness ... My brother seemed the happiest among us.[59]

Two days later John headed for Ireland, taking Grace Murray with him. Officially she acted as his servant but in practice she played a very active part in his ministry, visiting the sick, comforting the bereaved, and leading devotions among the bands created for women. Such had been Charles' success in Ireland that John and Grace spent ten happy weeks there. As a result John later agreed to visit the country at first annually and then, when Methodism was more established, about every two years. Grace's presence may partially explain why John chose this time to stress the importance of a loving spirit by publishing his *Letter to a Roman Catholic* and his sermon *Catholic Spirit*, both of which urged a more tolerant approach between Christian denominations and a recognition that all Christians shared the 'essentials' of the gospel.

Meanwhile Charles was busy proving his marriage was no restriction on his work. He spent his honeymoon preaching in the area around Garth and then resumed his travels with Sally riding behind him on horseback. He wrote to John:

> Never since I preached the Gospel have I been more owned and assisted of God than now. He is always with me in the work of the ministry; therefore I live by the Gospel. More zeal, more life, more power, I have not felt for some years ... so ... marriage has been no hindrance. You will hardly believe it sits so light upon me.[60]

In May he spent a very busy fortnight in London and told the Foundery members they could see he was not married to one person but to all of them. He then returned to a gruelling schedule in Bristol and the surrounding area. Sally was concerned about the impact on Charles' health but gave him her unqualified backing, even though the travelling made her 'spent with heat and fatigue'.[61] At the end of June Charles wrote in his journal: 'All look upon Sally with mine eyes.'[62]

The summer of 1749 saw the return of Whitefield's wife from America and she and George set up home in a new house adjacent to the Tabernacle. Once again he tried to reconcile the two branches of Methodism, asking Howell Harris to draw up possible terms of union. Charles was back in London in July but John was travelling in the North so the result was a delayed conference in Bristol at the start of August. The minutes record that most wanted 'a general union of our societies throughout England ... firmly united together by one spirit of love and heavenly mindedness'. Matters were helped by Whitefield's determination not to resume his role as leader of the Calvinistic Methodist Association. He made clear his sole desire was to be free to preach the gospel to any who would listen, whether they were atheists or agnostics, churchmen or dissenters, Wesleyans or Calvinists. To those who saw themselves as 'Whitefieldites', he made repeated comments like 'Let my name be forgotten, let me be trodden under the feet of all men, if Jesus may thereby be glorified'[63] and he tried to play down the theological differences: 'Let us look above names and parties: let Jesus be our all in all.'[64]

Unfortunately not even Whitefield's eloquence could produce complete unity. Nevertheless, he handed over the name of 'Methodist' to the Wesleys, leaving the brothers well placed to take over the religious societies created by him and the Calvinists. Just as importantly he agreed to become a preacher in their societies. It is important to note that it was Charles and not John who initiated the move that enabled this to happen. Charles invited his friend to preach in the Orphan House in Newcastle and Whitefield promptly accepted. Charles wrote:

> I gave him full possession of our pulpit and people's hearts ... The world is confounded. The hearts of those who seek the Lord rejoice ... Some at London will be alarmed at the news, but it is the Lord's doing.[65]

Seeing the huge crowds gather to hear Whitefield preach in the Midlands, John then acceded, if rather grudgingly, that Charles had been right to invite him. Publicly Whitefield reiterated he would be 'the head of no party'.[66] His contribution to the growth of the Wesleyan societies should not be underestimated because none could match his preaching.

During the summer the Gwynnes moved to a new home in Ludlow and Charles and John met there so John could formally sign the documentation providing Charles with his promised income. The money came from lay preachers selling hymnbooks and other publications so it was an arrangement which very much encouraged Charles to further cultivate his links with them – something John was particularly keen to promote. The agreement enabled the newly weds in September to take up residence in a small and narrow rented house in what is now called Charles Street in Stoke's Croft, Bristol. It was a very modest home but it had a garden with fruit trees at the back and Charles found this a particular source of pleasure. He consecrated his home by prayer and thanksgiving and sang a celebratory hymn:

> Me and mine I fain would give
> A sacrifice to thee,
> By the ancient model live,
> The true simplicity:
> Walk as in my Maker's sight,
> Free from worldly guile and care,
> Praise my innocent delight,
> And all my business prayer.[67]

Charles found that having his own home enabled members of Sally's family to become frequent visitors and this was not always to his liking. Within three days he was complaining to his friend Ebenezer Blackwell about the way Sally's overfashionable sisters, Betsy and Margaret, swallowed up his time.[68] To counter the social pressures Charles insisted on once more rising at four o'clock in the morning for prayer and on setting aside part of the day for reading and devotion. He also offered his home as a place where lay preachers could stay, calling it 'My own house, yet not my own'.[69] Despite her more genteel upbringing, Sally proved a great admirer of the preachers, saying they were living proof that God's grace was more effective in making true gentlemen than any amount of natural breeding. Sally was equally good when she met the Countess of Huntingdon and it has been suggested Selina's decision to lease a house in Clifton owed much to her desire to be near the married couple.

Charles' marriage continued to revitalize his ministry. In one of the new hymns published in 1749 he wrote of his own commitment:

> A faithful witness of thy grace,
> Long may I fill the allotted space,
> And answer all thy great design,
> Walk in the works by thee prepared,
> And find annex'd the vast reward,
> The crown of righteousness divine.[70]

And he captured the public's imagination with the more famous:

> Soldiers of Christ, arise,
> And put your armour on,
> Strong in the strength which God supplies
> Through his eternal Son.
> Strong in the Lord of hosts,
> And in his mighty power,
> Who in the strength of Jesus trusts
> Is more than conqueror.[71]

The success of Charles' marriage inevitably made John question his own continued celibacy. He and Grace had agreed to what was known as a 'spousal de praesenti', which meant that they were married bar engaging in sexual intercourse. Consequently Grace accompanied John on some of his travels, blind to the tittle-tattle this generated. Associating with her on a daily basis confirmed all John's feelings for her:

> I saw the work of God prosper in her hands. She lightened my burden more than can be expressed. She gave spiritual counsel to the women in the smaller societies and the believers in every place ... She was to me both a servant and a friend, as well as a fellow-labourer in the gospel. She provided everything I wanted.[72]

However, there was outspoken opposition when Grace accompanied John to London in August. Some openly told Grace she would never be accepted as John's wife and that marriage would destroy his effectiveness: 'If you love yourself, or if you love him, never think of it more.'[73] Despite this, John met up with John Bennet at Epworth in September to obtain his approval. It was only then that John discovered how extensively Grace had been in communication with Bennet, and he was especially shocked to hear that Grace had even been sending him copies of his own letters to her. Confused and angry, John told her to marry Bennet without delay. This reduced her to 'an agony of tears' and Grace said his harsh words would kill her. In reply John declared the passion 'which he had concealed too long'. Bennet responded by saying he would be destroyed if he did not marry her because she was his by right. Grace felt she was 'between two fires' and explained her dilemma to John:

> How can you think I love any one better than I love you! I love you a thousand times better than I ever loved John Bennet in my life. But I am afraid, if I don't marry him, he'll run mad.[74]

John opted out of making a decision about marriage. He left for New-castle saying he had to return to his preaching. This left Grace, who had become ill, with Bennet, who was able to plead his cause in his rival's absence. Concerned at the way Wesley had left her, fearful of what Bennet might do if he was refused, and weakened by sickness, Grace foolishly promised to marry him. Once recovered, she bitterly regretted this and rejoined John in Newcastle. They spent an emotional day discussing what to do. Grace urged they should quickly marry but John feared this would undermine his authority within the Methodist societies. Jealousy and envy were making too many women members prone to condemn her. John decided he ought to seek the consent of both Bennet and his brother Charles before declaring his reasons for marry-ing to all the Methodist societies. In the interim he agreed to renew his and Grace's 'spousal de praesenti' in front of a witness, a lay preacher called Christopher Hopper. This took place on 20 September in a village called Hineley Hill.

John wrote to Charles and asked Hopper to journey south to persuade Bennet to accede. While awaiting a response, John decided to leave Grace so she could examine the women bands in Allendale while he preached in the area around Whitehaven. Charles was devastated by the news. Some have alleged he selfishly feared the marriage would end his brother's financial support, but this ignores the fact that Charles' hymns were capable of bringing him in sufficient income. Others have specu-lated Charles was misled by the malicious gossip of ladies into thinking Grace was a scheming woman out to capture his brother, and that his wife Sally balked at Grace's humble origins and questionable relation-ship with Bennett. The explanation may be simpler. Already Charles was aware as a married man he was more reluctant to travel and, as he wrote to Grace, he feared marriage would put at risk John's leadership of the revival and thus destroy 'the whole work of God'.[75] Charles rode northwards as fast as he could. His resolve was strengthened at New-castle by having Grace's character blackened by a jealous woman called Jane Keith, who told him 'all the societies were ready to fly into pieces' if John married such an unsuitable wife.[76]

Charles caught up with John at Whitehaven. John assured him Grace was an ideal companion and an answer to the 'unholy desires and inord-inate affections' he had never entirely controlled:

She has every qualification that I desire. She understands all I want to have done. She is remarkably neat in person, in clothes, in all things. She is nicely frugal yet not sordid. She has much common sense, con-trives everything for the best, makes everything go as far as it will go, foresees what is wanting and provides for it all in time. She is a good work woman, able to do the finest, ready to do the coarsest work.[77]

Charles almost certainly replied that, whatever her qualities, Grace was not a person whom the Methodist societies would welcome as John's wife and that the religious revival required John's undivided attention. After much debate, the brothers had to agree to disagree and it was decided they would put the matter before their friend, Vincent Perronet.

However, Charles did not wait for such adjudication. He rode off to Hineley Hill where Grace was lodging in order to try and make her change her mind. We have no detailed account of what was said between them, but it is thought their meeting began with Charles collapsing in front of her from the strain of his journeys. His weakened state placed Grace at a disadvantage because she had no desire to further upset him. As far as we can tell Charles told her his brother would almost certainly decide against marriage and that she should therefore marry Bennet. He persuaded the distraught Grace to accompany him back to Newcastle. John put his preaching engagements ahead of chasing after them, convinced God would intervene if their marriage were intended. This left Charles free to use all his powers to persuade Grace and Bennet to marry.

Bennet had become angry at Grace's behaviour but Charles persuaded him the entire fault lay with John, who had abused his authority to seduce her. Members of the Newcastle society said John was 'a child of the Devil' and 'already in Hell Fire' over what he had done.[78] On 3 October Bennet married Grace at St Andrew's Church in Newcastle and both Charles and George Whitefield signed the register. Two days later the bridal party met up with John in Leeds. When the unsuspecting John shared his sorrow over his brother's opposition with Whitefield, George told him he should have long since married Grace, but that now it was his sad obligation to inform him Charles' 'impetuosity' had prevailed. It was Whitefield's oblique way of informing him of what had happened.

Once the real truth dawned on John, he vowed never to see his brother again. Both George and John Nelson used all their persuasive powers to alter his mind. At the resulting meeting neither brother could speak properly for weeping and both put the blame for what had happened primarily on Grace. As the bitter truth sunk home, John offered his 'deep unutter'd grief' to God and described himself as 'a drowning man'. He wrote a poem that reflected his hurt:

My soul a kindred spirit found
By Heaven entrusted to my care,

The Daughter of my faith and prayer ...
I saw her run, with winged speed,
In works of faith and labouring love;
I saw her glorious toil succeed,
And showers of blessings from above
Crowning her warm effectual prayer,
And glorified my God in her.[79]

When John met the couple he told Grace he would try to forgive her for committing a wrong that could never be remedied but he accused Bennet of acting dishonourably: 'I think you have done me the deepest wrong which I can receive on this side of the grave.'[80] Charles advocated that John should avoid ever meeting Grace again and told Bennet it was essential to 'pass an Act of Eternal Oblivion on all sides'.[81] Charles feared otherwise there would soon be scandalous stories circulated about John's passion for Grace. He told Bennet to ignore any attack by his brother: 'All private resentment must be sacrificed to public good ... For God's sake, and His people's, possess your soul in patience. I have need of patience too.'[82] Publicly Charles went out of his way to give the impression that nothing untoward had occurred: 'G. W. and my brother and I are one, a threefold cord which shall no more be broken.' Equally John never mentioned Grace's name in public again and only agreed to see her again many years later in 1788. There is no record of what passed between them on that occasion.

Behind the façade Charles knew John was bitterly resentful of what he had done and that their relationship was cruelly damaged. Charles fell into a deep depression and he claimed a throat infection made it impossible for him to preach. Understandably Vincent Perronet encouraged Charles to seek a reconciliation for the sake of his health and that of the revival:

Soothe his sorrows. Pour nothing but oil and wine on his wounds. Indulge no views ... but what tend to the honour of God ... and a healing of our wounded friend. How would the Philistines rejoice, could they hear that Saul and Jonathan were in danger from their own swords![83]

There is no doubt John's unhappiness was equally impinging on his effectiveness. By November George Whitefield was sufficiently alarmed to suggest the Countess of Huntingdon should take control of the Methodist movement: 'A leader is wanting. This honour hath been put upon your Ladyship by the great head of the church.'[84]

The loss of John's friendship made Charles increasingly turn to Whitefield. They agreed the countess' influence might turn the tide of church opinion in favour of supporting the religious revival and, once that happened, control of the Methodist societies would be assumed by the Anglican clergy, making the controversial use of lay preachers unnecessary. John's response was to show he was still leader by getting the Methodist Conference in November to agree to the very thing that would most scotch their plans – a radical increase in the number of lay preachers. He announced the minutes from previous conferences would be published as a handbook on what Methodism believed and that his *Sermons on Several Occasions* would become the movement's theological and ethical manual. Henceforth he would expect all the religious societies nationwide to look on the Foundery as 'the mother church'. Every circuit would have to appoint an 'Assistant' who was loyal to John and who would examine the spiritual health of the societies four times a year at a 'Quarterly Meeting'.

This deeply shocked Charles, who felt John was giving Methodism a status of its own outside of the Church of England. John then rubbed salt into the wound by demanding Charles and John Bennet should be at the forefront of the changes. Charles was asked to become the primary examiner of the new preachers and Bennet was told to travel the country encouraging all Methodist societies (whatever their origin) to join in a 'general union' with John Wesley as its 'Superintendent'. Charles declined and returned to Bristol from London 'exhausted ... with pain of body and vexation of spirit' and with little power or inclination to preach.[85] Despite being comforted by some of his closest friends, he records in December that he was 'quite sunk under the burden'.[86] He tried to keep a low profile rather than enter into any public confrontation with John and covered his refusal to travel by saying he wanted to focus his work in Bristol and London. Whitefield confided to John Bennet that Charles was 'doubtful of what he should do'[87] because John's conduct had become highly displeasing to God.

John may have felt he had pushed Charles and George too far because in January 1750 he offered an olive branch by granting permission for George to preach at the Foundery. This did not weaken their resolve to undermine what had happened at the 1749 Conference. Whitefield agreed with the countess that he would find Methodists worthy of ordination and she would use her influence to get them ordained. In this way Methodism could begin abandoning its use of travelling lay preachers and instead genuinely start transforming the Church from within. In February 1750 two events probably contributed to Charles' decision to become personally active in the revival again. Sally miscarried and, while taking her to her family to convalesce, he and Sally were almost killed while attempting to cross the swollen River Severn. Charles interpreted these events as signs of God's disapproval. He records in his journal that afterwards he received 'fresh strength for the work'.

All differences were temporarily laid aside when earthquakes struck London in February and March. It was generally accepted God was punishing the nation's continued sinfulness. Panic-stricken people rushed into the streets lest they be buried alive beneath their shaking homes, and begged God's forgiveness and mercy. Charles personally experienced the March earthquake:

> It shook the Foundery so violently that we all expected it to fall on our heads ... The earth moved westward, then east, then westward again, through all London and Westminster. It was a strong and jarring motion, attended with a rumbling noise, like that of distant thunder. Many houses were much shaken, and some chimneys thrown down, but without any further hurt. The alarm which it occasioned, as might be supposed, was deep and general.[88]

Family tragedy also occupied Charles' thoughts at this time. His much-loved sister Hetty died on 21 March. Her health had long been undermined by what she called 'the living death' of her disastrous marriage and she had asked that her epitaph should include the words 'a broken heart can bleed no more'.[89] The one consolation in her otherwise unhappy life had become seeing Charles and attending services at the Foundery. In her last letter to Charles she had written:

> It is almost incredible what a skeleton I am grown, so that my bones are ready to come through my skin ... I cannot say I desire life a minute longer ... [But] I trust to remember and bless you many times yet before I die ... Forgive all blunders. Adieu.[90]

He visited this 'gracious, tender, trembling soul'[91] every few days in her final illness for 'sweet fellowship ... [till] her spirit was set at liberty'.[92] It is not surprising that later that year Charles was to champion his other sister, Martha , and protect her from having to return to live with Westley Hall, whom he judged 'abandoned to every vice'.[93]

Hetty's death probably made Charles more prone to accept the increasingly held view that in April there would be a third earthquake heralding in the final Day of Judgement. Charles' mother-in-law wrote of the mounting panic in the city: 'Yesterday I saw the Westminster end of the town full of coaches, and crowds flying out of the reach of Divine justice ... London looked like a sacked city.'[94] Charles felt there was no question but that the earthquakes were God's punishment on a sinful world and he preached repentance to those who flocked to the Foundery to be saved: 'Kiss the Son, lest he be angry, and ye perish ... Confess with broken hearts the most damnable of your sins, your unbelief.'[95] He wrote 19 hymns on the earthquakes. Some reflected God's understandable anger over humanity's continued sinfulness:

So oft, and terribly reproved,
Our land is warn'd in vain,
For oh! The cause is unremoved,
The sin doth still remain.[96]

Others urged the need for confession in order to receive forgiveness:

Righteous Lord, Thy people spare
Lo! We turn at last to Thee,
Humbly the correction bear
Of our past iniquity,
Own the cause of our distress,
Mournfully our sins confess.[97]

On the day the world was thought to end, George Whitefield spoke to the gathered crowds in Hyde Park about God's coming judgement. However, the world did not end and almost immediately the divisions within the leadership of Methodism re-emerged. John's ill will towards Bennet publicly surfaced. He criticized his preaching and restricted his access to societies, even in those areas where Bennet was the acknowledged main preacher. John's character assassination began making inroads and Bennet understandably looked for support to Charles and George, but neither was prepared to further strain their already tenuous relationship with John. Charles wrote: 'You and your partner [Grace] must make amends for the loss of my brother ... whose love I have small hopes of recovering in this world.'[98] And Whitefield told him he should put up with whatever John said or did to him in the interests of the revival as a whole.

Bennet said it was time Whitefield appreciated that John was undermining the Calvinist thinking of most converts simply because he wanted personal control over all the Methodist societies. Whitefield said he was not concerned who ran the societies and again urged Bennet to be patient: 'Look to Jesus, and let not little things disappoint and move you ... [Satan] will be always trying to vex and unhinge you.'[99] Nevertheless, Whitefield confided to Selina, Countess of Huntingdon, that John was mistaking 'an overbearing spirit' for authority from God[100] and he emphasized the virtues of Charles. To John's annoyance, Charles clearly became the countess' protégé. He began preaching in Selina's mansion in Chelsea and administering communion to members of the nobility, though he lacked the real star quality of Whitefield to draw large numbers of the rich and famous.

Methodism's alleged link with Jacobitism was very much a thing of the past and some of the greatest figures in the government, including Lord North and William Pitt, Earl of Chatham, came to hear Whitefield. When Frederick, Prince of Wales, visited the countess' home, he commented to his sister: 'When I am dying I think I shall be happy to seize the skirt of Lady Huntingdon's mantle to lift me up with her to heaven.'[101] The court gossips were quick to declare 'his Royal Highness is fast verging towards Methodism'.[102] Unfortunately such success was marred by the failure of the countess to achieve the hoped-for ordination of existing lay preachers. The two eventual exceptions were Martin Madan, an able young lawyer who was related to the poet William Cowper, and Moses Brown, a less well-educated but equally fervent Christian.

In September John urged Charles to travel the country and identify which society members could be added to the ranks of the lay preachers. Charles put off this role by saying he would first have to check which of the existing preachers were still fit for their task. He reluctantly set out for the North as the first stage in a nationwide survey, but was thrown by his horse near Islington. Initially he tried to continue his journey but by the time he had reached St Albans it was clear he had severely injured himself. Charles returned to London to recuperate and then, in late October, set out for Ludlow, where his wife was staying with her family. After staying there a month, he returned first to Bristol and then to London in December.

Early in 1751 it was John's turn to be injured. He damaged his ankle in a fall on the icy road across London Bridge. He was nursed by one of Charles' acquaintances, a 41-year-old widow of Huguenot extraction called Mary Vazeille, in her home in Threadneedle Street. Charles had first met 'Molly' (as Mary was usually called) back in 1749 and he and Sally had shown her much kindness, escorting her on tours of Oxford and nearby Blenheim, and inviting her to the Gwynne family home in Ludlow. Molly was, in Charles' words, 'a woman of a sorrowful spirit'[103] and he thought she had nothing in common with his brother so it came as a complete shock when John announced he was going to marry her. On first appearance she appeared a sounder choice than Grace because she had independent means and higher social standing and her age precluded the possibility of children who might divert John from his work. But it did not take long for most to recognize she was entirely the wrong person for John. One preacher commented:

> Had he searched the whole kingdom he would scarcely have found a woman more unsuitable to the prospects of a happy marriage. There never was a more preposterous union. It is pretty certain that no loves lighted their torches on this occasion.[104]

John hurriedly married her on 18 February to avoid any discussion of the matter. Charles was mortified that John had not even consulted him:

> I was thunderstruck... [and] I retired to mourn with my faithful Sally. I groaned all the day, and several following ones, under my own and the people's burden. I could eat no pleasant food, nor preach, nor rest, either by night or by day.[105]

Molly never forgave Charles for not immediately welcoming the marriage, even though he afterwards made every effort to convince her he was 'perfectly reconciled to her'.[106] He was reduced to commenting on his delight when he managed to speak with her for two minutes before a Foundery service without her quarrelling with him.

Within a couple of months, Molly was openly complaining that hers was a loveless marriage. She thought no husband should expect his wife to risk life and limb on the treacherous roads or face the discomfort of eating and sleeping in shoddy inns. Wesley said hearing her complaints about his itinerant ministry were 'like tearing the flesh off his bones'.[107] In April 1751 John made his first journey to Scotland but he told Charles he might as well have been preaching to the stones. His unhappy marriage thus coincided with his first major failure since his time in Georgia. Given John's depression, it was probably fortunate for him there was no alternative leader. Charles still remained loyal and Whitefield took the decision to return to America (without his wife Elizabeth who was also finding the strain of constant travelling non-conducive to a happy life).

The only other commanding figure was Howell Harris, who was still travelling about 150 miles every week, preaching two to three times per day. However, at this critical juncture Harris was very badly injured by a blow to his head. It left him in such excruciating pain that he had to withdraw entirely from his work. He suffered what some have considered a mental breakdown and was confined to his bed for a number of years. John ruthlessly exploited Harris' absence to denigrate what he and Whitefield had achieved.

But John's real venom was reserved for Bennet, who had deprived him of Grace. In the face of this, Charles did all he could to show his continued affection for the couple. In September 1751 he convened a meeting of the northern preachers at Leeds without John's approval and encouraged Bennet to preach 'to the satisfaction of all'. He told him and Grace that he hoped his friendship with them would prove eternal. However, by October Bennet was sufficiently resentful of John's attitude to also question Charles' motives. He announced he was leaving Methodism. Charles wrote to Grace, saying 'My heart shall not be broken off from you' and begged Bennet to reconsider:

> I appeal to your calmer judgement ... I design never to quarrel with John Bennet, though John Bennet does all he can to force me ... The second blow makes the quarrel and that with God's help I will never give. Try again (if you are not weary of ceaseless provocations) ... If you loved me as I do you, you could not so hastily think evil of me.[108]

Bennet was not to be altered. He took with him some of the societies in which he had been most active and accused John of behaving as if he were a pope. Grace must have found all this very distressing. The main focus of Bennet's activities became a village chapel in Warburton, six miles east of Warrington and there he died aged only 45 from jaundice in May 1759. Grace thus became a widow again, but by then with five sons to look after. It was a harsh life, which she bore with her usual courage. In her later life she settled at Chapel-en-le-Frith and rejoined the Methodists, holding class meetings in her house until her death in 1803.

John's itinerant ministry came under increasing challenge from his wife. Jealous and possessive by temperament, Molly began claiming his travels were just an excuse for infidelity. She even accused him of having an affair with Charles' wife. John's habit of writing to women whom he had met fanned her fears, especially his correspondence with Sarah Ryan, the attractive young housekeeper at Kingswood. John's attempts to reason with Molly simply drove her into such fury that she sometimes struck him. One preacher recorded once seeing her and John locked in a fight on the floor. She was foaming at the mouth and holding in her fists some of John's hair, which she had torn out of his head. John denied this story, but that may have been because he was ashamed of such scenes. In one letter John begged Molly to be more reasonable:

> Suspect me no more, asperse me no more, provoke me no more. Do not any longer contend for mastery, for power, money, or praise ... Leave me to be governed by God and my conscience.[109]

Inevitably they ended up living separate lives. When Molly died in 1781, John had not seen her for a number of years and he was not even told 'till a day or two after'.[110] Such marital disharmony stood out in sharp contrast to Charles' continued happiness with Sally, whom he often called 'my best friend':

> I look back with delight on every step, every circumstance, in that whole design of providential love. I rejoice with great joy at our blessed union … [and] desire to thank my great Benefactor for giving you to my bosom.[111]

In another letter he wrote: 'Every hour of every day you are laid upon my heart; so that I make mention of you in all my prayers.'[112] Charles knew that if his marriage had been made in heaven, John's had been made in hell. Many years later he told one of his sons:

> If any man would learn to pray, let him think of marrying … No one step or action in life has so much influence on eternity as marriage. It is an heaven or an hell (they say) in this world much more so in the next.[113]

Though Grace Murray's name was never mentioned, the ghost of what might have been if John had married her instead of Molly Vazeille continued to cast a permanent shadow over the relationship between the brothers.

9

A Fear of Dissent

O Lord, our strength and righteousness,
Our base, and head, and corner-stone,
Our peace with God, our mutual peace,
Unite, and keep Thy servants one,
That while we speak in Jesus' name,
We all may speak, and think the same.

That Spirit of love to each impart,
That fervent mind, which was in Thee,
So shall we all our strength exert,
In heart, and word, and deed agree
To advance the kingdom of Thy grace,
And spread Thine everlasting praise ...

Pride, only pride, can cause divorce,
Can separate 'twixt our souls and Thee;
Pride, only pride, is discord's source,
The bane of peace and charity:
But us it never more shall part,
For Thou art greater than our heart.

Wherefore to Thine almighty hand
The keeping of our hearts we give,
Firm in one mind and spirit stand,
To Thee, and to each other cleave,
Fix'd on the Rock which cannot move,
And meekly safe in humble love.[1]

By the spring of 1751 the Wesleyan Methodists numbered still only about 10,000 among a population of some 10 million but their organization was becoming ever more complex and they were a recognized force in some regions of the country. The mainstay of the societies remained the lay preachers. John Wesley had recognized 85 of them and, despite all the persecution, 68 were still active. Charles could not understand why the Church could neither appreciate their worth nor admire their courage: 'Neither persuasions nor threatenings, flattery nor violence, dungeons or sufferings of various kinds can conquer them.'[2] Nevertheless, unlike John, he recognized the ordained clergy would never embrace the religious revival as long as the Methodists used them because they believed their use showed 'a wild and pernicious enthusiasm' which undermined 'true religion'. Charles therefore felt it was time to start reducing the number of lay preachers in order to encourage more evangelical clergy to join the movement.

This was not just wishful thinking. For example, Charles was well aware that there were at least three ministers in Bristol who were fully supportive of what Methodism was trying to achieve in the city. These were Richard Symes at St Werburgh's, Richard Hart at St George's, and, most influential of all, James Rouquet, the chaplain to the city gaol and St Peter's Hospital. The latter was a particular admirer of George White-field and a remarkably kind man, who for a time acted as headmaster of Kingswood School for the Wesleys. There it is said he guided the children 'by the persuasive influence of love ... [rather than by] the rod of iron' so they were 'not driven, but led, not alarmed but allured into obedience'.[3] When he died from typhoid fever in 1776 the streets of Bristol were lined with admirers of a man who 'was eyes to the blind, feet to the lame, and [who] caused thousands of drooping hearts to sing for joy'.

In London too Charles knew the Countess of Huntingdon was promoting the career of the Revd William Romaine, who had been his contemporary while a student in Oxford, though he had never joined the Holy Club. As a preacher at St George's in Hanover Square and later St Dunstan's in the West, Romaine was becoming a leading voice in the religious revival. Important evangelicals were also emerging at the universities. The Revd Thomas Haweis had created his own 'Holy Club' in Oxford and this was to produce a stream of ordained young men 'who went forth to preach the everlasting gospel in the land'. Cambridge also had its own evangelical religious society led initially by Rowland Hill.

Understandably Charles felt John's decision to call the Foundery 'a mother church' and to promote 'the general union of our societies throughout England' was a step in the wrong direction. The more the societies banded together the less they would remain attached to their local parish churches. Before his eyes he saw developing the potential for Methodism to become an independent dissenting church entirely reliant on its lay preachers. His brother tried to reassure him but he could not disguise his own increasing tolerance of dissent:

> Everyone must follow the dictates of his own conscience, in simplicity and godly sincerity ... and then act according to the best light he has ... I ask not, therefore, of him with whom I would unite in love, 'Are you of my Church?'[4]

Charles felt he was the only person able to place a brake on actions that might encourage Methodists to abandon the Church. For that reason he felt obliged to accept John's invitation to become the spiritual adviser to the preachers so he could urge them to retain a restricted role. We see this approach, for example, in records of his conversations with four Cornish preachers:

> [I] charged them not to stretch themselves beyond their measure by speaking out of the society, or fancying themselves ministers or public teachers. If they keep within their bounds as they promise ... they will be useful in the Church.[5]

Charles' first test case in controlling the preachers centred round a cobbler called James Wheatley who had been a successful preacher for about eight years. His plain and simple style was effective with the less intelligent. Unfortunately he decided that, because he was saved, his lifestyle was irrelevant. Charles tried to correct this but found Wheatley hopelessly stubborn: 'I threw away advice ... [on him] for I could make no impression on him, or in any degree bow his stiff neck.'[6] On 11 June 1751 two members of the Methodist society in Bradford on Avon accused Wheatley of being an adulterer. Seven women made damning statements to Charles about the preacher's immoral sexual behaviour. The cobbler admitted his guilt but, to Charles' consternation, tried to claim he had just been imprudent! Charles called him 'a wolf in sheep's clothing'[7] and John agreed Wheatley was a 'wonderful self-deceiver and hypocrite'.[8]

Charles was painfully aware that the actions of Wheatley played into the hands of Methodism's opponents. He announced he was temporarily revoking his right to preach until his conscience and behaviour improved. It was the first time such a serious disciplinary action had been taken against a lay preacher for moral (as opposed to theological) reasons. In reply Wheatley vowed he would continue to preach in the Methodist societies and that he would expose other preachers who were no better than himself. He made false allegations against ten. Charles was forced to investigate but found them innocent and Wheatley guilty of 'wilful lying'.[9] He then persuaded John to expel Wheatley altogether from Methodism for having 'grieved the Holy Spirit of God' and betrayed himself and others 'into temptation and sin'.[10] Wheatley left and set himself up as an independent preacher in Norwich.

Charles decided it was essential to undertake a far wider investigation to examine 'the life and moral behaviour of every preacher in connexion with us'.[11] He agreed to travel the country, hear all the preachers preach, and hold private conversations about their lifestyle. In many ways he was the better brother to do this because he was a popular figure with many of them, whereas some were increasingly resentful of John's high-handed approach. However, before this process was properly under way, Charles was taken seriously ill with a fever in July. Lying on his sick bed, Charles became very depressed and confided his anxieties to Lady Huntingdon. He believed by making the preachers give up their jobs to travel extensively John had given them no option but to wish to remain as preachers, whether they were suitable or not:

Unless a remedy be found, the preachers will destroy the work of God ... Will not each set up for himself, and make a party, sect, or religion? ... Who can stop them after our death? It does not satisfy my conscience to say, God look to that. We must look to that ourselves, or we tempt God.[12]

Charles proposed to John that all preachers should only be expected to allocate part of their time to preaching and to spend the rest of their time working at their original trade. No preacher should undertake the wider itinerant work unless he had the independent financial means to do so. In a remarkable letter for showing how far Charles now differed from his brother, Charles confided to Selina that he hoped his proposals would weaken John's authority:

It will break his power, their not depending on him for bread, and reduce his authority within due bounds, as well as guard against that rashness and credulity of his, which has kept me in continual awe and bondage for many years. Therefore I shall insist on their working ... because without this I can neither trust them nor him. If he refuses, I will give both preachers and society to his sole management, for this ruin shall not be under my hands. If he complies, I hope to take up my cross, and bear it more cheerfully than I have ever done heretofore.[13]

Somehow John discovered its contents and he was not amused by what it said or by Charles' veiled threat to desert him. However, he needed Charles and so he accepted his brother's terms in order to retain his services. It was agreed the next Methodist Conference should be used to create appropriate controls and guidelines for all the lay preachers. This climbdown by John was made easier by his awareness that some of the newer preachers were less reliable than the original sons of the gospel, who preached in 'the scriptural way, the Methodist way, the true way'.[14] Lest his brother prove too rigorous a judge, John reminded Charles that Methodism could not survive on less than 40 active preachers. Publicly he gave no such restriction:

> It is far better for us to have ten, or six preachers who are alive to God, sound in the faith, and of one heart with us and one another, than fifty of whom we have no such assurance.[15]

The strain on Charles over the next few months was considerable, even though he was accompanied and supported by Sally. Hearing all the preachers was a huge undertaking, especially as it was combined with his own preaching and an endless succession of discussions with individuals. Only a few instances of the latter are recorded in his journal but they show the variety of situations Charles faced. For example, he describes his attempt to make an elderly woman who was 'an old, self-righteous Pharisee' realize the need for humility, a task which required 'a greater miracle of grace than the conversion of a thousand harlots'.[16] On another occasion he mentions meeting an unmarried mother who was out to seek help from the father of her first child because of the poverty she faced in bringing up a child by a second partner. He encouraged her to take personal responsibility for her actions. Charles was constantly comforting the dying, the sick and the imprisoned to the extent that he often records being reduced to exhaustion. Sometimes he could scarcely speak or walk because he was so tired.

Charles could attract a bigger crowd than even the best of the lay preachers. This was exemplified at Birstal, where John Nelson had spent three weeks 'spending his strength in vain', but Charles drew such an immense crowd that 'they filled the valley and side of the hill ... [like] grasshoppers'.[17] Charles records he spoke with a God-given voice like a trumpet and many hearts were awakened. At a number of places he was touched by the warmth of reception he received. For example, he refers to the many hearers at Dudley drinking in his every word and to the society members at Darlaston being 'all in a flame of love'.[18] In some places, like Leeds and Bromidge Heath, the best response came from 'a multitude of the poor' [19] but sometimes, as at Birmingham, there was a good response from 'several of the better rank'.[20] However, not all received him well. For example, in Worcester he had to contend against 'lewd, hellish language' and had so much 'dust and dirt' thrown at him that he was 'covered from head to foot and almost blinded',[21] while at Sheffield he had to face 'a wild tumultuous mob'.[22]

Charles' investigation into the morality and suitability of the preachers mainly proved a reassuring one. Very few needed disciplining and most were outstandingly good Christians. There were only a few appalling exceptions. For example, he wrote of a preacher called Michael Fletcher:

Such a preacher I have never heard and hope I never shall again. It was beyond description. I cannot say he preached false doctrine, or true, or any doctrine at all, but pure unmixed nonsense. Not one sentence did he utter that could do the least good to any one soul. Now and then a text of Scripture or a verse quotation was dragged in by the head and shoulders. I could scarce refrain from stopping him ... Of this I am infallibly sure, that if he ever had a gift for preaching, he has now totally lost it.[23]

Charles set him up in a shop as a barber on condition he never preached again! Similarly, he said he was determined to return a former tailor called Robert Gillespie to his trade because of his 'utter unworthiness to preach the Gospel'.[24] And he wrote of a former drummer turned preacher that 'to set up for an itinerant, was, in my judgement, a step contrary to the design of God, as well as his own, and the church's interest'.[25]

Charles told John he was not setting a high enough standard in terms of the criteria for approving preachers. It was a mistake to judge appropriateness almost entirely on 'grace' (i.e. the ability to obtain conversions) when equally vital were 'gifts' (i.e. strength of character, intellectual ability and organizational capacity). John initially disagreed and it is clear he reinstated a number of the preachers Charles removed (including Michael Fletcher and Robert Gillespie). Nevertheless, Charles was right because over the next few years societies increasingly expressed their concerns that too many preachers had 'not weight enough'.[26] More worrying from Charles' perspective was the fact that in some areas, such as Leeds and Bolton, there were strong advocates for predestination. Notable among these was an energetic Scot called William Darney, who was creating his own societies in Yorkshire and Lancashire. Charles said he would ban Darney from preaching in any meeting-house unless he abstained from his ranting style of preaching and stopped using nonsensical hymns.

On 11 September Charles held a special meeting in Leeds so he could speak to all the preachers on 'the qualifications, work and trials of the Methodist ministry' and wrote a hymn for the occasion:

Arise, thou jealous God arise,
Thy sifting power exert,

Look through us with thy flaming eyes,
And search out every heart.

Do I presume to preach thy word
By thee uncalled, unsent?
Am I the servant of the Lord,
Or Satan's instrument?[27]

Given the need to control the preachers, Charles felt his own preaching should now take second place.[28] By the time he returned exhausted to London in October he knew more about the current state of the preachers and the societies than John did. He met up with his brother and Vincent Perronet, the Vicar of Shoreham, to agree new guidelines whereby nobody would be permitted to preach without being first examined 'as to grace and gifts' and winning the approval of Charles as well as John.[29] Perronet agreed to adjudicate if the brothers disagreed about an individual. Despite the decline in their relationship, John realized Charles was still the best vehicle he had for communicating what a preacher should believe and how he should live. There is no better example of this than Charles' 'Hymn for a Local Preacher':

Give me the faith which can remove
And sink the mountain to a plain ...
Enlarge, inflame and fill my heart
With boundless charity divine;
So shall I all my strength exert,
And love them with a zeal like thine;
And lead them to thy open side,
The sheep for whom their shepherd died.[30]

Charles' further reflections eventually led to the publication of a document which emphasized that Methodism was totally committed to staying within the Church. It was signed in March 1752 not only by John and Charles but also by four of the lay preachers whom they regarded as most reliable: John Nelson, John Downes, John Jones and William Shent. That same spring Charles also drew up statements designed to encourage key preachers to ignore malicious gossip about John's private life and remain loyal to his brother. Unfortunately John's continued attacks on the Calvinist preachers did little to generate unity. William Grimshaw wrote to Charles in despair: 'These intestine divisions are dreadful.'[31]

The return of Whitefield in May 1752 was welcomed by Charles, because his relationship with his brother was still at a low ebb. Publicly

George sought to play down what John had been saying, but privately he confessed: 'I have been supplanted, despised, censured, maligned, judged by and separated from my nearest, dearest friends.'[32] By August John was deeply concerned that Charles was being further drawn into Whitefield's circle despite their theological differences. The detail of what Charles and George were discussing is not known but it is likely they were debating whether Charles should remain permanently in London as the main minister for the Foundery and the three chapels in Seven Dials, Snowfields and Spitalfields. Another option was to take up the offer of the Countess of Huntingdon to make him her private chaplain. She said she would be 'deeply humbled' to have him as an adviser.[33] Clifton in Bristol was to become her chief home throughout most of the 1750s so she could be close to him.

Whitefield's remarkable response to Charles' possible desertion of John has survived in a letter dated December 1752:

> My dear friend ... The connection between you and your brother, hath been so close and continued, and your attachment to him so necessary to keep up his interest, that I would not willingly for the world do or say anything that may separate such friends. I cannot but help think that he is still jealous of me and my proceedings; but, thank God, I am quite easy about it ... [God] knows how I love and honour you, and your brother, and how often I have preferred your interest to my own. This, by the grace of God, I shall continue to do.[34]

Avoiding disunity dominated the discussions at the Methodist Conference in Leeds in May 1753. John Bennet's desertion had shown some were prepared to become dissenters rather than be dominated by John. William Grimshaw and many of the northern preachers demanded in future good relations should be maintained by minimizing doctrinal differences. They asked John to adopt a friendlier stance towards Benjamin Ingham and the Moravians and towards George Whitefield and the Calvinists. This evoked a blistering attack from John, who alleged that Whitefield's preaching in particular was creating 'not peace but confusion'. He wrongly asserted George was denigrating him 'in the most scoffing and contemptuous manner' and 'speaking lightly' of Methodist rules. He then demanded the 50 or so preachers in attendance should agree to exclude Whitefield from all Methodist pulpits. For once the Conference refused him. Instead they asked John to write a 'loving and respectful letter' to Whitefield asking him to curb his followers from preaching predestination. The Conference also declared that in future any preacher should consult their brethren before marrying 'hand over head' – this was a clear indicator it felt John's marriage had impaired his judgement.

John did not write a 'loving and respectful letter'. His very curt note deeply hurt Whitefield. In vain George tried to persuade John that he was not a baneful influence, yet contemporary accounts reveal most preachers could not speak highly enough of Whitefield's non-partisanship. One, Thomas Olivers, later wrote: 'When he preached in Mr Wesley's pulpits ... multitudes can tell what expressions of the highest esteem he frequently made use of, in exhorting Mr. Wesley's Societies.'[35] The one concrete thing John could point to as evidence that Whitefield was still a rival was the rebuilding of the Tabernacles in both London and Bristol in 1753. The former was completed in just 15 weeks between April and June and it was a far more impressive affair than the rather ramshackle Foundery. It could hold 4,000 people. The new Tabernacle in Bristol was smaller but just as impressive. However, these buildings were primarily the product of George's admirers and they were not in any way a sign of a wish to take over the leadership of Methodism. Moreover, Whitefield was far too itinerant to make full use of their potential.

Whitefield's respect for Charles was reflected in him choosing 24 of his hymns for inclusion in the Calvinists' *A Collection of Hymns for Social Worship*, which was published in 1753. These were drawn from the nine collections published by the Wesleys between 1739 and 1749 and Whitefield's selection helped publicize some of Charles' best hymns, including 'Christ from whom all blessings flow', 'Christ whose glory fills the skies', 'Ye Servants of God' and 'Rejoice the Lord is King'. Whitefield also altered one hymn and, in the process, improved its popularity. In 1739 Charles had written a hymn for Christmas Day which began with the line: 'Hark how all the Welkin rings'. Whitefield with one of his friends, Martin Madan, altered four of its opening eight lines. The result was:

> Hark! The Herald Angels sing
> Glory to the new-born King!
> Peace on Earth, and Mercy mild,
> God and Sinners reconcil'd!
> Joyful all ye Nations rise
> Join the triumphs of the skies,
> With the angelic Host proclaim
> Christ is born in Bethlehem![36]

Selina, Countess of Huntingdon, urged Charles to mediate between his brother and Whitefield: 'I hate everything that does not make for peace and ... I do think it best for us all to keep clear of anything that may be followed by a scrap of any kind.' [37] Selina hoped that she could persuade her aristocratic friends to fund the building of more chapels where evangelicals could preach without facing the strictures imposed by the church authorities. However, Charles was not well placed to sway John, given his role in preventing John's marriage to Grace Murray. Even their traditional collaboration over preaching engagements broke down when Charles made clear he no longer felt it was right to continue exposing his pregnant wife to the dangers and disease-ridden poverty of the lower classes. This may have come to the fore because Sally had been particularly upset in Leeds by having to sleep in a room whose only access was via a room that was let out as accommodation to the roughest of the labouring poor. Molly Wesley told John that Charles' wife was encouraging him to abandon itinerancy in favour of a luxurious lifestyle with the Countess of Huntingdon.

Charles' first son was born in September and, doubtless as a gesture of reconciliation, christened John. That autumn Charles travelled down to Cornwall for what was to prove the last time. He still appreciated the importance of his work but he missed 'the company of my true yoke-fellow' and his letters home reflect this. In October, John told Charles he wished him 'all peace, zeal, and love' but that he must do exactly what John wanted and not what Sally or the countess judged best:

> Take one side, or the other. Either act really in connection with me, or never pretend it. Rather disclaim it, and openly avow you do not ... Take counsel with me once or twice a year, as to the places where you will labour. Hear my advice before you fix whether you take it or no ... I am a better judge in this matter than either Lady Huntingdon, Sally ... or any other; nay, than your own heart.[38]

The next month John was taken seriously ill and some openly said it was a product of his unhappy marriage. His symptoms appeared to be those of consumption: a severe cough, pain, fever and a lack of strength to do anything. In his misery John lashed out unfairly at Charles, accusing him of undermining his work for ten years.[39] Initially Charles thought the illness was a ploy to bring him to heel but, when he realized this was not the case, he hurried to London as fast as he could. The brothers wept together and a remorseful John, believing he was about to die, asked for forgiveness, saying his epitaph should contain the phrase that he was 'an unprofitable servant' of God.[40] The generous Whitefield tried to convince John that he was deeply loved for what he had achieved:

The news and prospect of your approaching dissolution have quite weighed me down ... A radiant throne awaits you ... amidst an admiring throng of saints and angels ... [May you] die in the embraces of triumphant love! ... My heart is too big; tears trickle down too fast ... I commend you to His never-failing mercy.[41]

The illness stemmed the mounting criticism of John. Charles encouraged the members of the Foundery to pray for John's recovery and was moved by their response:

The whole society appear alive, so stirred up, so zealous, so prayerful, as I never knew them ... Many secret friends now show themselves. The strangers stop us in the street with their inquiries; and the people in general seem to find out the value of a blessing they are going to lose.[42]

Charles described his role as being 'a son of consolation'[43] and on 4 December Charles and John made their peace with each other:

This morning I got the long wished for opportunity of talking fully to him of all that had passed since his marriage; and the result of our conference was perfect harmony.[44]

Whitefield assumed Charles would take over from John and do 'double work'[45] but Charles was adamant he would not replace his brother as leader, saying he had 'neither a body, nor a mind, nor talents, nor grace for it'.[46] Whether he would have stuck to this resolution was not tested because the terrible news arrived that his wife Sally had caught smallpox. Charles hurried to Bristol to be by her side. It is tremendous testimony to his Christian faith that he agreed to take with him a mentally disordered man called John Hutchinson, whom he had been seeking to help and who was threatening suicide if Charles left him. The ranting and raving Hutchinson made the journey to Bristol a nightmare:

My flesh shrank at taking him in, a miserable comforter to me in my lowest distress ... Instead of comforting me all the way [he] insulted my sorrow and spoke against my wife. I was so hindered and distracted by him that I could pray very little.[47]

At Reading the coach stopped at a staging post inn and Charles seized the chance to go for a walk so he could pour out his heart in prayer, but he was not left alone for long because the behaviour of the demented

Hutchinson forced the people at the inn to find him. When they next stopped at Marlborough Charles ordered separate accommodation but Hutchinson then sought to drag Charles away from his room, screaming and shouting. Rather than physically hurt Hutchinson, Charles allowed himself to be dragged through a long chamber to the man's room. Hutchinson locked him in and the servants at the inn broke down the door, fearing Charles was about to be murdered. Hutchinson was then filled with remorse and Charles spent the night trying to prevent him committing suicide. He was understandably exhausted by the time they arrived in Bristol the next day.

When he saw Sally, Charles was shocked:

I found my dearest friend on a restless bed of pain, loaded with the worst kind of disease ... From the sole of the foot, even unto the head, there is no soundness in her; but wounds and putrefying sores.[48]

However, Hutchinson flew into a rage at the suggestion he should lodge in another house and leave Charles to comfort his wife:

He answered what was my wife more than another, that I made such a do with her ... and that it was the greatest cruelty in me thus to turn him out of my house desolate.[49]

Charles eventually managed to get him to stay elsewhere, and continued to help him. How many men would have been so charitable at such a time!

The next day Sally 'grew worse and worse' and Charles took comfort in 'powerful prayer'. George Whitefield, then in the final stages of preparation for another mission to America, was very solicitous and offered his prayers for Sally as well as John. On 8 December it became clear the disease had passed to Charles' son. Charles watched in agony 'while the glimmering lamp of life seemed every moment ready to go out'.[50] He records leaving the bedside only to take services among the society members at Kingswood, where he preached on the text 'Let not your heart be troubled'. On the Monday the disease became even more marked in Sally's features and she lay 'struggling as in the toils of death', but 24 hours later he recorded the crisis appeared over: 'The important die of life and death spun doubtfully ere it fell and turned up life! ... If she gets over another night we shall hope the worst is past.'[51]

The prayers of others were a real source of strength to Charles and none more so than that of Whitefield who wrote again to comfort him:

My Dear Friend, the Searcher of hearts alone knows the sympathy I have felt for you and yours; and in what suspense my mind hath been concerning ... your present circumstances. I pray and inquire, inquire and pray again ... To have the desire of one's eyes cut off with a stroke, what but grace, omnipotent grace, can enable us to bear it? But who knows? Perhaps the threatened stroke may be recalled; and my dear friend enjoy his dear yoke-fellow's company a little longer ... Pray let me know how it goes with you ... Night and day indeed you are remembered by ... [your dear friend].[52]

For over a fortnight Sally continued to fight for her life, assiduously attended by Dr John Middleton, who had become a real friend of the family. As usual Charles put as much faith in God as in human efforts:

Thy angels plant around her bed,
And let Thy hand support her head;
Thy power her pain to joy convert,
Thy love revive her drooping heart.
Thy love her soul and body heal,
And let her every moment feel
The atoning blood by faith applied,
The balm that drops from Jesu's side.[53]

He alternated between her bedside and visiting his sick brother in London. Sally survived but terribly scarred. Charles told her she need not fear the loss of her looks because he loved her more than ever. He jokingly commented that, having lost her youthful appearance, she would no longer be embarrassed by having to walk beside her old husband.

Their 16-month son was not so fortunate and he died from the smallpox. Sally retained a lock of his fair hair in an envelope, and wrote: 'I shall go to him, but he shall never return to me.'[54] Selina Countess of Huntingdon, who had faced the loss of some of her own children, comforted them as best she could: 'The chances against us parents for happiness is a hundred to one and the dear little creature is happy for eternity.'[55] Charles tried to comfort himself by saying the painful loss of his son would mean he was less distracted from doing God's work:

Those waving hands no more shall move,
Those laughing eyes shall smile no more:
He cannot now engage our love
With sweet insinuating power,
Our weak unguarded hearts ensnare,
And rival his Creator there ...[56]

Sally was sent to convalesce with her mother in Ludlow and this left Charles free to look after John at the Bristol Hotwell. The two brothers spent the next few months studying together in a life reminiscent of their early days together in Oxford. John used the opportunity to write his explanatory notes on the New Testament and Charles offered invaluable assistance. John's recovery was a very slow process and it was not until July 1754 that he set foot on the road again. Charles accompanied him to Norwich, where Methodism was being brought into disrepute by the sexual activities of the former lay preacher James Wheatley. They found the streets 'ringing all day with James' wickedness' as the mayor recorded the statements of the many women he had seduced. Charles bemoaned:

> He has, as much as in him lay, poisoned the fountain, debased the language, of God, hardened the people's hearts, palled their spiritual appetite, and made then even loathe religion and all that belongs to it.[57]

Wheatley told the local press about John Wesley's 'affair' with Grace Murray. This proved too much for John's health and he returned to Bristol, leaving Charles to spend several weeks fighting Wheatley's 'smooth words and flattering invitations'. A delighted Charles wrote that the local people increasingly listened to his field preaching and so 'did God bring good out of evil'.[58] A local ecclesiastical court eventually found Wheatley guilty of being 'a lewd, debauched, incontinent, and adulterous person'.[59]

However, it was two of Charles' close friends among the preachers, Charles and Edward Perronet, who posed a far greater challenge that autumn. They had grown tired of the continued opposition of most clergy to Methodism and resented the fact most Methodists found it difficult to take communion in many parishes. Supported by Thomas Walsh, a preacher who was a highly gifted biblical scholar, they urged the Wesleys to permit lay preachers to administer communion themselves. In October 1754 both Charles Perronet and Thomas Walsh took the law into their own hands and administered communion, one in London and the other in Reading. Charles knew that if this were to be repeated, the Church would view Methodism as no better than a dissenting organization. He was particularly distressed when Edward Perronet wrote a verse poking fun at the clergy's opposition to lay people administering communion:

> What, take the ordinance from them!
> Oh, what a frenzy of a dream
> Nor deacon nor a priest!

Sooner renounce our grace or friends,
Then take it from their fingers' ends
A lay, unhallowed beast.[60]

Charles tried to persuade John that those who wanted to perform holy offices should seek proper ordination and that all lay preachers who sought to administer communion were primarily motivated by false pride:

They now pre-eminence affect
Eager to form a rising sect ...
And thro' ambition blind, inspire
Without the cross to reign.[61]

However, John was clearly more sympathetic to the motives of his lay preachers. If he could authorize laymen to preach why could he not also ordain them to administer communion? His reading had convinced him that originally every Christian congregation had formed its own independent church and that there was no historical case for saying ordination required the authority of a bishop. The Church was essentially just an organization rather than something created by God. On 19 October 1754 Charles recorded his shock that John 'was inclined to lay on hands and to let the preachers administer'.[62]

Some historians have portrayed Charles as a reactionary fossil reluctant to accept the inevitable, but this is unfair. Only a few of the lay preachers as yet wanted to administer communion and they were hugely outnumbered by the 40 or so evangelical ministers sympathetic towards Methodism. Any chance of retaining such clerical support would be lost if John took on the function of a bishop and ordained lay preachers to administer communion. The criticism also ignores Charles' deeply held religious views. As far as he was concerned, the early Church had regarded communion as central to their daily worship and it was only the Catholic Church's later development of the 'monstrous' theory of transubstantiation which had undermined it. He felt both Calvin and Luther had failed to properly reassert communion's importance as a means of receiving God's grace. The last thing he wanted was to lower its status further by allowing laymen to take over its celebration.

After five days of debating Charles was able to record that John was 'wavering'. In effect this meant John had chosen not to publicly challenge Charles' views because he feared the consequences of a renewed quarrel between them. Charles had stopped John taking a step which would inevitably have caused a separation with the Church of England

and divided the Methodists. However, Charles knew he had won a battle and not the war. He referred to those who wanted to create Methodist ministers as 'Melchisedechians' – a reference to the biblical Melchisedech, who was 'without father, without mother, without descent'. He felt they wanted Methodism to become a distinct sect:

> They are continually urging ... [my brother] to a separation; that is, to pull down all he has built, to put a sword in our enemies' hands, to destroy the work, scatter the flock, disgrace himself, and go out like the snuff of a candle.[63]

In reply Charles sought to build up an opposition party. He particularly looked for support from two preachers who had become ministers specifically in order to be able to offer communion. One was a former doctor called John Jones and the other a former teacher at Kingswood called Walter Sellon. Charles wrote to the latter in December:

> Since the Melchisedechians have been taken in [to John's confidence] I have been excluded from his inner cabinet. They know me too well to trust him with me ... They are indefatigable in urging him to go so far that he may not be able to retreat.[64]

Charles felt all those opposed to John ordaining his preachers should make a stand at the next Conference. Howell Harris agreed:

> My dearest Charles ... I am glad true moderation dwells in your spirit ... I write in love & from a heart full of zeal for the work in England ... I really think the moment the work goes to be a Sect or Party or out of the Church let it be in whatever shape, it will be the Enemy [Satan] has carried his point and the blessing [of God] is no longer [ours].[65]

In the face of his brother's continued suspicions, John confirmed in the spring of 1755 he was opposed to preachers taking on the role of ordained clergy. Knowing his brother as well as he did, Charles did not believe him. Fearing his own voice was becoming too heated and therefore possibly counter-productive, Charles confessed to Sellon:

> There is ... danger of ... my opposing them too fiercely. It is a pity a good cause should suffer by a warm advocate. If God gives me meekness, I shall, at the conference, speak and spare not. Till then it is best the matter should sleep, or we should make the delinquents desperate ... We must [get to] know the heart of every Preacher.[66]

In April Charles met John at Birstal and extensively debated the issue with him prior to the Methodist Conference in May. William Grimshaw backed Charles, saying he would rather leave Methodism than work within an organization which overturned the authority of the Church to such a degree.[67]

Sixty-three preachers attended the Conference. This was the largest number ever but, apart from the Wesley brothers, the only clergyman present was Grimshaw. Such was the Conference's importance that Benjamin Ingham asked if he could attend as an observer. John presented the gathering with a treatise entitled 'Ought we to separate from the Church of England?' It was in favour of remaining loyal. On the crucial issue of communion, he said it would 'answer many good ends' to let the preachers administer it, but it was not worth the evil of separation and conflict. He also claimed it could not be justified from a historical viewpoint. The early Christian Church had recognized preachers and deacons who had 'extraordinary inspiration' but they had restricted the administering of the sacraments to those priests who stood in apostolic succession from St Peter.

Three days of heated debate followed, in which Charles and Grimshaw surprised many by declaring they would desert Methodism if its preachers began administering communion. Finally it was agreed that it was 'in no ways expedient' to separate. This phraseology neither pleased Charles nor impressed Ingham, who shortly afterwards decided to formally declare he was not a Methodist. He and Charles had wanted the Conference to declare separation a moral and legal impossibility. Charles was grateful to Grimshaw for his support and described him 'my worthy friend and fellow-labourer – a man after my own heart!'[68] But he was angry at John's soft stance during the debate. He felt this would encourage some preachers to ignore the decision. In protest Charles left the Conference early and condemned its proceedings to the members of the Foundery.

The Countess of Huntingdon vainly tried to calm him down but Charles insisted on writing an 'epistle' to his brother, denouncing John's behaviour and defending 'the church whose cause I serve, whose faith I approve, whose altars reverence, and whose name I love':

I tell thee, wise and faithful as thou art,
The fears and sorrows of a burden'd heart ...
Wilt thou with me in the old Church remain
And share her weal or woe, her loss or gain,
Spend in her service thy last drop of blood,
And die to build the temple of our God ...

Was it our aim disciples to collect,
To raise a party or to found a sect?
No, but to spread the power of Jesu's Name ...[69]

John told Charles the societies were 'far more firmly and rationally attached to the Church than ever they were before' and that the Conference had surrendered 'more than they could give up with a clear conscience [in order] not to separate from the Church'.[70] When this failed to silence Charles' opposition, John threatened to ordain some preachers unless Charles stopped making difficulties and abandoned his 'gross bigotry'.[71] Charles' response was to have his 'epistle' published. He told his wife Sally that she would have to accept him visiting 'every society throughout the land' to ensure the Conference decision was upheld: 'I have delivered my own soul in this society ... [and] my heart is more truly united to the true Methodists than ever.'[72]

Charles knew John would treat him as 'a deserter' but he felt cured of his earlier 'implicit regard' for his brother.[73] Not surprisingly John began writing to a number of the evangelical clergy to defend his actions. He wrote to the Revd Thomas Adam, Rector of Wintringham:

Many of the clergy, though called of man, are not called of God ... because they ... do not know what the Gospel is ... Whether I have gone far enough, I am extremely doubtful ... Soul damning clergymen lay me under more difficulties than soul saving laymen![74]

Adam replied that John had to understand that the creation of lay preachers in itself had been 'a manifest breach upon the order of the church, and an inlet to confusion'.[75] This was a view endorsed by the Revd Samuel Walker, a conscientious curate who was promoting a club for evangelical clergy in Cornwall. He told John that by using lay preachers he had already separated himself from the Church. The only issue now was whether there would be such 'a separation in all forms' that no regular churchman could have anything to do with Methodism.[76]

The debate on the use of lay preachers was temporarily put on hold when the country again was filled with rumours that the end of the world might be near. It was a time when the prophets of doom could point to many disturbing signs, including a major earthquake in Lisbon and the danger of invasion from a war-hungry France. Some of Charles' poetry took on an apocalyptic dimension:

Earth unhinged as from her basis,
Owns her great Redeemer nigh;

Plunged in complicated distresses,
Poor distracted sinners cry ...[77]

Through a series of poetic epistles Charles urged past and current friends to unite and redouble their missionary effort. His main focus rested on the Calvinists and he wrote to a recently recovered Howell Harris:

O what a Flame within thy Bosom burn'd
When to Himself thy Heart ye Saviour turn'd!
Thy Heart was simple Love, and pure Desire,
Thy lips were touch'd with consecrated.[78]

And to Whitefield, who had again returned to Britain:

Our hands, and hearts, and counsels let us join
In mutual league, to advance the work Divine,
Our one contention now, our single aim,
To pluck poor souls as brands out of the flame ...
Too long, alas! We gave to Satan place,
When party-zeal put on an angel's face ... .
With hasty blindfold rage, in error's night,
How did we with our fellow-soldiers fight![79]

As far as the Moravians were concerned, John Cennick had recently died so Charles challenged Count Zinzendorf to abandon his heretical thinking and encouraged George Stonehouse, the ex-Vicar of Islington, to come out of retirement:

Where hast Thou been so long? estrang'd from me,
By those with whom thy Soul could ne'er agree:
As soon might purest Light with Darkness dwell,
And Virtue match with Vice & Heaven with Hell.[80]

Charles expressed a desire for Christian unity that was remarkable in its breadth:

All sorts thou dost into Thy Service take,
Of all a wondrous Coalition make,
Where Luther's Partizans with Calvin's join,
And Orthodox & Heterodox combine,
Together jumbled in a common Mass ...
No matter which is wrong & which is right,

Suffice that in one Point they all agree,
To shut their eyes, and blindly worship Thee.[81]

Simultaneously the Countess of Huntingdon sought to unite the revival by promoting the talents of three ministers. One was inevitably White-field. An attempt by him to rent a chapel in the heart of the theatre district of London ended with mobs rioting outside it, so the countess agreed to fund the building of an entirely new chapel for her long-suffering friend in Tottenham Court Road. This was eventually completed in November 1756 but immediately proved too small and was enlarged, eventually making it the largest nonconformist building in the country. Although the church authorities refused to recognize it as a lawful public place of worship, Whitefield's 'Soul-Trap' (as it was nicknamed) became a very popular place, especially among the aristocracy who belonged to the countess' circle.

The countess' other two protégés were William Romaine, the minister at St George's in fashionable Hanover Square, and the less inspirational but very committed Martin Madan, who became chaplain of the Lock Hospital, a refuge for fallen and destitute women. In December 1755 Selina urged Charles to keep John 'in order' by persuading him to co-operate with Whitefield and the other evangelical clergy.[82] That John was failing to keep the lay preachers in line was evidenced in 1756 by Edward Perronet printing *The Mitre*, a vicious poetical attack on the corruption within the Church:

… thou'rt like a common shore
Filling and emptying, never pure
From pride, or pomp, or sin.

Perronet said the Church of England was just 'the ape of Rome' and its bishops had no authority from Christ and the apostles. The hierarchy of the Church was just 'a blended spawn of church and state' which had been created in the time of Constantine from 'the pride of priests'.[83]

Under pressure from Charles, John ordered Edward Perronet to cease selling his book and as many copies as possible were removed from circulation, but the damage had been done. Charles lobbied John to make use of the 1756 Conference to properly curtail the lay preachers. William Grimshaw and another evangelical clergyman, Henry Venn, added their weight. Charles wrote to the Cornish minister, Samuel Walker:

My brother ought, in my judgement, to declare in the possible strongest and most explicit manner, his resolution to live and die in the communion of the Church of England ... [and] take all proper pains to instruct and ground his preachers and his flock in the same.[84]

Walker said he was not optimistic because John had pinned too much of his hopes on using the preachers:

> He has had too great a hand in setting them up, to think of pulling them down. It has been a great fault all along to have made low people of your council; and if there be not power enough left in your brother's hands to do as he sees fit, they will soon show him they will be their own masters.[85]

To Charles' delight and surprise, calls for separation from the Church proved minimal at the Conference compared to the previous year. He attributed this to the fact that two or three of 'a forward, unhumbled spirit' had left the movement and most of the other delegates were of 'a humble teachable spirit'. To his satisfaction the Conference closed with a solemn declaration that Methodism would never embrace dissent. However, John refused to accept Charles' solution of encouraging the lay preachers to seek ordination. He felt this would encourage them to settle in a specific parish and so confine their talents to the detriment of the revival: 'I know were I myself to preach one whole year in one place, I should preach both myself and most of my congregation asleep.'[86] He also argued that he and Charles were better placed to retain their loyalty if the status quo was maintained: 'While we are with them, our advice has weight, and keeps them to the Church.'[87]

Charles confessed to Samuel Walker that he only remained within Methodism to prevent the catastrophe of separation:

> I stay not so much to do good, as to prevent evil. I stand in the way of my brother's violent counsellors, the object both of their fear and hate ... I know my brother will not hear of laying aside his lay preachers ... [I fear] the tide will be too strong for him, and bear him away into the gulf of separation ... The restless pains of bad men to thrust me from the Methodists seems a plain argument for my continuing with them.[88]

John agreed to let Charles purge any preacher who administered communion and he promised him a stronger say in selecting who was permitted to preach. A public document declared no more preachers would be created without the express approval of both brothers. John also promised to write a treatise on the importance of staying within the Church.

Charles saw it as his mission to convey the same message to ordinary society members by embarking on a national tour. He told John:

> The short remains of my life are devoted ... to follow your sons ... with buckets of water, and quench the flame of strife and division which they have, or may kindle.[89]

In the first instance he travelled into the Midlands to visit the main societies in Staffordshire, Yorkshire and Lancashire. He records constantly exhorting those who came to hear him preach that they should 'live and die in the Church of England'. He even went so far as to say there was 'no salvation out of the church'.[90] At times Charles felt greatly heartened by the response to his preaching. One of the highlights was probably preaching with Whitefield in Leeds:

> I rejoiced ... He beat down the separating spirit, highly commended the prayers and services of the Church, charged our peoples to meet their bands and classes constantly, and never to leave the Methodists, or God would leave them. In a word, he did his utmost to strengthen the hands of all the churches, for his abundant labour of love.[91]

That same year Whitefield published a significantly re-edited version of his journal. It was designed to play down his own role in the revival in favour of stressing it was the work of many led by God.

Sometimes Charles was deeply depressed by the number of societies who were considering breaking away from the Church. At Manchester, for example, he records:

> I challenged them to show me one Methodist who had ever prospered by turning Dissenter. I asked what would become of them when my brother should die, whether they would not then be scattered and broken into twenty sects old and new.[92]

It greatly upset him that he could still find copies of *The Mitre* circulating and he urged John to ban Perronet from visiting any societies so that he could not 'poison our children and wound us through the influence which we lend him':

> I intend to continue his friend, as far as he is capable of receiving good from me, but ... he has set himself against us ... counteracting us with our preachers, spiriting them up, poisoning, proselyting them to his own wretched notions.[93]

Both the Perronet brothers ceased to operate as Wesleyan preachers. True to his word, Charles kept in touch with them (while John equally typically from then on ignored them). By November a deeply depressed Charles confessed to Grimshaw: 'Nothing but grace can keep our children after our departure from running into a thousand sects, a thousand errors.'[94] On 6 November he wrote what was to be the last entry in his journal: 'God brought me safe to my friends in Bristol.' There is not a single document in his hand that dates from 1757. While this may be a historical fluke, it has been taken to show he had finally decided to distance himself from a movement which was headed towards separation. Howell Harris urged him to reconsider his inactivity because God was still using the lay preachers to effect a religious revival:

> Societies and exhorters are good for the present till a wider door is opened ... Your brother's pen speaks loud, let it carry the sound of a slighted gospel ... to a deistical licentious self-righteous generation ... [and] speak to the heart ... Let the spirit and simplicity in which the work was originally ushered in be kept up and maintained.[95]

Charles made clear he only wanted to work in the Bristol area, although he conceded he was willing to preach in London whenever John was absent. The truth was that Charles was tired of playing second fiddle to the dictatorial John and felt it was time to surrender to his physical infirmity. Successive bouts of pleurisy, gout, lumbago and dysentery had weakened his constitution. In addition, he was no longer prepared to spend such large amounts of time away from Sally. In July 1755 their second child, this time a daughter, Martha Maria, had died. In 1757 Sally was pregnant again and he was desperate not to risk causing her any anxiety by travelling far away from her: 'My heart is with you. I want you every day and every hour. I should be with you always, or not at all; for no one can supply your place.'[96] His and Sally's third child was born – and named Samuel after his grandfather – on 11 December 1757.

It must have been a hard decision to abandon his itinerant ministry because Charles' emotional nature thrived on the challenges it posed and it was a trait of his character that he tended to become more melancholic when reduced to staying in one place. His position stood in stark contrast now to both his brother and George Whitefield's continued constant travelling. The latter, for example, engaged in another tour of Scotland and then went to Ireland. It was while he was in Dublin in July that Whitefield suffered from an appalling attack in which he was violently stoned. He had to return to London to recuperate. This did not prevent him undertaking extensive work in sustaining societies, especially those based at the Tabernacle and his new chapel in Tottenham Court Road but, when he eventually left to undertake a tour of Wales, it was by chaise because he no longer had the strength to ride on horseback.

The gap between John and Charles inevitably widened. Based in Bristol and London, Charles increasingly was content with the traditional worship of the Church, whereas the still mobile John openly began to prefer the 'most clear, plain, simple, unaffected' worship organized by his lay preachers.[97] It did not help matters that John resented Charles' decision and that Charles became the recipient of correspondence from all those who disliked John's autocratic approach. Though Charles ceased extensive travelling, he remained in correspondence with many of the preachers. From the letters that have survived we know he wrote not only to old friends, such as John Nelson, Vincent Perronet, Howell Harris and Joseph Cownley, but also to a number of the new preachers, such as John Athay, Joseph Benson, James Creighton and Mark Davis. For virtually 30 years after his decision to cease travelling, he continued to receive letters from those who knew of his continued interest in their work and who valued his prayers and judgement. A good example is a letter sent from Ireland by Thomas Carhill in 1780, though Charles had not been there since 1748.

In the autumn of 1757 there was no way of telling Charles' decision to cease travelling would be permanent and so his views still therefore held some sway with John. Charles was able to persuade him to denounce any Methodist who attempted to make use of the terms of the Toleration Act of 1689, which offered legal protection to any person prepared to obtain a licence as a dissenting preacher and to any building registered as a meeting-house for dissenters. Nevertheless, John refused to act when a Wesleyan preacher called Jacob Rowell took out a preaching licence in Barnard Castle in January 1758. Understandably Charles feared his brother was conniving with what was happening: 'My brother applauds their skilfulness – and his own.'[98]

In the spring of 1758 Charles had an accident, which greatly hindered his mobility so, if he had intended a return to the itinerant ministry, it was ruled out. That summer the Conference made clear it accepted Charles could henceforth best serve the revival by becoming the permanent sole leader for the societies in Bristol. For family reasons the Countess of Huntingdon was also unable to play an active role at this time. Her 18-year-old youngest son Henry had been taken ill the previous year and he was going blind. Selina spent much of the year nursing him till his death in the September. He was the third of her six children to die young. The tragedy did not end there. That summer also saw her daughter Elizabeth give birth to her first child but the infant boy only lived a few days. Meanwhile the countess' eldest son Francis caused her endless worry because he was mixing with the wrong social set and becoming increasingly immoral.

One of those who visited the recuperating Charles was Thomas Walsh, one of the preachers whom Charles feared was generating secession. He called en route to Ireland and Charles gave him hospitality. According to one account, Charles used the opportunity to mercilessly harangue him, saying he 'had done more harm to religion than his life and labours had honoured it'.[99] In reality we know that, whatever their disagreements, Walsh felt well treated by Charles because he subsequently wrote thanking him for all his kindness and saying: 'I know it is God that gave us union and love. To the prayer of faith nothing is impossible. I trust love will abound.'[100] However, when Walsh shortly afterwards died from consumption in April 1759, some malicious voices alleged Charles had contributed to his death by reducing him to 'the utmost extremity of spiritual distress'.[101] In reply Charles wrote three hymns to show his admiration for Walsh:

> While Christ with all his heart he sought,
> And all his gifts from Christ received,
> A witness of the truths he taught,
> A pattern to the flock he lived ...[102]

It may have been Charles' continued absence that forced John to publish a tract called *Reasons Against a Separation from the Church of England* in 1758. It was extracted from a larger work which was not published because John was advised it had too many sections that provided arguments for separation! Even the shortened version is interesting because it does not argue that separation is wrong, merely that it is undesirable because divisions impair a religious revival. Charles welcomed the document but added his own postscript that separation was morally wrong:

> I am quite clear that it is neither expedient nor lawful for me to separate. I never had the least inclination or temptation to do so. My affection for the Church is as strong as ever; and I clearly see my calling; which is to live and die in her communion. This therefore I am determined to do, the Lord being my helper ... Would to God all the Methodist Preachers were, in this respect, like-minded.[103]

Charles added seven hymns which were all designed to encourage Methodists to stay loyal to the Church. He showed that he was fully aware it was not a perfect institution and that it suffered from clergy who were 'slaves of pride, ambition, [and] lust':

> O what a scene attracts our eyes!
> What multitudes of lifeless souls!
> An open vale before us lies,
> A place of graves, a place of skulls,
> The desolate house of England's sons,
> A Church – a charnel of dry bones![104]

But he asked for support to make the Church what Jesus wanted it to be. Dissent would simply destroy any chance of a successful religious revival.

Charles remained heartened by the rising number of clergy prepared to work with the Methodists. The most notable addition to the ranks of the evangelical clergy at this time was the kind-hearted if very eccentric John Berridge, Vicar of Everton, who commenced preaching out of doors up to 12 times a week and covered not only most of Bedfordshire, Cambridgeshire and Huntingdonshire, but also large sections of Hertfordshire, Essex and Suffolk. However, like Whitefield and the Wesleys before him, Berridge was soon reduced to building up his own team of lay preachers.

Charles decided it was time he played a larger role again. On a visit to London he tried to allay Sally's fears over the potential impact on his health:

> I am as careful of myself as you can wish me, and a good deal too careful in the judgement of some. My brother has set me down for preaching every night of the week at every quarter of the town. I regard not his commands in this, and plainly told him so.[105]

His return was timely because, in February 1760, three preachers in Norwich administered communion without seeking authorization from the Wesleys. Two were protégés of Grimshaw called Paul Greenwood and Thomas Mitchell. The other was a Cornishman, John Murlin. Charles saw their action as a deliberate attempt to drive Methodism into dissent and he again blamed John for not taking a stronger stand earlier. He declared either the men should agree to train for ordination or they should be expelled, despite their exemplary reputation. He told John:

> Dear Brother, We have come to the Rubicon. Shall we pass, or shall we not? ... The rest will soon follow their example, I believe because ... they think they may do it with impunity ... More and more will

give the sacrament, and set up for themselves, even before we die ...
You have connived at it too, too long.[106]

John was reluctant to take any decisive action and said the matter could wait until the next Conference.

Charles told Sally his brother was enabling the preachers concerned to spread their poison to others so that the Conference would find in their favour and vote for separation from the Church. He felt he had five months to prevent this happening and so he tried to use his power base in London to rally opposition by holding a meeting of the leaders of its societies. He promised those who attended he would not 'betray the cause of the Church' and was delighted by their backing: 'You cannot conceive what a spirit rose in all who heard me ... that they would ... live and die in the Church.'[107] Methodists in London were, of course, in a very different position from those elsewhere in the country because they had far easier access to evangelical clergy.

Charles still pinned his hopes on encouraging the preachers who wanted to administer the sacraments to train for the priesthood rather than seeking to license themselves as dissenting ministers. He looked to some of the very first lay preachers like John Nelson to support him:

> I think you are no weathercock ... John, I love thee from my heart, yet rather than see thee a Dissenting Minister, I wish to see thee smiling in thy coffin. What can de done to save our Preachers?[108]

Charles also wrote to many friends, including his traditional ally William Grimshaw:

> To leave them & things as they are, is to betray our charge – to undermine the Church – and, as far as in us lies, to destroy the work of God ... Will you not join hand & heart with us? ... Strengthen my hands by your counsel & by your prayers if you count me worthy to be called your affectionate & faithful brother.[109]

Grimshaw's response came as a blow. He told Charles it was too late to prevent separation, partly because the Church had been too slow to accept Methodism, and partly because John's inaction towards the Norwich preachers meant 'the Methodists are no longer members of the Church of England':

> They are as real a body of Dissenters from her as the Presbyterians, Baptists, Quakers, or any body of Independents ... It is time for me to

shift myself: to disown all connection with the Methodists ... [and] to stay at home and take care of my parish ... [I will] quietly recede without noise or tumult ... The thing is gone too far.[110]

Charles had no intention of letting Grimshaw go quietly. On 13 April he summoned all the leaders of London Methodism to the Foundery and he read out Grimshaw's letter. It caused consternation. Charles told his friends he understood the pressures on the preachers who after years of 'labouring like a horse and travelling like a post-boy' had exhausted themselves and now wished to settle into a parish and look after their families. It was incumbent on the Church to welcome them into its ranks rather than force them into becoming dissenting ministers. Ordination not separation was the answer and he for one would do all in his power to persuade the church authorities to recognize that 'or never blame him for turning Dissenter'.[111]

Most preachers did not share Charles' belief that the Church could be made to change its hostility towards ordaining them. For example, Joseph Cownley wrote to Charles: 'What Bishop, either in England or Ireland, will ever ... ordain a Methodist Preacher to be a Methodist Preacher?' He challenged Charles to stop wasting his time and to resume his itinerant ministry:

> Give me leave now to press you to do what I think is your bounden duty: I mean to visit the north this summer. We have excused you to the poor people, till we can do it no longer. If you refuse to come now, we can say neither more nor less about it, than, that you cannot because you will not.[112]

Pressure like this proved too much for Charles, who was taken ill. He was sent to Bath to recuperate.

John agreed that the 1760 Conference should be held in Bristol in order that the sick Charles could still attend. John knew he was in a very difficult position. Effectively Charles' control over the Methodists in London and Grimshaw's reputation in the North gave him little choice but to publicly support their views. He joked with Charles that he would 'gag the blatant beast' once and for all.[113] Consequently John made clear to the Conference he would also desert the organization if precipitate action by preachers caused a separation with the Church. This, according to Howell Harris, 'struck dumb'[114] those who wanted to see John ordain his preachers and enabled Charles' views to carry the day. A jubilant William Grimshaw agreed to remain as a Methodist preacher and John expressed his hope that, once Charles had recovered his health, he would also resume full active itinerancy now the separation issue had been resolved. John subsequently also wrote begging Charles not to pursue further their differences: 'I have done at the last Conference all I can or dare do. Allow me liberty of conscience, as I allow you.'[115]

Charles had effectively delayed a break with the Church of England on the issue of ordination for the next 20 years. It was a major achievement. Publicly John repeatedly said that God would desert Methodism if it left the Church, even though he did not believe that was true. In 1763 he created a 'Model Deed', by which he made clear preaching-houses were never to be called 'churches' and that the only preachers permitted within them were those authorized by him and Charles. Such preachers had to preach and act in accordance with what Conference had agreed or face expulsion. The sop to the preachers was that their welfare was more seriously considered. A Preachers' Fund was created to provide pensions for those who became too worn out to continue their work and to provide assistance to the widows and children of those who died. John also developed the habit of trying to write annually to each preacher.

Charles spent the next decade trying to encourage the Church to change its attitude towards Methodism. He told his wife: 'The converted clergy will be multiplied by the time my brother and I finish.'[116]

A Falling Away from Christian Perfection

Spirit of truth descend
And with thy church abide,
Our guardian to the end,
Our sure, unerring guide,
Us into the whole, counsel lead,
Of God reveal'd below,
And teach us all the truth we need,
To life eternal know ...

Descending from above,
Into our souls convey,
His comfort, joy, and love,
Which none can take away,
His merit, and his righteousness,
Which makes an end of sin;
Apply to every heart his peace,
And bring his kingdom in.

Thy plenitude of God
That doth in Jesus dwell,
On us thro' Him bestow'd
To us secure and seal:
Now let us taste our master's bliss,
The glorious, heavenly powers,
For all the Father hath is His,
And all He hath is ours.[1]

For a number of years France had been gradually encroaching on Britain's colonies, and when that 'insulting, enraged and perfidious enemy' (as Whitefield called them) gained control of the Great Lakes in North America, it was interpreted as evidence that France wanted to resurrect the Jacobite cause and force Britain to become Catholic. On 6 February 1756 a national fast was held and all businesses were suspended for prayers for the nation. Charles reprinted the patriotic hymns he had written in the 1740s and George Whitefield published an *Address to Persons of all Denominations* in which he made clear the Methodists would oppose any French attempt to invade Britain with the help of 'a Popish pretender and thousands of Romish priests'. John offered to raise at least 200 volunteers to help defend London in the event of any invasion. These moves reflected not just loyalty but a fear that Methodism might again be subjected to the charge of being a cover for Jacobitism.

In May 1756 Britain declared war only to have the French immediately seize Minorca, then Britain's principal Mediterranean base, without a fight and, in June, have British colonists suffer the disgrace of the 'black hole of Calcutta'. In August the colonial war acquired a European dimension when Frederick the Great of Prussia, who was in receipt of British subsidies to defend the interests of Hanover, launched a surprise attack on Saxony, a minor ally of France and Austria. By the autumn the patriotic William Pitt had been appointed prime minister to take charge of what later became known as the Seven Years' War. He had no doubt that Britain's future greatness lay in extending its colonies and becoming the world's major trading power, so he initiated hugely significant changes, including a ship-building programme designed to make Britain master of the seas. Nevertheless, by the summer of 1757 Prussia was fighting for survival while the British attacks on the French coast were farcically inept. Only in India was there some success and that was largely due to the military prowess of Robert Clive and the determination of the East India Company.

Charles felt Pitt should recognize 'no power less than that which defeated the Spanish Armada will rescue England now'[2] and called on the faithful to pray to God for their country's deliverance:

Against this evil day,
Ready prepared they stand,
To turn thy vengeful wrath away,
And save a guilty land.[3]

It was another 12 months before there was any cause for rejoicing. British forces seized control of Louisbourg, the strongest fortress in North America. However, fear of a French invasion remained very much in evidence. There was another national day of fasting and prayer on 16

February 1759 and John Wesley spearheaded Methodist participation
in this event. The Countess of Huntingdon invited him and Charles to
join her and Whitefield and other evangelical ministers in a fortnight of
prayer and reflection as to how the religious revival could be given fresh
impetus and so return the nation to God's favour. Thomas Maxfield
also joined the group and Whitefield said it was like old times again. To
Charles' delight, John was well received by William Romaine, Henry
Venn and Martin Madan: 'My brother preached, and won all our hearts.
I never liked him better, and was never more united to him, since his unhappy marriage.'[4]

Charles introduced into the countess' circle one of John's protégés, a
young Swiss ex-soldier and teacher called Jean Guillaume de la Flechere,
who became better known by his anglicized name of John Fletcher. John
had persuaded him to undertake ordination in March 1757 and he had
become a great friend of Charles, whom he deeply admired:

> I sense that I do not deserve your advice, much less the title of friend
> which you give me; you are a indulgent father to me, and the title of
> son would fit me much better than that of brother.[5]

Charles found Fletcher 'a great comfort and help'[6] in his work in London and soon treated him almost like a member of the family. Judging
from their later correspondence Fletcher also became fond of Charles'
wife. He was later to become godfather to Charles and Sally's daughter.
Both John and Charles judged him the most intellectually capable of the
younger generation of converts and therefore the one obvious clergyman
with the potential to become the next leader of Methodism.

Charles felt there was a golden opportunity to unite all the young
evangelical clergy in the common cause but John prevaricated, telling
the countess that her protégés were 'upright of heart' but lacked the
qualities of those 'whom we have known from the beginning, and who
have borne the burden and heat of the day'.[7] Charles was disappointed
but his greater concern was being in London away from his wife at a
time of threatened invasion, even though he judged Bristol to be 'one of
the safest places in England'. In June 1759 he wrote:

> My dear Sally, Trust in the Lord for yourself and children. They are in
> safe hands. The hairs of their heads, as well as yours, are all numbered
> ... All I meet with have great faith for the cause and people of God ...
> All expect the French ... My brother writes that I should give notice to
> all our society to spend Wednesday July 11 in fasting and prayer, that
> God may be entreated for the land.[8]

Charles' surviving letters show his interest in the war effort and knowledge of the defences being prepared against invasion, but he remained adamant that 'the matter will not be determined by numbers':

> If the French land, and the Lord of Hosts is with us, they will make more haste back than they came with ... We shall keep them off by prayer as long as we can ... If God is against them, what signify all their designs and threatenings?[9]

In fact the war was turning in Britain's favour by 1759 with the defeat of the French at Minden securing the safety of Hanover and the victories of the young British general James Wolfe ensuring a British victory in North America. Charles particularly rejoiced when he heard the news that Admiral Rodney had set fire in Havre-de-Grace to the French boats designed to transport an invading force.

Preachers continued to report how the country was full of rumour and panic. In October John Wesley visited Bristol and saw some of the 1,100 French prisoners being held captive at Knowle. He was shocked by their lack of adequate clothing and the appalling prison conditions. He immediately publicized their plight in the local newspaper and persuaded the Bristol societies to raise money to help them. Even the Corporation of Bristol City sent mattresses and blankets. The following spring Whitefield raised funds in London to assist those families affected by the war in Germany. Such compassion did not prevent Charles producing 8 hymns on 'The Expected Invasion' and 15 hymns 'To Be Used on Thanksgiving Day' when the British fleet defeated the French on 20 November 1759:

> Vainly invincible
> Their fleets the seas did ride,
> And doom'd our sires to death and hell,
> And Israel's God defied:
> But with His wind He blew,
> But with His waves He rose,
> And dash'd, and scatter'd, and o'erthrew,
> And swallow'd up His foes ...[10]

In January 1760 the whole of London society was shocked by the actions of the hot-tempered Lawrence Shirley, Earl of Ferrers, a cousin of the Countess of Huntingdon. When his maltreated wife successfully obtained a legal separation, the earl took exception that a family servant called John Johnson was appointed as the steward responsible for seeing she received her rightful income from his estate. Ferrars locked Johnson in a bedroom and demanded he sign papers saying he had wronged his master. When the servant refused, the earl shot him. Ferrars was charged with murder and his brother, the Revd Walter Shirley, sought comfort from Charles:

> I wish above all things that I may either meet with you or your dear brother ... I find this wretched man has refused to see any of his relations and friends. I am determined that I will not be so easily repulsed. I will carry him, spite of himself ... the message of everlasting peace ... I know ... you at least will not leave me to pray alone.[11]

Because the guilty man was an earl, the case was heard before the House of Lords. George Whitefield and Charles wanted to support the countess and Walter Shirley, and so they agreed to attend the trial. Both John Wesley and John Fletcher accompanied them. Virtually all of London society was there, including most of the royal family, the leading aristocracy, and even foreign ambassadors. Critics of the countess' attachment to the Methodists alleged there was clearly a streak of insanity in the family. Charles wrote of this experience:

> The pomp was quite lost upon me ... [The murderer] seemed undaunted; but as the proofs came up stronger and fuller, he lost his courage, and sunk visibly down into the lowest dejection ... I believe there was not a single person in the Court but believed the prisoner guilty ... My heart and that of most others bled for him.[12]

The earl was found guilty and he requested to die by decapitation as befitted a nobleman, but he was sentenced to be hung. George Whitefield, Walter Shirley and the countess visited him in prison and Charles wrote hymns of supplication for him, but the earl refused to be moved. He insisted on playing piquet with the warders of the prison rather than saying his prayers and went to his public hanging unrepentant:

> In doubt I lived, in doubt I die,
> Yet stand prepared the vast abyss to try,
> And undismayed expect eternity.[13]

In the summer of 1760 the countess left London to recover from her distress. While she was away, the Haymarket New Theatre launched a new play called *The Minor*, written by an actor called Samuel Foote. It contained a crude attack on Whitefield, who was depicted as a character called 'Dr Squintum'. George was inclined to ignore this but Selina sought to have the play banned by the Lord Chamberlain. The result-ing publicity led David Garrick, who was London's leading actor and theatre manager, to transfer the production to his own theatre in Drury Lane. This led to a heated exchange in the media by the defenders and opponents of Whitefield. George was referred to yet again in the press as 'the leader of Methodism' and this did little to encourage John Wesley to work more closely with him and the countess.

Charles had no such doubts and he was very active in both Bristol and London. However, his letters to Sally reveal his health was not good. For example, in May he told her he was suffering from sleeplessness and 'burning in my breast'. The medicine prescribed aggravated rather than helped:

> No sooner had I taken it, than it spread a flame throughout my body. Nature struggled against it for a while, but could not throw it off. Near eleven at night I was forced to alarm the family ... I was all over convulsions.[14]

Fletcher was concerned at how enfeebled Charles looked and a number of his letters to him reflect his continued concern over the next couple of years.

In 1761 Charles again encouraged John to try and attract more clergy to work with them, but they found many society members were reluc-tant to abandon using the lay preachers they liked in order to listen to relatively unknown clergy. This was exemplified in Huddersfield where John had to admit to the evangelical Henry Venn that, while he could restrict the number of visits being made by lay preachers into his par-ish, he could not ban them altogether. This did little to encourage Venn to join forces with the Wesleys. In March John confessed to the Bristol minister James Rouquet that almost all the evangelical clergy disliked him. Despite this, he invited a number to the Methodist Conferences in 1761 and 1762. Among those who attended the latter one in Leeds were Henry Venn, William Romaine and Martin Madan.

On 25 October King George II died and the Methodist societies held a day of fasting and prayer. The accession of George III meant William Pitt was replaced as chief minister by Lord Bute, who wanted peace. With the fear of invasion gone and the overseas empire saved, there was no need to keep Pitt in post or continue the war. Unfortunately the fight-ing was to drag on another three years because of the complications involved in ending the conflict between Prussia and its enemies. During this time Charles' hopes of greater unity among the evangelicals were shattered by two crises.

The first crisis affected the Moravian societies created by Benjamin Ingham. In 1760 Ingham was captivated by the writings of a Scottish minister called John Glas. These emphasized a lifestyle based very much on early Christianity. Members washed each other's feet, exchanged holy kisses, and shared all their belongings. Ingham introduced Glasite thinking into the societies under his control without fully appreciating that Glas laid great emphasis on each congregation deciding what it wanted to do in terms of worship and organization. By 1761 Ingham's authority was constantly being challenged and his societies were in chaos as conflicting groups sought to control them. His years of evangelical work were destroyed almost overnight.

Even more damaging to the religious revival was the controversy which arose over John Wesley's concept of Christian perfection. He had long believed men and women could be 'as perfect as our Father in heaven is perfect' and that such perfection was attained in stages as a person surrendered more and more to the action of God's Spirit in his or her life. Charles had frequently reflected his brother's thinking in his hymn-writing:

Thou wilt not leave Thy work undone,
But finish what Thou hast begun,
Before I hence remove;
I shall be, Master, as Thou art,
Holy, and meek, and pure in heart,
And perfected in love ...[15]

The man John held up as being an obvious example of perfection achieved was John Fletcher who, in 1760, had become Vicar of Madeley in Shropshire. In some respects this was odd, because John had bitterly opposed Fletcher's decision to take up a parish rather than itinerant preaching. Only Charles had encouraged Fletcher and been solicitous about the problems he faced. Fletcher's parish included the ironworks of the Darby family in Coalbrookdale and so was at the centre of the industrial revolution. He saw at first hand the appalling conditions in which coalminers and ironworkers lived. Most were asthmatic by the age of 30 and dead by 50. Fletcher did all he could to alleviate their suffering but, with Charles' approval, he refused to accept John's accolade that this made him a saint:

My perfection is to see my imperfection; my comfort to feel I have the world, flesh and devil to overthrow through the Spirit and merits of my dear Saviour; and my desire and hope is to love God with all my heart, mind, soul, and strength, to the last gasp of my life. This is my perfection. I know no other.[16]

Not all were so modest. In 1760 some Methodists in Otley began saying that they had reached a state of perfection. John went to examine them individually and rejoiced to accept their claim. He took such 'sanctification' (as he called it) to be a sign of God's approval of his work. By March 1761 he was receiving about 30 claims of perfection a week from London Methodists alone. Those who claimed perfection felt they had conquered their sinful nature. One commented:

[I can never say] 'sin will never enter more' for my everlasting life depends upon patiently continuing in well doing ... [but] 'tis long since I had a shadow of a doubt of my final acceptance with God ... [and] it is long since I felt a [sinful] desire inordinate either in kind or degree.[17]

Initially ill health prevented both Charles and George Whitefield challenging John's delight in the growing number of those judging themselves to be perfect. George had so overstrained his constitution by his constant itinerant preaching that in April it was felt he might die. In enforced convalescence he drank 'the bitter cup of continued silence'.[18] Charles' health was so poor he confided to Fletcher he was contemplating ending itinerant work and taking a parish, though he feared John's reaction. Fletcher told him to do what he thought was right: 'You are always your own master, once you have shown him the trust of a colleague and the warm affection of a brother.'[19] Charles tried to recover his health in the spa city of Bath, and used the opportunity to write over 2,000 *Short Hymns on Select Passages of the Holy Scriptures*.

Eventually Charles did voice his and others' concerns at John's ready acceptance of the claims of people to be perfect. John ignored him and asked the longest-serving of his lay preachers, Thomas Maxfield, to promote perfection among more society members in London. It was a huge error of judgement. Maxfield allied himself with a newly converted but emotionally volatile soldier called George Bell. Some found Bell's emotive demands for perfection attractive, but the more rational were repelled:

[He] soon ran into such an extraordinary strain, screaming in such a violent manner to compel a blessing upon the present meeting, that he seemed to be in a rapture and in fact as one raving with agony ... I cannot but esteem Mr Bell ripe for the most unscriptural extravagancies. I expect to hear of his prophecying, denouncing judgements and calling himself one of the witnesses. I hope he is honest at heart; but to me he appeared to be acting a part, whether out of vanity or mere delusion, I am not able to determine.[20]

It did not take long for Bell's actions to be labelled as evidence that no self-respecting clergyman should tolerate the nonsensical enthusiasm of Methodism.

By the time of the Methodist Conference of 1761 Charles had become an outspoken critic of Maxfield for permitting Bell to poison and destroy what he and John had struggled so long to achieve. As far as Charles was concerned, those claiming perfection were not only deceiving themselves and bursting 'with self-important pride' but also totally lacking in 'real grace'.[21] Charles said the shallow lifestyle of perfectionists stood in marked contrast to their arrogant boasts, and he argued the nature of perfect love was only fully understood and appreciated by the saints. For that reason anyone truly worthy of the name Christian accepted perfection was achievable only after death:

They never boast their grace, or dare
Their own perfection to declare,
But still their littleness maintain,
Till great in heaven with Christ they reign.[22]

Reluctantly John moderated his earlier enthusiasm by warning those who claimed to be perfect they could easily lose their state of perfection if, as was likely, sin re-entered their hearts:

To expect deliverance from wandering thoughts, occasioned by evil spirits, is to expect that the devil should die or fall asleep. To expect deliverance from those [temptations] which are occasioned by other men, is to expect either that all men should cease from the earth, or that we should be absolutely secluded from them. And to pray for deliverance from those [temptations] which are occasioned by the body, is, in effect, to pray that we may leave the body.[23]

It was too late because by then Bell had totally convinced Maxfield that God was now only working through the lives of the sanctified. He claimed the leadership of both John and Charles was a thing of the past.

To restore propriety and reason, Charles urged John to expel any perfectionist whose life was not perfect, but John was reluctant to take any strong action. He told Charles in January 1762 that the perfectionists required gentle handling: 'There is need of a lady's hand, as well as a lion's heart.'[24] Charles' opposition must have been weakened by having to deal with yet another family tragedy: the death of his daughter

Susanna, aged only 11 months. Fletcher did his best to console him: 'I hope that the weariness and sadness will not altogether beat down your wife. Greet her from me and tell her that I would with my heart bear a part of her burden'.[25]

In August John's complacent attitude led to a lost opportunity at the annual Conference in Leeds, which coincided with a visit of the Countess of Huntingdon to Yorkshire. Most of the leading evangelical clergy met together, but their growing concern at John's attitude towards the perfectionists prevented any progress towards greater co-operation with the Wesleys. John's naivety was made apparent when Bell announced he had cured a woman called Mary Spead, who had been terminally ill with breast cancer. John declared this was a miracle cure, even though many told him Bell's claim had no truth in it. About 100 Methodists decided to leave an organization which appeared to be descending into irrationality.

The normally loyal Charles was pushed into publicly challenging what John was permitting to happen. His normal practice was to let John edit his hymns for publication, but he now published some which he did not show in advance to his brother. Some of his *Short Hymns on Select Passages of the Holy Scriptures* clearly expressed his feelings about the danger of the 'loquacious, turbulent, and bold perfectionists'[26] and their false pride. He said they had allowed themselves to be 'by passion sway'd' and so were 'in Satan's cause employ'd ... against the truth and all its friends'.[27] The gospel was understandably discredited when people saw men and women falsely claiming to be perfect, even though it was wrong for some clergy to damn the whole Methodist movement because of the irrationality of a few:

> This does in no wise justify the men who put darkness for light, and light for darkness; who call the wisdom of God foolishness, and all real religion Enthusiasm.[28]

The hymns challenged John's theology as well as his actions. Whereas John believed God never deserted a true believer, Charles argued God sometimes deliberately withdrew his presence from people in order to test them and so periods of 'spiritual darkness' were to be expected by all, however strong their faith. Whereas John believed perfection was possible as soon as a believer's faith was strong enough, Charles reiterated his opinion it was only achievable after death:

> Perfection is my calling's prize,
> To which on duty's scale I rise;
> And when my toils are pass'd,

And when I have the battle won,
Thou in thy precious Self alone,
Shalt give the prize at last.[29]

John denounced Charles' hymns, saying he had seen 'five hundred witnesses' to the truth of Christian perfection and that Charles might as well join the Calvinists if he was to speak contrary to the doctrines he had long received.[30] He thought 'to set perfection too high (so high as no man that we ever heard or read of attained) is the most effectual ... way of driving it out of the world.'[31] The division between the brothers inevitably led to Charles receiving a number of letters from those who were equally unhappy with John's inaction.

John Fletcher tried to bridge the widening gulf between the two brothers. He tried to convince Charles not to place Maxfield in the same category as Bell, while acknowledging that some of the perfectionists in London sounded terrible:

> I do not willingly receive what is said against them; but allowing that what is reported is one half mere exaggeration, the tenth part of the rest shows that spiritual pride, presumption, arrogance, stubbornness, party spirit, uncharitableness, prophetic mistakes – in short, every sinew of enthusiasm is now at work among them.[32]

Fletcher showed he had no truck for false claimers of perfection by expelling two who had wrongly claimed perfection from his society in Madeley, but he reminded Charles that Maxfield had long been a true son of the gospel:

> I wish that we could discover a means to reconcile the deepest humility with the greatest hopes of grace. I believe that you insist on the one, and Maxfield on the other, and I believe you are both sincere in your view.[33]

Sadly George Whitefield was not in a position to use his immense conciliatory skills. His return to full-time itinerancy had caused a relapse and, when John met him, he commented that Whitefield was 'humanly speaking ... worn out'.[34] With the Seven Years' War over except for the formalities of a peace settlement, Whitefield announced he would return to America, hoping the sea voyage would enable him to more fully recuperate. However, he confided to one supporter:

> My breath is short, and I have little hopes, since my last relapse, of much further public usefulness. A few last exertions, like the last

struggles of a dying man, or glimmering flashes of a taper just burning out, is all that can be expected from me. But blessed be God the taper will be lighted up again in heaven.[35]

Conscious that there were still limits to Charles' willingness to publicly oppose John, William Grimshaw looked to Selina, Countess of Huntingdon to provide the leadership required to get the revival back on track: 'Come and animate us afresh – aid us by your counsels and prayers – communicate a spark of your glowing zeal, and stir us up to renewed activity in the cause of God.'[36]

On 2 November 1762 John finally wrote a letter criticizing the perfectionists in London. He said he admired their devotion but no one was as perfect as an angel and none were beyond temptation or the need for self-examination and private prayer. They therefore should cease regarding themselves as infallibly right on all matters and stop describing others who were growing in their faith as not true Christians. He condemned their meetings for being too full of pompous prayers and poorly written hymns and for being marred by their posturing and screaming behaviour which made much of what they said intelligible. He concluded:

I dislike something that has the appearance of enthusiasm, overvaluing feelings and inward impressions; mistaking the mere work of imagination for the voice of the Spirit; expecting the end without the means; and undervaluing reason, knowledge and wisdom in general ... But what I most dislike is your littleness of love ... your bigotry and ... your divisive spirit.[37]

The letter was insufficient to satisfy Charles or John's many other critics but it was strong enough to provoke animosity among the perfectionists. One woman returned her membership card, saying she would not be 'browbeaten any longer' and, because Maxfield was now her teacher, she would have no more to do with the Wesleys.[38] By December John was more outspoken, describing Maxfield as 'inimitably wrong-headed'.[39] He admitted the meetings of the enthusiastically sanctified were very unedifying affairs:

[They are] like a bear garden; full of noise, brawling, cursing, swearing, blasphemy and confusion ... Those who prayed were partly the occasion of this, by their horrid screaming, and unscriptural, enthusiastic expressions.[40]

He was especially shocked by Bell's preaching at the Foundery: 'He now spoke as from God what I knew God had not spoken.'[41]

But words were not deeds and many of the long-standing preachers, like John Downey, detested John's continued inaction:

I consider the follies and extravagance of the witnesses as the devices of Satan to cast a blemish on the real work of God ... As to the folly of the enthusiasts, Mr Charles hears every week less or more. Why his brother suffers them we cannot tell. He threatens, but cannot find in his heart to put execution. The consequence is the talk of all the town, and entertainment for the newspapers.[42]

Charles, Vincent Perronet and many others begged John to promote rational Christianity and to expel Bell and Maxfield 'lest delusions should overspread the Methodist church'.[43] Even Fletcher had to admit the perfectionists were reducing John's position to a shameful one by 'the magnitude of the evil'.[44]

Unfortunately John was now afraid to act because he feared action against Maxfield and Bell might cause Methodism in London to self-destruct, such was their level of support. However, even John could not ignore the press ridicule of Methodism in January 1763 when Bell announced he was sure the world would end on 28 February. He denounced Bell both in the press and from the pulpit and, on 9 January, expelled him from the Foundery. About 600 members threatened to leave with him and John begged Charles to return to London to support him. Charles refused, probably because John had not yet taken action against Maxfield. On 27 February matters got worse when the public authorities decided to arrest Bell for planning a mass meeting to await the end of the world. They felt they had to intervene to maintain public order. John preached to those who would listen that Bell's prophecy of the end of the world was a misguided vision.

Needless to say, the world did not end on 28 February and, shortly afterwards, William Grimshaw jokingly wrote to Charles:

Last Monday should have been the Day of Judgement. Therefore to have answered your [last] letter sooner would have been a waste of labour, time and paper ... But who was mistaken? God or Bell?[45]

Charles did not see the funny side. He bitterly resented that John had ignored his advice for four years on the matter. He commented: 'Sad havoc Satan has made of the flock ... [and] the flood of enthusiasm ... has now overflowed us.'[46] It was a view strongly shared by the Countess of Huntingdon's circle. William Romaine commented:

I pity Mr John from my heart. His societies are in great confusion; and the point, which brought them into the wilderness of rant and madness, is still insisted on as much as ever. I fear the end of this delusion ... Perfection is still the cry ... and brotherly love is almost lost in our disputes.[47]

Matters were not helped by the unexpected death of the 54-year-old William Grimshaw. The man who had once boasted he would never flag 'while I can ride, walk, creep, or crawl' had worn himself out.[48] His eyesight was failing and he was constantly troubled by bowel problems and arthritic pains. In his weakened state he contracted typhoid while visiting a sick parishioner. Benjamin Ingham, Henry Venn and many others risked their lives to see him, despite Grimshaw's protestations that this was unnecessary. Accounts of his last days are filled with the impact he had on those who saw him. Despite excruciating pain and fever, it is clear Grimshaw thought only of the welfare of his parishioners. Just before he died he told his housekeeper and nurse:

My flesh has, as it were, been roasting before a hot fire. But I have nothing to do but to step out of bed into heaven. I have my foot on the threshold already.[49]

In line with his wishes, he was buried in a poor man's burial sheet and coffin and given a simple funeral service. However, such was Grimshaw's reputation that he was still being talked about almost 50 years later in Haworth. Tales about him may have contributed to Emily Bronte's creation of the character of Heathcliff in her novel *Wuthering Heights*, as well as his name being partially echoed in another character in that book, Hindley Earnshaw. Tributes were expressed nationwide. Charles wrote two poetic tributes to his friend, though (as often was the case when Charles was emotionally deeply involved) neither were particularly well written. When he gave his own funeral oration on Grimshaw, he delivered it with such passion that he suffered from a heavy and protracted nosebleed. Aware of his own ill health, Charles wrote to his wife: 'Perhaps it is a blaze before death.'[50]

That same April Charles was further depressed by the death of the Countess of Huntingdon's 25-year-old daughter, and he clearly felt he had had enough of the world and all its sorrows:

O Saviour, descend, no longer delay,
Our sufferings to end, and bear us away,
Where death cannot sever, or sorrow molest,
Thy people for ever reposed on Thy breast![51]

Meanwhile John tried desperately to justify what he had done. In May he reminded a despondent Charles that, unlike the perfectionists, he had never said a person would always remain in a state of perfection because 'sinless perfection' was not scriptural.[52] He also defended himself to the countess and criticized Whitefield, Madan, Berridge, Haweis and others of her supporters for not helping him more in his hour of need.[53] They felt an apology would have served his cause better and the countess publicly stated John had significantly damaged the religious revival. Both Maxfield and Bell were bitter at John's treatment of them and Bell accused him of 'double dealings and unfaithful proceedings'.[54] About 200 left the Foundery to join Maxfield in creating their own chapel in Ropemakers' Alley, Little Moorfields. When Charles did return to London in May, he was heckled by some of Maxfield's supporters, who alleged his 'poverty of spirit' would 'destroy all our perfection'.[55]

Throughout the country the evangelical clergy were appalled at the way Methodism appeared to be descending into an unstoppable irrationality. For example, there were reports of how in Wales many societies were adopting the practice of jumping up and down in a wild fashion and singing a verse of a hymn repeatedly up to 40 times. Vincent Perronet tried to comfort Charles: 'Satan has certainly kindled a fire; but nothing except the chaff shall be consumed by it.'[56] Amazingly an unrepentant John chose to preach at the 1763 Conference on the subject of Christian perfection. He seemed to think any kind of enthusiasm was preferable to dull orthodoxy. It took the skills of Howell Harris to calm the resulting anger. He said that, if John had abused his power, it was for them as his children to weep rather than to condemn him. Having literally reduced the Conference to tears, Harris persuaded its members to abandon all discussion of the issue of perfection. John blandly commented: 'It was a great blessing that we had peace among ourselves, while so many were making themselves ready for battle.'[57]

The main outcome of the Conference was the publication of a far more detailed and accurate handbook of what Methodism was really about in the shape of a revised edition of the Minutes of previous Conferences. But the Conference's failure to deal with John's handling of the situation inevitably meant that criticism mounted after its closure. Only John Fletcher continued to urge for a reconciliation. He told Charles: 'The perfectionists and ourselves are not so far apart: clear definitions on both sides, and we shall draw much closer to each other.'[58] He reiterated his view that, although Maxfield had proved surprisingly inflexible, he was a sincere man with much to offer as a preacher.

In January 1764 a wounded John wrote to the countess, alleging she was treating him and his brother as being no better than 'a couple of postillions' and decrying her 'great narrowness of spirit'.[59] It may have been John's growing sense of isolation that led him into another error. He asked a man named Erasmus, whom he thought was a bishop in the Greek Orthodox Church, to ordain three of his best preachers: John Jones, Samson Staniforth and Thomas Bryant. Unfortunately Erasmus was a fraud. Once John realized his error, he denounced the bogus ordinations, but this did not stop a furore in Church of England circles over what had happened. Once again, John looked for support to his brother. Charles made clear his health would not permit him to return to London and that he very strongly disapproved of what John had done, even if Erasmus had been genuine.

John desperately used the only card he had left. He told Charles that his continued absence gave him no option but to use a lay preacher to administer communion to society members: 'I must do the best I can ... And insist upon John Jones assisting me on Sundays. I have delayed all this purely out of tenderness to you. Adieu!'[60] Charles under protest returned to London to take on the running of the divided London societies, but he avoided John's company as much as possible. In May John admitted he was 'sick of disputing'[61] and wrote to Charles:

> Dear Brother, Is there any reason why you and I should have no further intercourse with each other? I know none; although possibly there are persons in the world who would not be sorry for it ... I feel the want of some about me that are all faith and love.[62]

He failed to appreciate his brother was genuinely unwell. In a letter home to his wife Charles questioned whether he had much longer to live: 'My Doctor flattered me ... [but] I did not believe one word he said; feeling the contrary every day and hour.'[63] In a poem he contrasted the vigour of his youth:

> Swift on the wings of active zeal
> With Jesus' message flew
> O'erjoy'd with all my heart and will
> My Master's work to do ...
> I found no want of will, or power,
> In love's sweet task employ'd,
> And put forth, every day and hour,
> My utmost strength for God ...

with the weakness of age:

> But now enervated by age
> I feel my fierceness gone,
> And nature's powers no more engage
> To prop the Saviour's throne:
> My total impotence I see,
> For help on Jesus call,
> And stretch my feeble hands to Thee
> Who workest all in all.[64]

Arguably it was the return of George Whitefield from America which initiated an end to the crisis. He visited Bell and persuaded him to repress his 'furious bitter zeal' and seek his peace with John. The latter commented that Whitefield 'breathes nothing but love. Bigotry cannot stand before him, but hides its head wherever he comes.'[65] In similar conciliatory vein John Fletcher encouraged Maxfield to visit him in Madeley, telling Charles 'his faults will be corrected more easily through friendship than by aloofness'.[66] Across the country key Methodists urged unity and Selina, Countess of Huntingdon agreed to call a meeting in Bristol for those clergy still supportive of the religious revival. Twelve of the 39 invited agreed to attend the 1764 Conference. Most of these wanted a guarantee that if they supported Methodism they would be given control over the societies within their parish and control over which lay preachers (if any) visited. A notable exception was Fletcher, who commented he was happy to receive any lay preachers: 'I rejoice that the work of God goes on by any instrument or in any place.'[67]

The hostility of the lay preachers to the idea of losing their control over the societies hammered the last nail in the coffin of any hope that the evangelical clergy would support Wesleyan-style Methodism. Instead they placed their hope in the countess opening more chapels. Charles was very unhappy at the failure of the Conference and he was offended by John's false claim that the growth of overemotional behaviour had nothing to do with him. He was even more hurt by John's cruel assertion that Charles' emotional hymns were as much to blame as Maxfield's madness for what had happened: 'When your hymns on one hand were added to his talking and acting on the other, what was likely to be the consequence?'[68] Despite this provocative comment, John knew he required Charles' skills and support if he was to retain his authority and that Charles' skill as a preacher was essential if the mess in London was to be sorted:

You are made, as it were, for this very thing. Just here you are in your element ... in strong, pointed sentences you beat me. Go on, in your own way, what God has peculiarly called you to do.[69]

There is no doubt Charles was still recognized among the societies as one of Methodism's finest preachers and, unlike John, he was still highly regarded by the evangelical clergy. A lay preacher called John Valton, who went to London to hear Charles preach in July 1764, recorded the impact on him:

His word was with power; and I thought my Saviour was at hand, never being so sensibly affected under a discourse before. In the evening I heard him again at the Foundery, and all seemed to be comforted and affected by his word.[70]

Another listener, James Sutcliffe, was similarly impressed, saying that, though initially Charles appeared frail, once he began preaching 'he was on his high horse [and] age and infirmities were left behind. It was a torrent of doctrine, of exhortation and eloquence bearing down all before him.'[71]

John published *Further Thoughts on Christian Perfection* to reinstate confidence in perfection as a goal for all Christians. He made clear no human could be truly perfect because of 'unavoidable defects of human understanding' and humanity's innate capacity to make mistakes. Even the most religious were prone to do things wrong 'both in our tempers and words and actions'. He redefined perfection as 'the humble, gentle, patient love of God and man' ruling the heart,[72] and argued against 'that daughter of pride, enthusiasm' which encouraged people to assume that 'dreams, voices, impressions, visions, or revelations' must be from God when 'may be from the devil'.[73] This book satisfied no one and seemed to show John had no consistent view on perfection, though it (and Fletcher's encouragement) may explain why Maxfield was prepared to offer some conciliatory gestures to John in 1765.

The countess told Howell Harris, who was finally recovering from his illness, it was no longer possible to understand what truth John believed and compared him to a slippery eel. John Fletcher later commented that he had never understood what all the fuss about perfection was about because perfection 'is nothing but the acts of holiness, faith, love, prayer, praise, and joy so frequently repeated as to turn it into easy, delightful habits'.[74] If Wesley's book had any impact, it was to further promote a backlash against 'enthusiasm'. Some historians have argued that this explains why the growth of Methodism suffered a real setback. Certainly one Methodist preacher, writing in the 1790s, commented that the liveliness of the movement was hindered 'by the old members being so exceedingly afraid of George Bell's days. An excess of prudence has hindered it.' [75]

Charles' return to London as its main Methodist preacher did not lead to a better relationship with his brother because John was absent on the road preaching. But in December 1764 John pleaded with Charles for a reconciliation: 'I think vainly there is no need that you and I should be such strangers to each other. Surely we are old enough to be wiser.'[76] However, Charles had family preoccupations over the next couple of years that diminished his capacity to support John. Sally was pregnant in both 1765/6 and 1766/7. Charles chose to support her and retreat largely into hymnwriting. In 1766 and 1767 he published a new succession of hymnbooks. *Hymns for Children, and others of Riper Years* contained 100 hymns, *Hymns on the Trinity* 180, and *Hymns for the use of Families* a further 166, although some of these were reprints of hymns already published.

The hymns tried to find Christian meaning in all the trials of human existence: the uncertainty and danger of childbirth, cutting one's first teeth, going away to boarding school, the sickness or death of a child, moving house, a persecuting husband or unconverted wife, shortage of money to live, lack of certainty, an undutiful child, retirement, and so on. Some adopted an empathetic approach as in this extract from a hymn written from the viewpoint of a pregnant woman:

> I fear, lest in my trying hour
> The strength of pain should quite o'erpower
> My soul's infirmity,
> Lest, when my sorrows must prevail,
> My patience and my faith should fail,
> And leave me void of Thee ...[77]

The joys of life were also covered: a wedding, a successful and safe birth, baptism, birthdays, a family meal, recovery from sickness, patriotic celebrations, and so on. He offered hymns to cover the different stages of life: hymns for both the young child and the parent, for both the maiden and the young man, for both the servant and the master. Those on the Trinity tackled more complex theological considerations and included one that became particularly popular: 'Hail! Holy, holy, holy Lord!' Charles wrote too many hymns for them all to be good (indeed some are very repetitive and almost formulaic), but the best still showed a poetic inspiration few could match.

John felt Charles' hymnwriting was a wrong priority and expressed annoyance at Charles' dereliction of duty. In calmer vein Fletcher begged Charles not to stop preaching because there were many Methodists around the country who were counting upon him visiting them again. He also resumed his attempt to make Charles forgive Maxfield 'as the most simple, the most evangelical, and the most comforting preacher who has yet been seen in our Church'.[78] Charles' attitude may partially explain why when John published his *A Short History of Methodism* in 1765 it essentially ignored Charles' contribution. It also erroneously stated that George Whitefield had 'entirely separated' himself from the movement. A published sermon, 'The Lord our Righteousness', renewed John's long-standing attack on Calvinism. Alongside these, John published *The Scripture Way of Salvation*, which has been described as 'the maturation of his theology, hammered out during the years of contention and controversy'.[79]

At the Conference that year John told all the preachers they could not print anything of their own without his permission. With Charles' restraining hand removed, he felt free to dictate extensive detail on every aspect of Methodist living from the way to sing hymns to the role of women, and he deliberately demanded that all preachers should 'expect to be perfected in love in this life'.[80] All were told to accept whatever he said or leave. In the spring of 1766 this dictatorial approach was applied to Charles, who was instructed to stop placing his family before his Christian duty:

> Dear Brother, We must, we must, you and I at least, be all devoted to God! Then wives, and sons, and daughters, and everything else, will be real, invaluable blessings ... If I am (in some sense) the head, and you the heart, of the work, may it not be said, 'The whole head is sick, and the whole heart is faint?' Come, in the name of God, let us arise, and shake ourselves from the dust! Let us strengthen each other's hands in God, and that without delay.[81]

However, there was bluster behind John's dogmatism. Once it became clear Charles' lower profile was genuinely a product of ill health, John lost confidence. In a remarkably low moment he wrote: 'I do not love God. I never did. Therefore I never believed ... I am only an honest heathen ... one of the God-fearers.'[82] It did not help his morale that anti-Methodist publications were appearing on a regular basis. A poem called 'The Methodist' particularly focused on John's continued use of badly educated lay preachers:

> The bricklayer throws his trowel by,
> And now builds mansions in the sky.

The cobbler, touched with holy pride,
Flings his old shoes and lasts aside ...
The baker, now a preacher grown,
Finds man lives not by bread alone ...
Weavers inspired, their shuttles leave,
Sermons and flimsy hymns to weave.
Barbers unreaped will leave the chin,
To trim and shave the man within ...[83]

John asked John Fletcher to take over as leader because he was 'blessed with health, activity and diligence together with some degree of learning'. [84] Fletcher said he would 'gather the wreck' only if he could act as a co-worker with Charles.[85] This stipulation reflected Fletcher's huge regard for Charles. On one occasion he wrote to him:

I am so assured of your salvation that I ask for no other place in heaven than the one I might have at your feet. I even question whether Paradise would be Paradise if you were not there to share it with me. The very idea ... that we might one day be parted, grieves my heart and fills my eyes with tears.[86]

John therefore again tried to tempt Charles back to a wider role, saying it was a mistake that they had ceased properly speaking with each other:

Have we not known each other for half a century, and are we not jointly engaged in such a work as probably not two men upon earth are? Why then do we keep at such a distance? It is a mere device of Satan ... Let us therefore make the full use of the little time that remains ... We should help each other ... We must have a thorough reform of the Preachers ... I believe it would help, not hurt your health.[87]

It may have been Charles who persuaded Selina, Countess of Huntingdon to host a meeting of him and George with John in August 1766. Charles and George felt that if 'Pope John' could be persuaded to properly co-operate with 'Pope Joan' (as the countess was being nicknamed) Wesleyan and Calvinist could yet be brought together again. Charles wrote of the meeting: 'Last night my brother came. This morning we spent two hours together with G. Whitefield. The threefold cord, we trust, will never more be broken.'[88] Selina was less happy. She remained suspicious of John's motives. Nevertheless, the links between the two branches of Methodism were formalized into what Howell Harris called 'the Public Peace Union'. John agreed to preach in the countess' latest new chapel in Bath though, when he did so, he was not received particularly well because it was felt he acted with 'very vulgar enthusiasm'.[89]

The countess commenced a ministerial training college in the home of Howell Harris at Trevecca in Wales and placed John Fletcher in charge of it. It was her hope that this college would symbolize the new unity and provide Methodist lay preachers with the education they required to make them more eligible for ordination. Its official opening in the autumn of 1767 was marked by the translation of a recently written Welsh hymn into English: 'Guide Me O Thou Great Jehovah'. However, a rather jealous John expressed scorn on the enterprise to Joseph Benson, whom he had chosen to run his own school at Kingswood:

> Trevecca is much more to Lady Huntingdon than Kingswood is to me. 'I' mixes with everything. It is 'my' College, 'my' masters', 'my' students. I do not speak so of this school.[90]

Many others were doubtful of whether Trevecca would prove a worthwhile enterprise, but it soon acquired greater justification when, in 1768, six Methodist students were expelled from Oxford University for being religious 'enthusiasts'.

Charles was delighted at the creation of the Public Peace Union and agreed to act as leader for the societies in both London and Bristol while John and George travelled throughout England. John also toured Ireland and George Wales. It was almost like the old days in which the three offered 'the good methodistical, thirty year old medicine'.[91] Whitefield felt the younger generation of preachers needed to see that old Methodism had never been about creating preaching houses and an organization. It had all been about preaching in the open to those who would otherwise not hear the gospel: 'Ye Methodists of many years standing, shew the young ones, who have not the cross to bear, as we once had, what ancient Methodism was.'[92] Preaching was still, of course, what Whitefield did best, as one who heard him commented:

> In one way or another, the occurrence of the week or the day furnished him with matter for the pulpit ... He had a most peculiar art of speaking personally to you, in a congregation of four thousand people ... nor do I ever recollect his stumbling upon a word.[93]

In the spring of 1768 John travelled through the Midlands and the North, saying he preferred to work among the less fashionable, allowing George to focus his attention on preaching in London and Charles in

Bristol. John urged that he and Charles should 'come to a good under-standing, both for our sakes and for the sake of the people' on the sub-ject of Christian perfection[94] and avoid any further public disagreements 'if it can be avoided'.[95] By this stage he was becoming concerned that Methodism was becoming too comfortable. Treatises urged Methodists to adopt neat, plain, modest attire so that the bulk of their money could be given away to feed the hungry, clothe the naked, help the prisoner, and relieve the sick and the stranger. In this respect John had long set a personal example. When his income had been £30 per year he had lived on £28 and given away £2. When, largely through the sale of his books, he had £60 per year he gave away £32. Even when he had £120 per year he retained only £28 for his personal use.

Charles could be equally generous but he found John's uncompromis-ing example difficult when it was imposed on others, some of whom had more personal family commitments. On one occasion he actually com-plained at John's unreasonable expectations in this respect:

> How many collections think you my brother made between Thursday evening and Sunday? No fewer than seven. Five this one day from the same poor exhausted people. He has no mercy on them, on the GIV-ING poor I mean; as if he was in haste to reduce them to the number of the RECEIVING poor.[96]

This is not surprising. At varying times we have references in Charles' letters to concerns about being unable to pay his creditors and, on one occasion, even to having to pawn his coat. Only a legacy from Sally's family made matters eventually easier for Charles. John was always un-sympathetic. He once told Charles it was very unreasonable for him to take any money from the Preachers' Fund:

> I could not do it, if it were my own case. I should account it robbery. I have often wondered how either your conscience or your sense of honour could bear it ... I desire only to spend and be spent in the work which God has given to me to do.[97]

In July 1768 Whitefield set out for Scotland and Charles agreed to take over in London. His letters to Sally, who was left behind in Bristol, re-flect his continued passion for her and his love for his young children. Charles was greatly upset when he heard their seven-month-old baby, John James, was seriously ill, but before he could return home, the child had died. He confessed to Sally:

I should never have come hither, had I not depended on you to follow me. I cannot think of staying here without you ... Yet God prospers my labours at the beginning of my course. Perhaps it is a blaze before death.[98]

Tragedy also struck George because in August 1768 his wife was taken seriously ill and died. This made him return to London and start planning a return to America. Meanwhile, John made plans to tour the South-West and then the Midlands during the second half of the year, admitting to Charles that he was now prepared to abandon his emphasis on Christian perfection in the interests of Christian harmony.

Sally understandably felt it was time Charles stopped travelling between Bristol and London. John therefore encouraged Charles to move his family permanently to London and Charles agreed, partly because his surviving elder son was showing the kind of musical potential which only the metropolis could properly develop. Charles spent months trying to find a suitable home he could afford. He and his family eventually took up residence in a large four-storeyed house in Chesterfield Street in Marylebone. This was provided free of rent by a wealthy admirer called Mrs Gumley, who wanted to show her support for the Wesleys. The house, which was richly furnished and a far cry from Charles' home in Bristol, was about three miles from the Foundery and set in what was then still essentially a village surrounded by countryside. Charles was delighted that Mrs Gumley's generosity meant he could even afford to keep the house's caretaker as a servant for Sally: 'We shall keep her to keep up the fires, to keep the windows open, and to lie in the beds. When you come you will do as you like.'[99]

The house was to remain the family home for the rest of Charles' life and, once in situ, Charles quickly became the acknowledged main pastor to the London societies. He continued to regularly visit Bristol each summer when travelling was easier, but he ceased altogether going around the country. John thought three miles made the house too far away from the Foundery and he would have preferred Charles to have taken a less gracious home, but he expressed his delight at having Charles resident at the mother church of Methodism:

I rejoice to hear from various persons so good an account of the work of God in London. You did not come thither without the Lord, and you find your labour is not in vain. I doubt not that you will see more and more fruit.[100]

Charles agreed to attend the Methodist Conference in Leeds for the first time in a number of years. It was the first to be open to all the preachers (rather than just those selected by John). John said all the things that he knew would please Charles:

> We will not, dare not, separate from the Church ... We are not seceders ... and will do nothing willingly which tends to a separation from it ... Some may say 'Our own service is public worship'. Yes, in a sense; but not such as supersedes the church service. We never designed it should. We have a hundred times expressed the contrary ... I advise therefore all the Methodists in England and Ireland ... constantly to attend the service of the Church, at least every Lord's day.[101]

Unfortunately in 1769 the Public Peace Union collapsed once Whitefield left for America. John had no real desire for it and Calvinism's new leaders owed nothing to the Wesleys and were outspoken in their criticisms. Chief among these were Richard Hill and Augustus Montague Toplady, who both felt John placed too much emphasis on good works and not enough on the importance of salvation coming from God alone. At the Conference held in Leeds in August 1769, John announced he was abandoning his efforts to work with the Calvinists and unite the evangelical clergy behind Methodism: 'They are a rope of sand: and such they will continue.'[102] Given the Church's hostility he indicated he thought at best only a quarter of his preachers might eventually obtain ordination and it was likely the rest would be forced into dissent unless he made arrangements for how Methodism would be structured after his death.

John asked all the preachers to sign 'Articles of Agreement' promising to devote themselves entirely to God, and to both preach the old Methodist doctrines and enforce 'the whole Methodist discipline' as contained in the Minutes of the Conferences. He wrote to Selina, Countess of Huntingdon to try and persuade her to abandon her Calvinism. The letter has been lost but Fletcher described it as unkind in its tone, Harris called it very bitter, and even Charles felt obliged to apologize that his brother had written such a letter to her. It deeply offended her. John was unrepentant, saying 'as long as she resents the office of true esteem her grace can be but small'.[103]

John used the 1770 Methodist Conference to produce a definitive statement of what 'the old Methodist doctrines' actually were and to damn all links with the Calvinists. Selina denounced his unchristian behaviour and declared she would never again let him preach in her chapels. She asked all those who shared his views to leave her college at Trevecca. The final nail in the coffin of the Public Peace Union was the news of Whitefield's death in America on 30 September 1770, though initially the Wesleyans and Calvinists were united by grief at the loss of a man who had preached at least 18,000 times and always to great effect. In his last sermon George had proclaimed:

> I go to a rest prepared; my sun has arisen, and by aid from Heaven has given light to many. It is now about to set ... I shall soon be in a world where time, age, pain and sorrow are unknown. My body fails, [but] my spirit expands. How willingly would I live to preach Christ! But I die to be with him![104]

Tributes flowed from many in both Britain and America. At his memorial service in the London Tabernacle, John praised George's 'unparallel zeal, indefatigable activity, tender heartedness to the afflicted, and charitableness toward the poor', and he spoke of his 'most generous friendship' and 'unblemished modesty'. For once he said nothing about predestination but reminded everyone that the two different branches of Methodism shared the most important beliefs in common: that of the need for a new birth and justification by faith. Nevertheless, it was obvious to everyone that it was Charles and not John who genuinely felt the loss of Whitefield. He openly wept and made clear the debt all owed to 'his abundant labour of love'. Charles asked the countess to write an appreciation of their departed friend and she was glad to do so, describing him as a man without guile who single-mindedly always put Christ first.

Eventually Charles wrote his own thoughts in the form of a long poem in George's honour, of which this is a brief extract:

> His one delightful work and steadfast aim
> To pluck poor souls as brands out of the flame,
> To scatter the good seed on every side,
> To spread the knowledge of the Crucified,
> From a small spark a mighty fire to raise,
> And fill the continent with Jesu's praise ...
> In his unspotted life with joy we see
> The fervours of primeval piety:
> A pattern to the flock by Jesus bought,
> A living witness of the truths he taught.[105]

The spring of 1771 saw division return. In January Joseph Benson was dismissed from Trevecca because of his loyalty to John. By March John Fletcher felt honour-bound to resign from his post as president of the college. The strength of his affection for Charles meant his loyalty stayed with the Wesleys. The previous year he had travelled abroad and his comment to Charles was 'the waters of the ocean and the Mediterranean have not quenched my spark of brotherly love for you'.[106] About a third of the Trevecca students left with him. The countess was devastated but she told Fletcher she hoped they could remain as friends and not become open adversaries. Charles refused to become publicly involved in the disputes but we know from a private letter he wrote to the countess just after Whitefield's funeral that he was not happy with John's actions in destroying the Public Peace Union. In the letter he refers to the fact that 'one of the parties' to the Union [i.e. John] had never thought of upholding it from the day it had been signed. Charles assured the countess he at least still wanted peace.

The Wesleyan annual Conference was scheduled for August. The countess decided that she would encourage as many clergy as possible to attend it and challenge John's authority. Her chaplain, Walter Shirley, issued a circular to that effect. Selina mistakenly thought Charles would back this move and, in June 1771, she wrote to him:

> As you have had no part in this matter, I find it difficult to blame your brother to you, while as an honest man I must pity and not less regard you, as you suffer equal disgrace and universal mistrust from the supposed union with him.[107]

She had underestimated Charles' loyalty to his brother. He wrote on the letter: 'Lady Huntingdon's LAST. Unanswered by John Wesley's brother.'[108]

John was very concerned at what might happen in Bristol so he wrote a conciliatory letter to the countess:

> When I was much younger than I am now I thought myself almost infallible; but I bless God I know myself better now. To be short. Such as I am, I love you well. You have one of the first places in my esteem and affection.[109]

The countess naively cancelled her call to the evangelical clergy but slow communications meant that some still turned up to the Conference. On 6 August John wrote in his journal that he spoke with nine or ten of her followers and convinced them he was not a heretic. Shirley read out to Conference an apology from the countess for criticizing John and he said he and others had misinterpreted what John had said at the previous Conference.

With the threat of open criticism at the Conference behind him, John reverted to his true colours by publishing a work which he knew would cause immense upset. John Fletcher had produced a public defence of

Wesley's theological position in the form of five letters written to Shirley and these were already at the publishers. Charles had also had a hand in the writing of them. Fletcher and the countess now asked John to suppress their publication, knowing their content would merely inflame matters again. John cynically commented they 'could not be suppressed without betraying the honour of the Lord'.[110] Fletcher had styled himself as 'a Lover of Quietness and Liberty of Conscience' on the title-page of his *Vindication* (as the letters were called), but the contents smashed any hope of reconciliation.

Augustus Toplady was particularly incensed at John's duplicity:

He is like Mahommed for propagating his religion by the sword. Peals of anathemas are issued, and torrents of the lowest calumny are thrown out ... Not an inch beyond the purlieus of ignorance, prejudice, and superstition will his dictatorship extend ... His mode of phraseology is as pregnant with craft as his conduct is destitute of honour.[111]

In reply John commented that Toplady was 'too dirty a writer for me to meddle with; I should only foul my fingers'.[112] Open hostility between the two branches of Methodism was to become a sad feature of the 1770s. In this contest Charles defended John, saying the Calvinist attacks on his brother's character were unfair:

They blacken, not because he tries
To blind, but open, people's eyes;
They blacken, to cut short dispute,
With lies and forgeries confute,
And thus triumphantly suppress
The calm debate, and calm address.[113]

Fletcher warned Charles that he too had acquired enemies and there-fore needed to be careful: 'They complain of your love for music, com-pany, fine people, great folks, and of the wane of your former zeal and frugality.'[114]

Nevertheless, many Methodists on both sides of the doctrinal dispute still wanted to work together. Even John had to acknowledge that many Calvinists were fine Christians and that Calvinism was 'only an opin-ion, not subversive of the very foundations of the Christian experience, but compatible with a love to Christ and a genuine work of grace'.[115] The Calvinist James Hervey commented that theology bred division but in reality 'whosoever cometh to ... [God] ... will in no wise be cast out'.[116] Many hoped John Fletcher would become a unifying figure, even though, like Charles, he thought himself unworthy of becoming the national leader of Methodism. They knew Fletcher was a great believer in allowing people to have different theological views providing they served Christ and that he had no time for John's determination to reduce everyone to being either a supporter or an antagonist.

Influenced by Charles, Fletcher began to see his role as a biblical theologian who could mend the breaches between the members of the religious revival by his writings. He told Charles:

> I hope the time will come when all the breaches will be made up. I dreamt the other night I embraced Lady Huntingdon's knees and pleaded so for peace that she relented and cast the mantle of love over all grievances.[117]

Fletcher sent all his manuscripts to Charles for revisions, saying: 'Your every hint is a blessing to me.'[118] From Fletcher's perspective both Wesleyans and Calvinists were recipients of religious truths, but they were permitting their special emphases to become disproportionate in their thinking. Biblical truths needed a subtler approach. His reconciliatory reflections were to be embodied particularly in two short works called *The Doctrines of Grace and Justice* and *The Reconciliation or an Easy Method to Unite the Professing People of God*. In these he attempted to show what the Wesleyans could learn from the Calvinists and vice-versa.

Charles made his own unifying efforts by seeking to rekindle links with the Moravians. Preliminary negotiations began with his once close friend, James Hutton. However, from the outset Charles made clear his negotiations did not indicate he might consider abandoning his brother: 'Take it for granted that I am fixed, resolved, determined, sworn to stand by the M[ethodists] and my B[rother] right or wrong, through thick and thin.'[119] By the end of 1771 he had engineered a meeting between James and his brother and the negotiations between the two sides went on for two years. On Christmas Day 1773 Charles reaffirmed his total commitment to the Church of England as the home for both Methodism and Moravianism and his belief that this mattered more than who was leading the movements:

> God will look to that matter of successors. He buries His workers and still carries on His work. Let Him send by whom He will send. Rather than they should degenerate into a dead formal sect, I pray God the very name of Moravian and Methodist may die together! But I believe ... that God has a special regard to the Church of England ... and that

our Lord will have a true Church, a living people in this island, till He comes to set up His Universal Kingdom.[120]

In 1773 John asked Fletcher to take over leadership of the Wesleyan Methodists. Some have speculated that he did so under pressure from both Charles and Vincent Perronet. However, Fletcher was far too self-effacing to accept and, like Charles, he lacked the physical stamina that was John's huge strength. By 1776 Fletcher was thought to be terminally ill and doctors advised him to travel to Europe in the hope a warmer climate might yet save him. He was not to return until 1781. During those years the conflict between the two branches of Methodism was overshadowed by the far greater conflict that had emerged with the continent which Whitefield had so much loved – America.

II

Liberty and the American War
of Independence

Divided 'gainst itself so long
How could a kingdom stand,
Had we not a Redeemer, strong
To prop our tottering land?
Had He not left Himself a seed
Who deprecate the woe,
Who day and night for mercy plead,
And still suspend the blow.

Still let Thy praying seed prevail
Our evils to remove,
Till mercy turns the hovering scale,
And justice yields to love;
His king till every Briton owns
With warmest loyalty,
And faction's and rebellion's sons
Stretch out their hands to Thee ...

Open their eyes, almighty grace,
The latent snare to see,
That brethren may again embrace
In closest amity:
Britons! No more with Britons fight,
No more our God oppose!
Let Europe then their powers unite,
And all the world be foes.[1]

In the 1760s London was abuzz with the activities of a Member of Parliament called John Wilkes, who was a self-styled champion of liberty. A notorious libertine and a former member of the infamous Hellfire Club, he created his own London news-sheet to openly incite people to remove the monarchy in the name of freedom and liberty. High unemployment and rising bread prices made the artisans of London susceptible fodder. When he was arrested in 1768 there were massive public demonstrations in his defence. However, both John and Charles unreservedly condemned Wilkes as a man 'encumbered with no religion, with no regard to virtue or morality' and a promoter of civil war.[2] When the unrepentant Wilkes launched a campaign for a Bill of Rights and championed the cause of freedom of the press, Charles privately condemned such blatant manipulation of the masses:

> The Rabble-rout secures our quiet
> By threats and violence, and riot,
> Brings Ministers and Kings to reason
> By libels, Blasphemy, and Treason.[3]

He, like John, believed 'the wicked Wilkes' was playing on the fact that most ordinary people had no appreciation of the freedom already offered to them by the country's unwritten constitution. The cry for liberty masked Wilkes' desire for a licence that was destructive of real freedom. Charles thought treating the voice of the people as infallibly right was a nonsense born of the devil. He questioned how the cause of freedom was furthered by cursing and spitting in the king's face and urged people to appreciate the many qualities of George III, whom he judged to be a well-meaning monarch. He described the king as 'the father and friend' of rich and poor alike and pointed out that no reformation of the nation could stem from poisonous misinformation and 'insults on a gracious King'.[4]

Wilkes began backing the claims of Americans for freedom from taxes imposed by a British government. The Wesleys feared he was capitalizing on the political tensions which existed among the two and a half million people living in its colonies. The colonists understandably chafed under the restrictions and time-delays that were imposed by decisions having to be referred to a government based in faraway London. They resented the way in which ministers in London took decisions that affected them without having any real understanding of their way of life or the problems they faced. In particular they objected to attempts to make them pay taxation, even if that came in the guise of saying it would pay for their defence. Helping fund the British army seemed unnecessary once the French in Canada had been defeated in the Seven Years' War.

What was happening in the colonies now mattered more because in 1769 John had finally decided to accept he should send preachers out to

America. A cynic might argue he had waited till Whitefield was a spent force before taking over what he had achieved. The most effective of the first three Wesleyan lay preachers sent out to America was one particularly liked by Charles – Joseph Pilmoor. Indeed, Pilmoor acknowledged the importance of Charles' 'kindly' guidance before the three men embarked. Pilmoor travelled to Philadelphia and made sure the evangelical societies began adopting Wesleyan rules, but he soon requested more preachers should be sent because otherwise the Americans would abandon the Church of England in favour of dissenting groups. Charles therefore encouraged John to send out two more preachers in 1771. One of these was Francis Asbury, who began preaching widely across the colonies, travelling 40 to 50 miles a day. He was to earn himself the title 'the Wesley of American Methodism'. Not to be outdone, the Countess of Huntingdon sent out two ordained ministers and some of her Trevecca students in 1772 to transform the Bethesda Orphan House in Georgia into a training college for future ministers for the New World.

John and Charles were not unsympathetic to the American demands for more control over their own affairs. They found it very difficult to justify the so-called 'Boston Massacre' of 1770, when ill will between garrison troops and settlers led to British troops opening fire on some of the colonials. However, they refused to accept that legitimate American grievances justified retaliatory action or acceptance of Wilkes' demands for 'liberty'. They were shocked by the news of the famous 'Boston Tea-Party' in 1773 when colonists destroyed cargoes of tea rather than pay the tax on them. That same year saw Whitefield's Bethesda Orphan House in Georgia burn down, possibly as a result of arson. The general sense of foreboding that year was probably heightened by the death of Howell Harris and by John's ill health as a result of a riding accident the previous year. John authorized one of his favourite lay preachers, Thomas Rankin, to go to America and promote peace rather than conflict. Converted by Whitefield and strongly influenced by Maxfield, Rankin was a controversial choice because he had a reputation for brusqueness that ill suited him for the role of negotiator and Francis Asbury had a far greater claim to understand what was happening in the colonies.

Nevertheless, Rankin was warmly welcomed as Wesley's 'General Assistant' when he arrived in Philadelphia. He soon learned how the Methodists were operating in the provinces of New York, New Jersey, Pennsylvania, Maryland, Virginia and the Carolinas and he was impressed at the number of black as well as white members of the societies. In 1774 he published a letter from John Wesley urging all Methodists to promote peace:

My Dear Brethren, You were never in your lives in so critical a situation as you are at this time. It is your part to be peacemakers; to be loving and tender to all; but to addict yourselves to no party. In spite of all solicitations, of rough or smooth words, say not one word against one side or the other side ... Do all you can to help and soften all.[5]

Such action, of course, had no impact on the representatives from the various American colonies who met in Philadelphia. They decided to refuse to pay taxes to a parliament in which they had no representation and they imposed a ban on most exports and imports to Britain. Rankin began reporting back to the Wesleys how the more extreme opponents of British rule were talking of a possible war for independence. Charles wrote to Rankin:

I am of neither side, and yet of both; on the side of New England, and of Old. Private Christians are excused, exempted, privileged, to take no part in civil troubles. We love all, and pray for all, with a sincere and impartial love. Faults there may be on both sides; but such as neither you nor I can remedy: therefore let us, and all our children, give ourselves unto prayer.[6]

The refusal of both John and Charles to back the increasing demands of the colonists brought them into conflict with those supporters of John Wilkes who viewed achieving American liberty as a first step to British liberty. Wilkes was elected Lord Mayor of London in 1774 and Charles bemoaned how 'the reign of Wilkes and Liberty' offered only a route to rule by 'the many-headed Brute' of mass hysteria.[7] John said no one in Britain or America had any right to talk about liberty while engaging in the slave trade and that the problems in America were almost certainly God's punishment on the British nation for so actively participating in such a vile activity. In saying this he may have been partially influenced by Charles' positive experience in Bristol of helping two former African princes who had been enslaved for six years and who showed 'both the outward visible sign and the inward spiritual grace in a wonderful manner and measure'.[8]

Drawing from the anti-slavery writings of a French refugee called Anthony Benezet and other works, John wrote a pamphlet called *Thoughts Upon Slavery*. This outlined the history of slavery, portrayed the Africans as noble savages, and depicted the evil ways in which slaves were acquired and punished (including a graphic account of their transportation aboard the slave ships and the brutal use of torture and the whip on slave estates). John denied that slavery had any right to exist:

'Notwithstanding ten thousand laws, right is right and wrong is wrong. There must still remain an essential difference between justice and injustice.'[9] He challenged the economic arguments used to defend slavery and appealed to the sea captains, merchants and planters to put their conscience before their pocket:

> Give liberty to whom liberty is due, that is, to every child of man, to every partaker of human nature ... Away with all whips, all chains, all compulsion! ... Do with everyone else as you would he should do to you.[10]

Many Methodists responded to his arguments. For example, a radical group in Manchester campaigned for a boycott on the purchase of sugar as a means of forcing traders to abandon slavery. Most outside Methodism did not respond, although the pamphlet was partly instrumental in the conversion of the slave trader John Newton, who wrote the famous hymn 'Amazing Grace' about his change of heart. And many years later it was a letter from Wesley, written on his deathbed, which was to inspire William Wilberforce to persevere in fighting the slave trade: 'Go on in the name of God and in the power of His might, till even American slavery (the vilest that ever saw the sun) shall vanish away before it.'[11]

Rankin helped distribute over 10,000 copies of a leaflet called *A Calm Address to Our American Colonies*. In this John said he loved all Americans as 'my brethren and countrymen' but urged them to abandon their demand for no taxation without representation. They had to appreciate that most Englishmen were equally not entitled to vote but they still obeyed their government and paid their taxes. The American demand for liberty was therefore simply an excuse for creating anarchy. This leaflet was essentially an abridgement of a pro-government pamphlet by Dr Samuel Johnson, but it caused far more stir because until this time Wesley had been seen as pro-American. Its publication coincided with the time when the propaganda war between the Wesleyan and Calvinist branches of Methodism was at its height so the U-turn by Wesley provided his enemies with plenty of ammunition. Augustus Toplady accused him of being 'a low and puny tadpole in divinity who wants to be a high and mighty whale in politics'.[12]

In fact, neither John nor Charles had political ambitions. They merely wanted to avert a potential civil war by countering the arguments of those anti-monarchists out, in John's words, 'to inflame people to the pitch of madness'.[13] John Fletcher agreed and told Charles: 'The government protects us with the civil sword and we must protect it with the spiritual sword.'[14] In America the leaflet caused immense problems for the Methodists because they were immediately viewed as loyalists. Charles backed John, arguing that disloyalty to the Crown would only lead to disaster:

> Religion pure is chas'd away,
> General ungodliness succeeds,
> And treason walks in open day,
> And unprovok'd Rebellion spreads.[15]

Thomas Rankin held a meeting of the Methodist preachers from the different circuits in Philadelphia in May 1775. They resolved 'to follow the advice that Mr Wesley and his brother had given us' and to view the preparations for war as God's punishment for 'the dreadful sin of buying and selling the poor Africans'.[16]

At this critical juncture the normally fit John was taken seriously ill while on tour in Ireland and it was feared he might die. Even though she had been deeply hurt by John's anti-Calvinist actions, the Countess of Huntingdon immediately wrote to comfort Charles and say she had the humility to recognize his brother's immense contribution to Methodism:

> I do grieve to think his faithful labours are to cease yet on earth. How does an hour of loving sorrow swallow up the just differences our various judgements make ... I have loved him these five and thirty years and it is with pleasure I find he remains in my heart as a friend and a laborious beloved servant of Jesus Christ. I will hope yet the Lord may spare him ... May the Lord bless you and yours ... Forgive the hurried scrap wrote with bad eyes, pain of body and mind.[17]

John Fletcher told Charles they had to 'acknowledge the goodness of God in preserving him to undergo such labours as would have killed you and me ten times over' and recognize that Charles, despite his physical frailty, was his brother's natural successor:

> Should your brother fail on earth ... the Methodists will not expect from you your brother's labours, but they have (I think) a right to expect that you will preside over them while God spares you in the land of the living. A Committee of the oldest and steadiest preachers may help you to bear the burden ... and if at any time you should want my mite of assistance, I hope I shall throw it into the treasury with the simplicity and readiness of the poor widow, who cheerfully offered her next to nothing. Do not faint. The Lord God of Israel will give you

the additional strength for the day ... and his praying people will bear you up in their hands.[18]

To Charles' relief, John recovered. However, the faltering attempts to retain peace between Britain and America died. In June 1775 a clumsy British attempt to suppress some of the more rebellious colonists led to armed fighting at Bunker Hill outside Boston. A Virginian named George Washington agreed to become Commander-in-Chief of a 'Continental Army' to drive the British out. The threat of war immediately dislocated trade and this brought problems for many families in Britain. John Wesley said he saw thousands of unemployed 'standing in the streets, with pale looks, hollow eyes, and meagre limbs' and genteel families reduced to scavenging in the fields 'to pick up turnips which the cattle had left'.[19] He told Rankin to do all he could to hold the American Methodists together on the side of peace: 'We must speak the plain truth, wherever we are, whether men will hear, or whether they will forbear.'[20]

Realizing there were many colonists prepared to stay loyal, John wrote to the prime minister and colonial secretary and pleaded they withhold from using further force. The colonists were only asking for some legal rights and 'in the most modest and inoffensive manner that the nature of the thing would allow' so it was foolish to wage war. He rightly warned that, if that happened, the Americans would prove difficult to defeat, disputing every inch of ground: 'They are one and all ... enthusiasts for liberty ... [and] we know men animated with this spirit will leap into a fire, or rush into the cannon's mouth.'[21] He simultaneously published *A Seasonable Address by a Lover of Peace* in which he argued that no one would wish to see what amounted to a civil war, while urging Rankin in America to back any moves for peace: 'We must pour water, not oil, into the flame'.[22]

Privately John confessed to Charles that he was in danger of losing his 'love for the Americans' because it was difficult to continue promoting peace when the American leaders seemed set on war.[23] Certainly the outcome of initial British discussions for a peaceful settlement only encouraged more Americans to join the rebels because it was taken as a sign of weakness. On 4 July 1776 the American colonists formally produced their Declaration of Independence, declaring their faith in equal rights and their inalienable right to 'life, liberty, and the pursuit of happiness'.[24] The quality of its prose made some in London point out that the Americans were 'manifestly not those cowards and poltroons which our over-hasty, ill-judging, wrong-headed Administration styled them'.[25] However, most condemned both the act and the philosophy that lay behind it. Like many, Charles felt the French had had a big hand in encouraging the Americans and he wrote of 'the dire, malicious joy' of Britain's enemies:

> Against the public weal,
> They set the nation in a flame,
> And with the patriot's sacred name
> Their dark designs conceal.[26]

In *Some Observations on Liberty* John declared there was no true liberty to be found in a democracy, only the tyranny of misled masses. John Fletcher published three pamphlets criticizing the colonists in 1776: '[They] buy, and sell, and whip their fellow men as if they were brutes, and absurdly claim that they are enslaved.'[27] Such a stand against the rebels made life tough for the Methodists in America. Rankin wrote it was no longer safe for him to travel.

In September 1776 the war began in earnest with the British military Commander-in-Chief, General Sir William Howe, attempting to seize New York. His forces easily defeated the inexperienced rebel forces, forcing them back to their defences on Brooklyn Heights, but Howe failed to follow up his success and allowed Washington to evacuate his remaining 20,000 men. As a result a large part of New York was burnt to the ground in a fire almost certainly initiated by the rebels. Charles Wesley was furious that Howe had not realized the essential importance of totally crushing the rebels as quickly as possible:

> Not to destroy or conquer wholly,
> He check'd his Thunder in mid volley,
> Gave the unequal contest over,
> And time allow'd them to recover.
> Advantage he disdain'd to take
> Or hurt them, when they turn'd their back,
> Or push a victory too far ...
> He deem'd it prudenter by far
> Still to procrastinate the war.[28]

Charles also disapproved of Howe's failure to defend the loyalists among the colonists:

> He spurns their proffer'd services,
> Commands them tamely to sit still,
> While Rebels do whate'er they will,
> Roughly forbids them to resist,
> And quells the rising Loyalist.[29]

In October Howe won another battle but again failed to prevent Washington retreating with his forces to fight another day. Nevertheless, when a third victory followed in December many disheartened Americans began deserting Washington. It appeared the war for independence had been lost until, in January 1777, Washington revived the rebel hopes by defeating a British force at Princetown. Charles felt this was entirely due to Howe permitting Washington to act with 'full impunity'.[30]

It was therefore against a background of the prospect of a longer war that the Wesleys decided to commence building a new chapel in City Road as a replacement for the Foundery, whose lease was running out. The timing may have reflected their feeling that only through religion could the nation find peace. The foundation stone was laid in April 1777 and the chapel opened on 1 November 1778. While it was being built, the war took a serious turn for the worse. Throughout 1777 General Howe failed to capitalize on his military success and much valuable time was lost squabbling over what Britain should do next and which generals should be used. Charles thought Howe was deliberately prolonging the war to embarrass the politicians in Britain and he expressed his dislike of the general's decadent lifestyle in verse:

> Glory invites; but softer charms
> Detain him in Armida's arms;
> Wasting the time in careless ease,
> In revels, sports, and wantonness,
> In dear, luxurious dissipation,
> And doubly dear Procrastination.[31]

Howe eventually decided he should seize Philadelphia and then move on to Albany, where he could join forces with General John Burgoyne, who would have marched south with the British army which until then had been based in Canada. This complicated scheme meant the rebels were given time to regroup as Charles Wesley was quick to point out:

> Who can the secret drift discover
> Of such a wonderful manoeuvre?
> Unless he meant in special grace
> To give the Rebels longer space
> Their ruin'd army to recruit,
> And still continue the dispute ...
> Plainly his actions all declare
> He does not choose to end the war.[32]

Those loyal to the Crown were scattered across the colonies and so were exposed to the attacks of the rebels without the British army being able to defend them. Charles was pained by the accounts he received of the suffering of peaceful Methodists and bemoaned the way Howe was permitting the rebel forces to 'live by pillaging ... and to keep the country in a fright'.[33] All bar one of the Wesleyan preachers returned to England, shocked by the scenes of conflict. The exception was Francis Asbury, whose sympathies rested with the colonists even though, as a pacifist, he was in an unenviable position. Thomas Rankin told John and Charles how unpopular Methodism had become in the eyes of many Americans because of their public support for peace. It is estimated the number of Methodists in America had halved between 1775 and 1777.

By the time Howe's forces neared Philadelphia in September the British found Washington had raised an army of about 16,000 to block their path at Brandywine Creek. Moreover, both France and Spain had begun offering significant naval assistance to the Americans. Although Howe again defeated the rebels and took Philadelphia, he found himself under continual further attack. Even worse, Burgoyne's invasion from the north proved a disaster in the face of guerrilla tactics from the rebels. In October Burgoyne was forced to surrender at Saratoga. Charles was blistering in his condemnation of Howe's failed strategy, saying he had effectively 'made America independent'.[34] In parliament the voices against the war grew ever more strident but, to Charles' distress, few seemed interested in the fate of the loyal Americans (including most of the 7,000 members of the Wesleyan-controlled Methodist societies) who were now at most risk:

> Deserted at their utmost need,
> They for their King and Country bleed.
> By rebels arm'd with cruel power,
> As rebels judg'd, and doom'd to die,
> They lean on broken reeds no more,
> No more on public Faith rely ...
> As objects of the general hate,
> By all abandon'd to their fate.[35]

Nevertheless, neither Charles nor John engaged in public criticism of the government's handling of the war. Charles' poetry shows he feared the government's loudest critics were those with ulterior motives. He passionately believed Wilkes and others were using the war to discredit the monarchy in Britain and so create a republic. He said these 'Republican harpies' cared 'not a louse' for king and country,[36] and he compared

them to the supporters of Oliver Cromwell, who had executed Charles I
in order to seize absolute power for themselves:

> Such is the crooked Statesman's hire,
> The Traitors who their Country sell,
> Or in Rebellion's cause expire,
> They claim the hottest place in Hell,
> Unless the Saviour interpose,
> To snatch them from eternal woes.[37]

He was pleased when his brother openly defended King George III and
attacked the critics of the government. John's *A Calm Address to the
Inhabitants of England* pointed out that the war had not furthered the
cause of Liberty and that those who were criticizing the government
should remember 'the thousand benefits' they enjoyed as citizens of England under a benign king. Democracy was a false god and there was
nothing worse than masses misled by mischievous orators. John and
Charles' open support for the government led to them being viewed far
more favourably by the Anglican hierarchy. For example, in November
1777 the newly appointed Bishop of London, Robert Lowth, made a
point of inviting John to dinner and refusing to sit above him at table
because he would expect to sit at his feet in heaven. Remarkably, the
Wesleys' loyalty did not lead to the collapse of American Methodism.
This was largely because of the efforts of Francis Asbury, who managed
to maintain the 15 widely spread circuits with the help of 34 home-
grown American lay preachers. Most Wesleyans showed they were prepared to uphold a pacifist stance, even when most Calvinists joined the
rebels.

In 1778 Lord North's government tried desperately to produce a peace
settlement. They offered to abandon Britain's right to impose taxation
and to recognize the newly formed American Congress. In return it asked
the American rebels to withdraw their declaration of Independence, restore the confiscated property of loyalists, and accept that Britain had a
right to regulate American trade. The olive branch was too late and the
war continued in a desultory fashion, but with Sir Henry Clinton taking
over control as Commander-in-Chief from Howe. With great difficulty
and not without embarrassing losses Clinton withdrew the British army
from Philadelphia to make New York its base. It was widely known
that, as America's ally, France was seeking to create an alliance of Spain,
Austria, Prussia and Russia against England. To help quell the mounting panic at a possible invasion, John published *A Serious Address to
the People of England with Regard to the State of the Nation* to try

and reassure people by focusing on the country's 'eminent prosperity' and obvious freedoms: 'Let no sweet-tongued orator ... steal away your understanding; no thundering talker fill you with vain fears, of evils that have no being.'[38]

John also wrote a separate address to the people of Ireland in which he was more specific about the need to avoid panicking about a possible defeat. He said Washington's forces would 'melt away like snow in harvest'[39] and the British would easily defeat the French fleet. He argued it would be wrong to assume God would want to ensure Britain's defeat as a punishment because 'true, scriptural religion, the love of God and neighbour' was on the increase thanks to the efforts of Methodist preachers. In another leaflet entitled *Some Account of the Late Work of God in North America* he forecast that God would not permit the Americans independence because that would be 'a heavy curse'. Instead God would enable Britain to help them achieve 'a restoration of civil and Christian liberty'. It was probably no coincidence that John also launched *The Arminian Magazine* in 1778 as a vehicle to convey the nature of true 'Universal Redemption' (though his main motive was to counteract the influence of Calvinist Methodist magazines). It published the experiences and lives of the Methodist itinerant preachers, past and present, as a means of showing the importance of lives truly committed to serving Christ and transforming society for the better.

John tried to persuade Charles, who was working in Bristol, to undertake itinerant work again. With Sally in London and therefore not around to counter his arguments, John urged Charles to accept that travelling in a coach offered an older man a viable alternative when riding horseback was no longer an option because of health problems. However, Charles still demurred and wrote home to his wife: 'I cannot keep pace with him, and have therefore refused his kindness.' He knew his health was far too variable to return to the lifestyle John was still enjoying. He refers in one of his letters later in the year to his strength daily abating: 'I creep along the streets, tottering on the grave.'[40]

The war continued to go from bad to worse. Sir Henry Clinton was unable to devise any appropriate strategy given his limited forces and the ever-growing and increasingly well-trained ranks of the rebels. In 1779 there was resulting national alarm, not least because of stories that American agents were encouraging armed associations in Ireland. Press gangs were out in force as the government sought to increase the size of its navy, the armed forces, and the militia. A national day of prayer and fasting was called for – and the Wesleys were among those who complied. Charles had nothing good to say about the French whom he believed were providing such strong support for the rebels in order to create an opportunity to invade Britain and impose Catholicism:

A nation whom no oaths can bind,
The false corrupters of mankind,
The slaves of every lust,
Despiteful, insolent and proud,
Haters of the Redeeming God,
And murderers of the just
Fraught with the policy of Rome,
By the old felon led, they come
To scatter, steal, and slay;
Brethren and countrymen divide,
While with gigantic steps they stride
To universal sway ...[41]

The year 1779 saw the Wesleys face challenges to their leadership both in America and Britain. In America most of the remaining Methodist preachers in the south met in Conference at Fluvenna, Virginia, without Francis Asbury in attendance. They agreed it was time for Methodism to ordain lay preachers to administer communion. This deeply shocked both John and Charles. Fortunately the following year Asbury retaliated by holding a conference for the remaining preachers in the north and he got them to vote in favour of staying faithful to what the Wesleys wanted. However, Asbury bombarded John with letters pointing out that it was virtually impossible for most American Methodists to obtain communion and warning him that this problem had to be resolved quickly or the vote at Fluvenna would inevitably eventually win the day. In response John began lobbying the church authorities to send out ministers to America as a matter of urgency.

In Britain problems arose because the opening of the City Road chapel was accompanied by Charles and three other clergymen (Thomas Coke, John Richardson and John Abraham) being appointed as its officiating ministers. This made some of the lay preachers assigned to the London circuit feel they were now unwanted because they knew Charles was openly opposing their continued use. One of the offended preachers decided it was time to voice their unwillingness to be treated as second-rate citizens. The 40-odd-year-old John Pawson, who came from Leeds but who had been appointed as one of the main assistants in London, claimed he could not understand why the 70-odd-year-old Charles was still aiming to preach at the New Chapel every Sunday morning and evening. Pawson wrote to John asking for him to curtail Charles' activities because all the lay preachers were unhappy at Charles' 'suspicious temper' and rejection of their talents.

Pawson accepted that Charles was not blind to what the lay preachers had achieved or to their 'very considerable ministerial gifts' but he was 'much prejudiced in favour of the clergy'. For that reason Pawson felt Charles was inclined 'to find out and magnify any supposed fault in the lay preachers', whereas John was still treating them with respect and exercising 'a fatherly care over them'.[42] At one level this was unfair because it was Charles who had more consistently cared for the welfare of the preachers, but Pawson was right to think Charles was obsessed with reducing their role, especially in a chapel which he hoped would become a rallying place for those wishing to retain their links with the Church. Pawson found it easy to acquire allies because Charles' links with the Countess of Huntingdon's circle had always been a source of resentment among some of the lay preachers. Many also resented that Charles had not trained his two sons to become preachers and instead was promoting their musical talents by arranging concerts attended by the rich.

Charles defended his position to John:

I have served the chapel morning and evening, and met the society every other week ... I think myself bound to do so as long as I can; both by my duty as a clergyman, and by our agreement when the chapel was first opened ... Many of our subscribers, you know, were not of our society, but of the Church: out of good will to them and the Church, not out of ill will to the preachers, I wished the Church services continued there.[43]

Charles was confident that John's 'extraordinary strength' would ensure he outlived him and that his own work was 'very near at an end'.[44] For that reason he hoped John and the preachers would let him continue doing what he could still do at the chapel while he still had a little remaining strength. Unfortunately, his frailty forced Charles to use Pawson and others as stand-ins, especially if the weather was inclement. This understandably added salt to their wounds because they felt they were being used. Pawson resentfully wrote: '[Charles] would always have a lay preacher appointed as well as himself, lest a shower of rain or an agreeable visit should prevent his attending.'[45] He led a petition to make Charles cease altogether his evening preaching at the chapel, alleging that few wanted to hear sermons that had become 'dead and lifeless' and that Charles 'was like Samson shorn of his strength' because he had been corrupted by mixing with too many gentry.[46]

It seems reasonable to surmise that Charles' preaching had declined with the onset of old age and even frailer health, but Pawson's comments were almost certainly overstated. The decline in attendance at the chapel probably had nothing to do with Charles' preaching because most Methodist societies were recording a fall in attendance at this time. The reason for that was the impact of the continued conflict between the Wesleyan and Calvinist branches of Methodism and the unhappiness of some at the Wesley brothers' constant support for the government. Charles thought the dispute with Pawson had nothing to do with the quality or otherwise of his preaching, but was motivated by their desire to leave the Church. Charles felt John was far too naive:

> Your defect of mistrust needs my excess to guard it. You cannot be taken by storm, but may be by surprise. We seem designed for each other. If we could and would be more together, it might be better for both.[47]

And he defended his actions, saying he of all people had the best right to preach in the New Chapel and that, frail as he was, it should be understood he could 'do more good there than in any other place'. He told John he did not lack goodwill to the preachers and he would 'have no quarrel with them', but he did think their actions were motivated by pride and they were underestimating his remaining preaching skills: 'I thank God the chapel is well filled. Last Sunday I preached twice, never with greater and seldom with equal effect.'

Charles pleaded for John to support him:

> Convince them that it is impossible I should stand in their way long, for I cannot (should I live to the winter) serve the New Chapel Sundays and holy days in all weathers ... If God continues my strength, I shall take best care of the chapel I can till your return. Then I shall deliver up the charge to you and you alone.[48]

Despite this, John declared lay preachers should be used at the chapel and persuaded a reluctant Charles to relinquish the City Road pulpit in favour of preaching sometimes at the West Street Chapel. This climb-down led to a second challenge, this time directed against John by a Scotsman called Alexander McNab, who had been a lay preacher for 13 years and was superintendent of the Bristol circuit. When John told McNab that his services as a preacher were no longer required in Bath because the city had acquired a minister who was a supporter of Methodism, McNab retorted lay preachers were not just there to be used as a last resort. He went on to claim that neither John nor Charles had the authority to stop him preaching. John sent Charles to see McNab, who bitterly complained about John's excessive autocratic rule. McNab informed Charles that the preachers 'were resolved to have a meeting shortly, and to ... make a separation [from the Church of England], for their patience can hold out no longer'. Charles reported to John: 'One would think they took the Americans for their pattern.'[49]

The brothers travelled together to Bath in November and John, urged on by Charles, told McNab he could only preach 'when and where I appoint'. When McNab resisted, he was expelled. Charles prayed that John would be preserved 'from his rebellious sons' and that 'the curse of pride' would not destroy the preachers.[50] Hearing that McNab was praying for the death of his brother, Charles produced a special hymn to be sung in Bristol for John's protection:

Jesus, Thy hated servant own,
And send the glorious Spirit down,
In answer to our prayers;
While others curse, and wish him dead,
Do Thou Thy choicest blessings shed,
And crown his hoary hairs.[51]

He told John not to lose this opportunity of reasserting his authority:

You, single, are no match for near two hundred smooth-tongued ... Rouse yourself, before they flay you alive for your skin. Begin proving your sons one by one. Pray for wisdom, resolution and love. I would give up my wife and children, to cleave to you, if you stand firm and faithful to yourself, and the cause of God, and the Church of England.[52]

Charles thus expressed his readiness to play his part in another purge of the preachers on the lines of the one he had undertaken 20 years earlier. Pawson voiced the opposition of many preachers to this, saying McNab had been 'cruelly used' and there was no plot to usurp authority from John Wesley.[53] When John backed down and reinstated McNab, Charles was mortified. He genuinely believed there was a growing conspiracy among a section of the lay preachers to end the authority of his brother so that Methodism could be plunged into dissent. Aware he could no longer rely on John, Charles told his brother he would 'be always within call' if John required advice and help, but he was not prepared to attend the 1780 annual Conference and see everything he had worked for destroyed:

I can do no good ... [and] I am afraid of being a partaker of other men's sins, or of countenancing them by my presence ... I am afraid of myself; you know I cannot command my temper, and you have not the courage to stand by me. I cannot trust your resolution ... In the Bath affair you acted with vigour for the first time; but you could not hold out ... You yielded to the rebel, instead of his yielding to you.[54]

However, Charles did attend the Conference. His presence did not stop it reaffirming McNab as a lay preacher, but it may have contributed to its decision that 'none who leave the Church shall remain with us'.[55] John also promised that he would 'encourage all persons to go to church as much as they possibly can'.[56] Charles may also have been instrumental in calling a halt to the growing practice of letting women preach. John was happy at the unity shown at the Conference but Charles thought they should have forced into the open those preachers who wanted separation from the Church while he and John still had the strength and authority to overcome them. He confessed to John he had only gone to the Conference to please him and that he had gone resolved to say nothing rather than upset him, but he found the outcome very painful:

> Your design, I believe, was to keep all quiet ... By a very few words I could have provoked your preachers to lay aside the mask; but that was the very thing you guarded against; and I suppose, the reason for which you desired my presence was that I might be some sort of check on ... [those wanting independence from the Church of England].[57]

Charles felt his own role within Methodism had now effectively ended. He told his brother: 'I am perfectly satisfied with my own insignificancy. I have but one thing to do [i.e. die]. May the Lord make me ready for it.'[58] He vowed never to attend Conference again:

> Why should I longer, Lord, contend,
> My last important moments spend
> In buffeting the air?
> In warning those who will not see,
> But rest in blind security,
> And rush into the snare? ...
> Here then I quietly resign
> Into those gracious hands Divine
> Whom I received from Thee,
> My brethren and companions dear,
> And finish with a parting tear
> My useless ministry.[59]

There were, of course, far greater issues facing England in 1780. In May Clinton had successfully defeated the American forces and taken Charleston, the largest city in the southern states, but the British situation was still perilous. The worried government agreed to replace Clinton with one of his rivals, Charles Cornwallis. He found himself unable to control the remaining loyalists who wanted to use the British success to wreak revenge on the rebels in their midst. Atrocities on both sides were commonplace. Violence in London was also increasing because the fears of a potential invasion by France had generated strong anti-Catholic feeling. This was embodied in the creation of 'the Protestant Association' by a Scottish nobleman called Lord George Gordon. This organization plunged London into a frenzy of religious intolerance against all Catholics, who were held to be secretly undermining the country's war effort and co-operating in plans for an enemy invasion.

Both Charles and John had mixed feelings about the Protestant Association. They were both staunch Protestants and saw no reason to extend full toleration to Catholicism, but they abhorred violent religious persecution. They wanted the Church to remain moderate and not resort to excessive repression. John published a letter in the press making clear he felt the Association's fears of possible Catholic connivance with Britain's enemies was probably correct because the pope was always willing to 'pardon rebellions, high treasons, and all other sins whatsoever'. But he warned against responding to this by violent persecution of Catholics because that destroyed 'the right of private judgement, on which the whole Reformation stands'. This had no impact on the Protestant Association, which organized a march on 7 June to petition parliament to take stronger anti-Catholic measures.

This deteriorated into a major riot with initial attacks on Catholics subsequently degenerating into a pure orgy of mindless destruction, fuelled by alcohol from plundered breweries. Among the properties destroyed was the home of Charles' former schoolboy friend, William Murray, the Earl of Mansfield and Lord Chief Justice of the King's Bench. Gaols were burned and their inmates released. At least 210 people were killed and a further 75 died of the wounds they had received. Not surprisingly John urged Methodists to have nothing to do with the Protestant Associations that were springing up all over the country. However, it was Charles who was in London and so he saw at first hand the worst of what was happening. He was furious that the rabble was allowed to rampage unchecked while the justices of the peace looked on, begging only that their own homes escape destruction:

> The rabble speak, and spread their bands,
> To execute their own commands,
> Impetuous, as the torrent pours,

Resistless, as the flame devours,
And scattering ruin far and wide,
While terror is on every side,
With blasphemies they rend the sky,
And both their king and God defy ...
Where'er we turn our blasted eyes
The torrent roars, the flames arise:
The old, the sick, the women fear,
Or die through dread of death so near!
Swiftly the catching fire proceeds,
From house to house destruction spreads,
And streets entire are doom'd to fall,
And vengeance vows to o'erwhelm us all.[60]

He wrote to his brother John:

You read a very small part of the mischief done in the papers. It is nothing, they say, to what they intend to do. But they have made a good beginning. Brother Thackeray was an eyewitness. He saw them drag the Bishop of Lincoln out of his coach and force him to kneel down. They treated him unmercifully, began to pull the house down to which he fled for shelter, were scarcely persuaded to let him escape at eleven at night. Another bishop wisely called out, 'Huzza, no Popery', and was dismissed with shoutings. Lord Mansfield would have reasoned with them, but they would not hear him and handled him almost as roughly as the Bishop of Lincoln. They pulled off the Archbishop's wig ... Imagine the terror of the poor Papists.[61]

Charles bravely preached in public against what was happening, even though he knew he might be named as a secret papist for doing so. Calvinist Methodists at the Tabernacle expressed dismay that he was not standing up for the Protestant cause. However, Charles felt somebody had to openly denounce bigotry and preach 'for peace and charity' and 'for the trembling, persecuted Catholics'.[62] He wrote to one of his children, who rightly feared his father was risking his life:

If God had not rebuked the madness of the people at the very crisis, London had now been no more. No wonder your mother was terrified when I was proscribed as a Popish priest, for I never signed the petition or ranked among the patriots.[63]

Charles saw the mob as 'a vile, rebellious race' in a 'proud metropolis ...

where Satan's darkest works abound',[64] and he expressed his hatred for those who had misled the people:

> Confound their devilish art,
> Who leagued together rise,
> The poor unwary crowd pervert,
> And poison with their lies.[65]

Not surprisingly, he saw the hand of God in the eventual suppression of the Gordon riots. Lord George Gordon was imprisoned in the Tower of London. Interestingly among the people he asked to see was John Wesley. John eventually complied and spent an hour with him on 19 December, talking about 'popery and religion'. Of course, the Wesleys' credentials as supporters of the Crown and the war effort were now extremely well publicized. Charles produced a whole series of hymns in 1780 designed to express the loyalty of Methodists and their support for a much-maligned king and his government:

> God omnipotent arise,
> To scatter all Thy foes,
> Blast the rebels with Thine eyes,
> Who Thee and Thine oppose;
> Let the tools of anarchy,
> The daring sons of wickedness,
> Driven as by a whirlwind flee,
> Before Thine angry face.[66]

John wrote his own defence of true liberty, saying it would be hard to find a country where liberty meant more to people than Britain. He defined religious liberty as the right 'to choose our own religion, to worship God according to our conscience, according to the best light we have' and civil liberty as 'a liberty to enjoy our lives and fortunes in our own way; to use our property ... according to our choice'. He said it was shameful that some men pretended the king's government was not delivering these liberties when it clearly was. And he concluded:

> The many-headed beast, the people, roars for liberty of another kind
> ... the liberty of cutting throats ... the convenient liberty of plunder-
> ing ... the liberty of murdering their Prince ... The good people of
> England have, for some years past, been continually fed with poison
> ... turning reasonable men into wild bulls, bears and tigers! ... These
> dismal complaints that we are robbed of our liberty ... have not the

least foundation. We enjoy at this day throughout these kingdoms such liberty, civil and religious, as no other kingdom or commonwealth in Europe, or in the world, enjoys.[67]

Initially it appeared in 1781 as if the war was turning in Britain's favour. Many rebels were deserting from Washington's forces because they were tired of the conflict and the chaos of civil war. Those who remained knew they increasingly lacked the money and the supplies to effectively continue the conflict. Unfortunately an overconfident march through Virginia by General Cornwallis led to disaster and defeat. The failure of the British fleet to deliver the reinforcements he required led to the surrender of the British forces at Yorktown in October. When the news arrived, Lord North knew the war was lost. Charles Wesley interpreted Cornwallis' surrender as God's judgement on the pride and sinfulness of Britain, which had 'provoked the vengeance of the skies' and crowned 'the wicked with success'.[68]

Charles took comfort in events at the 1781 Methodist Conference in Leeds. It was unusually well attended by clergy (18 of them) and when a long-standing Methodist doctor called William Hey began reading out a paper outlining all the reasons why it was time for Methodism to break away from the Church of England, John shut him up and this time without any prodding by Charles. A disgruntled Hey quit the movement. The other bit of bright news was the marriage of John Fletcher and Mary Bosanquet on 12 November. By all accounts she was an extraordinarily kind and self-effacing yet dynamic woman, who was a fine preacher in her own right. For many years she had run a school in Leytonstone and its children had been chosen from the most destitute and friendless. Fletcher had long admired her but it took a near fatal illness to make him propose. Charles wrote to Mary of his immense pleasure at the marriage:

> Yours I believe is one of the few marriages that are made in heaven. Better late than never – my friend had thoughts of proposing to you (I am his witness) twenty years ago ... I sincerely rejoice that he has at last found out his Twin-soul, and trust you will be happier by your meeting thro' all eternity.[69]

Despite the catastrophe at Yorktown, George III refused to let his government surrender. The House of Commons descended into chaos as the opposition sought to bring the king to his senses and end what William Pitt called 'the accursed, cruel, unnatural, wicked American war, a war of injustice and moral depravity, marked by blood, slaughter, persecution and devastation'.[70] A motion was eventually carried that 'all further attempts to reduce the revolted colonies to obedience are contrary to the true interests of the Kingdom'. Charles was one of the few who still felt the war should continue, in part because he rightfully foresaw that the setting up of a Republic in America would have frightful consequences for the monarchies of Europe. Republicans in Britain, France, and elsewhere would be bound to urge the masses to seek a similar 'Liberty'.

To the so-called 'Patriots' in parliament who urged surrender Charles wrote:

> Their King they have conquered, and routed his friends,
> In pursuit of their own diabolical ends ...
> Our soldiers abroad they forbid to oppose,
> Or molest, or annoy their innocent foes,
> But tamely to give all the Loyalists up
> To the Rebels, or French, to the Sword, or the Rope,
> To keep out of harm's way, and their weapons lay down,
> Till the Mob has secured their Republican Crown.
> But true Englishmen hope, that the Nation o'erreached
> Will recover their wits, and awake unbewitched:
> Then the traitors at home, and the Agents of France
> Will finish their course with a sorrowful dance,
> Then we all shall unite in defence of our King,
> And Rebels at last, and the Patriots, swing.[71]

Lord North resigned but still the king insisted the war go on. Nevertheless, it was clear it was only a matter of time before Britain made peace with the Americans. Charles reflected his feelings in two collections of hymns published in 1782, one called *Hymns for the Nation* and the other *Hymns for the National Fast*. Even in defeat Charles looked to a God-given peace, which would end 'this dire intestine war'[72] and bring some hope from all the 'rebellions, massacres and blood'.[73] Such publications helped open the pulpits of London to his brother. John wrote: 'The tide has turned; so that I have now more invitations to preach in churches than I can accept thereof.'[74] It was a long way from the rejection that had first forced Whitefield and then the Wesleys into field-preaching.

Unlike many who thought only of Britain's loss, Charles gave thought to the poor Americans who had remained loyal and who were now in a parlous state, deserted by those they had supported. In 'By an American in New York' he imagined the feelings of the loyalist 'victims of fidelity':[75]

> We serv'd our King with warmest zeal:
> O had we serv'd our God so well

He would not have despised,
Or left us at our greatest need,
By Traitors now condemn'd to bleed,
By Britons sacrific'd.[76]

Meanwhile John Wesley was embroiled again in disputes over his authority within Methodism. This time the issue arose over the building of a
new chapel at Birstal, which the local society wanted under its control
rather than that of the Wesleys. This in effect meant that for the first
time John would have no final say over who preached within a Methodist building. Under pressure and now almost 80 years old, John weakly
agreed to assign control of the Birstal chapel to a board of 20 trustees
providing they accepted the chapel would remain part of the Methodist
plan and not use dissenting preachers. He confessed to Charles that he
had only agreed because they 'worried me down'[77] and Charles leapt
to his defence, alleging that technically the agreement also required his
assent. He refused to sign and challenged the so-called 'reformers', saying the Conference 'has no more business than the parliament to appoint
preachers at all'.[78]

Charles' action was not well received and there was an attempt to dis-
miss it as merely a product of sophistry and prejudice, but Thomas Coke,
the rising Welsh star in Methodism, supported Charles. He pointed out
that the money to build the chapel would not have been promised but
for its connection with Methodism and it was entirely reasonable to expect control of it to reside with both John and Charles Wesley as long as
they lived. He also argued that John's signature was inadequate and that
no legal agreement could be reached without also acquiring Charles'
assent. Charles must have been surprised because he and Coke had never
particularly got on with each other, ever since Coke had left his church
in South Petherton and taken up residency in London to help with the
construction of the City Road Chapel.

With Coke and Charles opposed and John clearly unhappy, those who
attended the November 1782 Conference felt they should avoid making
any conclusions over the Birstal chapel. This meant the matter remained
unresolved. It did not help matters that in the spring of 1783 John was
taken ill. He developed a fever and a distressing cough and lost all his
strength so that he had to confess 'the wheel of life seems scarcely able to
move'.[79] Soon there were exaggerated rumours of his impending death.
A convalescent trip to Holland did not restore his health and he was
seriously ill again at the time of the 1783 Conference. The negotiations
over the Birstal issue were not therefore finally resolved until January
1784 when a recovered John promised to underwrite the cost of the new

chapel on condition that the Conference was given the power to appoint its preachers. Confounding those who had written him off, John then once again resumed his active itinerant preaching, undertaking a seven-month programme that would have challenged a far younger man.

Even more complex negotiations were taking place internationally but these too eventually reached appropriate compromises. Peace was finally signed against the wishes of the king at the Treaty of Paris in September 1783. Immediately John Wesley had to decide what he would do to retain control of the Methodists in the newly independent country. Surprisingly the number of Methodists had significantly increased in the later war years and there were an estimated 15,000 members in 46 circuits run by 83 itinerant lay preachers. John's first action was to appoint Francis Asbury as his 'General Assistant' for America and urge the American Methodists to retain the doctrines and disciplines of English Methodism. However, retaining loyalty to the Church of England was virtually impossible, not least because most of its clergy had left America and it was almost impossible to take communion anywhere. Moreover, the Bishop of London, in whose diocese America lay, was refusing to take any steps to help the rebellious Americans.

John and Asbury were thus forced to consider creating a separate 'Methodist Church' in America which would not be tied to the Church of England. John knew this would make resisting English demands for a separation from the Church more difficult, especially as by this time events had forced the Countess of Huntingdon to take her societies into the ranks of dissent. Throughout the 1770s she had made her focus the college at Trevecca. John had unfairly dismissed its students as being 'raw lads of little understanding, little learning, and no experience',[80] but in practice they had proved very effective in founding more religious societies and in encouraging the countess to create more chapels across Britain. Unfortunately, the refusal of the church authorities to ordain any of them had forced a number into dissent. In 1779 the countess had taken over control of a dissenting chapel in Oxford Road with a view to returning it to the Church and establishing a Methodist society 'for the perishing thousands in that part of London'.[81] However, the Bishop of London had refused to accept this new 'Spa Fields Chapel' because its creation ignored the parish system. The resulting legal battle and attacks on her character had forced the frail Selina to accept she was 'cast out of the Church for what I have been doing these forty years – speaking and living for Jesus Christ'.[82]

As a result the countess had officially registered her Spa Fields Chapel as a dissenting meeting-house in 1782. It was a move that had cost her the support of almost all her clerical friends. William Romaine told her he would still pray for her but 'it would be better for you if you heard more truths and fewer lies'.[83] Henry Venn, John Berridge, Walter Shirley, Thomas Haweis and others knew she had been driven to it but they were adamant they would not become dissenting ministers in the 'Countess of Huntingdon's Connexion'. In March 1783 the first six dissenting ministers had been ordained in the Spa Fields Chapel (even though the countess herself had declined to attend). These ordinations were bound to encourage some Wesleyan preachers to seek the same.

This and the American issue meant it was obvious the Conference in 1784 was likely to prove a stormy affair. Charles felt physically unable to rise to the challenge of preventing a separation. He foresaw the Methodist movement breaking into 'a thousand pieces' and begged John Fletcher to take on the leadership of the Methodists from his ageing brother and himself and 'gather up the wreck'.[84] Fletcher agreed to attend the Conference and take on the role of mediator between conflicting parties. One preacher later recalled:

> Never shall I forget the ardour and earnestness with which Mr Fletcher expostulated, even on his knees, both with Mr Wesley and the preachers. To the former he said, 'My father! They have offended, but they are your children!' To the latter he exclaimed, 'My brethren! My brethren! He is your father!' and then, portraying the work in which they were unitedly engaged, he fell again on his knees, and with fervour and devotion engaged in prayer. The Conference was bathed in tears, many sobbed aloud.[85]

The result was a compromise embodied in the Deed of Declaration, which established the Conference as the ruling body of Wesleyan Methodism. Under the Deed it was agreed 100 preachers would meet annually in London, Bristol or Newcastle for a minimum of five days and a maximum of three weeks. To qualify for selection a preacher would have to have served Methodist societies for at least a year. The Conference would then choose an annual president and secretary and determine all issues relating to the societies. In this way the Deed was preparing Methodism for a future outside the Church, while avoiding a separation in the lifetime of the Wesleys. The Conference made this clear by saying it would have John Wesley as its annual president until he died. Not all the lay preachers accepted the Deed of Declaration because they resented their exclusion from the 100 chosen to attend future Conferences, but only 5 of the 91 rejected felt sufficiently strongly to resign.

Charles was no fan of the Deed but one suspects that his and Fletcher's views had a hand in the selection of the 100 preachers. Certainly some of the more contentious preachers were not listed among the 100 chosen, though in some instances they were long-serving preachers. The most obvious omission was the preacher John Hampson and he had long been an opponent of Charles. On one occasion when Charles had told Hampson if he had a parish he would never let Hampson preach there, Hampson had replied he would preach in Charles' parish without permission because he had as equal a right to preach as any minister. It was now left to John to defend the criteria used to nominate only half the preachers to attend future Conferences: 'I simply set down those that, according to the best of my judgement, were most proper. But I am not infallible.'[86]

In return for the support of most preachers over the matter of the Deed, John accepted he would send Thomas Coke to supervise the creation of a new Methodist Church in America. This must have been a blow to the loyal Francis Asbury, though Coke was in many ways a natural choice because he was an ordained minister with a strong interest in mission. Moreover, Coke had already backed abortive attempts to persuade the Conference to undertake a mission to Africa (in 1778) and to create 'a Society for the Establishment of Missions among the Heathen' (in 1784). In preparation for this new American Church, John agreed to reduce the Church's 39 articles of belief to 24 in order to accommodate the objections which many Methodists had to some of them (e.g. the article on predestination was omitted). A Service Book was produced with Coke's help. It was based on the Anglican liturgy with what Wesley called 'little alterations'. This included cutting or omitting a number of psalms because they were judged 'highly improper for the mouths of a Christian congregation'.[87] John even prepared a special American hymn-book, which was about a fifth the size of the British one he had recently produced with Charles' help.

Charles hated the creation of the Methodist Church in America, seeing it as a major step towards separation from the Church. As an alternative to what John was doing, he encouraged Joseph Pilmoor to return to America and seek proper ordination. Not surprisingly, John chose not to inform Charles that he was also considering making Coke 'a superintendent' (a Latinized form of 'bishop') so he could ordain American clergy. John discussed the issue with an inner circle of friends which included Fletcher and Coke. The latter was initially taken aback by the suggestion, but then welcomed it as a necessary expedient, saying: 'I may want all the influence in America which you can throw into my scale ... [and] my exercising the office of ordination, without that formal authority, may be disputed ... and opposed.'[88] In September 1784 John semi-secretly ordained Coke as 'superintendent' and appointed as 'elders' or 'presbyters' two other volunteer preachers chosen by Coke. These were

Richard Whatcoat and Thomas Vasey. John was not entirely sure what he had done was wise but he confessed he could see no alternative of helping 'those poor sheep in the wilderness'.[89]

From May 1783 to April 1785 there are no letters in existence between Charles and John and it is possible this is no accident of history but testimony to the deep division of opinion that had arisen between them. In November 1784 the news of the ordinations leaked out to Charles via one of his contacts in Bristol, Henry Durbin, who had heard what he called 'a report of a curious nature'.[90] When Charles received Durbin's letter he was astounded: 'I am thunderstruck [but] I can believe it.'[91] Not much later John published a vindication of his actions. He said in this *Apology* that the ending of English authority in America meant that country was 'at full liberty simply to follow the Scriptures and the Primitive Church'. They lacked bishops and ministers and so 'I violate no order and invade no man's right by appointing and sending labourers into the harvest'. He assured English Methodists he remained 'as firmly attached to the Church of England as ever I was'.[92]

Charles remained horrified by the ordinations. He asked Lord Mansfield for a legal judgement and his former schoolfellow confirmed Charles' judgement that the ordinations amounted to a separation from the Church. Charles believed that Coke must have somehow duped his brother and wrote to Henry Durbin that he wanted posterity to know he 'had no hand in this infamous ordination':

> The apology has so stunned and con[fuse]d me that I have not yet recovered the use of my brain ... He said he would never separate from the Church of England without my consent. Set this then to his age: his memory fails him ... I have the satisfaction of having stood in the gap so long, and staved off the evil for near half a century. And I trust I shall be able, like you, to leave behind me the name of an honest man. Which with all his sophistry he [i.e. John] cannot do.[93]

To a fellow clergyman Charles confided that John had never given him 'the least hint of his intention', but 'acted contrary to all his declarations, protestations, and writings ... and left an indelible blot on his name, as long as it shall be remembered'. Although he still loved John he had to accept 'our partnership is dissolved'. Sadly he concluded: 'I have lived on earth a little too long, who have lived to see this evil day.'[94] As ever, Charles also expressed his feelings in verse:

> Wesley himself and friends betrays
> By his own good sense forsook,

> While suddenly his hands he lays
> On the hot head of Coke ...
> The pious Mantle o'er his dotage spread,
> With silent tears his shameful Fall deplore,
> And let him sink, forgot, among the dead
> And mention his unhappy name no more ...
> So easily are Bishops made
> By man's or woman's whim?
> Wesley his hands on Coke hath laid,
> But who laid hands on him?[95]

Charles' concerns about Coke's motives were not entirely groundless. Coke was ambitious and he eventually did use John's action as justification to call himself a bishop. However, initially he had to be more cautious because he had to win over Francis Asbury and others. This he achieved because the American Conference met at Baltimore in December and not only gave their approval to become 'an Episcopal Church', but also appointed Asbury as a second superintendent to work with Coke. It also declared its loyalty to John Wesley and its determination to maintain its links with the Methodists in Europe. The dissident voices wrote to Charles, whom Coke soon regarded as an enemy. One American clergyman wrote:

> What is to become of all their professions of steadfast attachment to the Church? ... Can Wesley really suppose that he has a right to send men into this country invested with powers of ordination? We shall oppose their pretensions, and the consequence will be division and animosity.[96]

Charles confessed he felt the American Methodists had been 'betrayed into a separation from the Church of England' and were reduced to being 'a new sect of Presbyterians'.[97]

Even John was appalled when the Americans abandoned the term 'superintendent' in favour of the more controversial word 'bishop'. He knew this and the phrase 'Episcopal Church' would be extremely offensive to the Church of England. He wrote to Asbury and Coke:

> I study to be little; you study to be great. I creep, you strut along ... How can you, how dare you suffer yourselves to be called Bishops? I shudder, I start at the very thought. Men ... shall never by my consent call me Bishop![98]

Charles wrote of Coke's ordination of Asbury:

> A Roman emperor 'tis said,
> His favourite horse a consul made:
> But Coke brings other things to pass,
> He makes a bishop of an ass.[99]

Their shock was shared by some of the American Methodists and their spokesman became James O'Kelly, who had been a strong supporter of the move to independence. He said Americans had not shed their blood 'to free their sons from the British yoke' in order to become 'slaves to ecclesiastical oppression', and that 'it was a shame for a man to accept of such a lordship, much more to claim it'.[100]

The Wesleys had been united in their views on the American War of Independence, but its aftermath had driven them further apart than they had ever been. Charles began turning his back on the movement he had done so much to help create – it may help partially explain the fairly immediate decline in his health that was to shortly lead to his death. He wrote to one preacher: 'Young and healthy Christians are generally called to glorify God by being active in doing His will; but old and sick Christians in suffering it.'[101]

I2

Family and Finish

Beyond the bounds of time and space,
Look forward to that heavenly place,
 The saints' secure abode:
On faith's strong eagle-pinions rise,
And force your passage to the skies,
 And scale the mount of God.

That great mysterious Deity
We soon with open face shall see;
 The beatific sight
Shall fill heaven's sounding courts with praise,
And wide diffuse the golden blaze
 Of everlasting light.

The Father shining on His throne,
The glorious co-eternal Son,
 The Spirit, one and seven
Conspire our rapture to complete;
And lo! We fall before his feet,
 And silence heightens heaven.[1]

As late as 1773 Charles was writing: 'I do not want a heart to visit my very dear friends at Newcastle, but a body.'[2] Pleurisy, neuralgia, lumbago, piles, rheumatism, gout and various other ailments had cumulatively paid their toll. A decade later Charles referred to himself and his friend John Fletcher as being just 'human ruins tottering in the grave'.[3] His failure to remain an itinerant preacher made it easy for those who wanted Methodism to leave the Church to present him as an undesirable relic from the past. In reality his work in London and Bristol was still important and he continued to play a wider supportive role by communicating with those whom he deemed more worthy sons of the gospel. This, for example, is borne out by the young Irish preacher Henry

Moore, who was in London between 1784 and 1786. He commented that Charles treated him with 'a fatherly spirit' and never let Moore's different views produce 'any difference in his behaviour towards me'.[4]

The Irish clergyman James Creighton commented that Charles was astute enough to recognize that some preachers were flattering his brother in order to win his support for their wishes, and those preachers 'don't like him because he sees through them, for he is very discerning'.[5] Charles showed his life still had relevance by continued work on hymn-writing, even after the publication of his 1780 compilation, *Hymns for the Use of the People called Methodists*. This 'Methodist Manifesto'[6] quickly became the movement's definitive hymnbook, replacing Charles' earlier 1753 book, *Hymns and Spiritual Songs for the Use of Real Christians of All Denominations*. Charles was the author of 480 of the new hymnbook's 525 hymns. John wrote in its preface that the criteria for inclusion was that the hymns should contain 'no doggerel, no botches, nothing put in to patch up the rhyme, no feeble expletives ... nothing turgid or bombastic ... [and] no cant expressions, no words without meaning'. Instead there was elegant language which was simple and plain, 'suited to every capacity'.[7] Charles' hymns were, in the words of one historian, 'lyrical theology'.[8]

To these hymns were added tunes from a huge variety of sources, including German melodies and chorales, folk melodies from England, Scotland and Ireland, and adaptations of music by Handel, Purcell, Arne and others. Each tune had to be judged appropriately reverential and subordinate to the words. Some of the tunes were expressly written for the hymns, such as Handel's 'Rejoice the Lord is King'. The most prolific composer for Charles' hymns was the bassoonist John Frederick Lampe, and some of his work has stood the test of time, such as the tunes now called 'Derby', 'Crucifixion', 'Invitation' and 'Funeral'. When Lampe died, Charles wrote of the composer's welcome in heaven:

> The soul, by angel guards convey'd
> Has took its seat on high;
> The brother of my choice has gone
> To music sweeter than his own,
> And concerts in the sky.[9]

The hymnbook was a triumphant conclusion to the many hymns Charles had written, around 5,000 in the last 30 years alone. Most were poetic versions of scriptural passages because Charles more than John was a man of one book, the Bible. It is estimated there is only one allusion to a secular prose source about every 2,000 lines of his verse, but 'scriptural language and thought was the warp and woof of the texture of his poetry'.[10] He saw the Bible as a major channel through which the grace of God was experienced:

> Yet through the garment of His Word
> I humbly seek to touch my Lord.[11]

And one analyst has commented that 'a skilful man, if the Bible were lost, might extract it from Wesley's hymns'.[12] Certainly John viewed Charles' verse as 'the handmaid of piety' and as containing 'all the important truths of holy religion'.

The other passion of Charles' declining years was the welfare of his family. If anything, his love for his wife Sally had grown deeper with the passage of time. He regarded her as his best friend and confidante, and his letters show he missed her immensely whenever he was away on church matters. He was also fond of his children, though he tended not to show his affection for them in public. When Sally criticized him for this over their first son, he wryly answered: 'Why, I love him as well as you do. Only you make the most of a little love, by showing it, and I make the least of a great deal, by hiding it.'[13] Five of their children (John, John James, Martha Maria, Susanna and Selina) died in infancy and this clearly caused him considerable pain, though he tried to console both himself and his wife by saying that they were with God. For example, when John James died in 1768 he told Sally:

> I know the surest way to preserve our children is to trust them with Him who loves them infinitely better than we can do ... You must not deny my love to my sweet boy, if I am enabled to resign him for his heavenly Father to dispose of. I cannot doubt His wisdom or goodness. He will infallibly do what is best, not only for our children, but for us, in time and eternity.[14]

It made the three survivors, Charley (Charles), Sally (Sarah) and Sammy (Samuel), particularly precious. When his sons were very small Charles was still engaged in active itinerant preaching and so he was often absent. This made him understandably anxious whenever one of them was ill. For example, when Sally informed him in a letter that the infant Charley had an undiagnosed sickness which she hoped was not smallpox, he asked for 'constant intelligence ... till you think him out of danger'.[15] None of them were sent away to a boarding school, not even Kingswood. Instead they were educated at home by a mixture of their parents and private tutors. Like his mother, Charles feared that they might be led astray if allowed to mix with others because 'children are corrupters of each other'.[16] He wrote in 'A Father's Prayer for His Son':

When near the slippery paths of vice
With heedless steps he runs secure,
Preserve the favourite of the skies,
And keep his life and conscience pure:
Shorten his time for childish play,
From youthful lusts and passions screen,
Nor leave him in the wilds to stray
Of pleasure, vanity and sin.[17]

Sharing his mother Susanna's view that breaking the stubborn innate selfishness and wilfulness of children was part of a parent's educational role, Charles told his wife she should aim to cross their will 'in some one instance at least every day'.[18] When she told him that Charley was an amenable child who did not require such treatment, he told her she would still eventually find 'he has a will of his own', but that if she could persuade him, she need never compel him.[19] Where Charles was more liberal than his parents was in permitting his children to read not just the Bible but *Aesop's Fables* and novels like *Robinson Crusoe*, *Gulliver's Travels* and *Don Quixote*. It has been said that in some respects Charles treated his children more like a grandfather than a father. This is not surprising in that he was in his early 50s at the time of the birth of his sons and almost 60 by the time of his daughter's birth.

Charles was much criticized by some Methodists for not ensuring that his sons became evangelists, but he felt that their God-given talents lay in music and it should not be his role to suppress this. When one devout woman objected to him developing Charley's musical talent, he wrote that, while he had hoped his son would enter the Church, he had learned to accept that 'Nature has marked him for a musician':

My friends advised me not to cross his inclination. Indeed, I could not if I would. There is no way of hindering his being a musician but cutting off his fingers. As he is particularly fond of church music, I suppose if he lives he will be an organist.[20]

And he similarly defended his actions against a Quaker who criticized music as an undesirable and frivolous occupation: 'I can with a good conscience breed up my son to be a musician, not to please the giddy multitude, but to earn his bread.'[21]

It helped that both Charles and Sally enjoyed music. Charles played the flute and organ and Sally played the harpsichord and regularly sang, especially liking the oratorios of Handel. Charles wrote that Charley's inherited musical aptitude was almost immediately apparent from before he was aged three. He could play tunes he had heard sung by his mother or even just heard in the streets. Sally played the harpsichord to him from an early age and he soon was playing himself, tied to a chair so he would not fall off. Charles commented that 'from the beginning he played without study, or hesitation ... [and] he always played con spirito'.[22] Charles took Charley when he was four to audition before the actor and singer, John Beard, then a manager of Covent Garden. Beard suggested the lad be trained as a singer, and others were equally quick to admire the youthful talent, including the blind organist and composer, John Stanley, who was the manager of Handel's concerts. Lacking the money to fund a proper musical education, Charles handed over the development of his son's talent to a man in Bristol called Rookes, whom he judged would at least be a good-natured master.

On one of Charles' visits to London, his son was heard by Lady Gertrude Hotham, a sister of Lord Chesterfield and a contact of Selina, Countess of Huntingdon. She 'heard him with much satisfaction, and made him a present of all her music'.[23] Unfortunately her unexpected death shortly afterwards put pay to Charles' hopes that she might promote his son as a musical protégé. However, when the young Charles was ten, he was heard by a friend of Handel called Granville and he encouraged the boy to play before a number of musicians, including John Keeble, the organist of St George's in Hanover Square, Felice de Giardini, a noted Italian violinist, and Samuel Arnold, an up-and-coming young composer who years later was to become the main organist at Westminster Abbey. They recognized his potential but were not prepared to do anything themselves to promote it. That task fell largely to Joseph Kelway, the organist of St Martin-in-the-Fields, who told Charles his son was a genius with the spirit of Scarlatti and it was 'a pure pleasure' to teach a boy who was already better at playing sonatas than any master. Kelway informed his pupil that even Handel's hands 'did not lie on the harpsichord better than yours ... You have a divine gift.'[24]

Charles was anxious lest a musical career corrupt his son, but Kelway reassured him the boy was purity itself. Letting him proceed was encouraged by the fact his younger brother Sammy, eight years his junior, was also showing musical talent. In his case, the first signs were his singing songs he had heard from street organs when he was three years old. Sammy initially took up the violin and his father wrote he learnt to read at the age of four or five by looking at a copy of Handel's oratorio *Samson*.[25] The composer William Boyce described him as a potential

'English Mozart'[26] and once again Charles found himself taking a son to be heard by some of the leading musicians of the day. The young Samuel 'mastered the hardest music, without any pains or difficulty' and was very well received, especially as he could mimic the styles of Bach, Handel, Scarlatti and others. One of the aristocracy, the second Viscount Barrington, later recorded his impressions of hearing him play the harpsichord in 1775:

> Though he was always willing to play the compositions of others, yet for the most part he amused himself with extemporary effusions of his own most extraordinary musical inspiration ... His invention in varying passages was inexhaustible; and I have myself heard him give more than fifty variations on a known, pleasing melody.[27]

Charles commented that such praises 'bestowed so lavishly upon him did not seem to affect, much less to hurt, him'.[28] But he was concerned that playing music should not eventually lead to vanity or a decline in religious commitment and so he recommended Samuel study the Bible on a daily basis with his mother and be thankful for his gift, without being proud: 'Your brother has the same love of music; much more than you, yet he is not proud or vain of it. Neither, I trust, will you be.'[29] Inevitably it was not long before the young Charles and Samuel were playing publicly together. In 1779 they performed a series of concerts with Charles on the organ and Samuel on the violin at their father's house in Chesterfield Street, Marylebone. Among those who paid to hear them were not only a number of the aristocracy but also the Bishop of London and the Archbishop of Canterbury. Perhaps the most famous attendee was Dr Samuel Johnson, the creator of the first reputable English dictionary. It is said Johnson soon began reading a book because he did not know one tune from another and, when the boys had finished, he simply commented, 'Young gentlemen I am much obliged to you.'

A more attentive listener was Lord Mornington, the father of the future Duke of Wellington, who had a very high regard for their father, telling him on one occasion: 'I can say with truth that I esteem the commencement of your acquaintance as one of the happiest moments of my life.'[30] Mornington particularly liked Samuel and presented him with a special scarlet suit to wear at the concerts. Another admirer of Charles who came to hear his sons was the aged General Oglethorpe. Among newer acquaintances were some who were to become very famous in their time. These included William Wilberforce, the future opponent of slavery, and the writers Fanny Burney and Hannah More. John Wesley also attended some of his nephews' concerts, but confessed he felt 'a little out of my element among lords and ladies. I love plain music and plain company best.'[31]

Knowing his brother John viewed the concerts as a distraction from the main work of evangelism, Charles justified them by saying they would help pay for his sons' music lessons, encourage their independence, and keep them out of mischief:

> I am clear, without a doubt that my sons' concert is after the will and order of Providence. It has established them as musicians and in a safe and honourable way ... They may still make their fortunes if I would venture them into the world: but I never wish them rich. You also agree with me in this.[32]

Even though he could not afford the best teachers, Charles estimated he had spent hundreds of pounds on his sons' musical education. Not surprisingly, the concerts did not go down well among many of the Methodists. Fletcher felt he had to warn Charles that his fatherly love was weakening his reputation:

> They complain of your love for music, company and fine clothes, great folks, and the want of your former zeal and frugality. I need not put you in mind to cut off sinful appearances. You were taught to do this before I knew anything of the matter. Only see you abound more and more, to stop the mouths of your adversaries, or of your jealous friends.[33]

Though Charles was devoting some of his energies to the promotion of his children's talents, he was still regularly visiting the prisons and helping the poor, as well as undertaking his preaching engagements. The accusation about him living a richer lifestyle and turning his back on his former lifestyle was not really fair. Although he was living in a good house and mixing with aristocracy, he still had no real wealth himself. Whenever he was offered clerical positions that would have brought him a regular and good income, he refused them, saying he would not leave his work among the Methodists in London. On one occasion he also refused a large legacy from a woman who, having fallen out with her relatives, had decided to pass her fortune to him. He commented: 'I know what I am now, but I do not know what I should be if I were thus made rich.'[34] On another occasion when he was recounting his father's experience of being imprisoned for debt, his sister Martha told him not to shame the family by telling such stories. His reply was: 'If you are ashamed of poverty you are ashamed of your Master.'[35]

When the young Charles performed for the king at Windsor, his father feared those opposed to Methodism would seek to corrupt him, and he told him his interest should be to play 'least in sight'.[36] And he told his wife: 'I am not sanguine in my expectations of good from Windsor. If Charles has received no evil from it, it is a miracle, and I am satisfied.'[37] The young man's musical talents were much appreciated by both George III and the Prince of Wales. The latter made him his private organist and for a time the young Charles also taught music to the Princess Charlotte. Indeed there is a story (possibly apocryphal) that the king on one occasion took him aside when no one was present and confided:

> It is my judgement, Mr Wesley, that your uncle and your father, and George Whitefield and Lady Huntingdon, have done more to promote true religion in the country than all the dignified clergy put together.[38]

Nevertheless, both of his sons' musical careers suffered because of their father and uncle's involvement in Methodism. In part this was their father's fault because he did not permit them to perform in any aristocratic circles that might corrupt them. He once defined a 'Man of Fashion' in the following terms:

> A busy man without employment,
> A happy man without enjoyment ...
> In sleep and dress and sport and play,
> He throws his worthless life away ...
> Custom pursues, his only Rule
> And lives an Ape, and dies a Fool![39]

In part, they suffered from the opposition of some churchmen. For example, the young Charles' applications to pursue his talent in St Paul's Cathedral and Westminster Abbey were rejected with the words: 'We want no Wesleys here.'[40] The concertos, string quartets and church music he composed were largely ignored and he therefore gradually stopped writing. His last real chance to make a name for himself as a musician was to happen in 1788 when he could have been considered as the organist for the Chapel Royal – but his awareness of his father and uncle's dislike of the immorality of the court stopped him applying.

Charles was concerned that his elder son was attracted to the wrong sort of female, describing his choices as 'light' and 'inadvisable'. In August 1782 he urged him to seek God's guidance on his choice of wife so he would marry a person who would be a good influence on him and ensure his 'social happiness'.[41] However, a happy marriage, like a successful career, was to elude the younger Charles. According to Thomas Jackson, who was one of those who knew the family well, this was not entirely surprising because he had grown up to be a rather diffident and at times withdrawn young man who was notoriously eccentric. For example, he often appeared in public with his clothes awry because he was unable to dress himself properly without assistance.

While his elder brother was reduced to holding a number of second-rate musical posts as organist to various London chapels and churches, Samuel struggled to come to terms with his father's promotion of his talent. He had many of the qualities his brother lacked because he was a witty and engaging conversationalist, but he had no desire to be a minor professional musician, viewing it as a 'trivial and degrading business'.[42] In 1783 he rebelled against his father's restrictive evangelical approach by becoming a Roman Catholic, though initially he kept this a secret. There was no doctrinal reason for his actions. It was simply that he found the music of Methodist hymns and even the choral music performed in Anglican churches rather superficial compared to Gregorian chant. Samuel began composing music suited to Catholicism, including the mass *De Spiritu Sancto* and the motet *In Exitu Israel*, both of which are still performed.

Charles was very upset when he heard of Samuel's conversion to Catholicism. He poured out his feelings in a 25-stanza poem, which included the lines:

> Farewell, my all of earthly hope,
> My nature's stay, my age's prop,
> Irrevocably gone!
> Submissive to the will divine,
> I acquiesce, and make it mine;
> I offer up my son ...
> But while an exile here I live,
> I live for a lost son to grieve.[43]

John tried to persuade his nephew to change his mind, saying he feared he would never be born again as a Christian if he permitted himself to be distracted by 'a train of new notions, new practices, new modes of worship ... [all of which] put together do not amount to one grain of true, vital, spiritual religion'.[44] It made no difference, although, after his father's death, Samuel did abandon Catholicism.

Samuel's promising career was affected by an injury to his head in 1787 when he was still just 21. Coming home one night he accidentally fell into a hole which had been dug to lay the foundations for a new building, and spent the whole night insensible at the bottom of it. At first it was thought his life was in danger and the doctor suggested trepanning, an operation which removed portions of the bone of the skull in order to relieve the pressure on the brain. Charles refused his consent and the nasty head wound was allowed to heal naturally. However, Samuel appears to have subsequently suffered from fits of irritability and a nervous depression which adversely affected his music-making (though one of his best surviving compositions, *Exultate Deo*, dates from 1799). The fall may also have altered his character. The wife of the publisher Vincent Novello wrote that Samuel alternated between being a reasonable man who was a pious Catholic and being a madman who was a raving atheist and 'the dread of all wives and regular families'. She said he was 'a warm friend, a bitter foe, a satirical talker; a flatterer at times of those he cynically traduced at others; a blasphemer at times; a purling Methodist at others'.[45]

Like his elder brother, Samuel did not fulfil the musical hopes of his father, though some thought him the greatest organist of his day. Little of his output of religious works, symphonies, chamber music and piano pieces became popular. Historically his main claim to fame is now his promotion of the music of Bach. He criticized his brother and others for continuing to concentrate on the writings of Handel and the best of his own organ music looked to 'the transcendental merits' of Bach for inspiration. Samuel even named his own son Samuel Sebastian after him. As an old man Samuel also recognized the genius of Mendelssohn. Samuel Sebastian Wesley transformed his father's love of Bach and Mendelssohn into a unique contribution to British music, becoming one of the most significant figures in church music in the nineteenth century. Charles Wesley's hopes for his sons were thus to find their fulfilment in the grandson he never saw.

Charles' daughter Sally received almost as much attention as her brothers. Charles appears to have felt as strongly as John did that women deserved a better education than society gave them. Many years earlier John had written that women were just as much rational creatures as men and therefore in need of a proper education so they could better play their part in serving God. Charles ensured he personally educated his daughter Sally well beyond what was expected, including a strong grasp of Latin. There is a story that on one occasion he lost patience with her inability to grasp what he was teaching and he told her she was as stupid as an ass. When he saw the pain this caused her, tears came to his eyes and he immediately added the words 'and you are as patient'. She lacked her brothers' musical talents, but she had a great interest in literature and inherited her father's love of writing verse, though she lacked his gifts. Her aunt Martha Hall later introduced her to Hannah More and other leading literary women of the day. The writer Charles Lamb criticized the poet Coleridge for falsely encouraging 'that mopsy' (as he called Sally) 'to dance after you in the hope of having her nonsense put into a nonsensical anthology'.[46]

John Wesley showed particular affection to his niece. This is best illustrated by a story she herself later told of an event that took place in 1775. John had promised to take her with him to see Canterbury and Dover and she was very excited at the prospect. However, the day before they were due to go, her father discovered that John's estranged wife had sent some letters to the press designed to damage her husband's reputation. Charles advised John to postpone the trip so he could deal with this crisis, even though it would hugely disappoint Sally. John's reply was: 'Brother, when I devoted to God my ease, my time, my life, did I except my reputation? No. Tell Sally I will take her to Canterbury tomorrow.'[47]

Sally appears to have found irksome Charles' restrictions on what she could wear (he objected, for example, to her wearing fashionable but unpractical shoes) and do (he disliked her attending plays and balls). Rather than scold her in a confrontational manner, he relied on her love and respect not to want to offend and upset him: 'My not forbidding you, I thought was the strongest restraint to a generous mind, who knew what was most agreeable to me.'[48] A letter dated 1777 indicates her father was still overseeing her education when she was 18:

> I am not yet too old to assist you a little in your reading, and perhaps improve your taste in versifying. You need not dread my severity. I have a laudable partiality for my own children. Witness your brothers, whom I do not love a jot better than you; only be you as ready to show me your verses as they their music.[49]

He did not like it whenever Sally thought his links with Methodism were a social drawback, and he took pains to try and make her see why the movement was important:

> You gained by the despised Methodists, if nothing more – the knowledge of what true religion consists in; namely, in happiness and holiness; in peace and love; in the favour and image of God restored; in paradise regained; in a birth from above, a kingdom within you; a participation of the divine nature ... [A recognition that] faith is the gift of God, given to everyone that asks ... You have a thirst after

knowledge, and a capacity for it ... I would read something with you every day, and do what good I can for the little I shall be with you ... Ye might certainly more avail yourselves of my knowledge and dear-bought experience.[50]

At one level there was much to be proud of in what he and his brother John had achieved by the 1780s. There were 63 circuits with 178 itinerant preachers. The number of Methodist members had increased over the decade from 43,830 to 71,463 in England and Ireland and from 10,139 to 61,811 in America. Even larger numbers attended Methodist meetings. More importantly from Charles' perspective there was now a small but significant number of evangelical clergy who had learned from Methodism even if they had not adopted it. The most obvious example is the work of John Newton and William Cowper in producing the *Olney Hymns*, the first collection to remotely rival the Methodist hymnbooks. Among Newton's contributions were 'Amazing Grace', 'How sweet the name of Jesus sounds' and 'Glorious things of Thee are spoken'; while among Cowper's were 'God moves in a mysterious way', 'Hark, my soul, it is the Lord' and 'There is a fountain filled with blood'.

There was a sense in which Methodism was far more accepted by society and John Wesley commented he felt he was treated with a respectful courtesy which had long been lacking. However, this acceptance was still paper-thin in terms of the attitude of the church authorities towards the use of lay preachers so the pressure for separation was inevitably still growing, not least because the Calvinist Methodists had grown in popularity since becoming dissenters. Their preachers were running 116 chapels or 'preaching places' by 1788, scattered across the country from industrial areas like Walsall and Wolverhampton to traditional cathedral cities like Ely, Lincoln and York. Prominent among the successful Calvinist preachers were former students of Trevecca and this may partly explain why John's interest in Kingswood School resurfaced. He appointed the talented Thomas McGeary to develop the school so that it had the potential to become a Wesleyan Trevecca.

However, the main force pushing the Wesleyan Methodists towards separation from the Church was not Calvinist success but John's ordination of preachers for America in 1784. Charles felt betrayed by his brother's 'madness' and hoped desperately John would rescind his decision:

O that he had died before that day,
When W------ did himself betray
Did boldly on himself confer
The Apostolic Character!

O that we both had took our flight
Together to the realms of light,
Together yielded up our breath,
In life united, and in death! ...
God of unbounded power and grace ...
Thine energy of love exert
And change thy favour'd Servant's heart ...
Undo the evil he hath done ...
Stir up thy faithful people, Lord,
To urge their suit with one accord,
And rescue thro' the Strength of prayer,
Their Father, Guide, and Minister.[51]

Increasingly Charles felt he had outlived his usefulness. He was particularly upset in May 1785 by the death of the 92-year-old Vincent Perronet, Vicar of Shoreham, even though Perronet had been housebound for some time. Charles and John had often used Perronet as their confidential adviser, even jokingly calling him 'the Archbishop of the Methodists'. Charles conducted the burial service and preached the funeral sermon on the text: 'Mark, the perfect man, and behold the upright; for the end of that man is peace.' In June Charles told Fletcher's wife that he had lost the use of his hand and eyes and was 'useless'[52] and told Fletcher himself that he was 'far entered' on his last stage of life.[53] He began looking forward to his own death when he would be reunited with Perronet, Whitefield, Grimshaw, Harris and other friends who had died:

There all the ship's company meet,
Who sail'd with the Saviour beneath;
With shouting each other they greet,
And triumph o'er sorrow and death.[54]

Charles' unhappiness did not stop John deciding to ordain preachers to work in what he called 'the Methodist Church of Scotland' at the 1785 Conference. He argued this had no impact on his relationship with the Church of England and that he would not be stopped from 'doing what good I can while I live for fear of evils that may follow when I am dead'.[55] Charles vehemently disagreed with this decision, telling his wife:

To turn seventy thousand Church of England people Dissenters! ... Surely I am in a dream! Is it possible that J. W. should be turned Presbyterian? ... How would this disturb (if they were capable of being disturbed) my father and brother in Paradise![56]

He rightly appreciated that John was being naive if he thought the preachers ordained for Scotland would not soon also work in England. He bitterly commented: 'He has set open the flood-gates'[57] and expressed his grief at the extent to which he and John no longer worked in harmony:

> Happy the days, when Charles and John
> By nature and by grace were One,
> The same in office as in name,
> Their judgements and their will the same ...
> In infancy their hopes and fears,
> In youth, and in their riper years,
> Their hearts were to each other known
> Attun'd in perfect Unison.[58]

Charles placed no trust in the advice John was receiving from the 'hot-headed' Coke, who undoubtedly saw himself as John's potential successor. In August he poured out his sorrow, reminding John of how much he had constantly and unfailingly supported him and passionately begging his brother not to give in to the demands to ordain clergy in England in parishes where Methodists were denied communion:

> Alas! What trouble you are preparing for yourself, as well as for me, and for your oldest and best friends! Before you have quite broken down the bridge, stop and consider! ... Go to your grave in peace; at least suffer me to go first, before this ruin is under your hand. So much I think you owe to my father, to my brother [Samuel], and to me ... I am on the brink of the grave. Do not push me in, or embitter my last moments. Let us not leave an indelible blot [of separation from the Church] on our memory; but let us leave behind us the name and character of honest men. This letter is a debt to our parents, and to our brother, as well as to you, and to your faithful friend, Charles Wesley.[59]

John replied they might have to agree to disagree, but simultaneously tried to reassure Charles that he had no more desire to separate from the Church than he had 50 years before. He pointed out he was still urging all connected with him to observe the ordinances of the Church and accept the authority of the bishops, 'though sometimes with a doubting conscience' because of their continued hostility. He reminded Charles that he himself had once referred in his verse to the bishops as 'mitred infidels' so he should not oppose him doing what he believed was 'meet, right and my bounden duty':

I do nothing rashly ... If you will go on hand in hand with me, do. But do not hinder me, if you will not help. Perhaps if you had kept close to me, I might have done better. However, with or without help, I creep on.[60]

Charles replied that no one could have been more loyal than he had been: 'I kept as close to you as close could be for I was all the time at your elbow.' John was the last man on earth whom he would wish to quarrel with because 'my heart is as your heart'. As far as he was concerned no human agency could ever separate him from John because God had joined them together. However, John should not hide behind false pretences. His brother knew he had long recanted with a sense of shame 'that juvenile line of mine' about the bishops and it had been written when they had most opposed what he and John were doing. Now some bishops were 'quite friendly towards us, particularly toward you' so separation was totally unnecessary. His brother must know he 'might certainly have done better' if he had taken more heed of his advice, but he could always rely on him remaining 'your affectionate friend and brother'.[61]

John said there was no point he and Charles further disputing 'for neither of us is likely to convince the other' and that, if Charles persisted in opposing him, the only person to suffer would be Charles: 'You may thereby weaken a little my hands, but you will greatly weaken your own.' As far as he was concerned, Charles was too fearful of what might happen after they were dead: 'I must and will save as many souls as I can while I live without being careful about what may possibly be when I die ... I pray do not confound the intellects of the people in London.'[62] Charles insisted on having the last word, saying he was doing nothing by his actions to stop John, but pray 'for the Church of England, and for you, while breath remains in me'.[63] Someone had to be prepared to tell John the truth and who better than his brother: 'I cannot rest, living or dying, unless I deal faithfully with you as I am persuaded you would deal with me, if you were in my place, and I in yours.'[64]

It was no coincidence that Charles' health took a serious downturn from this time on, especially as he heard in the midst of this debate the devastating news of the death of his staunchest ally in maintaining the links with the Church. John Fletcher had chosen not to attend the Conference that year because he was tending to his parishioners, who were facing a typhoid epidemic. On 4 August he had collapsed suffering from a high fever and his body had become covered with spots. Ten days later he was dead, aged only 56. His wife Mary wrote to the Wesleys:

On my bleeding heart the fair picture of his heavenly excellence will be forever drawn. When I call to mind his ardent zeal, his laborious

endeavours to seek and serve the lost, his diligence ... [and] uninter-
rupted converse with heaven ... my loss is beyond the power of words
to paint ... From the time I have had the happiness and honour of
being with him, every day more and more convinced me he was the
Christian. I saw, I loved, in him the image of my Saviour; and thought
myself the happiest of women ... I never knew any one walk so closely
in the image of God as he did.[65]

John was also shocked by Fletcher's death and led a memorial service to
him in London. His sermon paid tribute to such a perfect Christian:

I never heard him speak an improper word, or saw him do an improper
action. Many exemplary men I have known, holy in heart and life,
within fourscore years. But one to equal him I have not known – one
so inwardly and outwardly devoted to God. So unblameable a character in every respect I have not found either in Europe or America.[66]

The following year John wrote a biography of Fletcher so that Methodists could seek to emulate such a saint. He hoped to publish this with
an accompanying elegy written by Charles, but Charles was so upset his
poetic talents for once deserted him. Charles despaired that the future
of Methodism now rested with Thomas Coke and others determined to
encourage John to ordain all the preachers.

In March 1786 John Pawson, one of the preachers ordained to work in
Scotland and a long-time critic of Charles' obsessive love for the Church,
urged John to accept the inevitable and ordain his preachers wherever
'the bulk of the people greatly desire it'.[67] Meanwhile Thomas Coke championed a more extensive worldwide mission, publishing his *Address to
the Pious and Benevolent*, which pleaded for the ordination of preachers
to undertake missionary work in the Highlands and Islands of Scotland,
the Channel Isles, the Leeward Islands, Quebec, Nova Scotia and New-
foundland. Charles preached as frequently as his strength permitted in
both London and Bristol to continue urging Methodists not to desert the
Church of England. He was painfully aware John was dismissive of his
stance, and so, in July, he wrote to the Revd Benjamin Latrobe, a prominent Moravian, to see if he could create a pro-Church party which combined both Methodists and Moravians in a last ditch stand to prevent
schism, 'the great evil I have dreaded for nearly fifty years'.[68] La Trobe
was under no illusion that Charles' move was one of sheer desperation,
born out of 'deep affliction of mind and sickness of body' as a result of
the Methodists 'setting up a new religion'.[69]

Charles attended the 1786 Methodist Conference but, according to
John Pawson, the one time he spoke was to utter the word 'No!' when

Thomas Coke tried to argue that it was better to let the societies in large towns hold their meetings at the same time as church services because the majority of evangelical clergy were Calvinists. John backed Charles and insisted that Methodists should cease the practice of holding services at the same time as the services of their local parish church. His only caveat was that he would not force any Methodist to attend a church because he had known too many examples where poor ministers made this too painful an experience. Charles' presence probably made a significant difference because John reaffirmed his control over doctrine and discipline within the connexion and insisted the Conference reaffirm its loyalty to the Church of England. Charles wrote to his wife:

> My brother is once more become a champion for the Church: and who so great as he and I? But – but – but! When the Conference is over we will see farther. It will cost me some of my last and precious hours.[70]

Immediately after the Conference Charles decided he would not attend another. He gave a sermon in which he predicted only about a third of the preachers would remain loyal to the Church after his brother's death, and he warned that God's blessing would only be given to the work of those who avoided dissent. He expressed his sadness that the Church was not doing more to prevent a schism: 'The bishops might, if they pleased, save the largest and soundest part of them back into the Church … but I fear … their lordships care for none of these things.'[71] He again told John that ordination was pushing their societies into dissent: 'I believe God left you to yourself in this matter … to show the secret pride which was in your heart. I believe … ordination is separation … Stop here; ordain no more.'[72]

In the autumn La Trobe's unexpected death ended any hope that the Moravians might help Charles prevent Methodism deserting the Church. Charles confided to one of the preachers with whom he still kept links that he felt those who had laboured inexhaustibly to separate him and John had now finally 'conquer'd' John, though not him: 'What God hath joined man cannot put asunder. Death itself cannot separate us … He is next in my heart to God and the Church.' He was devastated that John's so-called friends were just waiting 'impatiently for his dropping' to separate from the Church.[73] Entering his 80s Charles had to accept he had no longer the physical strength to continue personally opposing what John was doing. He told his brother:

> Let us agree to differ. I leave America and Scotland to your latest thoughts and recognitions … Keep your authority while you live; and after your death, detor digniori, or rather dignioribus.[74]

Charles felt his heart was broken:

> My brother does not and will not see ... that he has renounced the
> principles and practice of his whole life: that he has acted contrary
> to all his declarations, protestations and writings ... and left an in-
> delible blot on his name as long as it shall be remembered! Thus our
> partnership here is dissolved, but not our friendship. I have taken him
> for better, for worse, till death do us part – or rather re-unite in love
> inseparable. I have lived on earth a little too long, who have lived to
> see this evil day.[75]

Nevertheless, he continued to preach, even though sometimes he had to
pause and let the congregation sing until he had regained the strength
to continue. One of the young preachers has given us a portrait of him
at this time:

> He rode every day, clothed for winter even in summer, a little horse
> grey with age. When he mounted, if a subject struck him, he proceeded
> to expound and put it in order. He would write a hymn thus given him
> on a card (kept for that purpose) with his pencil in shorthand. Not
> infrequently he has come to the house in the City Road, and having
> left the pony in the garden in front, he would enter crying out, 'Pen
> and ink, pen and ink.' These being supplied, he wrote the hymn he had
> been composing. When this was done he would look round on those
> present and salute them with much kindness.[76]

Ordaining preachers was not the only action John took in defiance of
Charles' wishes at this time. John had long refused to officially sanction female preachers (such as Fletcher's wife, Mary Bosanquet) while
conniving at female involvement in leading services. To a certain extent
this had matched Charles' attitude. However, in 1787 John officially
authorized a woman called Sarah Mallet to preach in Norfolk. It was
another blow against remaining within the Church. The opponents of
female preachers were to have John's policy reversed after his death,
despite the work of women like Elizabeth Evans, whose evangelizing
tours in the Midlands and North were as demanding and as effective
as any of her male counterparts in the 1790s. She was later to be im-
mortalized as 'Dinah Morris' by the novelist George Eliot in her book
Adam Bede.

Charles did not attend the 1787 Conference. The week before it was
due to commence he preached in London about the 'self created bishops

and self made priests' who would tear Methodism apart, urging society members to refuse communion from any of them.[77] John Pawson recorded the dislike he and other preachers felt at 'such a hot, fiery spirit' and concluded: '[I] ... have nothing but love in my heart toward the old man. But really ... [his views] will not bear the light at all.' However, even he had to admit Charles was still able to show 'an astonishing degree of power'.[78] Those who listened to Charles decided to petition the church authorities, urging them to back Charles by making conciliatory gestures to prevent Methodism moving into dissent. In October 1787 James Creighton submitted a draft of a proposed letter to the archbishop and bishops, which was later called 'A Plan for Preserving the People Called Methodists in the Church of England'. It suggested the Church should avoid the Methodists breaking away by making John a bishop so that he could legally ordain a small number of his preachers to administer the sacraments.[79]

That autumn John records working alongside Charles in Bristol. Though very frail, Charles still retained his interest in the welfare of others. That is evidenced by one of his last surviving letters which was sent to a preacher whose wife was very sick. It was very short because Charles had to confess his failing eyesight made writing difficult, but in it he told him he 'hoped against hope that she be restored to you lest you should have sorrow on sorrow'.[80] On 23 October the two brothers shared duties at the Temple Church. In the morning Charles read the prayers and John preached, while in the evening it was Charles' turn to preach. John then set off for a week of itinerant preaching. A week later when he was back in Bristol Charles preached in the morning and John chose to speak in the open air in the afternoon. It may well not just be coincidence that following this John reasserted his own commitment to avoiding a separation with the Church of England in a sermon at Witney because 'every year more and more of the clergy are convinced of the truth and grow well-affected towards us'.[81]

John makes no reference in his journal to the state of Charles' health but Charles wrote to his daughter Sally that he felt this might be his last visit to Bristol: 'My eyes fail me for writing and reading. Perhaps they may not be quite darkened, till they are closed.'[82] And he said that she might have to play the same role as the daughter of John Milton in turning nurse to her blind father 'in my last days'. Shortly after his return to London, Charles took to his bed. He confessed to one of the London preachers: 'I am known as a dead man out of mind, and am content.'[83] He told his wife that he was 'going the way of all the earth' and that his 'night' was come. The failure of his sons to become staunch churchmen played on his mind: 'I have been of little use to my children. But it is too late to attempt it now.' He entrusted Sally and his family to God's grace, which was greater than anything he could offer:

> You married me, that you might be holier and happier to all eternity. If you have received less spiritual good than you expected, it is chiefly my fault. I have not yet set you the pattern I ought.[84]

As far as we know the last hymn Charles wrote with his own hand was one based on a text from Hosea about God taking away all iniquity. It concluded:

> O that the joyful hour was come
> Which calls Thy ready servant home,
> Unite me to the church above,
> Where angels chant the song of love,
> And saints eternally proclaim
> The glories of the heavenly Lamb![85]

In the spring of 1788 Charles' daughter Sally recorded that her aged and sick father seemed 'totally detached from earth' and that he 'spoke very little nor wished to hear anything read but the Scriptures':

> All his prayer was, 'Patience and an easy death.' He … said to us all, 'I have a good hope [of heaven]'. When we asked him if he wanted anything, he frequently answered, 'Nothing but Christ.' Some person observed that the valley of death was hard to be passed. 'Not with Christ', replied he.[86]

He became increasingly reliant on her to write for him. His last dictated letter was in February. It was to a music dealer who had billed him for something he had already paid. Charles said he would rather pay a bill 20 times than be thought not to have paid it at all. John was very solicitous, writing to advise him not to stint on the cost of any medicine required because he could rely on his financial support. Convinced that if Charles remained in bed, he would die, John urged him to go out for a walk every day, even 'if it may sometimes be a cross'.[87] And to Sally he recommended she give her father 'ten drops of elixir of vitriol in a glass of water' and that the family should avoid upsetting him in any way. Their 'tenderly respectful behaviour' would be 'the best cordial for him under heaven'.[88]

John recommended that Sally obtain the services of a Dr Whitehead, who was very highly regarded, but the doctor could do little to help because he found Charles' body was 'reduced to the last extreme state of weakness'. The doctor expressed his admiration at Charles' composure in the face of death and at his 'unaffected humility, and holy resignation to the will of God' and his 'unshaken confidence in Christ, which kept his mind in perfect peace'.[89] John, who was still engaged in itinerant preaching, continued to write all the homespun remedies he thought might help, ranging from binding a warm onion or thin slices of beef across the pit of his stomach to making a jelly from breadcrusts and lemon-juice mixed with sugar. Above all, he told the family to put their trust in God, who could do anything.[90]

By mid-March Charles was unable to keep anything in his stomach and he stopped eating. A few days before his death he called his wife to him and bid her write as he dictated:

In age and feebleness extreme,
Who shall a sinful worm redeem?
Jesus, my only hope thou art,
Strength of my failing flesh and heart;
Oh, could I catch a smile from thee,
And drop into eternity![91]

On the night of 26 March his health took a serious downturn and he prayed that God would spare him the pain of nights of agony. He became at times semi-conscious and was heard muttering 'Let me die. Let me die.' In a moment of greater lucidity he told his family not to worry because his brother John would look after them. On 28 March his wife asked him if he had any final message to give her and his children. His reply was 'Only thanks, love, blessing'. Samuel Bradburn, then the leading lay preacher in London, joined the family and sat beside his bedside all night. The next day Charles held first his wife's hand and then his beloved daughter's hand. Then he died. Sally told her uncle John that his last whispered words were 'Lord – my heart – my God' and that he died so peacefully 'that we knew not exactly the moment in which his happy spirit fled'.[92]

Charles had insisted his body should not be buried where John wanted in the City Road Chapel grounds, but in a properly consecrated cemetery: 'I have lived and I die in the communion of the Church of England, and I will be buried in the yard of my parish church.'[93] He died as passionate as ever that the Methodists should not become dissenters:

Exhort our people to keep close to the Church ... Warn them against despising the Prayers of the Church; against calling our society 'the

Church'; against calling our preachers 'ministers' ... Although we call sinners to repentance in all places of God's dominion, and although we frequently use extempore prayer, and unite together in a religious society, yet we are not Dissenters ... . [We do not] renounce the service of the Church. We do not, we dare not, separate from it. We are not Seceders ... [and] none who regard my judgement or advice will separate from it.[94]

Eight clergymen carried Charles' coffin to the churchyard of St Marylebone. John was not present because the letter informing him of his brother's death had been misdirected and so arrived too late for him to attend the funeral. Therefore Samuel Bradburn was chosen to give a funeral oration at City Road on 6 April. He preached on the text 'A Prince and a gentleman is fallen this day in Israel', 'to an inconceivable concourse of people of every description'. Bradburn had held very different views from Charles on the issue of the ordination of preachers but that did not prevent him admiring Charles' many qualities:

His general character was such as at once adorned human nature and the Christian religion. He was candid, without weakness; and firm, without obstinacy. He was free from the indifference of lifeless formality and the fire of enthusiastic wildness. He was never known to say anything in commendation of himself, and never was at a loss for something good to say of his divine Master. His soul was formed for friendship in affliction, and his words and letters were a precious balm to those of a sorrowful spirit. He was courteous without dissimulation, and honest without vulgar roughness. He was a great scholar without ostentation. He was a great Christian without any pompous singularity, and a great divine without the least contempt for the meanest of his brethren.[95]

A monument created in 1858 now marks the spot where Charles was buried. One face of the obelisk contains a verse which he had written in memory of a friend. It was felt it aptly applied to Charles himself:

With poverty of spirit blest,
Rest, happy saint, in Jesus' rest.
A sinner saved, through grace forgiven,
Redeem'd from earth to reign in heaven!
Thy labours of unwearied love,
By thee forgot, are crowned above,
Crowned, through the mercy of thy Lord,
With a full, free, immense reward.[96]

A simpler statement was inscribed on his memorial tablet in the City Road Chapel. It was a text which Charles had loved to use: 'God buries His workmen, but carries on his work.'

John was devastated. Preaching a fortnight later in Bolton, he broke down in the pulpit and publicly wept when he had to read out the lines from one of his brother's hymns:

My company before is gone
And I am left alone with Thee.[97]

He told the Methodist Conference that 'the weary wheels of life at last stood still'.[98] However, John did not do much for Charles' family. Initially he promised his sister-in-law he would continue to pay the annuity which had been part of her wedding settlement, but Sally asked for this to be converted into a one-off payment because she was fearful what might happen when John died. John was concerned she would not live modestly without the restraining influence of Charles and told her she would have to cut her costs in her reduced circumstances.[99] Some people thought John was being mean, especially as he was receiving income from publications to which Charles had contributed (most notably of course by his hymns). In December John defended himself in a letter to Sally, saying she should not listen to 'busy bodies on other men's matters' and that he knew he owed her 'one or two hundred pounds' and would be setting aside funds for her as soon as he could.[100] William Wilberforce says the family were in 'real want' and so he had to offer financial assistance. The Countess of Huntingdon also sent gifts to help and offered to assist his sons with their careers.

John was more concerned to press on with his work. In June he recorded his surprise that he was still so fit for a man of his age. Though his memory was at times faulty and his eyesight poor, he faced no signs of 'any decay in my hearing, smell, taste, or appetite', and the rheumatic pains in his right shoulder and arm did not hamper his continued ability to find travelling and preaching relatively straightforward.[101] More problematical was that Charles' death had encouraged those who wanted to cut their ties with the Church to believe their time had come. At the annual Conference Thomas Coke voiced their wishes for a 'formal separation from the Church'.[102] John resisted this on the grounds there were no doctrinal reasons for separation, but he offered a conciliatory gesture by for the first time ordaining one of the preachers, Alexander Mather, to work in England.

In May 1789 John told the still heavily grieving Sally that she had to accept Charles' death was God's will and recognize she still had in Christ a 'great Friend always at hand'.[103] John promised to write a biography of Charles and began collecting materials for this, but his own increasing frailty prevented this project ever happening. More practical help came eventually from the Methodist Conference which gave an annuity to the widow and her children. Sally survived on this till her death on 28 December 1822. Six years later her daughter died, while Charles died on 23 May 1834 and Samuel on 11 October 1837.

In 1789 John defeated those who wanted separation at the Conference and reiterated that 'the Methodists ... are not a sect or party' but, by January 1790, he felt his time was running out:

> I am now an old man, decayed from head to foot. My eyes are dim; my right hand shakes much; my mouth is hot and dry every morning; I have a lingering fever almost every day; my motion is weak and slow.[104]

Even so he continued his itinerant preaching and gave his cautious approval to Coke's wishes to send more designated preachers abroad. A committee was set up to manage the work and this is sometimes hailed as the real start of the Methodist worldwide mission. John had finally accepted a wider role for Methodism than either he or Charles had ever envisaged. This did not mean he had given up all hope of Methodism remaining within the Church of England. He wrote to some of the bishops about his pain at the way their hostility was driving Methodism into dissent.[105] These years also saw John attack the events of the anti-monarchical French Revolution: 'We are no republicans and never intend to be.'[106] He comforted himself with the hope that all the turmoil in Europe might be a sign of the second coming of Christ, even though 'the poor infidels ... know nothing of God'.[107]

By the time of the 1790 Methodist Conference it was obvious that John's faculties were considerably impaired and his memory failing. He was unable to preside over its sessions. Nevertheless, he made clear that he thought itinerancy should not be abandoned by himself or his preachers: 'If we do not take care, we shall all degenerate into milksops.'[108] On 24 November he ceased maintaining his journal but he continued writing sermons. Appropriately his last was a sermon 'On Faith' and it looked forward to the time when the veil that separated God from humanity would be removed by death.[109] He concluded it with some of Charles' verse:

> Faith lends its realizing light:
> The clouds disperse, the shadows fly;

Th' Invisible appears in sight,
And God is seen by mortal eye![110]

John's last appearance as a preacher at the City Road Chapel was on 22 February 1791. He made a journey to Leatherhead to preach and his frail health finally succumbed. He told his friends not to be concerned because 'The best of all is, God is with us!' Observers recorded he died 'without a struggle or groan ... [entering] His Master's joy' on 2 March, repeating the first words of a hymn by Isaac Watts:

I'll praise my Maker while I've breath,
And when my voice is lost in death,
Praise shall employ my nobler powers:
My days of praise shall ne'er be past,
While life, and thought, and being last,
Or immortality endures.[111]

John had requested a simple funeral with 'no pomp, except the tears of them that loved me'. The City Road Chapel was draped in black and the material later used to provide 'decent dresses for sixty poor women'. It is estimated 10,000 people filed by his coffin and special memorial services were held throughout the country. Even the secular press marked the passing of a man who was 'a blessing to his fellow creatures', recognizing that by his and his brother's efforts 'the ignorant were instructed, the wretched relieved, and the abandoned reclaimed'.

Martha Wesley, the last surviving sister, did not long outlive him. She died on 12 July 1791, saying she had the assurance of salvation she had always sought. Shortly before her, on 17 June, Selina Countess of Huntingdon died at the age of 83. One of those present at her death said 'she exhibited the greatest degree of Christian composure ever I witnessed'.[112] Her wishes were to be buried simply in an unmarked grave in the family vault at Ashby-de-la-Zouch alongside her husband's grave. Contemporaries were very much aware that her death brought to an end the era of Whitefield and the Wesleys. The Vicar of Everton, John Berridge, who was then in his 70s and partially deaf and blind, commented: 'Ah, is she dead? Then another pillar is gone to glory. Mr Whitefield is gone, Mr Wesley and his brother are gone, and I shall go soon.' The person who had brought him the news replied: 'Yes, sir, it is not probable you will long survive them; and although some little differences of opinion existed between you here, I have no doubt you will unite in perfect harmony in heaven.' Berridge agreed with the words: 'Ay, that we shall; for the Lord washed our hearts here and he will wash our brains there.'[113]

A few key preachers met in Halifax and agreed there could not be 'another King in Israel'. They issued a circular to all preachers saying that in future the Conference should elect its president and secretary on an annual basis, and they planned the division of the connexion into geographical districts, each under an annually appointed chairman. One of the Halifax group, an Irishman called William Thompson, was duly elected in 1791 as president. The majority of preachers wanted to remain loyal to the vision of the Wesleys, including remaining within the Church, and by 1793 the Conference was firmly stating it did not sanction ordination in England. Unfortunately, there was no reciprocal support from the Church and this enabled the separatists to begin winning a greater following. The 30-year-old son of a linen weaver from Epworth called Alexander Kilham urged Methodism to ordain its preachers and give them authority to offer holy communion within society meetings. He also argued in favour of a more Presbyterian approach to organization with authority vested at local level. In 1794 some of the other Methodist leaders, less egalitarian than Kilham, drew up a 'Bishop's Plan' whereby 'Superintendents' would take on a semi-episcopal role and ordain priests and deacons.

The 1795 'Plan of Pacification' tried to end the infighting. It accepted the creation of a separate Wesleyan Methodist Church, with its own ministry, while holding open the door to eventual reunion by saying it would not ordain by 'the laying on of hands', which only bishops could perform. Instead, Methodist preachers would be ordained by the recommendation of Conference. Initially, the majority so ordained even refused to take the name 'minister', preferring to describe themselves as 'helps to the regular clergy'. The rank and file largely accepted the Plan of Pacification and many continued to worship in their local parish church (where that was permitted) and looked to be married and to have their children baptized there. The Plan has been described as 'a triumph of the Wesleyan spirit in its pragmatism, its compromise, and its acceptance of the unavoidable'. Charles would not have viewed it in this light. Those who welcomed the separation were happy to reduce Charles' reputation to that of a hymnwriter and present John as the sole creator of Methodism.

It was left to Charles' wife to try and make people remember the warmth of Charles' character and appreciate that his willingness to always play second fiddle to John did not mean his contribution to Methodism had been less:

> His most striking excellence was humility; it extended to his talents as well as virtues; he not only acknowledged and pointed out but

delighted in the superiority of another, and if ever there was a human being who disliked power, avoided pre-eminence, and shrunk from praise, it was Charles Wesley.

She reminded people that her husband's contribution was as a preacher as well as a writer of richly poetic hymns which breathed 'the religion of the heart'. Sally described his preaching as 'impassioned and energetic', and designed to express 'the most important truths with simplicity, brevity, and force'. Even more memorable was his immense and constant kindness to friends and family, 'especially to those who were dependent upon him, or whom he thought neglected and oppressed'. She said Charles had been 'full of sensibility and fire', filled with divinely inspired 'patience and meekness':

> John affectionately discharged the social duties, but Charles seemed formed by nature to repose in the bosom of his family. Tender, indulgent, kind, as a brother, a husband, a father, and a master; warmly and inalienably devoted to his friend; he was a striking instance that general benevolence did not weaken particular attachments.[114]

She could easily have said more about how 'the man made for friendship' devoted himself more to John than anyone. For him he had undertaken many tasks which otherwise he would have declined. For him he had stayed within Methodism long after its development had ceased to please him because of its increasing independence from the Church he loved. His criticisms of John were always voiced in love and rarely did he criticize John in public. His bitterest attacks were reserved for people whom he judged to be misleading others, whether in a religious or a political sense, or for those he thought were being disloyal. At times Charles could be inconsistent, pessimistic and dogmatic, but he never put himself first and never sought wealth and power, nor did he ever complain at the many hardships he endured. Instead he used his unique gift with words to be not only a preacher of distinction but also a writer of hymns which uniquely embodied the spirit of Methodism by proclaiming the love and self-sacrifice of Christ.

In that sense Charles would be happy that his major role in creating the Methodist movement has been forgotten in favour of the hymnwriter who declared God's salvation open to all, regardless of their inadequacies and sinfulness:

Peace, righteousness, and joy Divine,
Thou dost with love impart,

That Thou art love, that Thou art mine,
Assure my happy heart:
Then am I meet for my reward,
Renew'd in holiness,
And live the image of my Lord,
And die to see Thy face.[115]

Notes

Chapter 1

1 Charles Wesley, Short Hymn on Matthew 19:13 in G. Osborn, *The Poetical Works of John and Charles Wesley*, Wesleyan Methodist Conference, London, 1870, Vol. X, p. 322

2 These were the words inscribed after his death on his tombstone.

3 Adam Clarke, *Memoirs of the Wesley Family*, London, 1823, p. 8

4 Daniel Defoe, *The Character of the Late Dr Samuel Annesley*, Preface and pp. 6 and 9, no date.

5 John Wesley, *A Christian Library*, London, 1819–27, Vol. XXIV, p. 453

6 J. B. Wakeley, *Anecdotes of the Wesleys*, Hodder and Stoughton, London, 1889, p. 22

7 Letter to Dr Sharpe, 28 December 1700, in George Stevenson, *Memorials of the Wesley Family*, Partridge & Co, London, 1876, pp. 79–80

8 Samuel Wesley, *The Life of Our Blessed Lord & Saviour Jesus Christ*, London, 1693, p. 41

9 Quoted in M. Edwards, *Family Circle*, Epworth, London, 1949, p. 36

10 Letter to J. W., 23 February 1725, in Charles Wallace, *Susanna Wesley: Complete Writings*, Oxford University Press, 1997, p. 106

11 31 July 1702, Letter from Susanna to Bishop Hickes discovered and printed in Manchester *Guardian* 2 July 1953

12 31 July 1702, Letter from Susanna to Bishop Hickes

13 Samuel's father quoted in Edwards, *Family Circle*, p. 100

14 Clarke, *Memoirs of the Wesley Family*, pp. 365–6

15 Letter to S. Wesley Jr, 11 March 1704, in Wallace, *Susanna Wesley*, pp. 47–8

16 John Kirk, *The Mother of the Wesleys*, Jarrold, London, 1868, p. 117

17 Emily Wesley to John Wesley, 31 December 1729, DDWF 6/2 John Rylands Library, University of Manchester

18 Stevenson, *Memorials of the Wesley Family*, pp. 95–6

19 Quoted in J. Newton, *Susanna Wesley and the Puritan Tradition in Methodism*, Epworth, London, 2002, p. 75–6

20 See Edwards, *Family Circle*, p. 47

21 Letter to Samuel quoted in Stevenson, *Memorials of the Wesley Family*, p. 101

22 Clarke, *Memoirs of the Wesley Family*, p. 262

23 Clarke, *Memoirs of the Wesley Family*, p. 265

24 Clarke, *Memoirs of the Wesley Family*, p. 264

25 No. 467 in *A Collection of Hymns for the Use of the People Called Methodists*, London, 1780.

26 'A Thought on the Manner of Educating Children 1783' in Thomas Jackson, *The Works of John Wesley*, Baker Book House, 1872 reprinted 1984, Vol. 13, p. 476

27 Clarke, *Memoirs of the Wesley Family*, p. 263

28 No. 468 in *A Collection of Hymns for the Use of the People Called Methodists*

29 *The Wesley Banner*, London, 1852, Vol. IV, p. 201

30 Quoted in Stevenson, *Memorials of the Wesley Family*, p. 282

31 G. V. Bennett, 'Conflict in the Church', in G. Holmes, *Britain After the Glorious Revolution*, London, 1969, p. 170

32 Stevenson, *Memorials of the Wesley Family*, p. 263

33 Letter to S. Wesley, 6 February 1712, in Wallace, *Susanna Wesley*, pp. 79–81

34 H. Wesley quoted in Clarke, *Memoirs of the Wesley Family*, p. 507

35 See 'Lessons for Children 1746' and 'Instructions for Children 1747', in Jackson, *The Works of John Wesley*, Vol. 14, pp. 217 and 218

36 Quoted in Eliza Clarke, *Susanna Wesley*, London, 1876, p. 28

37 Quoted in J. Telford, *Life of John Wesley*, Wesleyan Methodist Bookroom, London, 1899, p. 21

38 Clarke, *Memoirs of the Wesley Family*, p. 266

39 Letter to Sukey in Headingly Manuscripts, Vol. C, f. 59, Wesley College, Bristol

40 Quoted F. L. Wiseman, *Charles Wesley: Evangelist and Poet*, London, 1933, p. 226

41 Clarke, *Memoirs of the Wesley Family*, p. 176

42 Clarke, *Memoirs of the Wesley Family*, p. 197

43 Written to his brother John in 1738. See Edwards, *Family Circle*, p. 108

44 Quoted in Edwards, *Family Circle*, p. 122

45 Clarke, *Memoirs of the Wesley Family*, p. 374

46 Clarke, *Memoirs of the Wesley Family*, pp. 455–6

47 Edwards, *Family Circle*, p. 127–8

48 William Cowper. See G. M. Best, *Continuity and Change: History of Kingswood School*, Kingswood, 1998, pp. 20–1

49 *Journal of Revd Charles Wesley* (ed. Thomas Jackson), John Mason, London, 1849, Vol. II, p. 434

50 See Hymn XLVIII in *Hymns for Children 1763*, in Osborn, *The Poetical Works*, Vol. VI, p. 417

51 Clarke, *Memoirs of the Wesley Family*, pp. 457–8

52 Clarke, *Memoirs of the Wesley Family*, p. 435

53 *Unpublished Poetry of Charles Wesley* (ed. S. T. Kimbrough), Kingswood, 1998, Vol. II, p. 183

54 Henry Moore quoted in John Simon, *John Wesley and the Religious Societies*, Epworth, London, 1921, p. 85

Chapter 2

1 S. T. Kimbrough, *Songs for the Poor: Hymns by Charles Wesley*, New York, 1993, No 1

2 Quoted in M. Edwards, *Family Circle*, Epworth, London, 1949, p. 175

3 See A. Dallimore, *A Heart Set Free*, Evangelical Press, London, 1988, p. 176

4 Letter to John Wesley, 7 March 1725, Methodist Archives John Rylands Library, University of Manchester

5 Quoted in A. Quiller-Couch, *Hetty Wesley*, Arrowsmith, London, 1908

6 John Gambold quoted in Dallimore, *A Heart Set Free*, p. 31

7 L. Tyerman, *The Life and Times of John Wesley*, Hodder & Stoughton, London, 1878, Vol. 1, p. 57

8 G. Stevenson, *Memorials of the Wesley Family*, Partridge & Co, London, 1876, p. 303

9 Letter to J. Wesley, 12 October 1726, in Charles Wallace, *Susanna Wesley: Complete Writings*, Oxford University Press, 1997, p. 125

10 A phrase coined by Henry Rack in *Reasonable Enthusiast*, Epworth, London, 1989

11 Letter to John Wesley, 7 April 1725, in Tyerman, *The Life and Times of John Wesley*, Vol. 1, p. 33

12 6 December 1726, to Samuel Wesley, in F. Gill, *Selected Letters of John Wesley*, Epworth, London, 1956, pp. 8–9

13 Letter is in Stevenson, *Memorials of the Wesley Family*, p. 304

14 Quoted in A. Quiller-Couch, *Hetty Wesley*, pp. 215–16

15 Quoted in Tyerman, *The Life and Times of John Wesley*, Vol. 1, p. 36

16 Revd John Reynolds, 'Anecdotes of Wesley' in Tyerman, *The Life and Times of John Wesley*, Vol. 1, pp. 24–5

17 Charles Wesley to Dr Chandler in Methodist Archives and Research Centre, John Rylanda University Library of Manchester DDCW 1/38

18 In letter to his brother Samuel in Tyerman, *The Life and Times of John Wesley*, Vol. 1, p. 46

19 Quoted in V. H. H. Green, *The Young Mr Wesley*, Arnold, London, 1961, p. 145

20 Frank Baker, *Charles Wesley as Revealed by His Letters*, Epworth, London, 1948, p. 12

21 Baker, *Charles Wesley as Revealed by His Letters*, p. 9

22 Commemorative Hymn in *Journal of the Revd Charles Wesley* (ed. Thomas Jackson), John Mason, London, 1849, Vol. II, p. 434

23 Quoted in Green, *The Young Mr Wesley*, p. 138

24 Baker, *Charles Wesley as Revealed by His Letters*, pp. 11–12

25 Thomas Jackson, *Memoirs of the Revd Charles Wesley*, John Mason, London, 1862, Vol. 1, pp. 7–8

26 Commemorative Hymn in *Journal of the Revd Charles Wesley*, Vol. 2, p. 432

27 Commemorative Hymn in *Journal of the Revd Charles Wesley*, Vol. 2, p. 434

28 Baker, *Charles Wesley as Revealed by His Letters*, p. 11

29 Quoted in Green, *The Young Mr Wesley*, p. 151

30 5 May 1729, in Baker, *Charles Wesley as Revealed by His Letters*, p. 15

31 December 1728 at a meeting of the Vice-Chancellor, Heads of Houses, and Proctors of Oxford University in Statutes III.2

32 Quoted in Baker, *Charles Wesley as Revealed by His Letters*, p. 15

33 Quoted in Baker, *Charles Wesley as Revealed by His Letters*, p. 15–16

34 Quoted in Baker, *Charles Wesley as Revealed by His Letters*, p. 16

35 Diary 3 July and 13 August 1726, in Rack, *Reasonable Enthusiast*, p. 79

36 Jackson, *Memoirs of the Revd Charles Wesley*, Vol. 1, pp. 12–13

37 Quoted in Jackson, *The Life of Revd Charles Wesley*, Vol. I, p. 19

38 Quoted in Anthony Armstrong, *The Church of England, the Methodists and Society 1700–1850*, University of London Press, 1973, pp. 51–2

39 Richard Heitzenrater, *Mirror and Memory: Reflections on Early Methodist History*, Kingswood, 1989, p. 38

40 See Eric Baker, *A Herald of the Evangelical Revival*, Epworth, London, 1948, p. 72

41 Quoted in M. R. Brailsford, *A Tale of Two Brothers*, Rupert Hart-Davis, London, 1954, p. 67

42 Quoted in Green, *The Young Mr Wesley*, p. 11

43 J. Richardson, *The Works of Revd William Law*, London, 1762, Vol. IX, p. 65

44 *Journal of Revd Charles Wesley*, Vol. II, p. 463

45 Letter dated 28 Sept 1730 in Samuel Rogal, *A Biographical Dictionary of 18th Century Methodism*, Edwin Mellen Press, 1999, Vol. IX, p. 225

46 F. Baker, *Letters of John Wesley*, Oxford University Press, 1980–1, p. 339

47 *Methodist Magazine* 1798, reprinted in R. Heitzenrater, *The Elusive Mr Wesley*, Abingdon Press, 2003, pp. 234–41

48 1 December 1730, contained in Edwards, *Family Circle*, 1949, pp. 34–5

49 *Methodist Magazine* 1798, reprinted in Heitzenrater, *The Elusive Mr Wesley*, pp. 234–41

50 Sermon CVII 'On God's Vineyard' in *The Works of John Wesley*, Vol. 7, p. 203

51 R. Heitzenrater, *Diary of an Oxford Methodist: Benjamin Ingham 1733–41*, Duke University Press, 1985, p. 149

52 William Morgan's father quoted in Green, *The Young Mr Wesley*, p. 168

53 Quoted in T. R. Jeffrey, *John Wesley's Religious Quest*, Vantage Press, 1960, p. 111

54 John Telford, *The Letters of John Wesley*, Epworth, London, 1931, Vol. I, p. 176

55 See Jeffery, *John Wesley's Religious Quest*, pp. 110ff.

56 Quoted in J. F. Hurst, *History of Methodism*, Eaton & Mains, 1902, Vol. 1, p. 187

57 Quoted in Jeffery, *John Wesley's Religious Quest*, p. 136

58 Quoted in Frederick Gill, *Charles Wesley the First Methodist*, Lutterworth, 1964, pp. 20–1

59 Quoted in Stevenson, *Memorials of the Wesley Family*, p. 291

60 Quoted in Baker, *Charles Wesley as Revealed by His Letters*, p. 18

61 Sermon on 'The One Thing Needful' in Albert Outler, *The Works of John Wesley* (Sermons 133–51), Abingdon, 1984

62 Hymn on Jeremiah 32:39 in Osborn, *Poetical Works*, Vol. X, p. 43

63 Hymn XXVIII in *Hymns on the Lord's Supper*, 1745

64 Hymn LXXXVI, Hymn LIV, Hymn LVII and Hymn LIII in *Hymns on the Lord's Supper*, 1745

65 Phillips and Kersey, *The New World of Words*, London, 1706

66 Contained in full in Heitzenrater, *The Elusive Mr Wesley*, pp. 226–9

67 Susanna to John Wesley, 25 October 1732, in Clarke, *Memoirs of the Wesley Family*, p. 338–9

68 See Telford, *The Letters of Revd John Wesley*, Vol. I, p. 153

69 Telford, *The Letters of Revd John Wesley*, Vol. I, p. 143

70 Quoted in Green, *The Young Mr Wesley*, pp. 198–9.

71 Sermon on Phillippians 3:13–14 in Kenneth Newport, *The Sermons of Charles Wesley*, Oxford University Press, 2001, pp. 95–6

72 Quoted at length in Heitzenrater, *The Elusive Mr Wesley*, pp. 230–2

73 *Journals and Diaries* 1 (ed. Ward and Heitzenrater), Abingdon Press, 1988, p. 134

74 Quoted in Green, *The Young Mr Wesley*, p. 176

75 Heitzenrater, *Diary of an Oxford Methodist*, p. 109

76 Heitzenrater, *Diary of an Oxford Methodist*, p. 106

77 Heitzenrater, *Diary of an Oxford Methodist*, p. 166

78 Quoted in Green, *The Young Mr Wesley*, p. 189

79 'A Short Account of God's Dealings with the Revd George Whitefield from his Infancy to the time of his Entering Holy Orders' in L. Tyerman, *The Life of George Whitefield*, Hodder & Stoughton, 1876, Vol. I, p. 4

80 'A Short Account', Vol. I, p. 16

81 'A Short Account', Vol. I, pp. 16–17

82 'A Short Account', Vol. I, pp. 17–18

83 'A Short Account', Vol. I, pp. 18–19

84 'A Short Account', Vol. I, pp. 20–3

85 Quoted in Jackson, *Life of Revd Charles Wesley*, Vol. 1, p. 25

86 'An Elegy on the Late Revd George Whitefield' in *Journal of Revd Charles Wesley*, Vol. 2, p. 419

87 Rack, *Reasonable Enthusiast*, p. 95

88 Quoted in Edwards, *Family Circle*, p. 142

89 Letter to Samuel Wesley Snr, 10 December 1734, in Tyerman, *The Life and Times of John Wesley*, Vol. 1, p. 97

90 Quoted in Rack, *Reasonable Enthusiast*, p. 94

91 Heitzenrater, *Diary of an Oxford Methodist*, p. 256

92 Baker, *Charles Wesley as Revealed by His Letters*, p. 19

93 Clarke, *Memoirs of the Wesley Family*, p. 218–19

94 Clarke, *Memoirs of the Wesley Family*, p. 220

95 Clarke, *Memoirs of the Wesley Family*, pp. 222–8

96 Tyerman, *The Life and Times of John Wesley*, Vol. 1, p. 68

97 Quoted in Tyerman, *The Life and Times of John Wesley*, Vol. 1, p. 43

Chapter 3

1 C. Wesley, No 88 in *A Collection of Hymns for the Use of the People Called Methodists*, London, 1780

2 Quoted in Thomas Jackson's introduction to *Journal of the Revd Charles Wesley*, John Mason, London, 1849, Vol. 1, pp. xi–xv

3 Oglethorpe quoted in Jackson's introduction to *Journal of the Revd Charles Wesley*, Vol. 1, p. xxx

4 Quoted in L. Tyerman, *The Life and Times of John Wesley*, Hodder & Stoughton, London, 1878, Vol. 1, p. 109

5 John Telford, *Letters of John Wesley*, Epworth, London, 1931, Vol. 1, p. 188

6 Telford, *Letters of John Wesley*, Vol. 1, p. 188

7 C. Wesley to Dr Chandler DDCW 1/38, Methodist Archives, John Rylands Library, University of Manchester

8 Quoted in J. H. Overton, *John Wesley*, London, 1905, p. 45

9 See M. Edwards, *Family Circle*, Epworth, London, 1949, pp. 138–9

10 Letter to Charles, 21 September 1736, in Adam Clarke, *Memoirs of the Wesley Family*, London, 1823, p. 392

11 Charles Wesley to Dr Chandler in DDCW 1/38, Methodist Archives

12 Quoted in M. Brailsford, *A Tale of Two Brothers*, Oxford University Press, 1954, p. 85

13 Quoted in Tyerman, *Life and Times of John Wesley*, Vol. 1, p. 118

14 Letter 10 October 1735, in Tyerman, *Life and Times of John Wesley*, Vol. 1, p. 116

15 Quoted in Frederick Gill, *Charles Wesley the First Methodist*, Lutterworth, 1964, pp. 49–50

16 Sermon on 1 Kings 18:21 in Kenneth Newport, *The Sermons of Charles Wesley*, Oxford University Press, 2001, pp. 107–22

17 Tyerman, *Life and Times of John Wesley*, Vol. 1, p. 122

18 Frank Baker, *Charles Wesley as Revealed by His Letters*, Epworth, London, 1948, p. 21

19 Letter to Sally, 5 February 1736, in John Tyson, *Charles Wesley: A Reader*, Oxford University Press, 1988, p. 61–3

20 Letter to Sally, 5 February 1736, in Tyson, *Charles Wesley: A Reader*, p. 62

21 Written by Isaac Watts and quoted in Ralph Waller, *John Wesley*, SPCK, London, 2003, p. 34

22 Letter to mother, in Tyerman, *Life and Times of John Wesley*, Vol. 1, pp. 121–2

23 Sermon on Philippians 3:13–14 in Newport, *The Sermons of Charles Wesley*, pp. 95–106

24 Letter, 14 February 1736, in Tyson, *Charles Wesley: A Reader*, pp. 63–4

25 5 February 1736, Letter to Varanese, in Baker, *Charles Wesley as Revealed by His Letters*, p. 22

26 7 March 1736, in Jackson, *Works of John Wesley*, Vol. 1, p. 28

27 Mr Van Reck to John Wesley, June/July 1737, Autograph letter, Rylands Library, University of Manchester

28 Letter to Mrs Oglethorpe in Baker, *Charles Wesley as Revealed by His Letters*, p. 25.

29 9 March 1736, in Jackson, *Journal of Revd Charles Wesley*, Vol. 1, p. 1

30 *Journal of Revd Charles Wesley*, Vol. 1, p. 4

31 21 March 1736, *Journal of Revd Charles Wesley*, Vol. 1, p. 5

32 T. C. Mitchell, *Charles Wesley, Man with the Dancing Heart*, Beacon Hill Press, 1994, p. 52

33 21 March 1736, *Journal of Revd Charles Wesley*, Vol. 1, pp. 4–5

34 25 March 1736, *Journal of Revd Charles Wesley*, Vol. 1, p. 8

35 26 March 1736, *Journal of Revd Charles Wesley*, Vol. 1, p. 11

36 26 March 1736, *Journal of Revd Charles Wesley*, Vol. 1, p. 12

37 29 March 1736, *Journal of Revd Charles Wesley*, Vol. 1, p. 14

38 28 March 1736, *Journal of Revd Charles Wesley*, Vol. 1, p. 14

39 30 March 1736, *Journal of Revd Charles Wesley*, Vol. 1, p. 15

40 31 March 1736, *Journal of Revd Charles Wesley*, Vol. 1, p. 15

41 Sermon on Psalm 126:7 in Newport, *The Sermons of Charles Wesley*, pp. 125–9

42 Clarke, *Memoirs of the Wesley Family*, pp. 391–2

43 24 April 1736, *Journal of Revd Charles Wesley*, Vol. 1, pp. 19–20

44 24 April 1736, *Journal of Revd Charles Wesley*, Vol. 1, pp. 20–1

45 3 May 1736, *Journal of Revd Charles Wesley*, Vol. 1, p. 22

46 25 April 1736, *Journal of Revd Charles Wesley*, Vol. 1, p. 20

47 Phinizy Spalding, *Oglethorpe in America*, University of Georgia Press, 1984, pp. 454–6

48 2 December 1737, in Jackson, *Works of John Wesley*, Vol. 1, pp. 66–8

49 25 July 1736, *Journal of Revd Charles Wesley*, Vol. 1, p. 35

50 Quoted in Tyerman, *The Life and Times of John Wesley*, Vol. 1, p. 130

51 25 May 1736, *Journal of Revd Charles Wesley*, Vol. 1, p. 27

52 12 May 1736, *Journal of Revd Charles Wesley*, Vol. 1, p. 27

53 2 August 1736, *Journal of Charles Wesley*, Vol. 1, pp. 36–7

54 G. Osborn, *Poetical Works of J. and C. Wesley*, Vol. VII, pp. 168–9

55 Osborn, *Poetical Works of J. and C. Wesley*, Vol. VII, pp. 159–60

56 11 August 1736, *Journal of Revd Charles Wesley*, Vol. 1, p. 37

57 27 August 1736, *Journal of Revd Charles Wesley*, Vol. 1, p. 38

58 27 August 1736, *Journal of Revd Charles Wesley*, Vol. 1, pp. 38–40

59 4 September 1736, *Journal of Revd Charles Wesley*, Vol. 1, p. 41

60 24 September 1736, *Journal of Revd Charles Wesley*, Vol. 1, p. 44

61 2 October 1736, *Journal of Revd Charles Wesley*, Vol. 1, p. 46

62 Baker, *Charles Wesley as Revealed by His Letters*, p. 27

63 22 October 1736, *Journal of Revd Charles Wesley*, Vol. 1, p. 47

64 28 October 1736, *Journal of Revd Charles Wesley*, Vol. 1, p. 49

65 F. L. Wiseman, *Charles Wesley*, Epworth, London, 1933, pp. 33–4

66 9 November 1736, *Journal of Revd Charles Wesley*, Vol. 1, p. 51

67 3 December 1736, *Journal of Revd Charles Wesley*, Vol. 1, p. 55

68 5 December 1736, *Journal of Revd Charles Wesley*, Vol. 1, p. 56

69 Quoted in Mark Noll, *The Rise of Evangelicanism*, IVP, 2004, p. 79

70 *Journal of Revd Charles Wesley*, Vol. 1, p. 59

71 22 January 1737, *Journal of Revd Charles Wesley*, Vol. 1, p. 66

72 Quoted in Wiseman, *Charles Wesley*, pp. 38–9

73 Quoted in Jackson, *Life of Revd Charles Wesley*, Vol. 1, p. 108

74 'A Short Account of God's Dealings with the Revd George Whitefield from his Infancy to the Time of his Entering Holy Orders' in L. Tyerman, *The Life of Revd George Whitefield*, Hodder & Stoughton, London, 1876, Vol. I, p. 25

75 'Sermon on the Good Shepherd' in G. Whitefield, *Sermons on Important Subjects*, Baynes, London, 1825, p. 733

76 *Works of Revd George Whitefield*, Dilly, London, 1771, Vol. 1, pp. 18–19

77 A. Dallimore, *George Whitefield*, The Wakeman Trust, 1990, p. 27.

78 This was the nickname shouted out at Whitefield when he first arrived in London

79 Baker, *Charles Wesley as Revealed by His Letters*, p. 29

80 28 October 1737, *Journal of Revd Charles Wesley*, Vol. 1, p. 78

81 16 September 1737, *Journal of Revd Charles Wesley*, Vol. 1, p. 75

82 24 September 1737, *Journal of Revd Charles Wesley*, Vol. 1, p. 76

83 *George Whitefield's Journals*, Banner of Truth Trust, 1960, pp. 84–5

84 5 November 1737, *Journal of Revd Charles Wesley*, Vol. 1, p. 75

85 *Memoirs of the Life and Writings of Benjamin Franklin*, Yale University Press, 1959, Vol. 1, p. 87

86 'Sermon on Luke 9:23' in Whitefield, *Sermons on Important Subjects*

87 *George Whitefield's Journals*, pp. 89–90

88 V. H. H. Green, *The Young Mr Wesley*, Oxford University Press, 1961, p. 266

89 Letter to John Wesley, 19 October 1737, in Tyerman, *Life and Times of John Wesley*, Vol. 1, pp. 137–8

90 26 November 1737, quoted in Thomas Reed Jeffery, *John Wesley's Religious Quest*, Vantage Press, 1960, pp. 335–6

91 Letter to Ingham, 22 October 1737, in Jackson, *Life of Revd Charles Wesley*, Vol. I, p. 104

92 *Works of George Whitefield*, Vol. 1, p. 33

93 Tyerman, *Life of Revd George Whitefield*, Vol. I, p. 115

94 Noll, *The Rise of Evangelicanism*, p. 85

Chapter 4

1 *Methodist Hymns and Psalms*, 1983, No 216

2 Kenneth Newport, *The Sermons of Charles Wesley*, 2001, Oxford University Press, p. 364

3 Newport, *Sermons of Charles Wesley*, pp. 364–5

4 Newport, *Sermons of Charles Wesley*, p. 366

5 Letter to William Wogan, 28 March 1738, in L. Tyerman, *The Life and Times of John Wesley*, Hodder & Stoughton, London, 1878, reprinted 1984, Vol. 1, p. 138

6 Letter to Mrs Chapman, 29 March 1738, in Tyerman, *The Life and Times of John Wesley*, Vol. 1, pp. 138–9

7 Henry Rack, *Reasonable Enthusiast*, Epworth, London, 1989, p. 127

8 John Wesley, *Journal* (ed. E. Jay), Oxford University Press, 1987, Appendix B, p. 261

9 8 February 1737, *Journal*, Appendix B, p. 259

10 27 February 1737, *Journal*, p. 262

11 9 March 1737, *Journal*, Appendix B, pp. 263–4

12 2 December 1737, Thomas Jackson, *Works of John Wesley*, Baker Book House, 1872 reprinted 1984, Vol. 1, p. 61

13 29 January 1738, *Works of John Wesley*, Vol. 1, pp. 75–6

14 29 January 1738, *Works of John Wesley*, Vol. 1, pp. 75–6

15 'Sermon on 1 John 3:14' in Newport, *Sermons of Charles Wesley*, pp. 138–9

16 22 February 1737, in T. Jackson, *Life of Revd Charles Wesley*, John Mason, London, 1841, Vol. 1, p. 119

17 *Methodist Magazine*, London, 1854, p. 687

18 24 February 1738, Thomas Jackson, *Journal of the Revd Charles Wesley*, John Mason, London, 1849, Vol. 1, p. 82

19 24 February 1738, *Journal of Revd Charles Wesley*, Vol. 1, p. 82

20 *Methodist Magazine*, London, 1854, p. 687

21 Quoted in Thomas Jackson, *Memoirs of Revd Charles Wesley*, London, 1862, p. 57

22 28 February 1738, *Journal of Revd Charles Wesley*, Vol. 1, p. 84

23 Quoted in Thomas Reed Jeffrey, *John Wesley's Religious Quest*, Vantage Press, 1960, pp. 344–5

24 Quoted in Jeffrey, *John Wesley's Religious Quest*, pp. 344–5

25 Quoted in Jeffrey, *John Wesley's Religious Quest*, p. 348

26 Quoted in Jeffrey, *John Wesley's Religious Quest*, pp. 349–50

27 4 March 1738, *Works of John Wesley*, Vol. 1, p. 86

28 27 March 1738, *Works of John Wesley*, Vol. 1, p. 90

29 1 April 1738, *Works of John Wesley*, Vol. 1, p. 90

30 Quoted in Roy Hattersley, *A Brand from the Burning*, Little, Brown, 2002, p. 133

31 25 April 1738, *Journal of Revd Charles Wesley*, Vol. 1, p. 82

32 22 April 1738, *Works of John Wesley*, Vol. 1, p. 91

33 23 April 1738, *Works of John Wesley*, Vol. 1, p. 91

34 28 April 1738, *Journal of Revd Charles Wesley*, Vol. 1, p. 85

35 3 May 1738, *Works of John Wesley* Vol. 1, p. 93

36 Quoted in F. L. Wiseman, *Charles Wesley*, Epworth, London, 1933, pp. 43–4

37 Daniel Benham, *Memoirs of James Hutton*, London, no date, pp. 27–8

38 1–6 May 1738, *Journal of Revd Charles Wesley*, Vol. 1, pp. 85–6

39 This is Charles' description of John Bray, 11 May 1738, *Journal of Revd Charles Wesley*, Vol. 1, p. 86

40 11 May 1738, *Journal of Revd Charles Wesley*, Vol. 1, p. 86

41 11 May 1738, *Journal of Revd Charles Wesley*, Vol. 1, p. 86

42 Quoted in Wiseman, *Charles Wesley*, p. 47

43 17 May 1738, *Journal of Revd Charles Wesley*, Vol. 1, p. 88

44 William Holland, *A Narrative of the Work of the Lord in England*, manuscript in Moravian Church Library

45 17 May 1738, *Journal of Revd Charles Wesley*, Vol. 1, p. 88

46 19 May 1738, *Journal of Revd Charles Wesley*, Vol. 1, p. 89

47 20 May 1738, *Journal of Revd Charles Wesley*, Vol. 1, p. 90

48 21 May 1738, *Journal of Revd Charles Wesley*, Vol. 1, pp. 90f

49 21 May 1738, *Journal of Revd Charles Wesley*, Vol. 1, p. 91

50 *Journal of Revd Charles Wesley*, Vol. 1, pp. 92f

51 21 May 1738, *Works of John Wesley*, Vol. 1, pp. 96–7

52 22 May 1738, *Journal of Revd Charles Wesley*, Vol. 1, p. 94

53 23 May 1738, *Journal of Revd Charles Wesley*, Vol. 1, p. 94

54 24 May 1738, *Journal of Revd Charles Wesley*, Vol. 1, pp. 94–5

55 24 May 1738, *Works of John Wesley*, Vol. 1, p. 103

56 24 May 1738, *Journal of Revd Charles Wesley*, Vol. 1, p. 95

57 G. C. Cell, *The Rediscovery of John Wesley*, New York, 1935, p. 28

58 Hymns and Sacred Poems 1739, reprinted in John Tyson, *Charles Wesley: A Reader*, Oxford University Press, 2000, pp. 105–6

59 Letter to Charles, 6 December 1738, in Charles Wallace, *Susanna Wesley: Complete Writings*, pp. 175–7

60 Charles to his wife, Whitsunday 1760, in *Charles Wesley: A Reader*, p. 110

61 Quoted in Wiseman, *Charles Wesley*, pp. 162–3

62 14 October 1738, *Works of John Wesley*, Vol. 1, p. 162

63 4 January 1739, *Works of John Wesley*, Vol. 1, pp. 170–1

64 *Methodist Service Book*

65 6 June 1738, in R. Heitzenrater, *The Elusive Mr Wesley*, Abingdon Press, 2003, pp. 261–3

66 For full text, see Edward Sugden, *Wesley's Standard Sermons*, Epworth, London, 1921, pp. 35–52

67 George J. Stevenson, *Memorials of the Wesley Family*, Partridge & Co, London, 1876, pp. 273–4

68 Letter to Charles, 7 July 1738, in Jackson, *Life of Revd Charles Wesley*, Vol. 1, p. 160

69 Quoted in Heitzenrater, *The Elusive Mr Wesley*, p. 264

70 24 May 1738, *Memoirs of Revd Charles Wesley*, Vol. 1, p. 95

71 26 May 1738, *Memoirs of Revd Charles Wesley*, Vol. 1, p. 96

72 6 June 1738, *Memoirs of Revd Charles Wesley*, Vol. 1, p. 100

73 9 June 1738, *Memoirs of Revd Charles Wesley*, Vol. 1, p. 102

74 Tyson, in *Charles Wesley: A Reader*, p. 112

75 24 June 1738, *Journal of Revd Charles Wesley*, Vol. 1, p. 108

76 11 July 1738, *Journal of Revd Charles Wesley*, Vol. 1, pp. 118–19

77 21 June 1738, *Journal of Revd Charles Wesley*, Vol. 1, p. 108

78 11 June 1738, *Journal of Revd Charles Wesley*, Vol. 1, p. 105

79 4 September 1738, *Journal of Revd Charles Wesley*, Vol. 1, p. 129

80 2 July 1738, *Memoirs of Revd Charles Wesley*, Vol. 1, p. 115

81 27 July 1738, *Memoirs of Revd Charles Wesley*, Vol. 1, p. 125

82 27 June 1738, *Journal of Revd Charles Wesley*, Vol. 1, pp. 111–12

83 'Sermon on 1 John 3:14' in Newport, *Sermons of Charles Wesley*, pp. 133–52

84 21 August 1738, *Journal of Revd Charles Wesley*, Vol. 1, p. 128

85 'Sermon on Titus 3:8' in Newport, *The Sermons of Charles Wesley*, pp. 154–66

86 Quoted in Peter Linebaugh, *The London Hanged*, Verso, 2003, p. 28

87 12 July 1738, *Journal of Revd Charles Wesley*, Vol. 1, p. 120

88 18 July 1738, *Memoirs of Revd Charles Wesley*, Vol. 1, p. 122

89 19 July 1738, *Journal of Revd Charles Wesley*, Vol. 1, pp. 122–3

90 No 193, *Hymns and Psalms*, Methodist Publishing House, 1983

91 David Hempton, *Methodism: Empire of the Spirit*, Yale University Press, New Haven and London, 2005, p. 14

92 17 September 1738, *Journal of Revd Charles Wesley*, Vol. 1, p. 130

93 See Introduction to Tyson, *Charles Wesley: A Reader*, pp. 13–20

94 Quoted in A. Dallimore, *George Whitefield*, The Wakefield Trust, 1970, Vol. 1, pp. 195–6

95 Quoted in R. Heitzenrater, *Wesley and the People Called Methodists*, Abingdon Press, 1995, p. 120

96 Letter to Charles, 19 October 1738, in Wallace, *Susanna Wesley: Complete Writings*, pp. 174–5

97 8 November 1738, *Works of John Wesley*, Vol. 1, p. 163

98 7 November 1738, *Memoirs of Revd Charles Wesley*, Vol. 1, p. 134

99 8 November 1738, *Journal of Revd Charles Wesley*, Vol. 1, p. 134

100 12 November 1738, *Journal of Revd Charles Wesley*, Vol. 1, p. 135

101 14 November 1738, *Journal of Revd Charles Wesley*, Vol. 1, p. 135

102 *George Whitefield's Journals*, Banner of Truth Trust, 1960, p. 179

103 *George Whitefield's Journals*, p. 193

104 26 December 1738, *Journal of Revd Charles Wesley*, Vol. 1, p. 139

105 1 January 1739, *Works of John Wesley*, Vol. 1, p. 170

106 16 April 1739, in J. Priestley, *Original Letters by Revd John Wesley and His Friends*, Birmingham, 1791, p. 114

107 Letter of Samuel dated 4 January 1739, in Tyerman, *The Life and Times of John Wesley*, Vol. I, p. 190

108 'For the Anniversary Day of One's Conversion', reprinted in Tyson, *Charles Wesley: A Reader*, p. 108

109 Quoted in Jeffrey, *John Wesley's Religious Quest*, p. 345

110 No 744 in *Methodist Hymns and Psalms*

111 5 January 1739, *Journal of Revd Charles Wesley*, Vol. 1, p. 139

112 4 February 1739, *Journal of Revd Charles Wesley*, Vol. 1, p. 141

113 Quoted in A. C. H. Seymour, *The Life and Times of the Countess of Huntingdon*, London, 1840, Vol. I, p. 196

Chapter 5

1 *Charles Wesley*'s 'Hymn for a Preacher'

2 10 February 1739, 'Weekly Miscellany in L. Tyerman, *The Life of Revd George Whitefield*, Hodder & Stoughton, London, 1876, Vol. I, pp. 174–5

3 Thomas Oliver, quoted in D. Bruce Hindmarsh, *The Evangelical Conversion Narrative*, Oxford University Press, 2005, p. 136

4 See L. Tyerman, *The Life and Times of Revd John Wesley*, Hodder & Stoughton, London, 1878, Vol. 1, pp. 248–9

5 *George Whitefield's Journals*, Banner of Truth Trust, 1960, pp. 203–4

6 *George Whitefield's Journals*, p. 213

7 S. T. Kimbrough and O. A. Beckerlegge, *The Unpublished Poetry of Charles Wesley*, 1990, Vol. II, p. 183

8 8 March 1739, in Tyerman, *Life of Revd George Whitefield*, Vol. I, p. 176

9 13 February 1739, *Journal of Revd Charles Wesley* (ed. Thomas Jackson), John Mason, London, 1849, Vol. 1, p. 142

10 21 February 1739, *Journal of Revd Charles Wesley*, Vol. 1, p. 143

11 21 February 1739, *Journal of Revd Charles Wesley*, Vol. 1, pp. 143–4

12 H. J. Hughes, *Life of Howell Harris*, Nisbet, 1892, p. 12

13 Quoted in Arnold Dallimore, *George Whitefield*, Banner of Truth Trust, 1970, Vol. 1, p. 240

14 Quoted in R. Bennett, *The Early Life of Howell Harris*, Banner of Truth Trust, 1962, p. 48

15 Quoted in John Gillies, *Memoirs of the Life of Revd George Whitefield*, London, 1772, pp. 37–8

16 Quoted in Tyerman, *Life of Revd George Whitefield*, Vol. I, p. 180

17 24 February 1739, in Tyerman, *Life of Revd George Whitefield*, Vol. I, p. 182

18 6 March 1739, Letter from William Seward, in Tyerman, *Life of Revd George Whitefield*, Vol. I, p. 187

19 Mrs Edwards, quoted in Townsend, Workman and Eayrs, *A New History of Methodism*, Hodder & Stoughton, London, 1899, Vol. 1, p. 274

20 'Brief Account of the Life of Howell Harris', quoted in A. Skevington Wood, *The Inextinguishable Blaze*, Paternoster Press, 1960, pp. 31–2

21 H. Rack, *Reasonable Enthusiast*, Epworth, London, 1989, p. 190

22 Quoted in Dallimore, *George Whitefield*, p. 274

23 2 April 1739, *Works of John Wesley*, Vol. 1, p. 185

24 *Works of John Wesley*, Vol. 1, p. 185

25 11 June 1739, *Works of John Wesley*, Vol. 1, p. 201. It is believed the letter dates back to earlier in the year

26 'The Character of a Methodist' in *Works of John Wesley*, Vol. 8, pp. 340–7

27 See Tyerman, *Life of Revd George Whitefield*, Vol. I, pp. 208–10

28 4 June 1739, *Journal of Revd Charles Wesley*, Vol. 1, p. 151

29 See Tyerman, *The Life of Revd George Whitefield*, Vol. I, p. 230

30 25 April 1739, *Journal of Revd Charles Wesley*, Vol. 1, p. 148

31 19 June 1739, *Journal of Revd Charles Wesley*, Vol. 1, p. 154

32 7 June 1739, *Journal of Revd Charles Wesley*, Vol. 1, p. 152

33 7 June 1739, *Journal of Revd Charles Wesley*, Vol. 1, p. 152

34 12 June 1739, *Journal of Revd Charles Wesley*, Vol. 1, p. 153

35 Letter to the Fetter Lane Society dated 12 June 1739, in *Works of George Whitefield*, London and Edinburgh, 1771, Vol. 1, pp. 50–1

36 12 June 1739, *Journal of Revd Charles Wesley*, Vol. 1, p. 153

37 15 June 1739, *Works of John Wesley*, Vol. 1, p. 204

38 May 1740, Letters from Sarah Barber and Sarah Middleton to Charles Wesley, in *Early Methodist Volume* (chiefly letters to Charles Wesley 1738–88), John Rylands Library, University of Manchester

39 23 June 1739, *Journal of Revd Charles Wesley*, Vol. 1, p. 155

40 *Journal of Revd Charles Wesley*, Vol. 1, p. 155

41 'Sermon on Romans 3:23–25', in Newport, *The Sermons of Charles Wesley*, pp. 204–29

42 2 July 1739, *Journal of Revd Charles Wesley*, Vol. 1, p. 156

43 Maldwyn Edwards, *Family Circle*, Epworth, London, 1949, pp. 79–80

44 19 May 1740, in *Early Methodist Volume*

45 19 May 1740, in *Early Methodist Volume*

46 James Hutton, *Memoirs*, p. 42

47 John Whitehead, *Life of the Revd John Wesley*, London, 1793–6, Vol. 1, pp. 292 and 370

48 5 August 1740, *Journal of Revd Charles Wesley*, Vol. 1, p. 247

49 25 October 1739, *Works of John Wesley*, Vol. 1, p. 236

50 Letter to J. Wesley, 25 June 1739, in Tyerman, *Life and Times of John Wesley*, Vol. 1, p. 258

51 Quoted in Tyerman, *Life and Times of John Wesley*, Vol. 1, p. 243

52 27 June 1739, Letter to Dr Blackwell, in Tyerman, *Life of Revd George Whitefield*, Vol. I, p. 255

53 Sermon, in Tyerman, *Life of Revd George Whitefield*, Vol. I, p. 300

54 *George Whitefield's Journals*, p. 85

55 Quoted in Rack, *Reasonable Enthusiast*, p. 209

56 *George Whitefield's Journals*, p. 289

57 10 August 1739, *Journal of Revd Charles Wesley*, Vol. 1, pp. 158–9

58 Letter to Seward, 13 August 1739, in Jackson, *Life of Revd Charles Wesley*, Vol. 1, p. 186

59 26 August 1739, in *Journal of Revd Charles Wesley*, Vol. 1, p. 165

60 31 August 1739, *Journal of Revd Charles Wesley*, Vol. 1, p. 167

61 Quoted in Jackson, *Life of Revd Charles Wesley*, Vol. 1, pp. 195–6

62 Quoted in G. Nuttall, Charles Wesley in 1739, in *Proceedings of the Wesley Historical Society*, 42/1980, p. 184

63 Quoted in Jackson, *Life of Revd Charles Wesley*, Vol. 1, pp. 196–7

64 5 September 1739, *Journal of Revd Charles Wesley*, Vol. 1, pp. 168–9

65 Letter written in 1740 in *Accounts of Religious Experience of Early Methodists in Letters to Charles Wesley c.1740–86* (a folio of MS letters in John Rylands Library, Manchester)

66 *Journal of Revd Charles Wesley*, Vol. 1, pp. 168f

67 John Wesley, *Sermons on Several Occasions*, 1746

68 May 1740, Sarah Barber to Charles, in *Early Methodist Volume*

69 16 September 1739, *Journal of Revd Charles Wesley*, Vol. 1, pp. 173–4

70 Charles Wesley to Sarah Wesley, 18 June 1763, *Early Methodist Volume*

71 28 September 1739, *Journal of Revd Charles Wesley*, Vol. 1, p. 182

72 Letter to Charles, 17 October 1739, in Jackson, *Life of Revd Charles Wesley*, Vol. 1, p. 198

73 20 October 1739, in J. Priestley, *Original Letters by Revd John Wesley and His Friends*, Pearson, Birmingham, 1791, pp. 110–11

74 Quoted in Heitzenrater, *Wesley and the People Called Methodists*, p. 110

75 Contemporary account in G. J. Stevenson, *City Road Chapel*, London, 1872, p. 15

76 27 November 1739, *Works of John Wesley*, Vol. 1, p. 251

77 21 November 1739, *Works of John Wesley*, Vol. 1, p. 250

78 Clarke, *Memoirs of the Wesley Family*, p. 465

79 Quoted in Townsend, Workman and Eayrs, *A New History of Methodism*, pp. 59–60

80 19 March 1740, *Journal of Revd Charles Wesley*, Vol. 1, p. 200

81 Letter in *Journal of Revd Charles Wesley*, Vol. 1, pp. 222–3

82 Kimbrough and Beckerlegge, *Unpublished Poetry of Charles Wesley*, Vol. I, p. 183

83 'The Weekly Miscellany', quoted in Tyerman, *Life and Times of John Wesley*, Vol. 1, p. 248

84 Quoted in Faith Cook, *Selina Countess of Huntingdon*, Banner of Truth Trust, 2001, p. 41.

85 2 January 1740, *Works of John Wesley*, Vol. 1, p. 259

86 23 April 1740, *Works of John Wesley*, Vol. 1, p. 269

87 9 April 1740, *Journal of Revd Charles Wesley*, Vol. 1, p. 213

88 5 April 1740, *Journal of Revd Charles Wesley*, Vol. 1, p. 207

89 25 April 1740, *Journal of Revd Charles Wesley*, Vol. 1, p. 223

90 22 April 1740, *Journal of Revd Charles Wesley*, Vol. 1, p. 221

91 8 April 1740, *Journal of Revd Charles Wesley*, Vol. 1, p. 212

92 Kimbrough and Beckerlegge, *Unpublished Poetry of Charles Wesley*, Vol. I, pp. 182–3

93 4 May 1740, in Tom Beynon, *Howell Harris' Visits to London*, Cambrian News Press, 1960, p. 28

94 8 May 1740, *Journal of Revd Charles Wesley*, Vol. 1, p. 227

95 Letter to the Church of God at Herrnhut, 8 August 1740, in *Works of John Wesley*, Vol. 1, pp. 326–31.

96 11 June 1740, *Journal of Revd Charles Wesley*, Vol. 1, p. 238

97 Letter to Count Zinzendorf, 14 March 1740, in Tyerman, *Life and Times of John Wesley*, Vol. 1, pp. 298–9

98 24 July 1738, in *Early Methodist Volume*

99 Memoir of Susannah Claggett in *Fetter Lane Memoirs 1760–1850* in Moravian Church House, London

100 22 June 1740, *Journal of Revd Charles Wesley*, Vol. 1, pp. 242–3

101 15 June 1741, *Works of John Wesley*, Vol. 1, pp. 315–16

102 D. M. Jones, *Charles Wesley*, Skeffington, London, 1920, p. 96

103 Letter to George Whitefield, 1 September 1740, in Tyerman, *Life and Times of John Wesley*, Vol. 1, pp. 310–11

104 Letter to James Hutton, 24 November 1740, in Tyerman, *Life and Times of John Wesley*, Vol. 1, p. 311

105 Lady Mary Wortly Montagu in Cook, *Selina Countess of Huntingdon*, p. 48

106 Luke Wiseman, *Charles Wesley*, Abingdon Press, 1932, p. 100

107 Quoted in Wiseman, *Charles Wesley*, p. 101

108 Quoted in Wiseman, *Charles Wesley*, p. 137

109 *Journal of Revd Charles Wesley*, Vol. 1, p. 286

110 Quoted in Wiseman, *Charles Wesley*, p. 79

111 Originally part of a sermon preached in Oxford in July 1739, in *Charles Wesley: A Reader*, pp. 138–55

112 Originally part of a sermon preached in Oxford in July 1739, in *Charles Wesley: A Reader*, pp. 138–55

113 E. Bristow to Charles, 12 April 1740, in *Accounts of Religious Experience of Early Methodists in Letters to Charles Wesley c.1740–86* (a folio of MS letters in John Rylands Library, Manchester)

114 M. Sones to Charles, 1 June 1740, in *Accounts of Religious Experience of Early Methodists in Letters*

Chapter 6

1 G. Osborn, 'The Poetical Works of J and C Wesley', *1870 Wesleyan Methodist Conference*, Vol. XI, pp. 374–5

2 Letter to John Wesley, 18 August 1725, in C. Wallace, *Susannah Wesley: Complete Writings*, Oxford University Press, 1997, pp. 112–13

3 Epistle to a Friend Written in the Year 1743

4 S. T. Kimbrough and O. A. Beckerlegge, *The Unpublished Poetry of Charles Wesley*, Kingswood, 1990, Vol. II, p. 201

5 Letter to John Wesley, 26 March 1740, in L. Tyerman, *Life and Times of John Wesley*, Hodder & Stoughton, London, 1878, Vol. 1, pp. 313–14

6 Letter to John Wesley, 25 June 1740, in Tyerman, *Life and Times of John Wesley*, Vol. 1, p. 315

7 Letter to John Wesley, 16 July 1740, in Tyerman, *Life and Times of John Wesley*, Vol. 1, p. 315

8 Letter to George Whitefield, 9 August 1740, in Tyerman, *Life and Times of John Wesley* Vol. 1, pp. 315–16

9 19 June 1740, Thomas Jackson, *Works of John Wesley*, Baker House Books, 1872, reprinted 1984, Vol. 1, p. 274

10 22 June 1740, in *Works of John Wesley*, Vol. 1, p. 275

11 Kimbrough and Beckerlegge, *The Unpublished Poetry of Charles Wesley*, Vol. I, p. 176

12 *Works of John Wesley*, Vol. 7, p. 374

13 The entire verse is contained in T. Jackson, *Life of Revd Charles Wesley*, John Mason, London, 1841, Vol. 1, pp. 243–6

14 Thomas Jackson, *Journal of Revd Charles Wesley*, John Mason, London, 1849, Vol. 2, pp. 169–70

15 Letter to C. Wesley, in Jackson, *Life of Revd Charles Wesley*, Vol. 1, p. 255

16 26 August 1740 to J. L., in John Gillies, *The Works of George Whitefield*, London and Edinburgh, 1771, Vol. 1, p. 206

17 Ebenezer Pemberton, quoted in A. Dallimore, *George Whitefield*, Banner of Truth Trust, 1970, p. 436.

18 A Connecticut farmer called Nathan Cole, quoted in Mark A. Noll, *A History of Christianity in the United States and Canada*, SPCK, 1992, p. 93

19 6 August 1740, *Journal of Revd Charles Wesley*, Vol. 1, p. 247

20 6 August 1740, *Journal of Revd Charles Wesley*, Vol. 1, p. 248

21 Contained in Jackson, *Life of Revd Charles Wesley*, Vol. 1, p. 235

22 6 August 1740, *Journal of Revd Charles Wesley*, Vol. 1, p. 248

23 *Journal of Revd Charles Wesley*, Vol. 2, pp. 169–70

24 There is a vivid account of his 'awakening' in John Wesley's journal dated 21 May 1739

25 6 April 1740, *Journal of Revd Charles Wesley*, Vol. 1, p. 208

26 Quoted in Frank Baker, *John Wesley and the Church of England*, Epworth, London, 1970, p. 83

27 'Joseph Humphreys's Experience of the Work of Grace Upon his Heart, 1742, Bristol', quoted in F. Bruce Hindmarsh, *The Evangelical Conversion Narrative*, Oxford University Press, 2005, p. 82

28 Humphreys in Hindmarsh, *Evangelical Conversion Narrative*, p. 85

29 *Methodist Magazine*, 1822, p. 783

30 Quoted in T. Jackson, *Memoirs of Charles Wesley*, John Mason, London, 1862, p. 429

31 22 September 1740, *Journal of Revd Charles Wesley*, Vol. 1, p. 249

32 22 September 1740, *Journal of Revd Charles Wesley*, Vol. 1, p. 249

33 Hugh J. Hughes, *Life of Howell Harris*, London, 1892, pp. 142–3

34 See Tyerman, *Life and Times of John Wesley*, Vol. 1, p. 321

35 9 November 1740, *Journal of Revd Charles Wesley*, Vol. 1, p. 256

36 *Journal of the Historical Society of the Presbyterian Church of Wales*, Vol. XXXIII, p. 64

37 *Journal of the Historical Society of the Presbyterian Church of Wales* Vol. XXV, p. 17

38 18 November 1740, *Journal of Revd Charles Wesley*, Vol. 1, p. 261

39 Tyerman, *Life and Times of John Wesley*, Vol. 1, p. 320

40 Letter to Harris, in *Journal of Revd Charles Wesley*, Vol. 1, p. 256

41 18 November 1740, *Journal of Revd Charles Wesley*, Vol. 1, p. 259

42 30 November 1740, *Journal of Revd Charles Wesley*, Vol. 1, p. 263

43 *The Moravian Messenger*, Vol. XVL.

44 2 December 1740, *Journal of Revd Charles Wesley*, Vol. 1, p. 263

45 6 December 1740, *Journal of Revd Charles Wesley*, Vol. 1, p. 264

46 *Works of John Wesley*, Vol. 1, p. 303

47 *Works of John Wesley*, Vol. 1, p. 293

48 Letter to G. Whitefield, 17 January 1741, in Tyerman, *Life and Times of John Wesley*, Vol. 1, p. 344

49 Letter to John Wesley, 24 December 1740, in Tyerman, *Life and Times of John Wesley*, Vol. 1, pp. 322–4

50 Revd Alexander Gordon, quoted in Roy Hattersley, *A Brand from the Burning*, Little, Brown, 2003, p. 175

51 See *Works of John Wesley*, Vol. 1, p. 301

52 Letter to John Wesley, 28 February 1741, in G. M. Roberts, *Selected Trevecka Letters 1742–7*, Calvinist Methodist Bookroom, 1956, pp. 5–6

53 Letter to G. Whitefield, 9 August 1742, in Roberts, *Selected Trevecka Letters*, pp. 31–3

54 G. Whitefield, 21 August 1742, in Roberts, *Selected Trevecka Letters*, p. 38

55 Quoted in Jackson, *Life of Revd Charles Wesley*, Vol. 1, p. 260

56 Quoted in Dallimore, *George Whitefield*, Vol. II, p. 74

57 An Epistle to the Revd George Whitefield, in Osborn, *Poetical Works*, Vol. VI, p. 287

58 Letter dated 4 April 1740, in Gillies, *Works of George Whitefield*, Vol. 1, p. 161

59 Quoted in Jackson, *Life of Revd Charles Wesley*, Vol. 1, p. 260

60 Quoted in Dallimore, *George Whitefield*, Vol. II, p. 49

61 *Works of George Whitefield*, Vol. 1, p. 434

62 April 1741, *Journal of Revd Charles Wesley*, Vol. 1, p. 267

63 5 May 1741, *Journal of Revd Charles Wesley*, Vol. 1, p. 272

64 Quoted in Cook, *Selina Countess of Huntingdon*, p. 58

65 *Journal of Revd Charles Wesley*, Vol. 1, p. 277

66 *Journal of Revd Charles Wesley*, Vol. 1, p. 280

67 *Journal of Revd Charles Wesley* Vol. 1, p. 272

68 6 April 1741, in Jackson, *Works of Revd John Wesley*, Vol. 1, p. 306

69 Quoted in A. Skevington Wood, *The Inextinguishable Blaze*, Paternoster Press, 1960, p. 188

70 Letter to Charles, 21 April 1741, in Jackson, *Life of Revd Charles Wesley*, Vol. 1, pp. 271–2

71 Kimbrough and Beckerlegge, *Unpublished Poetry of Charles Wesley*, Vol. I, p. 179

72 L. Tyerman, *The Life of Revd George Whitefield*, Hodder & Stoughton, London, 1876, Vol. I, p. 478

73 4 May 1741, *Journal of Revd Charles Wesley*, Vol. 1, p. 272

74 Quoted in Tyerman, *Life of George Whitefield*, Vol. I, p. 479

75 Quoted in Tyerman, *Life of George Whitefield*, Vol. I, pp. 488–9

76 Gillies, *The Works of George Whitefield*, Vol. 1, p. 438

77 28 June 1741, *Journal of Revd Charles Wesley*, Vol. 1, pp. 283–4

78 4 July 1741, *Journal of Revd Charles Wesley*, Vol. 1, p. 285

79 23 July 1741, *Journal of Revd Charles Wesley*, Vol. 1, p. 290

80 10 September 1741, *Journal of Revd Charles Wesley*, Vol. 1, p. 298

81 'Hymns of God's Everlasting Love', 1741, in Tyson, *Charles Wesley: A Reader*, p. 294

82 28 September 1741, to John, in Tyerman, *Life of George Whitefield*, Vol. I, p. 482

83 22 September 1741, *Journal of Revd Charles Wesley*, Vol. 1, pp. 300–2

84 Letter in Jackson, *Life of Revd Charles Wesley*, Vol. 1, pp. 272–3

85 October 1741, Letter to John Wesley, in Tyerman, *Life of George Whitefield*, Vol. I, pp. 537–8

86 Letter to Gilbert Tennant, in Tyerman, *Life of George Whitefield*, Vol. I, p. 531

87 Tom Beynon, 'Howell Harris's Visits to Pembrokeshire', *Cambrian News Press*, 1966, p. 21

88 Duchess of Buckingham, March 1742, in Cook, *Selina Countess of Huntingdon*, p. 69

89 Historical Manuscript Commission, Hastings Family Papers, Vol. 3 ed. F. Buckley, HMSO, 1934, p. 32

90 See Tyerman, *Life and Times of John Wesley*, Vol. 1, pp. 239–52

91 2 January 1742, Letter to friend, in Tyerman, *Life of George Whitefield*, Vol. I, p. 548

92 See Cook, *Selina Countess of Huntingdon*, pp. 73–4

93 11 March 1742, unpublished letter in Methodist Archives, John Rylands Library University of Manchester

94 23 April 1742, in Jackson, *Works of John Wesley*, Vol. 1, p. 365

95 'Sermon on Ephesians 5:14' in Newport, *Sermons of Charles Wesley*, pp. 213–24

96 Quoted in Mrs Frank Stevens, *Lives of Early Methodist Preachers*, Marshall & Son, 1903, pp. 2–3

97 Quoted in Hindmarsh, *Evangelical Conversion Narrative*, p. 142

98 D. Macfarlan, *The Revivals of the Eighteenth Century, particularly at Cambuslang*, London and Edinburgh, no date, p. 74

99 Quoted in Dallimore, *George Whitefield*, Vol. II, p. 136

100 See Barrie Tabraham, *The Making of Methodism*, Epworth, London, 1995, p. 61

101 D. M. Jones, *Charles Wesley*, Skeffington and Son, London, 1920, p. 91

102 13 April 1742, in *Early Methodist Volume*

103 See Jackson, *Works of John Wesley*, Vol. 8, pp. 318–19

104 Quoted in Jackson, *Life of Revd Charles Wesley*, Vol. 1, p. 280

105 The whole poem is in Jackson, *Life of Revd Charles Wesley*, Vol. 1, pp. 314–18.

106 Address to Her Husband, in Edwards, *Family Circle*, pp. 157–9

107 Letter in Jackson, *Life of Revd Charles Wesley*, Vol. 1, p. 319

108 Jackson, *Life of Revd Charles Wesley*, Vol. 1, p. 319

109 Letter to Howell Harris, 6 August 1742, in Tyerman, *Life and Times of John Wesley*, Vol. 1, p. 375

110 Letter to Mrs Whitefield, 6 May 1742, in Tyerman, *Life and Times of John Wesley*, Vol. 1, pp. 419–20

111 Letter to G. Whitefield, 11 September 1742, in Roberts, *Selected Trevecka Letters*, p. 44

112 Kimbrough and Beckerlegge, *Unpublished Poetry of Charles Wesley*, Vol. I, p. 176

113 David Hempton, *Methodism: Empire of the Spirit*, Yale University Press, New Haven and London, 2005, p. 16

114 Kimbrough and Beckerlegge, *Unpublished Poetry of Charles Wesley*, Vol. I, p. 176

Chapter 7

1 'Charles on God's Defeat of the Forces of Bonnie Prince Charlie' in G. Osborn, *The Poetical Works of John and Charles Wesley*, Vol. IV, Wesleyan Methodist Conference Office, London, 1869, pp. 95–6

2 Minutes of First Conference, 28 June 1744, in Albert Outler, *Library of Christian Thought: John Wesley*, Oxford University Press, 1964, p. 144

3 Letter to Mr S. at Armagh, 24 April 1769, in T. Jackson, *Works of John Wesley*, 1872 Vol. 12, pp. 246–7

4 Minutes of Fourth Annual Conference, 18 June 1747, in Outler, *Library of Christian Thought*, pp. 175–6

5 'On Preaching Christ' in the *Arminian Magazine* 1779, in *Works of John Wesley*, Vol. 11, pp. 486–92

6 Minutes of the First Methodist Annual Conference, 29 June 1744

7 Sermon on John 8:1–11, in K. Newport, *The Sermons of Charles Wesley*, Oxford University Press, 2001, pp. 249–50

8 See T. R. Crichton Mitchell, *The Man with the Dancing Heart*, Beacon Hill Press, 1994, p. 136. The journal entry is 27 May 1743, *Journal* of *Charles Wesley*, Vol. 1, p. 312

9 20 May 1743, *Journal of Charles Wesley*, Vol. 1, p. 307

10 21 May 1743, *Journal of Charles Wesley*, Vol. 1, p. 308

11 25 May 1743, *Journal of Charles Wesley*, Vol. 1, p. 309

12 25 May 1743, *Journal of Charles Wesley*, Vol. 1, pp. 309–10

13 27 May 1743, *Journal of Charles Wesley*, Vol. 1, p. 312

14 29 May 1743, *Journal of Charles Wesley*, Vol. 1, p. 313

15 4 June 1743, *Journal of Charles Wesley*, Vol. 1, p. 314

16 8 June 1743, *Journal of Charles Wesley*, Vol. 1, p. 315

17 F. Gill, *Charles Wesley: The first Methodist*, Lutterworth, 1964, p. 110

18 *Works of John Wesley*, Vol. 8, pp. 270–1

19 Poem on Luke 16:8 in S. T. Kimborough and O. A. Beckerlegge, *The Unpublished Poetry of Charles Wesley*, Kingswood, 1990, Vol. II, p. 156

20 26 June 1743, *Journal of Revd Charles Wesley*, Vol. 1, p. 319

21 18 July 1743, *Journal of Revd Charles Wesley*, Vol. 1, p. 322

22 *Journal of Revd Charles Wesley*, Vol. 1, pp. 324–5

23 *Journal of Revd Charles Wesley*, Vol. 1, p. 325

24 *Journal of Revd Charles Wesley*, Vol. 1, pp. 326–7

25 30 July 1743, *Journal of Revd Charles Wesley*, Vol. 1, p. 330

26 *Works of John Wesley*, Vol. 8, pp. 3–4 and 6

27 Jackson, *Life of Revd Charles Wesley*, Vol. 1, p. 350

28 'Another Poem for One in Prison' in *Journal of Charles Wesley*, Vol. 1, p. 462

29 Eucharistic Hymn LXXII in *Hymns on the Lord's Supper*, London, 1745

30 *Journal of Revd Charles Wesley*, Vol. 1, p. 337

31 *Hymns for Times of Trouble and Persecution 1745* in Osborn, *Poetical Works*, Vol. IV, pp. 21–2

32 'A Prayer for His Majesty King George' in *Hymns for Times of Trouble and Persecution 1745* in Osborn, *The Poetical Works*, Vol. IV, pp. 21–2

33 No 9 in *Hymns for Times of Trouble and Persecution 1745* in Osborn, *The Poetical Works*, Vol. IV, p. 40

34 18 February 1744, Letter to James Beaumont, in G. M. Roberts, *Selected Trevecca Letters 1742–7*, Calvinist Methodist Bookroom, 1956, pp. 130–1

35 7 February 1744, *Journal of Revd Charles Wesley*, Vol. 1, p. 346

36 Quoted in Roy Hattersley, *A Brand Plucked from the Burning*, Little Brown, 2003, p. 216

37 10 March 1744, *Journal of Revd Charles Wesley*, Vol. 1, p. 355

38 14 March 1744, *Journal of Revd Charles Wesley*, Vol. 1, p. 356

39 14 March 1744, *Journal of Revd Charles Wesley*, Vol. 1, pp. 356–7

40 15 March 1744, *Journal of Revd Charles Wesley*, Vol. 1, p. 358

41 See M. R. Brailsford, *A Tale of Two Brothers*, Rupert Hart-Davies, 1954, pp. 146–8

42 F. Stevens, *Lives of Early Methodist Preachers*, Marshall & Son, London, 1903, p. 16

43 Osborn, *Poetical Works*, Vol. IV, pp. 43–4

44 No 1 in 'Hymns to be Sung in a Tumult' in *Hymns for Times of Trouble and Persecution 1744*

45 13 July 1744, *Journal of Revd Charles Wesley*, Vol. 1, p. 368

46 19 July 1744, *Journal of Revd Charles Wesley*, Vol. 1, p. 370

47 25 July 1744, *Journal of Revd Charles Wesley*, Vol. 1, p. 373

48 17 July 1744, *Journal of Revd Charles Wesley*, Vol. 1, p. 369

49 D. M. Jones, *Charles Wesley*, Skeffington, London, 1920, p. 133

50 Quoted in A. Dallimore, *A Heart Set Free*, Evangelical Press, London, 1988, p. 129

51 22 November 1744, *Journal of Revd Charles Wesley*, Vol. 1, p. 388

52 26 September 1745, *Journal of Revd Charles Wesley*, Vol. 1, p. 405

53 'A Brief Account of the Late Persecution and Barbarous Usage of the Methodists at Exeter', 1745

54 Letter, 11 September 1747, to John Wesley, in Tyerman, *Life of John Wesley*, Vol. 1, p. 535

55 Roberts, *Selected Trevecca Letters*, p. 183

56 31 March 1746, *Journal of Revd Charles Wesley*, Vol. 1, p. 411

57 4 February 1746, *Journal of Revd Charles Wesley*, Vol. 1, pp. 409–10

58 6 July 1746, *Journal of Revd Charles Wesley*, Vol. 1, p. 420

59 6 July 1746, *Journal of Revd Charles Wesley*, Vol. 1, p. 420

60 10 August 1746, *Journal of Revd Charles Wesley*, Vol. 1, p. 426

61 See 'The Emergence and Expansion of Methodism' in Henry Rack, *Reasonable Enthusiast*, Epworth, London, 1989, pp. 183–250

62 15 October 1746, *Journal of Revd Charles Wesley*, Vol. 1, p. 431

63 Frank Baker, *William Grimshaw*, Epworth, London, 1963, pp. 106–7

64 Quoted in Baker, *William Grimshaw*, p. 140

65 Baker, *William Grimshaw*, p. 113

66 27 November 1746, *Journal of Revd Charles Wesley*, Vol. 1, p. 435

67 30 November 1746, *Journal of Revd Charles Wesley*, Vol. 1, p. 436

68 No 781, *Hymns and Psalms*

69 6 January 1747, *Journal of Revd Charles Wesley*, Vol. 1, p. 438

70 G. F. Nuttall, *Correspondence of Philip Doddridge*, Northants Record Society, 1979, Vol. 29, p. 251

71 25 February 1747, *Journal of Revd Charles Wesley*, Vol. 1, pp. 443–9

72 25 February 1747, *Journal of Revd Charles Wesley*, Vol. 1, pp. 443–9

Chapter 8

1 C. Wesley: *Hymns for the Family* in G. Osborn, *The Poetical Works of John and Charles Wesley*, Wesleyan Methodist Office, London, 1870, Vol. VII, pp. 198–9

2 A. G. Ives, *Kingswood School in Wesley's Day and Since*, Epworth, London, 1970, p. 6

3 'A Plain Account of Kingswood School 1781' in Thomas Jackson, *The Works of John Wesley*, Baker Book House, 1872, reprinted 1984, Vol. 13, p. 292

4 Hymn XLVII in 'Hymns for Children, 1763' in Osborn, *Poetical Works*, Vol. VI, p. 416

5 Hymn XLIII in 'Hymns for Children' in Osborn, *Poetical Works*, Vol. VI, pp. 410–11

6 Hymn LVI in 'Hymns for Children' in Osborn, *Poetical Works*, Vol. VI, p. 424

7 'Lessons for Children, 1746' in Jackson, *Works of John Wesley*, Vol. 7, pp. 86–98

8 'Thought on Educating Children, 1783' in Jackson, *Works of John Wesley*, Vol. 13, pp. 476–7

9 Hymn XXIV in 'Hymns for Children, 1763' in Osborn, *Poetical Works*, Vol. VI, p. 393

10 Hymn L in 'Hymns for Children' in Osborn, *Poetical Works*, Vol. VI, p. 419

11 Mary Davey, housekeeper at Kingswood, quoted in *The History of Kingswood School by Three Old Boys*, Kelly, 1898, p. 37

12 Hymn XL in 'Hymns for Children' in Osborn, *Poetical Works* Vol. VI, pp. 407–8

13 'A Plain Account of Kingswood School' in Jackson, *Works of John Wesley*, Vol. 13, p. 293

14 Letter to J. Benson, November 1768, in Ives, *Kingswood School*, p. 64

15 Hymn LII in 'Hymns for Children' in Osborn, *Poetical Works*, Vol. VI, p. 421

16 'A Short Account of Kingswood School' in Jackson, *Works of John Wesley*, Vol. 13, p. 285

17 Hymn LV in 'Hymns for Children' in Osborn, *Poetical Works*, Vol. VI, p. 423

18 Hymn LXVI in 'Hymns for Children' in Osborn: *Poetical Works*, Vol. VI, p. 434

19 'A Plain Account' in Jackson, *Works of John Wesley*, Vol. 13, p. 293

20 Letter, 3 March 1749, in *Watchman*, 18 February 1835

21 Diary of J. Bennett, 27 January 1750, in S. R. Valentine, *Mirror of the Soul*, Methodist Publishing House, 2002, p. 198

22 To Mrs Robert Jones, quoted in Ives, *Kingswood School*, p. 36

23 Hymn C in 'Hymns for Children' in Osborn, *Poetical Works*, Vol. VI, p. 462

24 Hymn VII in 'Hymns for Children' in Osborn, *Poetical Works*, Vol. VI, pp. 377–8

25 Hymn LX in 'Hymns for Children' in Osborn, *Poetical Works*, Vol. VI, pp. 428–9

26 Hymn LXXII in 'Hymns for Children' in Osborn, *Poetical Works*, Vol. VI, p. 462

27 Published in 1746 *Hymnbook*. See L. Tyerman, *The Life of Revd John Wesley*, Hodder & Stoughton, London, 1878, Vol. 1, p. 529

28 Quoted in M. R. Brailsford, *A Tale of Two Brothers*, Hart-Davies, London, 1954, p. 160

29 Quoted in Frank Baker, *Charles Wesley as Revealed by His Letters*, Epworth, London, 1949, p. 46

30   19 April 1748, *Journal of Revd Charles Wesley*, Vol. 2, p. 12

31   9 September 1747. See *Life of Revd Charles Wesley*, Vol. 1, p. 473

32   *Journal of Revd Charles Wesley*, Vol. 1, p. 462

33   8 February 1748, *Journal of Revd Charles Wesley*, Vol. 2, p. 2

34   18 April 1748, Letter to C. W., in G. M. Roberts, *Selected Trevecka Letters 1747–94*, Calvinist Methodist Bookroom, London, 1962, p. 14

35   11 September 1747, to Charles, in L. Tyerman, *The Life of Revd George Whitefield*, Hodder & Stoughton, London, 1877, Vol. II, p. 177

36   *Journal of Revd Charles Wesley*, Vol. 2, p. 441

37   25 March 1748, *Journal of Revd Charles Wesley*, Vol. 2, p. 11

38   Published in his *Hymns and Sacred Poems*. See Baker, *Charles Wesley as Revealed by His Letters*, p. 58

39   Quoted in Tyerman, *Life of John Wesley*, Vol. 2, p. 6

40   Tom Beynon, *Howell Harris' Visits to London*, Cambrian News Press, 1960, p. 202

41   Quoted in Tyerman, *Life of George Whitefield*, Vol. II, pp. 211–12

42   Quoted in Faith Cook, *Selina Countess of Huntingdon*, The Banner of Truth Trust, 2001, pp. 110–11

43   Quoted in Cook, *Selina Countess of Huntingdon*, p. 110

44   J. Gillies, *Works of George Whitefield*, London, 1771, Vol. II, p. 216

45   J. Gillies, *Works of George Whitefield*, Vol. II, p. 196

46   Baker, *Charles Wesley as Revealed by His Letters*, pp. 58–9

47   21 August 1748, *Journal of Revd Charles Wesley*, Vol. 2, p. 19

48   22 August 1748, *Journal of Revd Charles Wesley*, Vol. 2, p. 20

49   1 September 1748, *Journal of Revd Charles Wesley*, Vol. 2, p. 24

50   12 September 1748, *Journal of Revd Charles Wesley*, Vol. 2, p. 32

51   27 August 1748, *Journal of Revd Charles Wesley*, Vol. 2, p. 22

52   For whole hymn called 'Shepherd of Souls' see *Journal of Revd Charles Wesley*, Vol. 2, pp. 27–9

53   10 October 1748, *Journal of Revd Charles Wesley*, Vol. 2, p. 39

54   10 October 1748, *Journal of Revd Charles Wesley*, Vol. 2, p. 40

55   Quoted in Brailsford, *A Tale of Two Brothers*, pp. 167–8

56   Baker, *Charles Wesley as Revealed by His Letters*, p. 62

57   14 January 1749, *Journal of Revd Charles Wesley*, Vol. 2, pp. 50–1

58   3 April 1749, *Journal of Revd Charles Wesley*, Vol. 2, p. 54

59   7 April 1748, *Journal of Revd Charles Wesley*, Vol. 2, pp. 55–6

60   Letter to Charles Wesley, 29 April 1740, in Jackson, *Life of Revd Charles Wesley*, Vol. 1, p. 529

61   1 July 1749, *Journal of Revd Charles Wesley*, Vol. 2, p. 61

62   24 June 1749, *Journal of Revd Charles Wesley*, Vol. 2, p. 61

63   Gillies, *Works of George Whitefield*, Vol. II, p. 193

64   Gillies, *Works of George Whitefield*, Vol. II, p. 428

65   Letter dated 8 October 1749, Thomas Jackson, *Memoirs of Revd Charles Wesley*, London, 1862, p. 178

66   Gillies, *Works of George Whitefield*, Vol. II, p. 283

67   4 September 1749, *Journal of Revd Charles Wesley*, Vol. 2, p. 65

68   Quoted in Brailsford, *A Tale of Two Brothers*, p. 172

69   1 September 1749, Jackson, *Journal of Revd Charles Wesley*, Vol. 2, p. 64

70 The whole hymn is in Jackson, *Life of Revd Charles Wesley*, Vol. 1, pp. 543–5

71 *Hymns and Sacred Poems* 1749. Now No 719 in *Hymn and Psalms*, Methodist Publishing House, 1983

72 Tyerman, *Life of Revd John Wesley*, Vol. 2, p. 50

73 Quoted in Brailsford, *A Tale of Two Brothers*, p. 185

74 Tyerman, *Life of Revd John Wesley*, Vol. 2, pp. 50–1

75 Baker, *Charles Wesley as Revealed by His Letters*, p. 72

76 Quoted in Brailsford, *A Tale of Two Brothers*, p. 191

77 Quoted in Maldwyn Edwards, *My Dear Sister*, Penwork (Leeds) Ltd, Manchester, 1976, p. 33

78 Quoted in Brailsford, *A Tale of Two Brothers*, p. 198

79 'Reflection upon Past Providence, 1749' in John Telford, *The Life of John Wesley*, London, 1902, p. 251

80 Quoted in Stanley Ayrling, *John Wesley*, Collins, London, 1979, p. 195

81 Baker, *Charles Wesley as Revealed by His Letters*, p. 74

82 Baker, *Charles Wesley as Revealed by His Letters*, p. 73

83 Jackson, *Memoirs of Charles Wesley*, p. 227

84 Gillies, *Works of George Whitefield*, Vol. II, p. 294

85 1 December 1749, *Journal of Revd Charles Wesley*, Vol. 2, p. 66

86 18 December 1749, *Journal of Revd Charles Wesley*, Vol. 2, p. 66

87 Letter in Methodist Archives in John Rylands Library, Manchester. See A. Dallimore, *George Whitefield*, London, 1980 Vol. II, pp. 337–8

88 Jackson, *Memoirs of the Revd Charles Wesley*, p. 230

89 Jackson, *Life of Revd Charles Wesley*, Vol. 1, p. 557

90 Letter to Charles, 4 October 1745, in Jackson, *Life of Revd Charles Wesley*, Vol. 1, pp. 558–60

91 5 March 1750, *Journal of Revd Charles Wesley*, Vol. 2, p. 68

92 21 March 1750, *Journal of Revd Charles Wesley*, Vol. 2, p. 69

93 See Jackson, *Life of Revd Charles Wesley*, p. 563

94 5 April 1750, *Journal of Revd Charles Wesley*, Vol. 2, p. 70

95 'Sermon on Psalm 46:8' in Kenneth Newport, *The Sermons of Charles Wesley*, Oxford University Press, 2001, pp. 236–7

96 See 'Hymns occasioned by the Earthquake' in Osborn, *Poetical Works*, Vol. VI, pp. 21–3

97 Osborn, *Poetical Works*, Vol. VI, pp. 39–40

98 15 March 1751, in Baker, *Charles Wesley as Revealed by His Letters*, p. 75

99 Letter, 29 June 1750, to J. Bennett, contained in Tyerman, *The Life of the Revd John Wesley*, Vol. 2, pp. 42–3

100 Gillies, *Works of George Whitefield*, Vol. II, p. 316

101 Quoted in Cook, *Selina Countess of Huntingdon*, p. 127

102 Lord Bolingbroke, quoted in Cook, *Selina Countess of Huntingdon*, p. 127

103 See Jackson, *Memoirs of Revd Charles Wesley*, p. 234

104 John Hampson, *Life of Wesley*, London, no date, Vol. II, p. 124

105 2 February 1751, quoted in Tyerman, *The Life of the Revd John Wesley*, Vol. 2, p. 104

106 13 March 1751, *Journal of Revd Charles Wesley*, Vol. 2, p. 79

107 Quoted in A. Dallimore, *A Heart Set Free*, Evangelical Press, 1988, p. 168

108 See forthcoming article by John Lenton, 'Charles Wesley and the Preachers' in the Symposium being edited by Kenneth Newport and planned for publication by Epworth Press 2007

109 Letter, in Tyerman, *Life of John Wesley*, Vol. 2, pp. 111–12

110 Quoted in Tyerman, *Life of John Wesley*, Vol. 2, p. 114

111 Letter to his wife dated 1756 in Dallimore, *A Heart Set Free*, p. 147

112 *Journal of Revd Charles Wesley*, Vol. 2, p. 195

113 Baker, *Charles Wesley as Revealed by His Letters*, p. 78

Chapter 9

1 Hymn I in 'Hymns for Preachers 1758' in G. Osborn, *The Poetical Works of John and Charles Wesley*, Wesleyan Methodist Conference, London, 1870, Vol. VI, pp. 99–100

2 Thomas Jackson, *Journal of Revd Charles Wesley*, John Mason, London, 1849, Vol. 1.

3 See G. M. Best, *Continuity and Change: A History of Kingswood School*, Kingswood, 1998, pp. 31–2

4 'Sermon on Catholic Spirit' preached in 1749, in Thomas Jackson, *Works of John Wesley*, Baker Book House, 1872, reprinted, 1984, Vol. 5, pp. 495–7

5 30 June 1746, *Journal of Revd Charles Wesley*, Vol. 1, p. 419

6 *Journal of Revd Charles Wesley*, Vol. 2, p. 61

7 Frank Baker, *Charles Wesley as Revealed by His Letters*, Epworth, London, 1949, p. 83

8 Quoted in L. Tyerman, *Life and Times of John Wesley*, Hodder & Stoughton, London, 1878, Vol. 2, p. 122

9 *Journal of Revd Charles Wesley*, Vol. 2, p. 84

10 25 June 1751, in Tyerman, *Life and Times of John Wesley*, Vol. 2, p. 123

11 *Journal of Charles Wesley*, Vol. 2, p. 84

12 Baker, *Charles Wesley as Revealed by His Letters*, p. 83

13 Baker, *Charles Wesley as Revealed by His Letters*, p. 84

14 Letter, 20 December 1751, in Tyerman, *Life and Times of John Wesley*, Vol. 2, pp. 130–1

15 21 August 1751, Letter to a friend, in Tyerman, *Life and Times of John Wesley*, Vol. 2, p. 129

16 18 July 1751, *Journal of Revd Charles Wesley*, Vol. 2, p. 88

17 21 July 1751, *Journal of Revd Charles Wesley*, Vol. 2, p. 89

18 9–11 July 1751, *Journal of Revd Charles Wesley*, Vol. 2, p. 86

19 8 July 1751, *Journal of Revd Charles Wesley*, Vol. 2, p. 86

20 12 July 1751, *Journal of Revd Charles Wesley*, Vol. 2, p. 87

21 5–6 July 1751, *Journal of Revd Charles Wesley*, Vol. 2, p. 86

22 17 July 1751, *Journal of Revd Charles Wesley*, Vol. 2, p. 88

23 *Journal of Revd Charles Wesley*, Vol. 2, p. 90

24 Letter to John Bennet, September 1752

25 *Journal of Revd Charles Wesley*, Vol. 2, pp. 90–1

26 Minutes of Methodist Conference, London, 1862, p. 52

27 Tyerman, *Life and Times of John Wesley*, Vol. 2, p. 128

28 9 August 1751, *Journal of Revd Charles Wesley*, Vol. 2, p. 91

29 Full document in Tyerman, *Life and Times of John Wesley*, Vol. 2, pp. 129–30

30 No 767 *Hymns and Psalms*, Methodist Publishing House, 1983

31 Letter, January 1752, in Frank Baker, *William Baker*, Epworth, London, 1963, pp. 247–8

32 J. Gillies, *Works of George Whitefield*, London and Edinburgh, 1771, Vol. II, p. 466

33 Letter to Charles in Faith Cook, *Selina Countess of Huntingdon*, The Banner of Truth Trust, 2001, p. 143

34 Gillies, *Works of George Whitefield*, Vol. II, p. 464

35 Thomas Olivers, *A Rod for the Reviler*, London, 1777, p. 58

36 For more detail on Whitefield's use of Charles' verse see S. T. Kimborough, *Charles Wesley Poet and Theologian*, Abingdon Press, 1992, pp. 168–74

37 Letter 23 in folio containing the Countess' correspondence with Charles Wesley and others, John Rylands Library, University of Manchester

38 Letter 20 October 1753 to Charles, in T. Jackson, *Life of Revd Charles Wesley*, Vol. 2, pp. 24–5

39 Quoted in M. Brailsford, *A Tale of Two Brothers*, Hart-Davis, London, 1954, p. 244

40 *Journal of Revd Charles Wesley*, Vol. 2, p. 97

41 Letter 3 December 1753, in Tyerman, *Life and Times of John Wesley*, Vol. 2, p. 175

42 *Journal of Revd Charles Wesley*, Vol. 2, p. 98

43 *Journal of Revd Charles Wesley*, Vol. 2, p. 98

44 *Journal of Revd Charles Wesley*, Vol. 2, p. 99

45 3 December 1753, letter to William Shent, in L. Tyerman, *The Life of Revd George Whitefield*, Hodder and Stoughton, London, 1876, Vol. II, p. 319

46 *Journal of Revd Charles Wesley*, Vol. II, p. 99

47 From Charles' secret diary contained in J. R. Tyson, *Charles Wesley: A Reader*, Oxford University Press, 1989, pp. 329–30

48 *Journal of Revd Charles Wesley*, Vol. 2, p. 100

49 From Charles' secret diary, in Tyson, *Charles Wesley: A Reader*, pp. 330–1

50 From Charles' secret diary, in Tyson, *Charles Wesley: A Reader*, p. 331

51 From Charles' secret diary, in Tyson, *Charles Wesley: A Reader*, p. 331

52 Letter 13 December 1753 to Charles in Jackson, *Life of Charles Wesley*, Vol. 2, pp. 32–3

53 Osborn, *Poetical Works*, Vol. VIII, pp. 403–4

54 Jackson, *Life of Charles Wesley*, Vol. 2, p. 34

55 Letter 33 in Countess' correspondence with Charles Wesley and others in folio in John Rylands Library

56 'On the Death of a Child' in *Funeral Hymns* (2nd series) 1759 in Osborn, *Poetical Works*, Vol. VI, p. 253

57 11 July 1754, *Journal of Revd Charles Wesley*, Vol. 2, p. 101

58 *Journal of Revd Charles Wesley*, Vol. 2, pp. 105–7

59 *Gentleman's Magazine*, London, 1756, p. 89

60 Edward Perronet, *The Mitre*, 1756. See Tyerman, *Life and Times of John Wesley*, Vol. 2, pp. 241–3

61 G. Smith (ed.), *History of the Methodists in Great Britain*, Vol. IV, Longmans, 1862, p. 190

62 Quoted in Frank Baker, *John Wesley and the Church of England*, Epworth, London, 1970, p. 163

63 Letter quoted in Jackson, *Life of Revd Charles Wesley*, Vol. II, p. 71

64 Letter 14 December 1754 in Jackson, *Life of Revd Charles Wesley*, Vol. 2, p. 71

65 14 February 1755, Letter to C. W., in G. M. Roberts, *Selected Trevecka Letters 1747–94*, Calvinist Bookroom, London, 1962, p. 59

66 Letter 4 February 1755, in Jackson, *Life of Revd Charles Wesley*, Vol. 2, pp. 72–3

67 2 May 1755, Letter to Mrs Gallatin, in Frank Baker, *William Grimshaw*, Epworth, London, 1963, pp. 249–50

68 Quoted in Baker, *William Grimshaw*, p. 251

69 An Epistle to the Revd Mr John Wesley by Charles Wesley Presbyter of the Church of England 1755, reprinted in Jackson, *Life of Revd Charles Wesley*, Vol. 2, pp. 545–51

70 Letter 20 June 1755 to Charles, in Jackson, *Life of Revd Charles Wesley*, Vol. 2, pp. 82–3

71 Letter 28 June 1755 to Charles, in Jackson, *Life of Revd Charles Wesley*, Vol. 2, p. 83

72 Jackson, *Life of Revd Charles Wesley*, Vol. 2, pp. 78–80

73 30 May 1755, manuscript letter in Drew University published in Baker, *John Wesley and the Church of England*, p. 168

74 Letter 31 October 1755 to Revd Thomas Adam, in Tyerman, *Life and Times of John Wesley*, Vol. 2, p. 210–11

75 Quoted in Baker, *John Wesley and the Church of England*, p. 170

76 Letter 16 August 1756 to Charles, in Tyerman, *Life and Times of John Wesley*, Vol. 2, pp. 245–6

77 Hymn XV in 'Hymns for the Year, 1756' in Osborn, *Poetical Works*, Vol. VI, p. 93

78 S. T. Kimbrough and O. A. Beckerlegge, *The Unpublished Poetry of Charles Wesley*, Kingswood, 1988, Vol. I, p. 195

79 Osborn, *Poetical Works*, Vol. VI, p. 67

80 Kimbrough and Beckerlegge, *Unpublished Poetry of Charles Wesley*, Vol. I, p. 196

81 Kimbrough and Beckerlegge, *Unpublished Poetry of Charles Wesley*, Vol. I, p. 206

82 Letter 52 in the Countess' correspondence with Charles Wesley and others in John Rylands Library

83 Tyerman, *Life and Times of John Wesley*, Vol. 2, p. 242

84 7 August 1756 to Revd Samuel Walker, in Tyerman, *Life and Times of John Wesley*, Vol. 2, pp. 244–5

85 Quoted in Tyerman, *Life and Times of John Wesley*, Vol. II, pp. 250–1

86 3 September 1756 to Samuel Walker, in Tyerman, *Life and Times of John Wesley*, Vol. 2, p. 249

87 Letter 16 September 1757 to Samuel Walker, in Tyerman, *Life and Times of John Wesley*, Vol. 2, p. 280

88 21 August 1756 to Revd Sanmuel Walker, in Tyerman, *Life and Times of John Wesley*, Vol. 2, pp. 247–8

89 Baker, *Charles Wesley as Revealed by His Letters*, p. 97

90 See Tyerman, *Life and Times of John Wesley*, Vol. 2, p. 252

91 25 October 1756, *Journal of Revd Charles Wesley*, Vol. 2, pp. 133–4

92 Journal, 21 October 1756. See Jackson, *Life of Revd Charles Wesley*, Vol. 2, p. 121

93 Letter 16 November 1756 to John, in Tyerman, *Life and Times of John Wesley*, Vol. 2, pp. 253–5

94 29 October 1756, in Jackson, *Life of Revd Charles Wesley*, Vol. 2, p. 126

95 Letter to C. W. in Roberts, *Selected Trevecka Letters*, pp. 67–8

96 Quoted in Frank Gill, *Charles Wesley the First Methodist*, Lutterworth, 1964, p. 165

97 Letter 20 September 1757, in Tyerman, *Life and Times of John Wesley*, Vol. 2, pp. 282–3.

98 Manuscript letter quoted in Baker, *John Wesley and the Church of England*, p. 176

99 Quoted in Jackson, *Life of Revd Charles Wesley*, Vol. 2, p. 141

100 Letter 17 April 1758 to Charles, in Jackson, *Life of Revd Charles Wesley*, Vol. 2, pp. 142–3

101 Quoted in F. Bruce Hindmarsh, *The Evangelical Conversion Narrative*, Oxford University Press, 2005, p. 258

102 Hymn XLI in 'Funeral Hymns' in Osborn, *Poetical Works*, Vol. VI, pp. 283–4

103 Quoted in Jackson, *Life of Revd Charles Wesley*, Vol. 2, p. 138

104 Hymn V in 'Hymns for Preachers, 1758' in Osborn, *Poetical Works*, Vol. VI, pp. 104–5

105 Quoted in Brailsford, *A Tale of Two Brothers*, p. 232

106 Undated but probably March letter to John in Jackson, *Life of Revd Charles Wesley*, Vol. 2, pp. 180–1

107 Letter 13 April 1760 to Sally, in *Methodist Magazine*, London, 1848, p. 1205

108 Letter 27 March 1760 to John Nelson, in Tyerman, *Life and Times of John Wesley*, Vol. 2, p. 383

109 Quoted in Baker, *William Grimshaw*, p. 255

110 Letter 31 March 1760 to Charles, in Jackson, *Life of Revd Charles Wesley*, Vol. 2, pp. 189–92

111 Letter 27 March 1760 to Christopher Hopper, in Jackson, *Life of Revd Charles Wesley*, Vol. 2, pp. 185–6

112 Joseph Cownley to Charles, in Tyerman, *Life and Times of John Wesley*, Vol. 2, p. 387

113 23 June 1760, Letter to Charles, in Tyerman, *Life and Times of John Wesley*, Vol. 2, p. 358

114 Quoted in Baker, *John Wesley and the Church of England*, p. 178

115 Letter 8 September 1761 to Charles, in Jackson, *Works of John Wesley* Vol. 12, p. 121

116 Quoted in Baker, *John Wesley and the Church of England*, p. 185

Chapter 10

1 'Hymn on John 16:14-15' in John Tyson, *Charles Wesley: A Reader*, Oxford University Press, 1989, pp. 392-4

2 Letter 5 July 1759 to Sally, in Thomas Jackson, *The Life of Revd Charles Wesley*, John Mason, London, 1841 Vol. 2, p. 164

3 'From Hymns on the Expected Invasion 1759'. See Jackson, *Life of Revd Charles Wesley*, Vol. 2, p. 166

4 L. Tyerman, *The Life and Times of Revd John Wesley*, Hodder & Stoughton, 1878, Vol. 2, p. 323

5 Letter 15 November 1759, in Patrick Strieff, *Reluctant Saint*, Epworth, 2001, p. 55

6 Quoted in Strieff, *Reluctant Saint*, p. 63

7 John Telford, *The Letters of John Wesley*, Epworth, 1931, Vol. IV, p. 57

8 Letter 29 June 1759 to Sally, in Jackson, *Life of Charles Wesley*, Vol. 2, p. 161

9 Letter July 1759 to Sally, in Jackson, *Life of Charles Wesley*, Vol. 2, pp. 162-3

10 Hymn 1 in 'Hymns on the Expected Invasion' in G. Osborn, *The Poetical Works of John and Charles Wesley*, Wesleyan Methodist Conference Office, 1870, Vol. VI, pp. 149-50

11 Letter 23 February 1760 to Charles, in Jackson, *Life of Charles Wesley*, Vol. 2, pp. 168-70

12 For a detailed account, see Jackson, *Life of Charles Wesley*, Vol. 2, pp. 169-79

13 Words left behind in his cell and quoted in *London Magazine* in 1760.

14 15 May 1760, in Thomas Jackson, *The Journal of the Revd Charles Wesley*, John Mason, London, 1849, Vol. 2, p. 238

15 'For One in a Declining State of Health, 1749', contained in full in Tyson, *Charles Wesley: A Reader*, p. 368

16 Letter to C. Wesley, 31 October 1760, in F. Cook, *William Grimshaw of Haworth*, Banner of Truth Trust, 1997, p. 237

17 Testimony of Hannah Harrison, in Tyerman, *Life and Times of John Wesley*, Vol. 2, p. 421

18 *Works of George Whitefield*, London and Edinburgh, 1771, Vol. III, p. 272

19 Letter 12 October 1761, translated in Strieff, *Reluctant Saint*, p. 326

20 W. Biggs to Charles Wesley, 28 October 1762, in Gareth Lloyd and Kenneth Newport, *George Bell and Early Methodist Enthusiasm: A New Manuscript Source*, Bulletin of the John Rylands University Library of Manchester, 1998, pp. 89-101.

21 'Hymn on Matthew 9:17' in S. T. Kimbrough and O. A. Beckerlegge, *The Unpublished Poetry of Charles Wesley*, Kingswood Books, 1990, Vol. II, pp. 23-4

22 'Hymn on Matthew 18:6' in Kimbrough and Beckerlegge, *Unpublished Poetry*, Vol. II, p. 31

23 Sermon on 'Wandering Thoughts'. See Tyerman, *Life and Times of Revd John Wesley* Vol. 2, p. 424

24 5 January 1762, Letter to Charles, in T. Jackson, *Works of John Wesley*, Baker House Books, 1872, reprinted 1984, Vol. 12, pp. 122–3

25 Letter 16 May 1762 to Charles, in P. Forsaith, *Correspondence of Revd John W. Fletcher*, thesis submitted for DPhil at Oxford University, 2003, p. 68

26 'Hymn on Acts 20:30' in Kimbrough and Beckerlegge, *Unpublished Poetry of Charles Wesley*, Vol. II, p. 402

27 'Hymn on Acts 21:27' in Kimbrough and Beckerlegge, *Unpublished Poetry of Charles Wesley*, Vol. II, p. 405

28 'Preface to Short Hymns on Select passages of Scripture, 1762' in Tyson, *Charles Wesley: A Reader*, pp. 378–9

29 'Short Hymn on Matthew 5:14' in Tyson: *Charles Wesley: A Reader*, p. 379

30 Letter quoted in Jackson, *Life of Charles Wesley*, Vol. 2, p. 209

31 15 September 1762 letter, in Tyerman, *Life and Times of John Wesley*, Vol. 2, pp. 452–3

32 22 November 1762 letter, in Tyerman, *Life and Times of John Wesley*, Vol. 2, p. 437

33 Letter 20 September 1762 to Charles, in Forsaith, *Correspondence of Revd John W. Fletcher*, p. 83

34 Quoted in A. Dallimore, *George Whitefield*, Banner of Truth Trust, 1980, Vol. II, p. 422

35 *Works of George Whitefield*, Vol. III, p. 293

36 A. C. H. Seymour, *The Life and Times of the Countess of Huntingdon*, London, 1840, Vol. I, p. 284

37 Jackson, *Works of John Wesley*, Vol. 3, pp. 119–20

38 Tyerman, *Life and Times of John Wesley*, Vol. 2, p. 433

39 Letter 23 December 1762 to Charles, in Jackson, *Works of John Wesley*, Vol. 12, p. 124

40 Letter 11 December 1762 to Charles, in Jackson, *Works of John Wesley*, Vol. 12, p. 123

41 26 December 1762, in Jackson, *Works of John Wesley* Vol. 3, p. 124

42 John Downey to Joseph Connley, reprinted in *Methodist Magazine*, 1794, p. 565

43 Letter 1 January 1763 to Charles, in Jackson, *Life of Charles Wesley*, Vol. 2, pp. 210–12

44 Letter 5 January 1763 to Charles, in Forsaith, *Correspondence of Revd John W. Fletcher*, p. 87

45 Quoted in Faith Cook, *Selina Countess of Huntingdon*, Banner of Truth Trust, 2001, p. 209

46 Letter dated 1 February 1763, in *Methodist Magazine*, 1794, p. 566

47 William Romaine to the countess, 26 March 1763, in Seymour, *Life and Times of the Countess of Huntingdon*, Vol. I, p. 330

48 Quoted in Frank Baker, *William Grimshaw*, Epworth, 1963, p. 259

49 Quoted in Baker, *William Grimshaw*, p. 262

50 Quoted in T. Jackson, *Memoirs of Revd Charles Wesley*, John Mason, London, 1862, p. 317

51 'Another Hymn on the Death of Revd William Grimshaw' in *Journal of Revd Charles Wesley*, Vol. 2, pp. 365–6

52 Letter 12 May 1763 to Mrs Maitland, in *Methodist Magazine 1797*, p. 351

53 Seymour, *Life and Times of the Countess of Huntingdon*, Vol. I, p. 329

54 In 'Vindication', published in 1767

55 Letter to Sally, 27 May 1763, in Tyson, *Charles Wesley: A Reader*, p. 383

56 Letter 6 July 1763 to Charles, in Jackson, *Life of Charles Wesley*, Vol. 2, p. 219

57 W. R. Ward and R. Heitzenrater, *John Wesley: Journal and Diaries*, Abingdon Press, no date, Vol. XXI, p. 421

58 Letter 9 September 1763 to Charles, in Forsaith, *Correspondence of Revd John W. Fletcher*, p. 92

59 Ms letter in Cheshunt Foundation Archives, Westminster College

60 Letter 1 March 1764 to Charles, in Tyerman, *Life and Times of John Wesley*, Vol. 2, p. 507

61 Letter 16 May 1764 to the Countess, in Tyerman, *Life and Times of John Wesley*, Vol. 2, pp. 508–9

62 Letter 25 May 1764 to Charles, in Tyerman, *Life and Times of John Wesley*, Vol. 2, pp. 506–7

63 Letter 17 May 1764 to Sally, in Jackson, *Life of Revd Charles Wesley*, Vol. 2, p. 221

64 Kimbrough and Beckerlegge, *Unpublished Poetry of Charles Wesley*, pp. 281–2

65 Quoted in Dallimore, *George Whitefield*, Vol. II, p. 462

66 Letter 22 August 1764 to Charles, in Forsaith, *Correspondence of Revd John W. Fletcher*, p. 104

67 Luke Tyerman, *Wesley's Designated Successor: Life of William Fletcher*, Hodder & Stoughton, 1882, p. 107

68 Letter to Charles, 9 July 1764, in Telford, *Letters of Rev. John Wesley*, Vol. V, p. 19

69 Quoted in Maldwyn Edwards, *Sons to Samuel*, Epworth, 1961, p. 78

70 Quoted in John Telford, *Wesley's Veterans*, Kelly, London, 1912, Vol. VI, p. 19

71 Quoted in C. W. Flint, *Charles Wesley and His Colleagues*, Washington Public Affairs Press, 1957, p. 148

72 See Jackson, *Life of Charles Wesley*, Vol. 2, p. 209

73 Quoted in Tyerman, *Life and Times of John Wesley*, Vol. 2, p. 467

74 Letter 16 January 1773 to Charles, in Forsaith, *Correspondence of Revd John W. Fletcher*, p. 144

75 John Pawson writing in January 1796, in Tyerman, *Life and Times of John Wesley*, Vol. 2, p. 444

76 7 December 1764, in Jackson, *Works of John Wesley*, Vol. 12, p. 127

77 G. Osborn, *The Poetical Works of John and Charles Wesley*, Wesleyan Methodist Conference Office, 1870, Vol. VII, pp. 54–5

78 Letter 8 August 1765 to Charles, in Forsaith, *Correspondence of Revd John W. Fletcher*, p. 116

79 R. Heitzenrater, *Wesley and the People Called Methodists*, Abingdon Press, 1995, p. 220

80 Minutes 1:54, cf Book of Discipline

81 28 February 1766 to Charles, in Jackson, *Works of John Wesley*, Vol. 12, p. 130

82 Quoted in Heitzenrater, *Wesley and the People Called Methodists*, pp. 224–5

83 Tyerman, *Life and Times of John Wesley*, Vol. 2, pp. 592–3

84 Telford, *Letters of John Wesley*, Vol. VI, p. 10

85 Quoted in R. Hattersley, *A Brand from the Burning*, Little Brown, 2003, pp. 338–9

86 Letter to Charles undated, but c. 1759, original in French. Translated in Streiff, *Reluctant Saint*, p. 59

87 27 June 1766 to Charles, in Jackson, *Works of John Wesley*, Vol. 12, pp. 130–1

88 Quoted in Cook, *Selina Countess of Huntingdon*, pp. 227–8

89 John Chute in *Private Correspondence of Horace Walpole*, London, 1820, Vol. III, p. 192

90 J. Curnock, *Letters of John Wesley*, Epworth, 1931, Vol. V, p. 166

91 *Works of George Whitefield*, Vol. III, p. 345

92 Luke Tyerman, *Life of George Whitefield*, Hodder & Stoughton, 1876, Vol. II, p. 460

93 *Memoirs of the Late Revd Cornelius Winter*, ed. William Jay, 1808, Bath, pp. 37f

94 Letter to Charles 27 January 1767, in Telford, *Letters of John Wesley*, Vol. V, pp. 38–9

95 12 February 1767 to Charles, in Jackson, *Works of John Wesley*, Vol. 12, p. 132

96 Letter to his wife Sarah, 2 March 1760. Methodist archives in John Rylands University Library of Manchester

97 Quoted in F. Gill, *Charles Wesley, the First Methodist*, Lutterworth, 1962, p. 175

98 Quoted in Gill, *Charles Wesley, the First Methodist*, p. 177

99 Quoted in Gill, *Charles Wesley, the First Methodist*, p. 178

100 14 June 1768 to Charles, in Tyerman, *Life and Times of John Wesley*, Vol. 3, pp. 12–13

101 See Tyerman, *Life and Times of John Wesley*, Vol. 2, p. 576

102 Minutes of Conference in Frank Baker, *John Wesley and the Church of England*, Epworth, 1970, p. 196.

103 Telford, *Letters of John Wesley*, Vol. V, p. 215

104 Joseph Belcher, *A Biography of George Whitefield*, New York, 1857, p. 435

105 *Journal of Revd Charles Wesley*, Vol. 2, pp. 418–31

106 Letter 10 August 1770 to Charles, in Forsaith, *Correspondence of Revd John W. Fletcher*, p. 125

107 8 June 1771, in Jackson, *Memoirs of Revd Charles Wesley*, p. 331

108 Cited in Jackson, *Life of Revd Charles Wesley*, Vol. 2, p. 256

109 Telford, *Letters of John Wesley*, Vol. V, pp. 264–5

110 Telford, *Letters of John Wesley*, Vol. V, pp. 274–5

111 Quoted in Tyerman, *Life and Times of John Wesley*, Vol. 3, p. 139

112 Quoted in Anthony Armstrong, *The Church of England, the Methodists and Society 1700–1850*, University of London Press, 1973, p. 105

113 Jackson, *Memoirs of Revd Charles Wesley*, p. 357

114 Letter 13 October 1771 to Charles, in Forsaith, *Correspondence of Revd John W. Fletcher*, p. 133

115 Curnock, *Letters of John Wesley*, Vol. IV, p. 298

116 *Arminian Magazine*, 1778, p. 34

117 Letter 12 March 1772 to Charles, in Forsaith, *Correspondence of Revd John W. Fletcher*, p. 140

118 Quoted in D. M. Jones, *Charles Wesley*, Skeffingtons, p. 223

119 Letter to James Hutton, 1771, in Frank Baker, *Charles Wesley as Revealed by His Letters*, Epworth, 1948, p. 130

120 Baker, *Charles Wesley as Revealed by His Letters*, p. 131

Chapter 11

1 'Hymn VII for Concord' in 'Hymns for the Nation' in 1782 in G. Osborn, *The Poetical Works of John and Charles Wesley*, Wesleyan Methodist Conference, 1870, Vol. VIII, pp. 300–2.

2 'Free Thoughts on the Present State of Affairs, 1768' in Thomas Jackson, *The Works of John Wesley*, Baker House Books, 1872, reprinted 1984, Vol. 11, pp. 26–9

3 S. T. Kimborough and O. A. Beckerlegge, *The Unpublished Poetry of Charles Wesley*, Kingswood Books, 1988, Vol. I, p. 150

4 Kimborough and Beckerlegge, *Unpublished Poetry*, Vol. I, p. 153

5 Letter 1 March 1775 to Thomas Rankin. See L. Tyerman, *The Life and Times of John Wesley*, Hodder & Stoughton, 1878, Vol. 3, p. 194

6 Letter 1 March 1775 to T. Rankin. See Tyerman, *Life and Times of John Wesley*, Vol. 3, pp. 194–5

7 Kimborough and Beckerlegge, *Unpublished Poetry*, Vol. I, p. 152

8 Frank Baker, *Charles Wesley as Revealed by His Letters*, Epworth, 1948, p. 122

9 Jackson, *Works of John Wesley*, Vol. 11, p. 70

10 Jackson, *Works of John Wesley*, Vol. 11, pp. 78–9

11 John Telford, *The Letters of John Wesley*, Epworth, 1931, Vol. VIII, p. 7

12 Quoted in Tyerman, *Life and Times of John Wesley*, Vol. 3, p. 190

13 Letter in *Lloyd's Evening Post*. See Tyerman, *Life and Times of John Wesley*, Vol. 3, p. 192

14 Letter 4 December 1775 to Charles, in P. Forsaith, *Correspondence of Revd John W. Fletcher*, thesis submitted for DPhil at Oxford University 2002, p. 160

15 Hymn VI in 'Hymns on Patriotism' in Kimbrough and Beckerlegge, *Unpublished Poetry*, Vol. I, p. 65

16 Mrs Frank Stephens, *Lives of the Early Methodist Preachers*, Marshall & Son, London, 1903, pp. 188–9

17 28 June 1775, quoted in Faith Cook, *Selina Countess of Huntingdon*, Banner of Truth Trust, 2001, p. 352

18 2 July 1775, in Thomas Jackson, *Memoirs of Revd Charles Wesley*, John Mason, London, 1862, pp. 369–70

19 A sermon preached at St Matthew's, Bethnal Green, 12 November 1775, 'published for the benefit of the widows and orphans of the soldiers who recently fell near Boston, in New England'

20 Letter 19 May 1775 to T. Rankin, in Tyerman, *Life and Times of John Wesley*, Vol. 3, pp. 195–6

21 Letter 15 June 1775 to Lord North, in Tyerman, *Life and Times of John Wesley*, Vol. 3, pp. 197–200

22 20 October 1775, in Jackson, *Works of John Wesley*, Vol. 12, p. 330

23 19 October 1775 in Jackson, *Works of John Wesley*, Vol. 12, p. 144

24 The wording was largely produced by Thomas Jefferson, later to become the country's third president.

25 The *Public Advertiser*, a newspaper which fiercely attacked the government's handling of the issue.

26 Hymn IV in 'Hymns on Patriotism' in Kimbrough and Beckerlegge, *Unpublished Poetry*, Vol. I, pp. 61–2

27 'The Bible and the Sword' (1776) in Ellis Sandoz, *Political Sermons of the American Founding Era 1730–1805*, Liberty Press, Indianapolis, 1991, p. 567

28 'The American War' in Kimbrough and Beckerlegge, *Unpublished Poetry*, Vol. I, pp. 42 and 45

29 'The American War' in Kimbrough and Beckerlegge, *Unpublished Poetry*, Vol. I, p. 43

30 'The American War' in Kimbrough and Beckerlegge, *Unpublished Poetry*, Vol. I, p. 47

31 'The American War' in Kimbrough and Beckerlegge, *Unpublished Poetry*, Vol. I, p. 47

32 'The American War' in Kimbrough and Beckerlegge, *Unpublished Poetry*, Vol. I, p. 51

33 'The American War' in Kimbrough and Beckerlegge, *Unpublished Poetry*, Vol. I, p. 54

34 'The American War' in Kimbrough and Beckerlegge, *Unpublished Poetry*, Vol. I, p. 57

35 'Prayer for the Loyalists' in Kimbrough and Beckerlegge, *Unpublished Poetry*, Vol. I, pp. 120–1

36 'The Patriots' King' in Kimbrough and Beckerlegge, *Unpublished Poetry*, Vol. I, p. 165

37 'Non Tali Auxilio' in Kimbrough and Beckerlegge, *Unpublished Poetry*, Vol. I, pp. 156–7

38 Jackson, *Works of John Wesley* Vol. 11, pp. 141–6

39 Jackson, *Works of John Wesley* Vol. 11, p. 150

40 Quoted in F. Gill, *Charles Wesley, the First Methodist*, Lutterworth, 1964, p. 183

41 Hymn XII in 'Hymns for the Nation', 1782, in Osborn, *Poetical Works* Vol. VIII, pp. 300–2

42 Quoted in Tyerman, *Life and Times of John Wesley*, Vol. 3, pp. 297–9

43 Baker, *Charles Wesley as Revealed by His Letters*, p. 132

44 23 April 1779 in Tyerman, *Life and Times of John Wesley*, Vol. III, p. 296

45 Quoted in D. M. Jones, *Charles Wesley*, Skeffington & Co, London, 1920, p. 238

46 Quoted in Tyerman, *Life and Times of John Wesley*, Vol. III, p. 301

47 23 April 1779 to John, in Tyerman, *Life and Times of John Wesley* Vol. 3, p. 296

48 Quoted in Jones, *Charles Wesley*, pp. 238–9

49 Baker, *Charles Wesley as Revealed by His Letters*, p. 132

50 Quoted in Tyerman, *Life and Times of John Wesley*, Vol. 3, p. 310

51 Osborn, *Poetical Works*, Vol. VIII, p. 415

52 Baker, *Charles Wesley as Revealed by His Letters*, p. 133

53 Quoted in Tyerman, *Life and Times of John Wesley*, Vol. 3, p. 311

54 Letter to John, in Tyerman, *Life and Times of John Wesley*, Vol. 3, pp. 311–12

55 Telford, *Letters of the Revd John Wesley*, Vol. VII, p. 29

56 Telford, *Letters of the Revd John Wesley*, Vol. VII, p. 115

57 Quoted in Tyerman, *Life and Times of John Wesley*, Vol. 3, p. 312

58 Quoted in Tyerman, *Life and Times of John Wesley*, Vol. 3, p. 312

59 Osborn, *Poetical Works*, Vol. VIII, pp. 416–17

60 'The Protestant Association Written in the Midst of the Tumults June 1780' in Osborn, *Poetical Works*, Vol. VIII, pp. 453, 458 and 460

61 Quoted in Jones, *Charles Wesley*, p. 243

62 Quoted in Jones, *Charles Wesley*, p. 243

63 Quoted in Jones, *Charles Wesley*, p. 242

64 Hymn X in 'Hymns Written in the Time of Tumults June 1780' in Osborn, *Poetical Works*, Vol. VIII, p. 277

65 Hymn VIII in 'Hymns Written in the Time of Tumults June 1780' in Osborn, *Poetical Works*, Vol. VIII, p. 273

66 Hymn IV in 'Hymns Written in the Time of Tumults June 1780' in Osborn, *Poetical Works*, Vol. VIII, p. 268

67 Jackson, *Works of John Wesley*, Vol. 11, pp. 34–46

68 Hymn 1 in 'Hymns for the Nation in 1782' in Osborn, *Poetical Works*, Vol. VIII, p. 283

69 Letter to John and Mary Fletcher, 13 March 1782, in Patrick Strieff, *Reluctant Saint*, Epworth, 2001, p. 268

70 Quoted in C. Hibbert, *Redcoats and Rebels*, Penguin, 2001, p. 334

71 'Written After the Next Vote' in Kimbrough and Beckerlegge, *Unpublished Poetry*, Vol. I, pp. 146–7

72 Hymn XIV in 'Hymns for the National Fast' in Osborn, *Poetical Works*, Vol. VIII, p. 335

73 Hymn XV in 'Hymns For The Nation in 1782' in Osborn, *Poetical Works*, Vol. VIII, pp. 304–5

74 19 January 1783, in Jackson, *Works of John Wesley*, Vol. 4, p. 242

75 Hymn II in 'Hymns for the Nation in 1782' in Osborn, *Poetical Works*, Vol. VIII, pp. 284–6

76 Kimbrough and Beckerlegge, *Unpublished Poetry*, Vol. I, p. 137

77 28 May 1782, in Tyerman, *Life and Times of John Wesley*, Vol. 3, p. 376

78 Quoted in Tyerman, *Life and Times of John Wesley*, Vol. 3, pp. 376–7

79 16 March 1783 letter to Hester Ann Roe, in Tyerman, *Life and Times of John Wesley*, Vol. 3, p. 392

80 Quoted in Cook, *Selina Countess of Huntingdon*, p. 350

81 Quoted in Cook, *Selina Countess of Huntingdon*, p. 368

82 A. C. H. Seymour, *The Life and Times of the Countess of Huntingdon*, London, 1840, Vol. II, p. 315

83 Quoted in Cook, *Selina Countess of Huntingdon*, p. 377

84 21 June 1784, letter to John and Mary Fletcher, in Streif, *Reluctant Saint*, p. 273

85 Charles Atmoor, quoted in L. Tyerman, *Wesley's Designated Successor*, London, 1882, pp. 545–6

86 Thoughts Upon Some Late Occurrences, published in *Methodist Magazine*, 3 March 1785, p. 269

87 J. A. Vickers, 'Documents and Source Material' in Rupert Davies, *A History of the Methodist Church*, Epworth, 1988, Vol. IV, p. 201

88 Letter 9 August 1784 to John, in Tyerman, *Life and Times of John Wesley*, Vol. 3, p. 429

89 10 September 1784, in Tyerman, *Life and Times of John Wesley*, Vol. 3, p. 435

90 Baker, *Charles Wesley as Revealed by His Letters*, p. 134

91 Baker, *Charles Wesley as Revealed by His Letters*, p. 134.

92 *Methodist Magazine*, 1786, p. 677

93 Baker, *Charles Wesley as Revealed by His Letters*, p. 135

94 Letter 28 April 1785 to Dr Chandler, in Tyerman, *Life and Times of John Wesley*, Vol. 3, pp. 439–40

95 'Ms Ordination Hymns': Hymn I, Hymn III and Hymn V Epigrams, in John Tyson, *Charles Wesley: A Reader*, Oxford University Press, 1989, pp. 428–9

96 Quoted in Frank Baker, *John Wesley and the Church of England*, Epworth, 1970, p. 274

97 15 August 1785 to Dr Smith, in Baker, *John Wesley and the Church of England*, p. 275

98 Quoted in J. Vickers, *Thomas Coke: Apostle of Methodism*, Abingdon Press, 1969, p. 91

99 Frank Baker, *The Verse of Charles Wesley*, Epworth, 1989, p. 367

100 Quoted in A. Noll, *America's God*, Oxford University Press, 2002, p. 339

101 Letter to John Pritchard, in Mrs Frank Stephens, *Lives of the Early Methodist Preachers*

Chapter 12

1 'Come On, My Partners in Distress' in S. T. Kimbrough, *Charles Wesley: Poet and Theologian*, Kingswood, 1992, p. 33

2 Frank Baker, *Charles Wesley as Revealed by His Letters*, Epworth, 1948, p. 105

3 Letter 13 March 1782 from Charles to Fletcher, in P. Forsaith, *Correspondence of Revd John W. Fletcher*, thesis submitted for DPhil at University, of Oxford 2003, p. 160

4 See J. Lenton's forthcoming article on 'Charles Wesley and His Preachers' to be published in symposium edited by Kenneth Newport, Epworth Press, 2007

5 Ms copy of letter to his sister, 7 February 1788, in Creighton Letter Book, p. 47, in the Clark Collection, Lake Junaluska Museum, North Carolina

6 Ernest Rattenbury, *The Evangelical Doctrines of Charles Wesley's Hymns*, Epworth, 1941

7 *A Collection of Hymns for the Use of the People Called Methodists*, London, 1780, pp. 74–5

8 Carlton R. Young, *Music of the Heart*, Carol Stream, Illinois, 1995, p. 191

9 Quoted in T. Crichton Mitchell, *Man with the Dancing Heart*, Beacon Hill, 1994, p. 247

10 Luke Wiseman, *Charles Wesley*, Epworth, 1932, p. 210

11 G. Osborn, *The Poetical Works of John and Charles Wesley*, Wesleyan Methodist Conference, 1870, Vol. X, p. 225

12 J. E. Rattenbury, *The Evangelical Doctrines of Charles Wesley's Hymns*, Epworth, 1941, p. 48

13 Baker, *Charles Wesley as Revealed by His Letters*, p. 105

14 Letter to Sally, in J. Tyson: *Charles Wesley: A Reader*, Oxford University Press, 1989, p. 346

15 Baker, *Charles Wesley as Revealed by His Letters*, p. 108

16 Baker, *Charles Wesley as Revealed by His Letters*, p. 109

17 'Hymns For a Family', 1767

18 Baker, *Charles Wesley as Revealed by His Letters*, p. 109

19 Baker, *Charles Wesley as Revealed by His Letters*, p. 109

20 Baker, *Charles Wesley as Revealed by His Letters*, p. 110

21 Baker, *Charles Wesley as Revealed by His Letters*, p. 110

22 Charles' Account of his two sons, in Jackson, *Journal of Revd Charles Wesley*, John Mason, London, 1849, Vol. 2, p. 140

23 Charles' Account, in Jackson, *Journal of Revd Charles Wesley*, Vol. 2, p. 142

24 Charles' Account, in Jackson, *Journal of Revd Charles Wesley*, Vol. 2, pp. 143–6

25 Charles' Account of Samuel, in Jackson, *Journal of Revd Charles Wesley*, Vol. 2, p. 153

26 Charles' Account of Samuel, in Jackson, *Journal of Revd Charles Wesley* Vol. 2, p. 154

27 Daines Barrington's full account in Jackson, *Journal of Revd Charles Wesley*, Vol. 2, pp. 151–66

28 Charles' Account of Samuel, in Jackson, *Journal of Revd Charles Wesley*, Vol. 2, pp. 155–7

29 Frank Baker, *Charles Wesley as Revealed by His Letters*, p. 111

30 F. Gill, *Charles Wesley the First Methodist*, Lutterworth, 1964, p. 185

31 Quoted in D. M. Jones, *Charles Wesley*, Skeffington & Co, London, 1920, p. 235

32 Baker, *Charles Wesley as Revealed by His Letters*, p. 113–14

33 Quoted in Jones, *Charles Wesley*, p. 235

34 Quoted in Jones, *Charles Wesley*, p. 254

35 Quoted in Jones, *Charles Wesley*, p. 255

36 Baker, *Charles Wesley as Revealed by His Letters*, p. 114

37 Baker, *Charles Wesley as Revealed by His Letters*, p. 114

38 Story contained in Thomas Jackson, *Memoirs of Revd Charles Wesley*, John Mason, London, 1862, p. 397

39 Quoted in Gill, *Charles Wesley the First Methodist*, p. 210

40 Erik Routley, *The Musical Wesleys*, Herbert Jenkins, 1968, p. 58

41 John Tyson, *Charles Wesley: A Reader*, Oxford University Press, 1989, pp. 351–2

42 Quoted in Routley, *The Musical Wesleys*, p. 65

43 A. Dallimore, *A Heart Set Free*, Evangelical Press, 1988, p. 245

44 19 Aug 1784, in Jackson, *Memoirs of Revd Charles Wesley*, pp. 402–3

45 Quoted in *Musical Opinion*, February 1966, p. 299

46 Quoted in Jones, *Charles Wesley*, p. 229

47 Quoted in Jones, *Charles Wesley*, pp. 222–3

48 Baker, *Charles Wesley as Revealed by His Letters*, p. 115

49 Baker, *Charles Wesley as Revealed by His Letters*, pp. 115–16

50 Tyson, *Charles Wesley: A Reader*, pp. 354–5

51 'Ms Brothers': Hymn IX in Tyson: *Charles Wesley: A Reader*, pp. 432–33

52 Letter 21 June 1785, in P. Forsaith, *Correspondence of Revd John W. Fletcher*, p. 172

53 Letter 21 June 1785, in Forsaith, *Correspondence of Revd John W. Fletcher*, p. 174

54 Henry Moore, *Life of Mr Wesley*, London, 1824 Vol. II, p. 369

55 *Arminian Magazine*, 1786, p. 678

56 Baker, *Charles Wesley as Revealed by His Letters*, p. 138

57 To E. Johnson, in Baker, *Charles Wesley as Revealed by His Letters*, p. 139

58 'Ms Brothers': Hymn IX in Tyson: *Charles Wesley: A Reader*, pp. 430–31

59 Letter 14 August 1785 to John in L. Tyerman, *Life and Times of John Wesley*, Hodder & Stoughton, 1878, Vol. 3, pp. 443–4

60 Letter 19 August 1785 to Charles, in Tyerman, *Life and Times of John Wesley*, Vol. 3, pp. 444–5

61 Letter 8 Sept 1785 to John, in Tyerman, *Life and Times of John Wesley*, Vol. 3, pp. 446–7

62 15 September 1785, in Tyerman, *Life and Times of John Wesley*, Vol.3, p. 447

63 19 September 1785, in Tyerman, *Life and Times of John Wesley*, Vol. 3, pp. 447–8

64 27 July 1786, in Tyerman, *Life and Times of John Wesley*, Vol. 3, p. 448

65 Wesley's Life of Fletcher in Thomas Jackson, *The Works of John Wesley*, Baker Book House, 1872 reprinted 1984, Vol. 11, pp. 362–4

66 L. Tyerman, *Wesley's Designated Successor*, London, 1882, p. 567

67 Frank Baker, *John Wesley and the Church of England*, Epworth, 1970, p. 308

68 Baker, *Charles Wesley as Revealed by His Letters*, p. 131

69 Quoted in M. Brailsford, *A Tale of Two Brothers*, Hart-Davies 1954, p. 274

70 Baker, *Charles Wesley as Revealed by His Letters*, p. 139

71 Letter to Rev Latrobe, in Tyerman, *The Life and Times of John Wesley*, 1878, Vol. 3, p. 479

72 Letter 27 July 1786 to John, in Tyerman, *Life and Times of John Wesley*, Vol. 3, p. 448

73 Letter to Michael Callendor, 25 November 1786, in Tyson: *Charles Wesley: A Reader*, p. 438

74 Letter 9 April 1787 to John, in Tyerman, *Life and Times of John Wesley*, Vol. 3, p. 523

75 Quoted in Brailsford, *A Tale of Two Brothers*, p. 275

76 Quoted in Jones, *Charles Wesley*, pp. 253–4

77 As reported by Joseph Pawson in 8 August 1787 Letter to Charles Atmore, in Tyerman, *Life and Times of John Wesley*, Vol. 3, p. 497

78 8 August 1787, Letter to Charles Atmore, in Tyerman, *Life and Times of John Wesley*, Vol. 3, pp. 497–8

79 James Creighton to Charles Wesley, 6 October 1787, in Methodist Archives, London. See Baker, *John Wesley and the Church of England*, pp. 279–80

80 Letter dated August 1787. See J. Lenton's article in symposium edited by K. Newport, Epworth Press, 2007

81 Quoted in Baker, *John Wesley and the Church of England*, p. 309

82 Baker, *Charles Wesley as Revealed by His Letters*, p. 116

83 13 January 1788 to Samuel Bradburn, *Methodist Manuscript Book*, World Methodist Museum, Lake Junaluska, North Carolina, p. 8

84 Quoted in Jackson, *Memoirs of Revd Charles Wesley*, pp. 474–5

85 Tyson, *Charles Wesley: A Reader*, p. 480

86 Tyson, *Charles Wesley: A Reader*, p. 481

87 5 March 1788, Letter to Charles, in Jackson, *Memoirs of Revd Charles Wesley*, p. 453

88 7 March 1788, Letter to Charles, in Jackson, *Memoirs of Revd Charles Wesley*, p. 454

89 Tyson, *Charles Wesley: A Reader*, pp. 480–1

90 20 March 1787, in Jackson, *Memoirs of Revd Charles Wesley*, pp. 454–5

91 Jackson, *Memoirs of Revd Charles Wesley*, p. 455

92 Tyson, *Charles Wesley: A Reader*, p. 482

93 Quoted in Jones, *Charles Wesley*, p. 259

94 Source unknown

95 Quoted in Jackson, *Memoirs of Revd Charles Wesley*, pp. 460–1

96 Quoted in Jackson, *Memoirs of Revd Charles Wesley*, p. 459

97 From the hymn 'Wrestling Jacob'.

98 Baker, *Charles Wesley as Revealed by His Letters*, p. 141

99 25 July 1788, in Jackson, *Memoirs of Revd Charles Wesley*, p. 463

100 21 December 1788, in Jackson, *Memoirs of Revd Charles Wesley*, pp. 463–4

101 28 June 1788 journal, in *Works of John Wesley*, Vol. 4, p. 427

102 Quoted in Baker, *John Wesley and the Church of England*, p. 311

103 29 May 1789, in Jackson, *Memoirs of Revd Charles Wesley*, p. 464

104 1 January 1790 journal, in *Works of John Wesley*, Vol. 4, p. 478

105 Henry Moore, *Life of the Rev. John Wesley*, Vol. II, pp. 383–4

106 John Telford, *The Letters of John Wesley*, Epworth, 1931, Vol. VIII, pp. 196–7

107 Telford, *Letters of John Wesley*, Vol. VIII, p. 199

108 Telford, *Letters of John Wesley*, Vol. VIII, p. 206

109 Tyerman, *Life and Times of Revd John Wesley*, Vol. 3, p. 642

110 A. C. Outler, *Sermons of John Wesley*, Abingdon Press, 1984, Vol. IV, p. 200

111 No 439 *Hymns and Psalms*, Methodist Publishing House, 1983

112 John Lettsom to Lady Anne Erskine, in Faith Cook, *Selina Countess of Huntingdon*, Banner of Truth Trust, 2001, p. 423

113 See R. Whittingham, *Introduction to Whole Works of John Berridge*, London, 1864, p. liii

114 In the introduction to the 1816 edition of his sermons

115 Hymn No 3, 'Preparations for Death in Several Hymns', 1772, in *Poetical Works*, Vol. VII, p. 355

Index